THINK
CRITICALLY

THINK CRITICALLY

PETER FACIONE

Prentice Hall

Boston   Columbus   Indianapolis   New York   San Francisco   Upper Saddle River
Amsterdam   Cape Town   Dubai   London   Madrid   Milan   Munich   Paris   Montréal   Toronto
Delhi   Mexico City   São Paulo   Sydney   Hong Kong   Seoul   Singapore   Taipei   Tokyo

Editorial Director: Craig Campanella
Editor in Chief: Dickson Musslewhite
Publisher: Nancy Roberts
Editorial Project Manager: Vanessa Gennarelli
Editorial Assistant: Nart Varoqua
Director of Marketing: Brandy Dawson
Senior Marketing Manager: Laura Lee Manley
Marketing Assistant: Patrick Walsh
Managing Editor: Maureen Richardson
Senior Project Manager/Production: Harriet Tellem
Operations Specialist: Amanda Smith
Manager of Design Development: John Christiana
Art Director and Text Designer: Laura Gardner
Cover Designer: John Christiana
Line Art and Illustrations: Words & Numbers

Manager, Visual Research: Beth Brenzel
Photo Researcher: Kathy Ringrose
Manager, Rights and Permissions: Zina Arabia
Image Permission Coordinator: Debbie Latronica
Manager, Cover Visual Research & Permissions: Karen Sanatar
Cover Art: *The Science of Speed*, Drew Wilson
Text Research and Permissions: Lisa Black
Senior Media Editor: David Alick
Full-Service Project Management: Bernadette Enneg, Ally Brocious, Katherine Hoover, Adam Noll, Russ Hall, Salimah Perkins/ Words & Numbers
Composition: Words & Numbers
Printer/Binder: Courier/Kendallville
Cover Printer: Lehigh-Phoenix Color/Hagerstown
Text Font: Helvetica 45 Light

Credits and acknowledgments borrowed from other sources and reproduced, with permission, in this textbook appear on appropriate page within text (or on pages 231–232).

Library of Congress Cataloging-in-Publication Data
Facione, Peter A.
THINK critically / Peter Facione.—Student ed.
    p. cm.
Includes bibliographical references and index.
ISBN 978-0-205-73845-8
1. Critical thinking—Study and teaching (Secondary) I. Title.
BF441.F23 2011
160—dc22
                                        2009042642

10 9 8 7 6 5 4 3 2 1

Prentice Hall
is an imprint of

www.pearsonhighered.com

Student Edition
ISBN 10:   0-205-73845-1
ISBN 13:   978-0-205-73845-8
Examination Edition
ISBN 10:   0-205-71187-1
ISBN 13:   978-0-205-71187-1

To students and teachers everywhere,
may developing critical thinking help you stay
forever young.

BRIEF CONTENTS

CONTENTS

 01

PURPOSEFUL, REFLECTIVE JUDGMENT 2

02

THE "ABLE" IN "WILLING AND ABLE" TO THINK CRITICALLY 14

03

THE "WILLING" IN "WILLING AND ABLE" TO THINK CRITICALLY 26

04

CLARIFYING IDEAS 40

05

USING MAPS TO ANALYZE ARGUMENTS AND DECISIONS 58

SPECIAL FEATURES

Just as teaching and learning critical thinking is a collaboration, so is putting together all the words, images, exercises, video clips, page layouts, and Web site materials for THINK Critically. This project could not have happened were it not for the wonderful participation, support, and guidance of a great many people.

I want to thank the collaborators who drew upon their talents and experience as teachers to provide so much essential supporting material to instructors and to students.

Carol Gittens, Ph.D., author of the Instructor's Manual for THINK Critically, is the director of assessment at Santa Clara University, where she has taught in the Liberal Studies Program, the Department of Psychology, and the Department of Education, and where she has served as an associate dean. Dr. Gittens's research focuses on the development and measurement of students' learning motivation and critical thinking skills. Her Instructor's Manual is a wonderful tool because of all the strategies she offers on teaching for thinking.

Douglas J. Eder, Ph.D., developed the PowerPoint supplements. A neuroscientist researcher and faculty member at Southern Illinois University Edwardsville (SIUE) for more than 30 years, he presents regularly at regional, national, and international conferences, and has advised over a hundred institutions of higher learning on learning outcomes assessment. During his academic career, Dr. Eder served in leadership positions at Arizona State University and the University of North Florida.

Supplementary materials available at www.TheThinkSpot.com come from the generous participation of these experienced instructors.

Rick Chew, Ph.D., is an assistant professor of Humanities and Philosophy at the University of Central Oklahoma. He contributed supplementary material for the three introductory chapters.

Kurt Erhard is a member of the Department of Philosophy at Prince George's Community College and a Ph.D. candidate at the University of Miami. Kurt has also served in pastoral ministry since 1982, having pastored the same Maryland church for the past 10 years. Kurt contributed supplementary material for Chapters 4–6.

Stephanie Semler currently teaches philosophy at Virginia Tech. She has been teaching courses in reasoning, argument, and logic for the past 12 years. She contributed supplementary materials for the two chapters on evaluating arguments, Chapters 7 and 8.

John Gibson, Ph.D., is an associate professor of philosophy at the University of Louisville in Kentucky. John contributed supplementary exercises for Chapters 9–13. His research focuses on various intersections of the philosophy of language, aesthetics, and ethics.

I benefited immensely from the insightful comments and suggestions of the people Pearson Education used to review in detail each chapter of the manuscript. Later I learned their names, and I want to thank them publicly for their guidance and help. This book is so much stronger because of the wisdom they shared. They are:

Deborah Boyle, College of Charleston
Ann Glauser, University of Georgia
John Gibson, University of Louisville
Michael Monge, Long Beach City College
Stephanie Semler, Virginia Tech

This is the twelfth book I've written, but never have I had a more skilled, insightful, and productive group of professionals working on the project than the people at Pearson Education and at Words & Numbers. I am truly grateful to each and every one of them, but two deserve special acknowledgment: Salimah Perkins at Words & Numbers, because early in the process she recognized the vision for this book and did everything necessary to help the vision be realized, and Vanessa Gennarelli, who "got it" and systematically worked long and hard on every detailed aspect of this project, coordinating all aspects of its editorial production so that everyone else could "get it," too. Without these two extraordinary and dedicated people, this book would not be.

For me, good ideas come from thinking and discussing things with other people. Great ideas come when that other person happens to be brilliant and wise. The ideas in this book come from a lifetime of those kinds of experiences, but mostly from talking and thinking with the one brilliant and amazing person who has shared that lifetime with me. Through her words and ideas, she contributed inestimably to this book, to other books, to a myriad of projects both professional and domestic, and to every other part of my life. No "thank you" can do justice to all that I owe to her. But let me say it anyway. Thank you, Noreen.

PREFACE

In "Forever Young," the songwriter Bob Dylan expressed my hopes for all who learn from and teach from *THINK Critically.* What more could one person wish for another than that he or she should always seek to know the truth, walk in the light of well-trained reason, be courageous, and have the intellectual integrity to stand strong, and that, no matter what the chronological age, that he or she should stay forever young?

This book aims to strengthen critical thinking skills and nurture the courageous desire to seek truth by following reasons and evidence wherever they lead. We all may have different beliefs, values, per-spectives, and experiences influencing our problem solving and decision making. But we share the human capacity to be reflective, analytical, open-minded, and systematic about thinking through our problems and choices so that we can make the best judgments possible about what to believe or what to do. That process of well-reasoned, reflective judgment is critical thinking. I also think that exercising our critical thinking helps our minds become stronger, healthier, and more youthful.

My approach is simple, practical, and focused. To strengthen critical thinking skills, we have to use them. To build positive critical thinking habits of mind, we have to engage our beliefs, intentions, and values around the importance of thinking critically as the optimal means of solving problems and making decisions, particularly in contexts of risk and uncertainty. Every chapter of this book builds critical thinking skills and engages critical thinking habits of mind in every way possible. Questions, exercises, video clips, controversial examples, contemporary issues, practical life problems, classic questions, science, technology, religion, politics—all of these, and more, are represented.

Why? Because I believe with every fiber of my being that critical thinking is all about real life, so the only way to build up one's skills and desire to engage practical problems and important deci-sions is to use material from real-life situations in teaching and learning critical thinking.

It is more important, in my judgment, that a person use all of his or her strength as a critical thinker to try to make the best judgments possible than that the person memorize a lot of vocab-ulary or theory about critical thinking. Learning about critical thinking certainly helps one become a better critical thinker. But it is not sufficient just to know something about music to play a musi-cal instrument well, nor is it sufficient to know the rules of a game or the strategies of a sport to be good at that game or sport. A person must pick up the instrument and practice, or play the game, or take the field and engage in the sport. The same goes for critical thinking. We learn it by doing it, not just reading about it or watching someone else do it.

So, to hone your critical thinking skills through practice, I put more than 100 exercises in the text itself, and there are more for you at **www.TheThinkSpot.com**. Some are group exercises and some are individual exercises, because critical thinking is something we do individually on occa-sion and with others in the process of group problem solving or group decision making on other occasions. The exercises in the textbook and the supplementary exercises, which faculty col-leagues from around the nation contributed, are crafted to be engaging, fascinating, entertaining, and provocative as well as instructional.

The THINKSpot Web site includes the nearly 50 links to video clips, news stories, and Internet URLs that are called out in the body of the chapters and in some of the exercises. Text is not enough by itself; critical thinking in real life calls for analyzing and interpreting images, body lan-guage, gestures, contexts, and much more. The video clips and other links build upon the words in print to give you a more well-rounded body of examples and exercises from which to learn.

Why critical thinking in real life and what I hope for you are bound together in the Dylanesque blessing that you should have a strong foundation, even in the shifting winds of change, that joy should fill your heart and learning guide your life, and, of course, that by using your mind to reflect on what to believe and what to do, that you should stay forever young.

Chapters 1, 2, and 3, while introductory, are vital to understanding what critical thinking is and why it is important to all of us individually and collectively everyday. Don't underestimate the value of these short chapters. They show how critical thinking connects to our academic studies and to our personal, professional, and civic lives.

Chapters 4 and 5 focus on interpretation and analysis so we can understand what people are saying so we can articulate the reasons being advanced on behalf of a particular claim or choice. These are vital skills. Without these, we wander in a cloud of confusion, not really knowing what things might mean or why people, including ourselves, think what they think.

Chapters 6, 7, and 8 are essential building block chapters. In these, we focus on how to evaluate claims, assess the trustworthiness of so-called experts, and recognize reasoning patterns that are logical and strong as contrasted with those that are misleading and fallacious.

Chapters 9 and 10 explain the importance of snap judgments and the grip of our previous decisions on how we live and act as we go through our day. These two chapters emphasize the essential critical thinking skills of self-monitoring and self-correction, along with the habits of truth seeking and open-mindedness, as the best defense against mistaken snap judgments and unreflective decision making.

Chapters 11, 12, and 13 are the three most important chapters of this book. Why? Because comparative reasoning, ideological reasoning, and empirical reasoning are the three most fundamental and most widely used methods human beings have for supplying reasons on behalf of their beliefs and ideas. These three chapters focus on inference and explanation, because drawing conclusions and explaining one's reasons in real life are the products of comparative, ideological, and empirical reasoning. The other chapters enable you to get the most out of these three chapters.

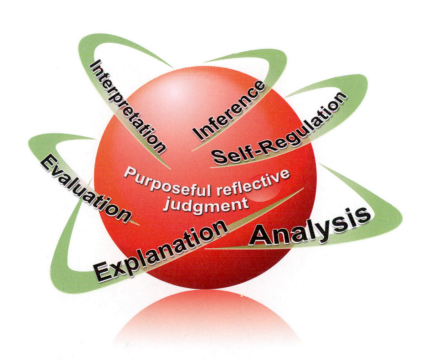

PETER FACIONE, Ph.D., wants to help all people build up their critical thinking skills, for their own sakes, and for the sake of our freedom and democracy. Facione draws on decades of experience as a teacher, consultant, business entrepreneur, university dean, grandfather, husband, and avid "old school" pickup basketball player. Now he is taking his message about the importance of critical thinking directly to students. For improving reasoning skills for use in one's personal, professional, and civic life, there may never before have been a more practical, enjoyable, important, comprehensive, and engaging text than this.

"I've paid very close attention to the way people make decisions since I was 13 years old," says Facione. "Some people were good at solving problems and making decisions; others were not. I have always felt driven to figure out how to tell which were which." He says that this led him as an undergraduate and later as a professor to study psychology, philosophy, logic, statistics, and information systems as he searched for how our beliefs, values, thinking skills, and habits of mind connect with the decisions we make, particularly in contexts of risk and uncertainty.

"As a professor and as a college administrator, I focused on problem-solving and decision-making strategies so that I could be a more effective teacher-scholar and a more capable leader. I found it was always valuable when working with groups or individuals to be mindful of how they applied their cognitive skills and habits of mind to solve a problem, make a decision, or troubleshoot a situation. Careful analysis and open-minded truth seeking always worked better than any other way of approaching problems."

A native Midwesterner, Facione earned his Ph.D. in philosophy from Michigan State University and his B.A. in philosophy from Sacred Heart College in Detroit. He says, "Critical thinking has helped me be a better parent, citizen, manager, teacher, writer, and friend. It even helps a little when playing point guard!"

In academia, Facione served as provost of Loyola University–Chicago, dean of the College of Arts and Sciences at Santa Clara University, and dean of the School of Human Development and Community Service at California State University–Fullerton. "As a dean and provost, I could easily see that critical thinking was alive and well in every professional field and academic discipline."

"I've focused my research on the teaching and measurement of critical thinking since my earliest years as a faculty member in the 1960s and 1970s. But before you can measure something that crosses into every aspect of life, you have to be sure that you understand what it is. So, in the 1980s, I first had to see whether there was a consensus among experts about the term *critical thinking*. After two years of research, a solid consensus emerged. That plus all the stats and behavioral science research I had studied and taught for years enabled me and my research team, during the 1990s, to design and validate tools to assess critical thinking skills and habits of mind. In the first decade of this century, our team has explored the connections between critical thinking and human decision making in its broadest sense."

In fact, Facione spearheaded the international study to define critical thinking, sponsored by the American Philosophical Association. His research formed the basis for numerous government policy studies about critical thinking in the workplace, including research sponsored by the U.S. Department of Education. Today, his tools for assessing reasoning are used around the world in educational, business, legal, military, and health sciences.

Today, Peter operates his own business, *Measured Reasons*. He is a speaker, writer, workshop presenter, and consultant for organizations large and small. His work focuses on strategic planning and leadership decision making, in addition to teaching and assessing critical thinking. With his wife, who is also his closest research colleague and coauthor of many books and assessment tools, he now lives in sunny Los Angeles, which suits him just fine. He welcomes questions from students and instructors—you can reach him at pfacione@measuredreasons.com.

<<< Michelle Obama participates in volunteer service with local elementary school students. What decision-making factors contribute to our own choices to participate in service?

WHAT DOES "CRITICAL THINKING" MEAN?
WHY IS CRITICAL THINKING IMPORTANT?
HOW CAN WE EVALUATE OUR CRITICAL THINKING?

Walking

down 10th Street in Hermosa Beach the other day, I saw a helmetless young man skillfully slalom his skateboard downhill toward the beach. Ignoring the stop sign at Hermosa Boulevard, he flashed across all four lanes of traffic and coasted on down the hill. My immediate reaction was, "Whew! Lucky that dude wasn't killed!" since I had often seen cars on Hermosa roll through that particular stop sign. Whatever was occupying his attention, the skateboarder did not appear to have self-preservation on his mind that day!

Whether he reflected on it or not, the skater *decided* to run the stop sign. Similarly, we all make decisions all the time, with some of our choices made more thoughtfully than others. We've

all underestimated obstacles, overlooked reasonable options, and failed to anticipate likely consequences. Life will continue to present us with our full share of problems, and when we err, we often think about the better decisions we could have made if we'd given it a little more thought.

Critical thinking is the process of reasoned judgment. Because this book is about that process, it is about *how to go about deciding* what to believe or what to do. This is not a book about what we should believe or do. The purpose of the book is to assist you in strengthening your critical thinking skills and habits of mind. Why should you strengthen these skills and habits? To solve problems and make decisions more thoughtfully.

PURPOSEFUL, REFLECTIVE JUDGMENT

CHAPTER 01

> You will recall how you were inspired to **THINK CRITICALLY** and to question without fear, to seek out radically different solutions and to voice them without reprisal, to read widely and deeply, and to examine without end and grow intellectually. . . . What I ask is this: pass it on.

Navy Adm. Mike Mullen, June 11, 2009[i]

Risk and Uncertainty Abound

We might not skateboard through an intersection, but none of us can escape life's risks and uncertainties. Uncertainties apply to potentially good things, too. For example, people might be uncertain when choosing a major, taking a part time job, making a new friend, or responding to President Obama's call for volunteer service. You never know what new friendships you will make, what new skills you will acquire, what new opportunities might emerge for you, how your efforts will benefit other people, or how much satisfaction you may feel. Whenever a choice is being contemplated, to maximize our chances for welcome outcomes and to minimize our chances for undesirable outcomes, we need to employ purposeful, reflective judgment. Sure, winning is great, but it's just not a good idea to play poker unless we can afford to lose. We need to think ahead, to plan, and to problem solve. This means we need **critical thinking**.

All of us encounter opportunities in our daily lives to engage problems and decisions using strong critical thinking. In a nation that values self-reliance and initiative, the stronger our critical thinking skills and habits of mind, the greater our prospects for success. Imagine a population that made thoughtful and informed judgments about the policy issues and social questions of its day. It is unlikely that such a citizenry would blindly accept whatever the authorities said was true or unquestioningly comply with whatever those leaders commanded. Some have argued that corporations that hope to succeed in a global high-tech world will have to cultivate exactly the kind of internal culture that fosters strong critical thinking.[ii] Fortunately, a great many leaders in government, business, education, military, and religious organizations truly value critical thinking. The quote from Admiral Michael Mullen, Chairman of the Joint Chiefs of Staff, is only one example.[iii]

Obviously, a society of knowledgeable people determined to apply strong critical thinking skills to evaluate the policy decisions of their leaders might pose major difficulties for those in power. Not everyone in a leadership position has the confidence and the wisdom to want to cultivate critical thinking. A master of irony, the late George Carlin says it could be "Dangerous!" Go to **www.TheThinkSpot.com**

the **THINK SPOT**
www.thethinkspot.com

<<< **George Carlin offers** his comical take on education and critical thinking. He ironically speaks about feeding mental junk food to the masses so that people in power can maintain control.

Positive Examples of Critical Thinking

- A person trying to interpret an angry friend's needs, expressed through a rush of emotion and snide comments, to give that friend some help and support

- A manager trying to be as objective as possible when settling a dispute by summarizing the alternatives, with fairness to all sides to a disagreement

- A team of scientists working with great precision through a complex experiment in an effort to gather and analyze data

- A creative writer organizing ideas for the plot of a story attending to the complex motivations and personalities of the fictional characters

- A person running a small business trying to anticipate the possible economic and human consequences of various ways to increase sales or reduce costs

- A soccer coach during halftime working on new tactics for attacking the weaknesses of the other team when the match resumes

- A student confidently and correctly explaining exactly to his or her peers the methodology used to reach a particular conclusion, or why and how a certain methodology or standard of proof was applied

- An educator using clever questioning to guide a student to new insights

- Police detectives, crime scene analysts, lawyers, judges, and juries systematically investigating, interrogating, examining, and evaluating the evidence as they seek justice

- A policy analyst reviewing alternative drafts of health care legislation determining how to frame the law to benefit the most people at the least cost

- An applicant preparing for a job interview thinking about how to explain his or her particular skills and experiences in a way that will be relevant and of value to the prospective employer

- Parents anticipating the costs of sending their child to college, analyzing the family's projected income, and budgeting projected household expenses in an effort to put aside some money for that child's education

to access a video clip of Carlin on critical thinking. Some are so worried about the risks to their own power and position that they do not see the benefits to their organization's core purposes if its people are strong critical thinkers. Unscrupulous Machiavellian leaders might well ponder the question of how to distract, divert, or derail other people's critical thinking so that they can maintain their own power and control. After viewing the George Carlin clip we can almost hear the answer he might have imagined: Force-feed the population mental junk food by filling the popular media with celebrity inanities, sports trivia, exaggerated reports of imminent catastrophes, and outrageous opinions pumped out by extremist talk-show hosts like methane over a Coalinga cattle yard.

CRITICAL THINKING AND A FREE SOCIETY

Information is power. As we saw with the Iranian elections in 2009, an organization that can withhold information or distort it to fit official orthodoxy is in a much better position to suppress dissenters and maintain its position of control. The Iranian government curtailed Internet access, blamed the United States and Great Britain for fomenting opposition, and used the coercive power of the police and the social status of the ruling clergy to maintain its control. Thus, the desire to know who truly won the election, voiced by the hundreds of thousands who at first protested in the streets of Teheran, soon dissipated. Even those with strong critical thinking skills could not get the information needed to make a correct application of those skills. It was hard to know what to think. And the fear of imprisonment and retaliation put major damper on efforts to find out. History has many similar examples to offer. The bottom line is that it is difficult to foster the free and open questioning and the fair-minded search for the truth that is characteristic of critical thinking in any civil, religious, or corporate society that equates education with uniformity of belief, that punishes people who question authority, or that withholds the truth from its own people.[iv]

By contrast, in a free society, where education is about learning to think, where the powers of the state are used to protect the right to free and open inquiry, where people have the courage and the brains to ask hard questions, and where there is unfettered access to accurate information, then "perception management" is far more difficult. *Perception management* is the carefully choreographed manipulation of the beliefs and feelings of large numbers of people. Going beyond marketing and spin, perception management uses fear, anger, distortion, disinformation, and deceit, whatever it takes, including creating martyrs for the cause, faking enemy threats, lying to the media, destroying documents, etc., to achieve its goals. Those goals are always to influence people's beliefs and behavior, typically toward one

>> To get a sense of perception management in action, rent the movies, *Wag the Dog* starring Robert De Niro and Dustin Hoffman, or *Syriana* with George Clooney. The novel, *The Whole Truth,* by the *NY Times* bestselling author, David Baldacci, does a superb job of showing the extent to which some could take perception management to achieve their self-interested purposes.

outcome rather than another. The important thing is that the people would probably not believe those things nor do those things if they had access to all of the relevant information. We will see an example of this kind of dishonesty in Chapter 3 with a video clip of an interview with a Victor Crawford, a man who spent his career doing perception management on behalf of the tobacco industry.

One reason higher education in America is internationally admired and yet feared is that it has the potential to teach critical thinking. The upside is great progress in learning and culture, and hence huge benefits for society. Problem solvers using critical thinking have achieved massive breakthroughs in science, technology, commerce, and the arts, such as G3 cell phone technology, cancer treatments individualized to a person's unique DNA, global e-business, and new forms of music and architecture. But, at the same time, all that critical thinking can make interactions awkward at times. Not only is it harder for tyrants when people begin thinking for themselves, but people are apt to disagree, policy issues become more complicated to resolve, public discourse is more confusing, and decision making takes more time.

History shows what happens when people are not vigilant defenders of open, objective, and independent inquiry. We saw the results to a greater or lesser extent in Hitler's Germany, in Communist Russia, and, sadly, even in early 21st-century United States: Governments aggrandize their own power by fear-mongering and alarming people with doomsday scenarios. They wage wars of choice (e.g., the U.S. invasion of Iraq in 2003), not of necessity (e.g., United States' entry into WWII). They spy on their own citizens (e.g., the powers granted to the executive branch of government by the Patriot Act to monitor phone calls and e-mail), ignore the rights of various groups of people (e.g., the profiling by law enforcement agencies of Muslim Americans, Mexican Americans, and Blacks),

> Our whole constitutional heritage rebels at the thought of giving government the power to control men's minds.

Thurgood Marshall,
Former U.S. Supreme Court Justice[v]

forbid research on certain topics (e.g., stem cell research aimed at benefiting the victims of spinal cord injuries or Parkinson disease), accuse those who ask hard questions of disloyalty, and brand critics as traitors (e.g., the extreme rhetoric of the 2008 election, which became so vicious that Senator John McCain, a true American hero, had to speak out against it).

THE ONE AND THE MANY

Individual decisions can seem isolated and yet when they accumulate, they can have a far-reaching impact. For instance, in China the one-child policy has been in force for about 30 years. Culturally, there has always been a strong preference for male children and if families could only have one child, most wanted a boy. In household after household, family after family made the choice to do whatever seemed necessary, including infanticide, to ensure a male heir. The collective impact of those millions of individual decisions now burdens that nation. In some villages, the ratio of unmarried men to unmarried women is twenty to one. Today brides fetch payments as high as five years of family income. Those parents who decided to raise their first-born daughters sure look smart now.

Six billion of us share a planet in which economic, cultural, political, and environmental forces are so interconnected that the decisions of a few can impact the lives of many. Short-sighted and self-interested decisions made by corporate executives, bankers, stock traders, legislators and government regulatory agencies plunged the world into a global economic depression, which has cost trillions of dollars, devastated honest and well-run companies, bankrupted pension plans, destroyed families, and put tens of millions of people out of work. What were the decision-makers thinking? What blinded all of us to the foreseeable consequences of our choices?

Another reason why we need to think critically: Acting on beliefs accepted without reflection and decisions made thoughtlessly can be devastating to us and to our families, friends, co-workers, society, environment, and planet. We might believe that, in the great sweep of history, we generally are making progress toward the good.

Karl Popper argues that this notion can be comforting particularly to authoritarian and totalitarian organizations.[vi] But the evidence suggests that civilizations rise and fall, that economies flourish and flounder, that the arts are encouraged and suppressed, that advances in learning are made and then forgotten. As a species we have very few advantages, other than our oversized brain and the critical thinking it can generate. We would be unwise not to use what little we have.

What Do We Mean by "Critical Thinking"?

EXPERT CONSENSUS CONCEPTUALIZATION

At this point you might be asking yourself, "OK, so critical thinking will change our habits of mind, but what *is* critical thinking, exactly?" To answer that question precisely, an international group of 46 recognized experts in critical thinking research collaborated. The men and women in this group were drawn from many different academic disciplines, including philosophy, psychology, economics, computer science, education, physics, and zoology. For more than a year and a half, from February 1988 through September 1989, the group engaged in a consensus-oriented research process developed by the Rand Corporation known as the "Delphi" method.[viii] The challenge put to the experts was to come up with a working consensus about the meaning of "critical thinking," which could serve instructional and assessment purposes from K-12 through graduate school and across the full range of academic disciplines and professional fields. They also asked themselves questions that relate to Chapters 2 and 3, namely: "What are the core critical thinking skills and subskills? How can we strengthen those skills in students? Who are the best critical thinkers we know, and what habits of mind do they have which lead us to consider them the best?"

Long story short, the expert consensus forged defined *"critical thinking"* as *"the process of purposeful, self-regulatory judgment."*[ix] The purpose is straightforward: to form a well-reasoned and fair-minded judgment regarding what to believe or what to do. The "self-regulatory" part refers to our capacity to monitor our own thinking process and to correct any mistakes we might detect.[x]

The first realization emerging from this definition was that critical thinking was a "pervasive human phenomenon." Critical thinking is occurring whenever an individual or a group of people makes a reasoned and reflective judgment about what to believe or what to do.

How important did the experts think critical thinking was? They put their answer to that question this way: "Critical thinking is essential as a tool of inquiry. As such, critical thinking is a liberating force in education and a powerful resource in one's personal and civic life. While not synonymous with good thinking, critical thinking is a pervasive and self-rectifying human phenomenon."

So long as people have problems to solve and decisions to make, so long as they have things to learn and issues to resolve, there will be ample opportunities to use our critical thinking skills and habits of mind.

"CRITICAL THINKING" DOES NOT MEAN "NEGATIVE THINKING"

Critical thinking is not about bashing what people believe just to show how clever we are. Nor is critical thinking about using our skills to defend beliefs that we know are untrue or decisions we know are poor. Critical thinking is intended to be used to seek truth (small "t") with intellectual energy and with integrity. Thus, critical thinking is skeptical without being cynical. It is open-minded without being wishy-washy. It is analytical without being nitpicky. Critical thinking can be decisive without being stubborn, evaluative without being judgmental, and forceful without being opinionated.

HOW TO GET THE MOST OUT OF THIS BOOK

Growth in critical thinking is about becoming more skillful and mentally disciplined. To maximize your growth, this book offers a variety of exercises, examples, and topics to think about. Some of these are intentionally jarring. Those among us who find it frightening to follow reason and evidence wherever they may lead, even if they go against cherished beliefs, will find it difficult to make progress in critical thinking. The same is for those of us who try to avoid making decisions that involve uncertainty or risk or who try to live without ever questioning our own assumptions.

Think for a moment about learning to play a musical instrument or learning to play a sport. In both, improvement comes from practicing the requisite skills and strengthening our resolve to keep at it until we begin to see improvements. As we experience success at the skills part, enjoyment increases, and our disposition to keep applying ourselves

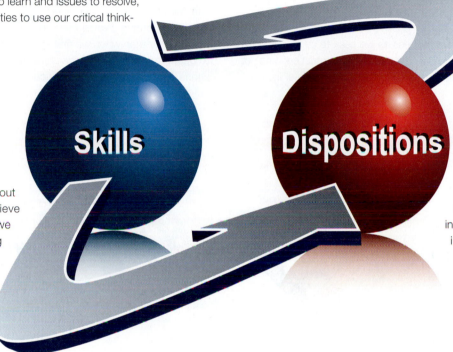

Critical Thinking Willing and Able

Thinking Critically

Group Discussion: George Carlin and Admiral Mike Mullen

1 Watch the classic George Carlin commentary on the seven words you cannot say on television. Give reasoned and fair-minded consideration to the question "What exactly makes a word a 'dirty word'?" Is there a difference between using the word and simply mentioning that word? Why is it acceptable to use one of those seven words in some contexts or with a particular intent, but not in other circumstances? Who has the authority to forbid other people from enunciating or writing certain individual words, and how did they get that power over others?

2 Discuss George Carlin's hypothetical question: "What if there were no hypothetical questions?"[xi]

3 George Carlin warned that those with great power and control would fear critical thinking. But, if that is so, what are we to make of the address by Navy Admiral Mike Mullen, who is the Chairman of the Joint Chiefs of Staff, to a group of graduating senior military officers at the National Defense University on June 11, 2009? Access the clip of George Carlin's "Seven Words You Can Never Say on Television" at www.TheThinkSpot.com.

the THINKSPOT
www.thethinkspot.com

> We need your service, right now, at this moment in history. I'm not going to tell you what your role should be; that's for you to discover. But I am asking you to stand up and play your part. I am asking you to help change history's course.

President Barack Obama, April 21, 2009[xii]

grows. And, having an ever more positive attitude about striving to improve, we tend to enjoy more success as we seek to refine our skills. Each aspect feeds the other. To be a success the player must become not only able but willing, not just skillful but disposed to use those skills.

We learn to play a musical instrument so we can enjoy making music. We learn a sport to enjoy playing the games. We work on our skills and mental dispositions not for their own sake, but for the sake of making music or playing the game. This is true with critical thinking, too. The defining purpose of critical thinking is to make reflective judgments about what to believe or what to do. We will work on both the skill part and the dispositional part as we move through this book. But we want to keep in mind that our purpose is to use them as tools to come to good judgments about what to do or what to believe.

Evaluating Critical Thinking

Even when we are first learning a musical instrument or a sport, we can tell that some of our peers are better at the instrument or the sport than others. We all make progress, and soon we are all doing much better than when we first started. We do not have to be experts to begin to see qualitative differences and to make reasonable evaluations. This, too, is true of critical thinking. There are some readily

Selected National Service Organizations
Find out more at http://www.serve.gov/

available ways to begin to make reasonable judgments concerning stronger or weaker uses of critical thinking. The following example illustrates some of these methods.

THE STUDENTS' ASSIGNMENT

Imagine a professor has assigned a group of four students to comment on the Edward M. Kennedy Serve America Act. Among other things, this bill, signed into law on April 21, 2009, designates September 11th as a national day of service. The group has access to the information about the bill reproduced here and on the Internet.

- "The bill encourages voluntary service. The legislation provides for gradually increasing the size of the Clinton-era AmeriCorps to 250,000 enrollees from its current 75,000. It outlines five broad categories where people can direct their service: helping the poor, improving education, encouraging energy efficiency, strengthening access to health care, and assisting veterans."

- "AmeriCorps offers a range of volunteer opportunities including housing construction, youth outreach, disaster response and caring for the elderly. Most receive an annual stipend of slightly less than $12,000 for working 10 months to a year."

- "The bill also ties volunteer work to money for college. People 55 and older could earn $1,000 education awards by getting involved in public service. Those awards can be transferred to a child, grand-child, or even someone they mentored."

- "Students from sixth grade through senior year of high school could earn a $500 education award for helping in their neighborhoods during a new summer program."[xii]

More information is available at **http://www.americorps.gov/**, and a summary of the legislation can be downloaded from **http://www.nationalservice.gov/about/serveamerica/index.asp**. The site **http://www.serve.gov/** is a clearinghouse of volunteer opportunities.

THE STUDENTS' STATEMENTS:

Student #1: "My take on it is that this bill requires national service. It's like, . . . a churchy-service-sorta-thing. But, you know, like run by the government and all. We all have to sign up and do our bit before we can go to college. That's a great idea. Think about it, how could anyone be against this legislation? I mean, unless they are either lazy or selfish. What excuse could a person possibly have not to serve our country? The president is right, we need to bring back the draft so that our Army has enough soldiers, and we need to fix health care and Social Security. I don't want to pay into a system all my working life only to find out that there's no money left when it's my time to retire."

Student #2: "Well I think this bill is a stupid idea. Who's going to agree to work for a lousy $12,000 a year? That's nuts. I can earn more working at Target or by enlisting in the Navy. This legislation is just more foolish liberal nonsense that takes our nation one step closer to socialism. Socialism is when the government tries to control too many things. And now the president is trying to control volunteer service. Maybe you want to build houses for poor people or clean up after hurricanes, but I don't see how any

of that is going to help me pass physics or get me a better job after college."

Student #3: "I think there are problems with the legislation, too. But you're wrong about people not wanting to volunteer. The number of hits on the AmeriCorps Web site keeps going up and up each month. Retired people, students, and people who just want to make a difference go there and to Serve.gov to see what opportunities might exist near where they live. On the other hand, I do have issues with the government being the organizing force in this. Volunteerism was alive and well in America before Big Brother got involved. I don't see why we need to spend 5.7 billion dollars getting people to do what they were already going to do anyway. We shouldn't pay people to be volunteers."

Student #4: "That's the point, some of them wanted to do volunteer service but they need a small incentive. Nobody is going to get rich on the stipends the government is offering. I think that people who want to keep government at arm's length are going to have problems with this bill. They are right that it is another way that government is worming itself into every facet of our lives. But a lot of people feel that way about religion, too; that's why they do not want to volunteer in programs sponsored by religious groups, because they don't want to be seen as agreeing with all the beliefs or that group. The real question for me is the effect that this legislation might have on the future politics of our nation. All these volunteers could become, in effect, people the Administration can call on in the next election. Organizing tens of thousands Americans who basically agree with the idea of public service at public expense is like lining up the Democratic voters who will want to be sure these policies are not reversed by the Republicans. I'm not talking about a vague idea like "socialism," I'm talking about clever politics, positioning the Democratic Party for success in 2012. On balance, that's OK with me. But we need to understand that this legislation will result in more than just a lot of wonderful work by a large number of generous Americans who are willing to give of their time to help others."

Having reviewed the information about this legislation and read the statements by each of the four students, how would you evaluate those statements in terms of the critical thinking each displays?

The Holistic Critical Thinking Scoring Rubric

A Tool for Developing and Evaluating Critical Thinking
Peter A. Facione, Ph.D., and Noreen C. Facione, Ph.D.

Strong 4. Consistently does all or almost all of the following:

- Accurately interprets evidence, statements, graphics, questions, etc.
- Identifies the salient arguments (reasons and claims) pro and con.
- Thoughtfully analyzes and evaluates major alternative points of view.
- Draws warranted, judicious, non-fallacious conclusions.
- Justifies key results and procedures, explains assumptions and reasons.
- Fair-mindedly follows where evidence and reasons lead.

Acceptable 3. Does most or many of the following:

- Accurately interprets evidence, statements, graphics, questions, etc.
- Identifies relevant arguments (reasons and claims) pro and con.
- Offers analyses and evaluations of obvious alternative points of view.
- Draws warranted, non-fallacious conclusions.
- Justifies some results or procedures, explains reasons.
- Fair-mindedly follows where evidence and reasons lead.

Unacceptable 2. Does most or many of the following:

- Misinterprets evidence, statements, graphics, questions, etc.
- Fails to identify strong, relevant counterarguments.
- Ignores or superficially evaluates obvious alternative points of view.
- Draws unwarranted or fallacious conclusions.
- Justifies few results or procedures, seldom explains reasons.
- Regardless of the evidence or reasons, maintains or defends views based on self-interest or preconceptions.

Weak 1. Consistently does all or almost all of the following:

- Offers biased interpretations of evidence, statements, graphics, questions, information, or the points of view of others.
- Fails to identify or hastily dismisses strong, relevant counterarguments.
- Ignores or superficially evaluates obvious alternative points of view.
- Argues using fallacious or irrelevant reasons and unwarranted claims.
- Does not justify results or procedures, nor explain reasons.
- Regardless of the evidence or reasons, maintains or defends views based on self-interest or preconceptions.
- Exhibits close-mindedness or hostility to reason.

Reprinted with permission from The California Academic Press / Insight Assessment. – *Assessing Critical Thinking Worldwide*

www.insightassessment.com   USA Phone: (650) 697- 5628

Remember, base your evaluation on what the statements reveal about the quality of the reasoning, not on whether you agree or disagree with their conclusion.

THE HOLISTIC CRITICAL THINKING SCORING RUBRIC

Every day we all make decisions about what to believe or what to do. When we are being reflective and fair-minded about doing so, we are using our critical thinking skills. The idea behind a critical thinking course is to help us strengthen these skills and fortify our intentions to use them when the occasion arises.

If that is true, then, like other things we do that we may not have formally studied, there probably is room for improvement. But we are not starting from zero. We have critical thinking skills, even if we have not yet refined them to their maximum potential. We know what it means to be open-minded and to take a systematic and objective look at an issue. We are familiar with the ordinary English meanings of common words for talking about thinking such as "interpret," "analyze," "infer," "explain," "reason," "conclusion," and "fallacy" "argument." And, in a broad sense, a lot of the time we can tell the difference between strong reasoning and weak reasoning, even if we do not yet know all the details or terminology.

So, given that none of us are novices at critical thinking, we should be able to make a reasonable first stab at an evaluation of the thinking portrayed by the four students in the example on page 9. Just using our experience and common sense we can agree that #4 and #3 are stronger than #2 and #1.

A tool was designed to help us with this process of evaluation. It relies on the ordinary meanings of common terms used to talk about thinking. Called "The Holistic Critical Thinking Scoring Rubric (HCTSR)," this tool can aid us in evaluating real-life examples of critical thinking because it requires us only to describe an example of the four descriptions as "strong," "acceptable," "unacceptable," and "weak" and see which of the four fits best. At this point, before we have worked through any of the other chapters of the book, this simple tool/approach is sufficient to get us started evaluating critical thinking. Naturally, as we learn more about critical thinking, we will become better at applying the rubric and more facile at using the terminology it contains. Our evaluative judgments will improve, and our ability to explain our judgments will improve as well. In this way, the rubric actually become one of the tools we can use to improve our critical thinking. Where we may disagree with one another at first about the evaluative levels that best fit, in time as we work with the rubric and with others on applying it, we will begin to form clearer ideas of the differences not only between the extreme examples, but between examples that fall between the extremes.

To apply the HCTSR, take each student's statement and see which level of the Rubric offers the best description of the reasoning evident in that statement. You will see that they line up rather well with the four levels of the HCTSR. Statement #4 is a good example of the top level, "strong –4"; student statement #3 is "acceptable"; student statement #2 is "unacceptable" because it displays the problems listed in the HCTSR in category 2; and statement #1 is so far off base that it qualifies as "weak –1."

The HCTSR is a great tool to use to evaluate the critical thinking evident in lots of different situations: classroom discussions, papers, essays, panel presentations, commercials, editorials, letters to the editor, news conferences, infomercials, commentator's remarks, speeches, jury deliberations, planning sessions, meetings, debates, or your own private thoughts. Keep the focus on the reasoning, and do not let the fact that you may agree or disagree with the particular conclusions being advocated sway you. Do not worry if you feel unsure of yourself, having used the HCTSR only this one time. There will be plenty of additional opportunities for you to practice with it in the exercises in this chapter and in future chapters. Like a new pair of shoes, you will get comfortable with the tool. Think of it this way: The more you use the HCTSR, and the more adept you become at sorting out why something represents stronger or weaker critical thinking, the more you will improve your own critical thinking.

Thinking Critically — Apply the Holistic Critical Thinking Scoring Rubric

1 On April 27, 2009 only six days after the bill was signed by President Obama, NPR's Michel Martin interviewed Deepak Bhargava about the Edward M. Kennedy Serve America Act on "Tell Me More." With one or two classmates, or individually, listen to the interview and then use the HCTSR to evaluate the critical thinking evident in their conversation. Evaluate the discussion as a whole rather than evaluating the two people's thinking separately. Access the interview at www.TheThinkSpot.com.

2 Each year, the U.S. Supreme Court decides which cases it will hear. In June 2009 it declined to review a case that would have brought before it the question of gays in the military. *The New York Times* published an editorial about that decision. Using the HCTSR, evaluate the critical thinking evident in that editorial. Remember to separate your personal views about gays in the military

and your opinion about the Supreme Court's decision from your evaluation. Access the article at www.TheThinkSpot.com.

3 When people first begin using a rubric like the HCTSR, it is important to calibrate their scoring with one another. Some individuals might initially rate something higher and 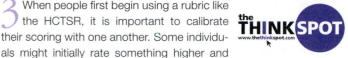 others rate it lower. However, through mutual discussion, it is possible to help one another come to a reasonable consensus on a score. Identify two editorials and two letters to the editor that appear in your campus newspaper. Working with four classmates, individually rate those four things with the HCTSR. Then compare the scores that each of you initially assigned. Where the scores differ, discuss the critical thinking evident in the editorials or letters, and come to consensus on a score.

CRITICAL THINKING is purposeful, reflective judgment that is focused on deciding what to believe or what to do. Critical thinking is a pervasive human phenomenon. We all have some level of skill in critical thinking and we have the capacity to improve those skills. Critical thinking skills, which are the topic of Chapter 2, are used to engage purposeful and reflective judgment. Critical thinking habits of mind motivate us to use those skills and incline us toward adopting critical thinking, rather than using some other approach, when we must make important decisions about what to believe or what to do. Chapter 3 explores the critical thinking habits of mind that, like the skills, can be fostered and strengthened.

Neither negative nor cynical, but thoughtful and fair-minded, critical thinking is essential for inquiry and learning. Critical thinking is a liberating force in education and a precondition for a free and democratic society. Strong critical thinking is a powerful resource and tremendous asset in one's personal, professional, and civic life.

KEY TERMS

critical thinking is purposeful, reflective judgment that manifests itself in giving reasoned and fair-minded consideration to evidence, conceptualizations, methods, contexts, and standards in order to decide what to believe or what to do.   *4*

FIND IT ON THE THINKSPOT

This chapter features the ironic and at times caustic observations of the late George Carlin, comedian and social critic. I invite you to view video clips for this chapter and the dozens of other video clips cited throughout this book by going to **www.TheThinkSpot.com**.

Why am I inviting you to The Think Spot? You have the right to ask, given that this is a book about giving reasons and making strong arguments. Strengthening our critical thinking for use in real-life contexts requires that we practice with realistic examples. As valuable as text-based examples will be for us in this book, we must also use examples that are visual, auditory, and culturally complex. The best examples require us to analyze and interpret body language, gestures, and unspoken but implicit assumptions. Video clips, particularly if we watch them carefully and analyze them in detail, are powerful devices for engaging our critical thinking.

In this chapter I put George Carlin side by side with Admiral Mullen, whom we can consider a strong and articulate representative of a more conservative political perspective. This juxtaposition is intentional. There are strong critical thinkers on all sides of the political spectrum. We cannot say that people who agree with us are necessarily strong critical thinkers and those who disagree are necessarily weak critical thinkers. Please be careful to remember this as you view the video clips and work through the exercises in this chapter and throughout the book. In this book, as in real life, we often encounter vivid images, topics, issues, people, and events that trigger positive or negative emotional responses. Critical thinking in real life must find its way through our initial emotional reactions and locate that place in our minds where reason, facts, and wise judgments guide what we believe and what we do. This takes practice.

- I invite you to visit **www.TheThinkSpot.com** to hear what George Carlin has to say about critical thinking. (p. 4)

- I ask that you watch a George Carlin clip and then discuss his views about the use of language that some may find offensive. (p. 7)

- The third discussion topic in that page 7 exercise refers to Admiral Mullen's quote from page 4. The quotation is taken from a speech that is available to you at **www.TheThinkSpot.com** too.

- Please use the NPR radio interview for the first HCTSR exercise. (p. 11)

Exercises

REFLECTIVE LOG EXERCISES

Think back over today and yesterday. Describe a problem you faced or a decision which you considered. Who was involved, and what was the issue? Describe how you thought about that problem or decision—not so much what you decided or what solution you picked, but the process you used. Were you open-minded about various options, systematic in your approach, courageous enough to ask yourself tough questions, bold enough to follow the reasons and evidence wherever they led, inquisitive and eager to learn more before making a judgment, nuanced enough to see shades of gray rather than only stark black and white? Did you check your interpretations and analyses? Did you draw your inferences carefully? Were you as objective and fair-minded as you might have been? Explain your decision in your log with enough detail that would permit you to go back a week or two from now and evaluate your decision for the quality of the critical thinking it demonstrates.

EXPLAIN WHAT IS WRONG WITH EACH

1. Critical thinking has no application in day-to-day life.
2. "Critical thinking" means making criticisms of other people's ideas.
3. Democracies get along just fine even if people do not think for themselves.
4. Decisions about how I want to live my life do not affect other people.
5. Reflective decision making requires little or no effort.
6. Deciding what to believe or what to do is not possible without critical thinking.
7. If we disagree on something, then one of us is not using critical thinking.
8. Every time I make a judgment I am engaged in critical thinking.

GROUP DISCUSSION

Critical thinking takes effort! Why work so hard? Imagine what would it be like to live in a community where critical thinking was illegal? What might the risks and benefits of such a life be? How would the people living in that community redress grievances, solve problems, plan for the future, evaluate options, and pursue their individual and joint purposes? Now imagine what it would be like to live in a community where critical thinking was unnecessary? Can there be such a place, except perhaps as human specimens in some other species' zoo?

In the fall

of 2008, the presidential campaign was in full swing. Journalists were interviewing all the candidates to inform the American public, and Katie Couric, the anchor and managing editor of *CBS Evening News*, wrestled with how to conduct the interviews both informatively and objectively. She knew this would not be easy. Reflecting on her preparation, she comments, "I realized I had to control my words and my facial expressions." While asking probing questions to uncover vague generalities and practical implications, she did not want viewers to interpret her reactions as agreeing or disagreeing with what her interviewees said.

Couric had to ask questions creatively to display the candidate's depth of understanding, or lack thereof. A skillful and highly experienced journalist, Couric said, "I wanted to showcase candidates' ideas, but not to evaluate their merit." That assessment, Couric believes is best left to the viewing audience. What better way, she decided, than to give the candidates the opportunity to speak for themselves in response to questions aimed at clarifying reasons and drawing out the implications? Couric knew she had a unique responsibility with the relatively unknown Governor Sarah Palin. Couric said, "The interview would be worthless if it turned out to be either a conservative puff piece or a liberal hatchet job." In the video clip, Couric explains how she prepared to interview candidate Palin. View the interview at **www.TheThinkSpot.com**.

the **THINK** SPOT
www.thethinkspot.com

THE "ABLE" IN "WILLING AND ABLE" TO THINK CRITICALLY

Core Critical Thinking Skills

When thinking about the meaning and importance of the term "critical thinking" in Chapter 1, we referenced an expert consensus. That consensus identified certain cognitive skills as being central to critical thinking. Their research puts it this way[i]:

INTERPRETING AND ANALYZING THE CONSENSUS STATEMENT

Let's unpack that quote. The experts identify six skills:

- Interpretation
- Evaluation
- Analysis
- Explanation
- Inference
- Self-Regulation

When thinking critically, we apply these six skills to:

- Evidence   (facts, experiences, statements)
- Conceptualizations   (ideas, theories, ways of seeing the world)
- Methods   (strategies, techniques, approaches)
- Criteria   (standards, benchmarks, expectations)
- Context   (situations, conditions, circumstances)

We are expected to ask a lot of tough questions about all five areas. For example, "How good is the evidence? Do these concepts apply? Were the methods appropriate? Are there better methods for investigating this question? What standard of proof should we be using? How rigorous should we be? What circumstantial factors might lead us to revise our opinions?" Good critical thinkers are ever-vigilant, monitoring and correcting their own thinking.

THE JURY IS DELIBERATING

In the American classic film, *12 Angry Men*[ii] a jury deliberates the guilt or innocence of a young man accused of murder. The jury room is hot, the hour is late, and tempers are short. Ten of the twelve jurors have voted to convict when we join the story. As one of the two jurors who are still uncertain, Henry Fonda's character first *analyzes* the testimony of a pair of witnesses, putting what each said side by side. Using all his critical thinking skills, he tries to reconcile their conflicting testimony. He asks how the old man could have heard the accused say "I'm going to kill you" with the El train roaring by the open window. In this statement, Fonda *infers* that the old man could not have been telling the truth. Fonda then *explains* that inference to the other jurors with a flawless argument. But, the other jurors still want to know why an old man with apparently nothing to gain would not tell the truth. One of the other jurors, an old man himself, *interprets* that witness's behavior for his colleagues. The conversation then turns to the question of how to *interpret* the expression "I'm going kill you!" that the accused is alleged to have shouted. One juror wants to take it literally as a statement of intent. Another argues that context matters, that words and phrases cannot always be taken literally. "Why did the defense attorney not make these arguments?" someone says. In their *evaluation*, the jury does seem to agree

> We understand critical thinking to be purposeful, self-regulatory judgment which results in interpretation, analysis, evaluation, and inference, as well as explanation of the evidential, conceptual, methodological, criteriological, or contextual considerations upon which that judgment is based. "

The Delphi Report, American Philosophical Association[iii]

on the quality of the defense—namely, that it was poor. One juror draws the conclusion that this means the lawyer thought his own client was guilty. But is that so? Could there be some other explanation or interpretation for the half-hearted defense?

The jury has the authority to question the quality of the *evidence*, to dispute the competing *theories* of the case that are presented by the prosecution and the defense, to find fault with the investigatory *methods* of the police, to dispute whether the doubts some members may have meet the *criterion* of "reasonable doubt" or not, and to take into consideration all the *contextual and circumstantial* elements that may be relevant. In other words, a good jury is the embodiment of good critical thinking that a group of people practice. The stronger their collective skills, the greater justice will be done. Access the El Train video clip from *12 Angry Men* at **www.TheThinkSpot.com**.

the THINK SPOT
www.thethinkspot.com

CRITICAL THINKING SKILLS FIRE IN MANY COMBINATIONS

One way to present critical thinking skills is in the form of a list, as we did on page 16 when we listed the six skills. But lists typically suggest that we move from one item to another in a predetermined step-by-step progression, similar to pilots methodically working down the mandatory list of preflight safety checks. Critical thinking is not rote or scripted in the way that a list of skills might suggest.

Critical thinking is a form of judgment, namely reflective, purposeful judgment. The skills are what we use to make that judgment. Imagine for a moment what it is like looking for an address while driving on a busy and unfamiliar street. To do this, we must simultaneously be coordinating the use of many skills, but fundamentally our focus is on the driving and not on the individual skills. We are concentrating on street signs and address numbers while also interpreting traffic signals such as stoplights, and controlling the car's speed, direction, and location relative to other vehicles. Driving requires coordinating physical skills such as how hard to press the gas or tap the brakes and

EL - LINE

BEDROOM

mental skills such as analyzing the movement of our vehicle relative to those around ours to avoid accidents. In the end, however, we say that we drove the car to the destination. We do not list all the skills, and we certainly do not practice them one by one in a serial order. Rather, we use them all in concert. Critical thinking has certain important features in common with looking for an address while driving on a busy and unfamiliar street. The key similarity to notice here is that critical thinking requires using all the skills in concert, not one at a time sequentially.

The intricate interaction of critical thinking skills in real-life problem solving and decision making may begin with an analysis, an interpretation, an inference, or an evaluation. Then, using self-regulation, we may go back and check ourselves for accuracy. On other occasions, we may first draw an inference on the basis of an interpretation and then evaluate our own inference. We may be explaining our reasoning to someone and realize because we are monitoring our own thinking, that our reasoning is not adequate. And this may lead us to recheck our analyses or our inferences to see where we may need to refine our thinking. That was what the jury, considered as a whole, was doing in *12 Angry Men*—going back and forth among interpretation, analysis, inference, and evaluation, with Henry Fonda as the person who called for more careful self-monitoring and self-correction. The jury's deliberation demanded reflection and an orderly analysis and evaluation of the facts, but deliberation is not constrained by adherence to a predetermined list or sequencing of mental events. Nor is critical thinking.

No, it would be an unfortunate and misleading oversimplification to reduce critical thinking to a list of skills, such as the recipe on the lid of dehydrated soup: first analyze, then infer, then explain, then close the lid and wait five minutes. To avoid the misimpressions that a list might engender, we need some other way of displaying the names of the skills.

For nearly 20 years now, I have found it helpful when talking with college students and faculty around the world about critical thinking skills to use the metaphor of a sphere with the names of the skills displayed randomly over its surface,[iv] Why a sphere? Three reasons: First, organizing the names of the skills on a sphere is truer to our lived experience of engaging in reflective judgment, as indicated above. We have all experienced those moments when, in the mental space of a few seconds, our minds fly from interpretation to analysis to inference and evaluation as we try to sort out our thoughts before we commit ourselves to a particular decision. We may go back and forth interpreting what we are seeing, analyzing ideas and drawing tentative inferences, trying to be sure that we have things right before we make a judgment. Second, a sphere does not presume any given order of events, which, for the present, is truer to the current state of the science. Third, a sphere reminds us about another important characteristic of critical thinking skills, namely that each can be applied to the other and to themselves.[v] We can analyze our inferences. We can analyze our analyses. We can explain our interpretations. We can evaluate our explanations. We can monitor those processes and correct any mistakes we might see ourselves making. In this way, the core critical thinking skills can be said to interact.

Core Critical Thinking Skills Interact

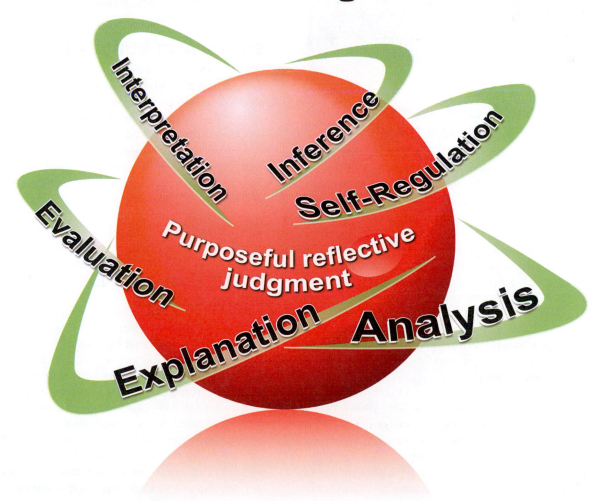

Professionals Measure Outcomes

Musicians	→	Quality of the concert
Salesperson	→	Number of sales
Athletes	→	Games won
Nurses	→	Health care outcomes achieved
Teachers	→	Learning accomplished
Soldiers	→	Success of the mission

STRENGTHENING OUR CORE CRITICAL THINKING SKILLS

Musicians, salespeople, athletes, nurses, teachers, and soldiers strive to improve their likelihood of success by strengthening the skills needed in their respective professions. Even as they train in one skill or another, working people must not lose sight of how those skills come together in their professional work. The quality of the concert, the number of sales made, the games won, the health care outcomes achieved, the learning accomplished, and the success of the mission—these are the outcomes that count. The same holds for critical thinkers. Success consists of making well-reasoned, reflective judgments to solve problems well and to make good decisions. Critical thinking skills are the tools we use to accomplish those purposes.

In the driving example, our attention was on the challenges associated with reaching the intended address. In real-world critical thinking, our attention will be on the challenges associated with solving the problem or making the decision at hand.

To strengthen our critical thinking skills, we will emphasize first one and then another in future chapters. Here is our plan: We will focus on strengthening our skills of **interpretation** and **analysis** in Chapters 4 and 5 when we examine how to clarify the meanings of individual claims and how to visually display the reasoning we use to support our claims and conclusions. In Chapters 6, 7, and 8 we will work on **evaluation**, looking first at how to assess the credibility of individual claims

and then at how to evaluate the quality of arguments. Strengthening our **self-regulation** skill will be our emphasis in Chapters 9 and 10 as we take a closer look at decision making in real life, particularly at the differences between snap decisions and reflective decisions. In Chapters 11, 12, and 13, we will work on improving our **inference** and **explanation** skills. Those chapters focus on how human beings use their powers of reasoning to acquire new knowledge using analogies, ideologies, and investigative inquiry.

The Art of the Good Question

There are many familiar questions that invite people to use their critical thinking skills. We can associate certain questions with certain skills. The table on page 20 gives some examples.[vi] Often, our best critical thinking comes when we ask the right questions.[vii]

Katie Couric used the art of good questioning in her interviews with Governor Palin. For example, the next clip, which you can access at **www.TheThinkSpot.com**, shows Couric asking about how Palin interprets the word "sexist." It also shows Couric using her critical thinking skills to learn the implications of the governor's views on global warming, abortion, and other domestic issues. After you view that clip, watch the next clip in which the topics shift to international issues. Notice that the questions Couric uses are not limited to just "Tell us what you think about X." Rather, Couric asks questions intended to evoke deeper analysis, evaluation, and self-regulation. Her use of critical thinking questioning, always with respect, is exemplary. As you watch these two clips, write down each of Couric's questions. Watch both of these clips at **www.TheThinkSpot.com**.

SKILLS AND SUBSKILLS DEFINED

The six core critical thinking skills each has related subskills, as shown in the table on page 21. The descriptions in the table of each core skill come from the expert consensus research referenced earlier.[viii] The experts provided this more refined level of analysis of the concept of "critical thinking skills" to assist students and teachers in finding examples and exercises that could help strengthen these skills. But, remember that "critical thinking" does not refer to a package of skills. Rather, critical thinking is what we do with the skills, which is making purposeful reflective judgments about what to believe or what to do. So, make sure to use this table as an awareness tool, not a map.

Inductive and Deductive Reasoning

The table on page 21 describing the core critical thinking skills mentions "inductive or deductive reasoning" in the subskill column. Conceiving of reasoning as being either induction or deduction has a long and rich history going back to Aristotle (384–322 BCE).[x] Over the centuries, logicians studying deductive reasoning developed deductive logic systems that are useful in fields like mathematics and computer science.[xi] Statisticians have developed advanced techniques of statistical analysis that are useful for the kinds of probabilistic inductive inferences characteristic of scientific research and economics.[xii] But, as you will see from the examples in this section and later in the book, we all use inductive and deductive reasoning in making everyday inferences

Couric's Questions

1 The *CBS Evening News* on September 24, 2008 ran this segment of the Sarah Palin interview. The main topic of the interview was the pending economic bailout legislation proposed by the Bush administration. Watch the video of the interview and see whether you can spot questions being asked by Katie Couric inviting the use of critical thinking. Access Katie Couric's interview with VP candidate Governor Sarah Palin at **www.TheThinkSpot.com**.

2 Here is a transcript of that video.[ix] Questions that evoke critical thinking skills are highlighted. Which skills does each invoke? [My observations are in brackets.]

Sarah Palin: My understanding is that Rick Davis recused himself from the dealings of the firm. I don't know how long ago, a year or two ago that he's not benefiting from that. And you know, I was—I would hope that's not the case.

Katie Couric: But he still has a stake in the company **so isn't that a conflict of interest?**

Palin: Again, my understanding is that he recused himself from the dealings with Freddie and Fannie, any lobbying efforts on his part there. And I would hope that's the case because, as John McCain has been saying, and as I've on a much more local level been also rallying against is the undue influence of lobbyists in public policy decisions being made.

Next, Couric asked about the $700 billion government bailout of bad debt—and whether she supports it.

Palin: I'm all about the position that America is in and that we have to look at a $700 billion bailout. And as Sen. McCain has said unless this nearly trillion dollar bailout is what it may end up to be, unless there are amendments in Paulson's proposal, really I don't believe that Americans are going to support this and we will not support this. The interesting thing in the last couple of days that I have seen is that Americans are waiting to see what John McCain will do on this proposal. They're not waiting to see what Barack Obama is going to do. Is he going to do this and see what way the political wind's blowing? They're waiting to see if John McCain will be able to

see these amendments implemented in Paulson's proposal.

Couric: Why do you say that? Why are they waiting for John McCain and not Barack Obama?

Palin: He's got the track record of the leadership qualities and the pragmatism that's needed at a crisis time like this.

Couric: But polls have shown that Sen. Obama has actually gotten a boost as a result of this latest crisis, with more people feeling that he can handle the situation better than John McCain. [Implicit question: How do you reconcile apparently divergent evidence?]

Palin: I'm not looking at poll numbers. What I think Americans at the end of the day are going to be able to go back and look at track records and see who's more apt to be talking about solutions and wishing for and hoping for solutions for some opportunity to change, and who's actually done it?

Couric: If this doesn't pass, do you think there's a risk of another Great Depression?

Palin: Unfortunately, that is the road that America may find itself on. Not necessarily this, as it's been proposed, has to pass or we're going to find ourselves in another Great Depression. But, there has got to be action—bipartisan effort—Congress not pointing fingers at one another but finding the solution to this, taking action, and being serious about the reforms on Wall Street that are needed.

Couric: Would you support a moratorium on foreclosures to help average Americans keep their homes? [Depending upon the interpretation, this could either be a question asking only for a statement of fact regarding Governor Palin's views, or it could be a question asking for her views and her reason.]

Palin: That's something that John McCain and I have both been discussing—whether that ... is part of the solution or not. You know, it's going to be a multi-faceted solution that has to be found here.

Couric: So, you haven't decided whether you'll support it or not? [Couric herself uses her critical thinking skills to draw this inference and then seeks confirmation.]

Palin: I have not.

Couric: What are the pros and cons of it, do you think?

Palin: Oh, well, some decisions that have been made poorly should not be rewarded, of course.

Couric: By consumers, you're saying? [Self-monitoring. Couric is trying to clarify the interpretation.]

Palin: Consumers—and those who were predator lenders also. That's, you know, that has to be considered also. But again, it's got to be a comprehensive, long-term solution found ... for this problem that America is facing today. As I say, we are getting into crisis mode here.

Couric: You've said, quote, "John McCain will reform the way Wall Street does business." Other than supporting stricter regulations of Fannie Mae and Freddie Mac two years ago, can you give us any more example of his leading the charge for more oversight?

Palin: I think that the example that you just cited, with his warnings two years ago about Fannie and Freddie—that, that's paramount. That's more than a heck of a lot of other senators and representatives did for us.

Couric: But he's been in Congress for 26 years. He's been chairman of the powerful Commerce Committee. And he has almost always sided with less regulation, not more. [In context, asking how apparently divergent evidence can be reconciled with the claim put forth.]

Palin: He's also known as the maverick though, taking shots from his own party, and certainly taking shots from the other party. Trying to get people to understand what he's been talking about—the need to reform government.

Couric: But can you give me any other concrete examples? Because I know you've said Barack Obama is a lot of talk and no action. Can you give me any other examples in his 26 years of John McCain truly taking a stand on this? [Asking for any additional evidence for the claim being made.]

Palin: I can give you examples of things that John McCain has done, that has shown his foresight, his pragmatism, and his leadership abilities. And that is what America needs today.

Couric: I'm just going to ask you one more time—not to belabor the point. Specific examples in his 26 years of pushing for more regulation. [Checking credibility of the claim.]

Palin: I'll try to find you some and I'll bring them to you.

about what to believe or what to do. Let's take a quick look first at inductive reasoning and then at deductive reasoning. In later chapters we will return again and again to explore how critical thinking skills relate to induction and deduction.

NURSES' HEALTH STUDY—DECADES OF DATA

One powerful example of research conducted using inductive reasoning is the Nurses' Health Study. This project is perhaps the most comprehensive descriptive investigation of health-related behavior ever conducted. Since its inception in 1976, over 238,000 nurses have provided information.[xiii] The details in the box entitled "Early Life Factors and Risk of Breast Cancer," on page 22, report findings based on statistical analyses of millions of data. As you can see, some remarkable, unexpected, and important correlations were discovered.[xiv] Measured expressions like "investigations . . . suggested . . .", ". . . is associated with reduced risk . . .", and "strong correlations . . . support . . ." characterize the report. The scientists who conducted this research are presenting probabilistic conclusions. Their conclusions are warranted because the statistical analyses provide sufficient confidence to assert that the relationships on which they report are highly unlikely to have occurred by random chance.

Questions to Fire Up Our Critical Thinking Skills	
Interpretation	• What does this mean? • What's happening? • How should we understand that (e.g., what he or she just said)? • What is the best way to characterize/categorize/classify this? • In this context, what was intended by saying/doing that? • How can we make sense out of this (experience, feeling, statement)?
Analysis	• Please tell us again your reasons for making that claim. • What is your conclusion/What is it that you are claiming? • Why do you think that? • What are the arguments pro and con? • What assumptions must we make to accept that conclusion? • What is your basis for saying that?
Inference	• Given what we know so far, what conclusions can we draw? • Given what we know so far, what can we rule out? • What does this evidence imply? • If we abandoned/accepted that assumption, how would things change? • What additional information do we need to resolve this question? • If we believed these things, what would they imply for us going forward? • What are the consequences of doing things that way? • What are some alternatives we haven't yet explored? • Let's consider each option and see where it takes us. • Are there any undesirable consequences that we can and should foresee?
Evaluation	• How credible is that claim? • Why do we think we can trust what this person claims? • How strong are those arguments? • Do we have our facts right? • How confident can we be in our conclusion, given what we now know?
Explanation	• What were the specific findings/results of the investigation? • Please tell us how you conducted that analysis. • How did you come to that interpretation? • Please take us through your reasoning one more time. • Why do you think that (was the right answer/was the solution)? • How would you explain why this particular decision was made?
Self-Regulation	• Our position on this issue is still too vague; can we be more precise? • How good was our methodology, and how well did we follow it? • Is there a way we reconcile these two apparently conflicting conclusions? • How good is our evidence? • OK, before we commit, what are we missing? • I'm finding some of our definitions a little confusing; can we revisit what we mean by certain things before making any final decisions?

Source: © 2009. Test Manual for the California Critical Thinking Skills Test, published by Insight Assessment. Used with permission.

SKILL	Experts' Consensus Description	Subskill
Interpretation	"To comprehend and express the meaning or significance of a wide variety of experiences, situations, data, events, judgments, conventions, beliefs, rules, procedures, or criteria"	Categorize Decode significance Clarify meaning
Analysis	"To identify the intended and actual inferential relationships among statements, questions, concepts, descriptions, or other forms of representation intended to express belief, judgment, experiences, reasons, information, or opinions"	Examine ideas Identify arguments Identify reasons and claims
Inference	"To identify and secure elements needed to draw reasonable conclusions; to form conjectures and hypotheses; to consider relevant information and to educe the consequences flowing from data, statements, principles, evidence, judgments, beliefs, opinions, concepts, descriptions, questions, or other forms of representation"	Query evidence Conjecture alternatives Draw conclusions using inductive or deductive reasoning
Evaluation	"To assess the credibility of statements or other representations that are accounts or descriptions of a person's perception, experience, situation, judgment, belief, or opinion; and to assess the logical strength of the actual or intended inferential relationships among statements, descriptions, questions, or other forms of representation"	Assess credibility of claims Assess quality of arguments that were made using inductive or deductive reasoning
Explanation	"To state and to justify that reasoning in terms of the evidential, conceptual, methodological, criteriological, and contextual considerations upon which one's results were based; and to present one's reasoning in the form of cogent arguments"	State results Justify procedures Present arguments
Self-Regulation	"Self-consciously to monitor one's cognitive activities, the elements used in those activities, and the results educed, particularly by applying skills in analysis, and evaluation to one's own inferential judgments with a view toward questioning, confirming, validating, or correcting either one's reasoning or one's results"	Self-monitor Self-correct

Source: Critical thinking skill definitions cited are from APA Report: Expert Consensus Statement on Critical Thinking. (ERIC ED 315 423)

INDUCTIVE REASONING

Drawing probabilistic inferences regarding what is most likely to be true or most likely not true, given certain information, is known as **inductive reasoning**. Here are some examples.

- When I stop at a traffic light, I hear this funny, rattling sound coming from under my car. It is sort of in the middle or maybe toward the back, but definitely not toward the front. I only hear it when the car is idling, not when I'm driving along at a reasonable speed. My Dad said once that the metal baffles inside a muffler can loosen up if the muffler is old and rusty. He said that a loose baffle makes a rattling sound when it vibrates, like when the engine is idling or when the tires are out of alignment. My muffler is at least nine years old. So, I'm thinking that probably the rattling sound is coming from the muffler.

- We interviewed three people, and each one was very personable. I think that the first person had the strongest resume. But the second person seemed a lot smarter. I liked the enthusiasm and energy that the third person had, but that person never worked for an organization like ours before. It's a tough choice. But I'm thinking that probably the second person would be the best of the three for us to hire since innovative ideas are more important to us than experience or enthusiasm.

- In the past whenever the TV news programs in Chicago ran headline stories featuring a sketch artist's drawing of a fugitive, the Chicago Police Department (CPD) hotline received over 200 phone calls from people all over the city who said that they spotted the person. Tonight the Chicago TV news programs are going to feature a sketch artist's drawing of a fugitive whom the police are trying to locate. This will probably yield hundreds of calls to the CPD hotline.

- Suppose we imagine electricity flowing through wires in the way that water flows through pipes. With this analogy in mind, it would be reasonable to infer that wires that are larger in circumference should be capable of carrying greater electrical loads.

Inductive reasoning is used when we are trying to diagnose what the problem might be or deciding which of several promising options would be the most reasonable to select. Scientists use inductive methods, such as experimentation, and inductive tools, such as statistics. The Nurses' Health Study report was an example of scientific findings derived inductively. When we base our predictions on our past experiences about how things will happen in the future, we are using inductive reasoning. Reasoning by analogy, exemplified in the example about electricity being like water, is inductive. In strong, inductive reasoning, the evidence at hand gives us a reasonable assurance that the conclusion we are drawing is probably true. *As long as there is the possibility that all the reasons for a claim could be true and yet the claim itself could turn out to be false, we are in the realm of inductive reasoning.*

COSMOS VS. CHAOS

The idea that the earth is a planet revolving around the sun is often attributed to the 15th-century Polish astronomer–priest named Copernicus. But, in fact, the first scientist known to have reasoned to that view of the solar system was the Greek astronomer mathematician Aristarchus, who lived more than two millennia earlier. Carl Sagan describes the reasoning Aristarchus used in a clip from the *Cosmos* series, which you can access at **www.TheThinkSpot.com**.

Sagan tells us that Aristarchus "deduced that the Sun had to be much larger" from "the size of the Earth's shadow on the Moon during a lunar eclipse." Aristarchus used deduction to infer that the Sun was much larger than the Earth because there was no other possible explanation for the size of the shadow of the Earth on the Moon during a lunar eclipse than that the shadow is being made by a hugely larger source of light shining toward the Earth and the Moon from a very great distance away.

Early Life Factors and Risk of Breast Cancer

"Epidemiologic investigations conducted by our group and others have suggested that during childhood and early adult life breast tissue is particularly sensitive to factors that influence the likelihood of developing cancer many years later. For example, if the breast is exposed to multiple x-rays or other types of radiation during this early period, the risk of breast cancer rises steadily with higher doses, but after age 40 radiation has little effect. Also, we have seen that being overweight before age 20 is paradoxically associated with a reduced risk of breast cancer for the rest of a woman's life, although subsequent weight gain and becoming overweight after menopause increases risk of breast cancer in these later years. These findings led us to develop sets of questions focusing on diet and physical activity during the high school years. . . . In addition, to assess the validity of the recalled dietary data, we invited a sample of mothers of NHS II participants to also compete a questionnaire about the high school diets of their NHS II daughters; strong correlation between the mother–daughter reports supported the validity of our dietary data.

We have now begun to examine the relation of high school diet and activity patterns to subsequent risk of breast cancer. We have seen that higher intake of red meat during high school years is related to a greater risk of premenopausal breast cancer. Also, higher levels of physical activity during high school were associated with lower risk of breast cancer before menopause. This is particularly important, as many schools do not include regular physical activity in the curriculum, and many girls are now quite inactive during these years."

What are Your Professors and Textbooks Asking of You?

1 A good education includes learning content knowledge and learning skills. Because there is so much to learn, it is understandable that many instructors focus a lot of attention on helping students get the content knowledge right. These profs often call on students in class to answer questions that show that they know the meanings of technical terms or have learned the material from a previous lesson. Sprinkled in among those questions from time to time are critical thinking skills questions like those given in the table on page 20. Here is your challenge: In each of your classes over the next two class days, keep a list of the questions that the instructors ask students. Then, take the complete list and evaluate each question to see which were intended to evoke the use of critical thinking skills. Which skills were most often evoked?

2 Some textbooks include exercises at the end of each chapter or unit. Those exercises can address content knowledge to be sure it is well understood. They can also invite students to apply their critical thinking skills to that knowledge, for example to interpret some data, to analyze arguments, to draw out the consequences of certain principles or facts, or to explain the right methods to apply. Take the textbooks for your other subjects and review the exercises at the end of the unit or chapter you are on. Identify those questions, if any, that are intended to evoke critical thinking skills. In the case of each textbook, write five additional "exercise questions" that evoke critical thinking about the content of the chapter.

DEDUCTIVE REASONING

Drawing inferences in which it appears that the conclusion cannot possibly be false if all of the premises are true is called **deductive reasoning**. Here are some examples:

- San Francisco is west of Denver. Denver is west of Detroit and Newark. Therefore, we can infer with deductive certitude that San Francisco is west of Newark.

- Every successful president of the United States was both diplomatic and decisive. General Dwight D. Eisenhower served in WWII as the Commander of the Allied Armies in Europe and then went on to become a successful U.S. president. Therefore, President Eisenhower was decisive and diplomatic.

- Either we attended the campus Halloween party last year or we were in Texas visiting your folks that day. We did not go to Texas at all last year. So, we must have attended the campus Halloween party last year.

- Assume that 'a,' 'b,' and 'c' are any three numbers. Where 'w' and 'y' are numbers, assume that 'f' is a mathematical function such that 'fwy' yields 'z' where 'z' is the number that is the product of 'w' multiplied by 'y.' It follows deductively then that '(fa(fbc))' yields to the product of 'a' multiplied by the product of 'b' multiplied by 'c.'

- If God intended marriage for the sole purpose of human reproduction, and if same-sex couples are entirely incapable of human reproduction, then it follows that God did not intend marriage for same-sex couples.

- Not every argument is of equal quality. Therefore, at least one argument is better than at least one other argument.

Mathematics, algebra, geometry, and computer programming rely heavily on deductive reasoning. Activities that require us to apply strict protocols, rules, or regulations that leave no room for independent judgment call on our deductive reasoning skills. People often enjoy games and puzzles that test their deductive reasoning skills, such as Sudoku. When we seek to resolve questions and doubts by appeal to first principles, commandments, or beliefs that are assumed to be absolute certitudes, we are often using our deductive powers.

Deductive reasoning is a very important form of inference, as is inductive reasoning. We require both forms of inference to be successful in critical thinking.

In Chapter 1, we said that strong critical thinking requires the application of a set of cognitive skills. In this chapter, we identified those core critical thinking skills as interpretation, analysis, inference, evaluation, explanation, and self-regulation. By asking good questions, as the clips with Katie Couric and Henry Fonda illustrate, we fire up those skills. The skill of inference included both of the domains that are traditionally known as "inductive reasoning" and "deductive reasoning." We clarify the difference between induction and deduction using examples and definitions. Being skilled at thinking is only part of the story. Being willing to engage our critical thinking skills is the other part. In the next chapter, we will look closely at those habits of mind that incline us toward using our critical thinking skills to make reflective, fair-minded judgments in real-life contexts about what to do.

KEY TERMS

interpretation is an expression of the meaning or significance or a wide variety of experiences, situations, data, events, judgments, conventions, beliefs, rules, procedures, or criteria. *18*

analysis identifies the intended and actual inferential relationships among statements, questions, concepts, descriptions, or other forms of representation intended to express belief, judgment, experiences, reasons, information, or opinions. *18*

evaluation assesses the credibility of statements or other representations that are accounts or descriptions of a person's perception, experience, situation, judgment, belief, or opinion; also assesses the logical strength of the actual or intended inferential relationships among statements, descriptions, questions, or other forms of representation. *18*

self-regulation is a process in which one monitors one's cognitive activities, the elements used in those activities, and the results educed, particularly by applying skills in analysis, and evaluation to one's own inferential judgments with a view toward questions, con-

firming, validating, or correcting either one's reasoning or one's results. *18*

inference identifies and secures elements needed to draw reasonable conclusions; it forms conjectures and hypotheses, considers relevant information and educes the consequences flowing from data, statements, principles, evidence, judgments, beliefs, opinions, concepts, descriptions, questions, or other forms of representation. *18*

explanation states and justifies reasoning in terms of the evidential, conceptual, methodological, criteriological, and contextual considerations upon which one's results were based; also presents one's reasoning in the form of cogent arguments. *18*

inductive reasoning is drawing probabilistic inferences regarding what is most likely to be true or most likely not true, given certain information. *21*

deductive reasoning is drawing inferences in which it appears that the conclusion cannot possibly be false if all of the premises are true. *23*

FIND IT ON THE THINKSPOT

Three video clips in this chapter feature Katie Couric from *CBS Evening News*, winner of the Edward R. Murrow Award for best newscast in 2008 and 2009.

I invite you to access a video clip of Couric describing her preparations for the fall 2008 interview with then-Vice Presidential candidate Sarah Palin. Access this at **www.TheThinkSpot.com**. (p. 15)

• Earlier I asked you to watch part of the interview itself, and a third clip shows how Couric uses good questioning to probe for the reasoning behind Palin's opinions about the economic stimulus legislation proposed by the Bush administration. (p. 18, 19)

The video clip of the El train scene from *12 Angry Men* is a classic. Please view that scene and analyze it carefully, noticing how the argument unfolds and how the "train of reasoning" is often interrupted, but yet always stays on track. The movie itself is terrific, and I urge you to watch it all the way through. Do you think we've made much progress on the issue of racial profiling in the past 50 years? How about on a citizen's duty to render service as a thoughtful and diligent juror? (p. 16)

Exercises

SMALL GROUP DISCUSSIONS

1. Consider this claim: *"If textbooks used more critical thinking exercises, students would learn the material better."* What are the best arguments for and against that claim? Do not take a position on this. Rather, work to develop the strongest arguments possible for both sides. What additional information would you need to investigate in order to ground each side's arguments in solid facts? What assumptions about learning and schooling are required to make each side's arguments as strong as possible. Again, do not evaluate (yet).

2. Consider this claim: *"Professors should ask content questions, not critical thinking questions. It's the responsibility of the professor to lay out the content, but it's the job of the student to think critically about the subject matter."* What are the best arguments for and against that claim? As with the question above, do not take a position on this. Rather, work to develop the strongest arguments possible for both sides. What additional information would you need to investigate in order to ground each side's arguments in solid facts? What assumptions about learning and schooling are required to make each side's arguments as strong as possible? Again, do not evaluate (yet).

REFLECTIVE LOG

1. You were specifically asked not to "defend" "evaluate" or to "argue for" one side or the other in the previous two exercise items. Here's your new challenge: Keeping an open mind and maybe stirring up a bit of courage, too, interview two professors and two students *not* in your critical thinking class. Present them with the same two claims, but invite them to agree or disagree with each one and to give their reasons. Note their reasons respectfully, and like Katie Couric did, ask follow-up questions aimed at evoking more critical thinking. You should be able to base your follow-up questions on the group work you did earlier when you developed the best arguments for and against each claim. Then, in your reflective log, record the conversations and highlight some of the places where the people you interviewed did, in fact, engage in some deeper critical thinking about the topic.

2. Using the "Holistic Critical Thinking Scoring Rubric" from Chapter 1, how would you evaluate the critical thinking displayed by each of the four people you interviewed? Quote some of the things each side said that led you to evaluate them in the way that you did. [I know you caught it, but just in case you didn't, that was another critical thinking skills question. This one asked you to *explain* the evidence you used for your *evaluation*.]

OPTIONAL BONUS EXERCISE

When a skilled professional journalist of national stature, Katie Couric, interviews a high profile political figure, Sarah Palin, a subtle competition occurs. Each hopes that the interview will advance his or her own purposes. Couric hoped to inform the viewing audience about the candidate, and Palin hoped to showcase her views on key issues. Obviously, here Couric was the veteran journalist, and Palin was the relative newcomer to the national political scene.

By contrast, the 2008 film *Frost/Nixon* shows a somewhat naïve and overconfident young entertainer, David Frost, interviewing the politically savvy ex-president, Richard M. Nixon. The film portrays both men agreeing to do the interview for their own personal reasons: Frost as hoping to advance his TV career and Nixon as wanting to positively shape his otherwise tarnished presidential legacy. Their critical thinking skills are severely tested as each tries to choreograph the conversation with the cameras rolling.

View this 2008 cinematic recreation of the Frost-Nixon interviews and see if you can spot places in the film where Frost considers using or does use the critical thinking skills questions discussed in this chapter. Or locate the real 1977 interview on the web to see what actually happened when Frost confronted Nixon about his role in the Watergate break in and cover up. What questions does Frost use to evoke Nixon's revealing responses? Which critical thinking skills (analysis, interpretation, evaluation, inference, explanation, or self-regulation) does each person display most strongly?

WHAT DOES IT LOOK LIKE WHEN A GROUP IS ENGAGED IN CRISIS-LEVEL CRITICAL THINKING?

WHAT IS A PERSON LIKE WHO IS STRONGLY PREDISPOSED TOWARD CRITICAL THINKING?

WHAT DOES THE RESEARCH TELL US ABOUT SPECIFIC POSITIVE HABITS OF MIND?

HOW CAN I CULTIVATE THE SEVEN POSITIVE CRITICAL THINKING HABITS OF MIND?

After training

for every conceivable contingency, the unexpected happened. Initially, the challenge was simply to figure out what the problem was. If it could be correctly identified, then there might be some slim chance of survival. If not, the outcome could be tragic.

As you watch the video clip at **www.TheThinkSpot.com**, keep in mind that you are seeing a dramatic reenactment. The actors, music, camera angles, staging, props, and lighting all contribute to our overall experience. That said, this portrayal of individual and group problem solving is highly consistent with the research on human cognition and decision making.[i] The clip dramatizes a group of people engaged in thinking critically together about one thing: *What could the problem be?* Their approach is to apply their reasoning skills to the best of their ability. But, more than only their thinking skills, their mental habits of being analytical, focused, and systematic enabled them to apply those skills well during the moment of crisis. I suggest that you watch the brief video prior to reading the summary analysis of *Apollo 13* beginning on page 28.

THE "WILLING" IN "WILLING AND ABLE" TO THINK CRITICALLY

A Group Engaged in Crisis-Level Critical Thinking

The *Apollo 13* sequence opens with the staff at Mission Control in Houston and the three-person crew of Apollo 13 well into the boredom of routine housekeeping. Suddenly, the crew of Apollo 13 hears a loud banging noise and their small, fragile craft starts gyrating wildly. The startled look on Tom Hanks's face in the video re-enactment is priceless. A full 15 seconds elapses before he speaks. During that time his critical thinking is in overdrive. He is trying to interpret what has just happened. His mind has to make sense of the entirely unexpected and unfamiliar experience. He neither dismisses nor ignores the new information that presents itself. His attention moves between checking the craft's instrument panel and attending to the sounds and motions of the spacecraft itself. He focuses his mind, forms a cautious but accurate interpretation, and with the disciplined self-control we expect of a well-trained professional, he says, "Houston, we have a problem."

At first they call out information from their desk monitors and from the spacecraft's instrument displays. They crave information from all sources.

They know they must share what they are learning with each other as quickly as they can in the hope that someone will be able to make sense out of things. They do not yet know which piece of information may be the clue to their life-or-death problem, but they have the discipline of mind to want to know everything that might be relevant. And they have the confidence in their collective critical thinking skills to believe that this approach offers their best hope to identify the true problem.

One member of the ground crew calls out, "O_2 Tank Two not reading." That was the vital bit of information, which had washed by in the torrents of data. Soon a number of people begin proposing explanations: "They may have been hit by a meteor." "Their antenna is broken." "This can't be happening, it must be instrumentation."

The vital critical thinking skill of Self-Regulation is personified in the movie by the character played by Ed Harris. His job is to monitor everything that is going on and to correct the process if he judges that it is getting off track. For example, he says, "These guys are talking about bangs and shimmies up there. Don't sound like instrumentation to me." His argument is brief, powerful, and effective. The reason—"These guys are talking about bangs and shimmies up there"—is based on what he has

Critical Thinking Disposition Self-Rating Form

Answer yes or no to each. Can I **name any specific instances over the past two days** when I:

1 _____ was courageous enough to ask tough questions about some of my longest held and most cherished beliefs?

2 _____ backed away from questions that might undercut some of my longest held and most cherished beliefs?

3 _____ showed tolerance toward the beliefs, ideas, or opinions of someone with whom I disagreed?

4 _____ tried to find information to build up my side of an argument but not the other side?

5 _____ tried to think ahead and anticipate the consequences of various options?

6 _____ laughed at what other people said and made fun of their beliefs, values, opinion, or points of views?

7 _____ made a serious effort to be analytical about the foreseeable outcomes of my decisions?

8 _____ manipulated information to suit my own purposes?

9 _____ encouraged peers not to dismiss out of hand the opinions and ideas other people offered?

10 _____ acted with disregard for the possible averse consequences of my choices?

11 _____ organized for myself a thoughtfully systematic approach to a question or issue?

12 _____ jumped in and tried to solve a problem without first thinking about how to approach it?

13 _____ approached a challenging problem with confidence that I could think it through?

14 _____ instead of working through a question for myself, took the easy way out and asked someone else for the answer?

15 _____ read a report, newspaper, or book chapter or watched the world news or a documentary just to learn something new?

16 _____ put zero effort into learning something new until I saw the immediate utility in doing so?

17 _____ showed how strong I was by being willing to honestly reconsider a decision?

18 _____ showed how strong I was by refusing to change my mind?

19 _____ attended to variations in circumstances, contexts, and situations in coming to a decision?

20 _____ refused to reconsider my position on an issue in light of differences in context, situations, or circumstances?

If you have described yourself honestly, this self-rating form can offer a rough estimate of what you think your overall disposition toward critical thinking has been in the past two days.

Give yourself 5 points for every "Yes" on odd numbered items and for every "No" on even numbered items. If your total is 70 or above, you are rating your disposition toward critical thinking over the past two days as generally positive. Scores of 50 or lower indicate a self-rating that is averse or hostile toward critical thinking over the past two days. Scores between 50 and 70 show that you would rate yourself as displaying an ambivalent or mixed overall disposition toward critical thinking over the past two days.

Interpret results on this tool cautiously. At best this tool offers only a rough approximation with regard to a brief moment in time. Other tools are more refined, such as the *California Critical Thinking Disposition Inventory*, which gives results for each of the seven critical thinking habits of mind.

heard monitoring the radio conversation. The conclusion he draws from that information has the effect of directing everyone's energy and attention toward one set of possibilities, those that would be "real problems" rather than toward another set of possibilities. Had he agreed that the problem was instrumentation, then everyone's efforts would have been directed toward checking and verifying that the gauges and computers were functioning properly.

There is a very important lesson for good critical thinking in what we see Ed Harris doing. Judging correctly what kind of problem we are facing is essential. If we are mistaken about what the problem is, we are likely to consume time, energy, and resources exploring the wrong kinds of solutions. By the time we figure out that we took the wrong road, the situation could have become much worse than when we started. The Apollo 13 situation is a perfect example. In real life, had the people at Houston Control classified the problem as instrumentation, they would have used up what little oxygen there was left aboard the spacecraft while the ground crew spent time validating their instrument readouts.

Back on the spacecraft, Tom Hanks, who personifies the critical thinking skills of interpretation and inference, is struggling to regain navigational control. He articulates the inference, "If we'd been hit by a meteor, we'd be dead by now." A few moments later he glances out the craft's side window. Something in the rearview mirror catches his attention. Again, his inquisitive mind will not ignore what he's seeing. A few seconds pass as he tries to interpret what it might be. He offers his first observation, "We are venting something into space." The mental focus and stress of the entire Houston ground crew are etched on their faces. Their expressions reveal the question in their minds: What could he possibly be seeing? Seconds pass with agonizing slowness. Using his interpretive skills, Tom Hanks categorizes with caution and then, adding greater precision, he infers, "It is a gas of some kind . . . It must be the oxygen." Kevin Bacon looks immediately to the oxygen tank gauge on the instrument panel for information that might confirm or disconfirm whether it really is the oxygen. It is.

Being by habit inclined to anticipate consequences, everyone silently contemplates the potential tragedy implied by the loss of oxygen. As truth-seekers, they must accept the finding. They cannot fathom denying it or hiding from it. Their somber acknowledgment comes in the response, "Roger, we copy you're venting."

OK, now we have the truth. What are we going to do about it? The characters depicted in this movie are driven by a powerful orientation toward using critical thinking to resolve whatever problems they encounter. The room erupts with noise as each person refocuses on their little piece of the problem. People are moving quickly, talking fast, pulling headset wires out of sockets in their haste. The chaos and cacophony in the room reveal that the group is not yet taking a systematic, organized approach. Monitoring this, Ed Harris interjects another self-correction into the group's critical thinking. He may not yet know how this problem of the oxygen supply is going to be solved or even whether this problem can be solved, but he is going to be sure that the ground crew addresses it with all the skill and all the mental power it can muster. "Wake up anybody you need. Let's get them in here. Let's work the problem, people."

As depicted in this excerpt, the combined ground crew and spacecraft crew, as a group, displayed a top score on "Holistic Critical Thinking Scoring Rubric." The emotions and stresses of the situation are unmistakable. The group's powerfully strong critical thinking habits of mind enable the group to use that energy productively. It gives urgency to the efforts. Thus, the message about our thinking processes that emerges is that emotion need not be the antithesis to reason; emotion can be the impetus to reason.

> If we were compelled to make a choice between these personal attributes and knowledge about the principles of logical reasoning together with some degree of technical skill in manipulating special logical processes, we should decide for the former.

John Dewey, *How We Think*[iv]

The Spirit of a Strong Critical Thinker

The video clip was well staged. Skillful actors displayed the behaviors and responses of strong critical thinkers engaged in problem solving at a moment of crisis. Authors of screenplays and novels often endow their protagonists with strongly positive critical thinking skills and dispositions. The brilliantly insightful Sherlock Holmes or the lead character on CBS series *The Mentalist,* Patrick Jane, played by Simon Baker, comes to mind as examples. A key difference, however, is that fictional detectives always solve the mystery, while, as we all know, in the real world there is no guarantee. Critical thinking is about *how* we approach problems, decisions, questions, and issues even if ultimate success eludes us. Being disposed to engage our skills as best we can is the "willing" part of "willing and able" to think. We looked at the "able" part in Chapter 2. Here we examine the "willing" part, beginning with taking a closer look at the overall disposition toward critical thinking.

POSITIVE AND NEGATIVE HABITS OF MIND

A person with a strong *disposition* toward critical thinking has the *consistent internal motivation* to engage problems and make decisions by using critical thinking.[ii] Operationally this means three things: The person consistently *values* critical thinking, *believes* that using critical thinking skills offers the greatest promise for reaching good judgments, and *intends* to approach problems and decisions by applying critical thinking skills as best as he or she can. This combination of values, beliefs, and intentions forms the habits of mind that dispose the person toward critical thinking.[iii]

Someone strongly disposed toward critical thinking would probably agree with the following statements:

- "I hate talk shows where people shout their opinions but never give any reasons at all."

- "Figuring out what people really mean by what they say is important to me."

- "I always do better in jobs where I'm expected to think things out for myself."

- "I hold off making decisions until I have thought through my options."

- "Rather than relying on someone else's notes, I prefer to read the material myself."

- "I try to see the merit in another's opinion, even if I reject it later."

- "Even if a problem is tougher than I expected, I will keep working on it."

- "Making intelligent decisions is more important than winning arguments."

Persons who display a strong positive disposition toward critical thinking are described in the literature as "having a critical spirit," or as people who are "mindful," "reflective," and "meta-cognitive." These expressions give a person credit for consistently applying their critical thinking skills to whatever problem, question, or issue is at hand. People with a critical spirit tend to ask good questions, probe deeply for the truth, inquire fully into matters, and strive to anticipate the consequences of various options. In real life our skills may or may not be strong enough, our knowledge may or may not be adequate to the task at hand. The problem may or may not be too difficult for us. Forces beyond our control might or might not determine the actual outcome. None of that cancels out the positive critical thinking habits of mind with which strong critical thinkers strive to approach the problems life sends their way.

A person with weak critical thinking dispositions might disagree with the previous statements and be more likely to agree with these:

- "I prefer jobs where the supervisor says exactly what to do and exactly how to do it."

- "No matter how complex the problem, you can bet there will be a simple solution."

- "I don't waste time looking things up."

- "I hate when teachers discuss problems instead of just giving the answers."

- "If my belief is truly sincere, evidence to the contrary is irrelevant."

- "Selling an idea is like selling cars; you say whatever works."

- "Why go to the library when you can use made-up quotes and phony references?"

- "I take a lot on faith because questioning the fundamentals frightens me."

- "There is no point in trying to understand what terrorists are thinking."

When it comes to approaching specific questions, issues, or problems, people with a weak or negative critical thinking disposition are apt to be muddle-headed, disorganized, overly simplistic, spotty about getting relevant information, likely to apply unreasonable criteria, easily distracted, ready to give up at the least hint of difficulty, intent on a solution that is more detailed than is possible, or too readily satisfied with some uselessly vague response.

PRELIMINARY SELF-ASSESSMENT

It is only natural to wonder about our own disposition. The "Critical Thinking Disposition Self-Rating Form" on page 28 offers us a way of reflecting on our own values, beliefs, and intentions about the use of critical thinking. As noted on the form itself, "This tool offers only a rough approximation with regard to a brief moment in time." Before reading further in the chapter about the disposition toward critical thinking, I invite you to take a moment and compete the self-assessment. Keep in mind as you interpret the results that this measure does not assess critical thinking skills. Rather, this tool permits one to reflect to himself or herself whether, over the past two days, the disposition manifested in behavior was positive, ambivalent, or averse toward engaging in thoughtful, reflective, and fair-minded judgments about what to believe or what to do.

Research on the Disposition toward Critical Thinking

The broad understanding of being disposed toward using critical thinking or away from using critical thinking has been the object of empirical research in the cognitive sciences since the early 1990s. The purpose of this research has been to give greater precision to the analysis and measurement of the dispositional dimension of critical thinking.

SEVEN POSITIVE CRITICAL THINKING HABITS OF MIND

One research approach involved asking thousands of people to indicate the extent to which they agreed or disagreed with a long list of statements not unlike those in the two short lists on pages 29–30. Using factor-analytic statistical methods, these researchers identified seven measurable aspects within the overall disposition toward critical thinking. We can think of these as the seven positive critical thinking habits of mind.[v] Using this research, we can describe someone who has all seven positive critical thinking habits of mind as a person who is:

- **Truth-seeking** – meaning that the person has intellectual integrity and a courageous desire to actively strive for the best possible knowledge in any given situation. A truth-seeker asks probing questions and follows reasons and evidence wherever they lead, even if the results go against his or her cherished beliefs.

- **Open-minded** – meaning that the person is tolerant of divergent views and sensitive to the possibility of his or her own possible biases. An open-minded person respects the right of others to have different opinions.

- **Analytical** – meaning that the person is habitually alert to potential problems and vigilant in anticipating consequences and trying to foresee short-term and long-term outcomes of events, decisions, and actions.

- **Systematic** – meaning that the person consistently endeavors to take an organized and thorough approach to identifying and resolving problems. The systematic person is orderly, focused, persistent, and diligent in his or her approach to problem solving, learning, and inquiry.

- **Confident in reasoning** – meaning that the person is trustful of his or her own reasoning skills to yield good judgments. A person's or a group's confidence in their own critical thinking may or may not be warranted, which is another matter.

- **Inquisitive** – meaning that the person habitually strives to be well-informed, wants to know how things work, and seeks to learn new things about a wide range of topics, even if the immediate utility of knowing those things is not directly evident. The inquisitive person has a strong sense of intellectual curiosity.

- **Judicious** – meaning that the person approaches problems with a sense that some are ill-structured and some can have more than one plausible solution. The judicious person has the cognitive maturity to realize that many questions and issues are not black and white and that, at times, judgments must be made in contexts of uncertainty.

NEGATIVE HABITS OF MIND

After the measurement tools were refined and validated for use in data gathering, the results of repeated samplings showed that some people are strongly positive on one or more of the seven positive dispositional

The Disposition toward Critical Thinking

Inquisitive   Judicious
Systematic   Truth-seeking
Analytical   Confident In Reasoning
Open-minded

Access this clip at www.TheThinkSpot.com.

In the film *Philadelphia*, Denzel Washington plays a personal liability litigator who is not above increasing the amount a client seeks for "pain and suffering" by hinting to the client that he may have more medical problems than the client had at first noticed. Watch the scene where a new potential client, played by Tom Hanks, visits Washington's office seeking representation. Access this clip at **www.TheThinkSpot.com**.

The clip from *Philadelphia* starts out with Denzel Washington talking to a client who wants to sue the city over a foolish accident that the man brought upon himself. The scene establishes that Washington is a hungry lawyer who will take almost any case. Tom Hanks comes into the office and says that he wants to sue his former employer, believing that he was wrongly fired from his job because he has AIDS. You would think that Washington would jump at this opportunity. There is a lot of money to be made if he can win the case. Truth-seeking demands that the real reason for the firing be brought to light. But at this point in the story, Washington declines to take the case.

Notice what the film makers do with the camera angles to show what Washington is thinking as he considers what to do. His eyes focus on the picture of his wife and child, on the skin lesion on Hanks's head, and on the cigars and other things Hanks touches. The story takes place during the early years when the general public did not understand AIDS well at all. It was a time when prejudices, homophobia, and misinformation surrounded the disease. Washington's character portrays the uncertainty

aspects. Some people are negative or ambivalent on one or more of the seven attributes.

There is a name associated with the negative end of the scale for each of the seven attributes, just as there is a name associated with the positive end of the scale. The "Critical Thinking Habits of Mind" chart on page 33 indicates the full set of names, for both positive and negative attributes. A person's individual dispositional portrait emerges from the seven, for a person may be positive, ambivalent, or negative on each.

Thinking Critically

How Does TV Portray Critical Thinking?

1 **You can do this exercise by yourself or with a classmate.** This exercise requires watching TV for two hours. Begin with a clean piece of paper and draw a line down the page. Mark one side + and the other −. With pencil and paper in hand, watch CBS, NBC, or ABC or a cable network that shows commercials along with its regular programming. Pay close attention to the commercials, not the regular programming. Note each of the people who appear on screen. If you judge that a person is portrayed as a strong critical thinker, note it, e.g., Woman in car commercial +. If you think a person is portrayed as a weak critical thinker, note that, e.g., Three guys in beer commercial − − −. If you cannot tell (e.g., in the car commercial there were two kids riding in the back seat but they were not doing or saying anything), do not make any notation. After one hour of watching, total up the plusses and the minuses. Now do the

same thing for another hour, but this time pay attention only to the regular programming, not the commercials. Again note every character who appears and indicate on the paper if the person is portrayed as a strong critical thinker (e.g., evil bad guy +, clever detective +) or a weak critical thinker (e.g., victim who foolishly walked into the dark alley alone −). Tally up the plusses and minuses. Based on your observations, is there a tendency or pattern that might be evident regarding the critical thinking strengths or weaknesses of children, adolescents, young adults, middle-aged people, and senior citizens?

2 **Group Project–four-page mini-paper:** Attitudes, while not immutable, are shaped and formed as we mature. To the extent that the disposition toward critical thinking is attitudinal, it can be affected by our experiences growing up. Begin by locat-

ing research reports (not just opinion pieces) in which credible experts report findings based on solid data about the impact of the images of ourselves we see on television and whether those images influence how we behave. Research on the power of TV stereotypes, for example, can be a good place to start. Consider what you learn through your review of the materials that you were able to find and draw on your own life experience to formulate your response to this question: What is the potential impact that the characters portrayed on TV have on the disposition toward critical thinking, which is developing in adolescents? Explain your opinion on this by providing reasons, examples, and citations. In the last part of your short paper, respond to this question: What kind of evidence would lead you to revise or reverse the opinion which you have been presenting and explaining?

∧
∧   In *Philadelphia,* the plaintiff, played by Tom Hanks, and his lawyer, played by Denzel Washington, wade
∧   through a crowd of reporters. How does Denzel Washington's character use critical thinking throughout
the course of the film?

and misplaced fears of the U.S. public at that time. Not understanding AIDS or being misinformed, Washington's character is frightened for himself and for his family. Notice how he stands in the very far corner of his office, as physically far away from Hanks's character as possible. He wipes his hand against his trousers after shaking hands. The nonverbal thinking cues are so well done by the filmmakers that we are not surprised when Washington, having thought things through, refuses to take the case.

There is no question that critical thinking is wonderfully powerful. Yet, by itself it is incomplete. We need knowledge, values, and sensitivities to guide our thinking. Washington's character is sensitive to what he thinks are the dangers of the disease and what he believes (wrongly) about the ways it might be transmitted. His character uses his critical thinking skills, which turn out to be quite formidable as the film progresses. But his beliefs about AIDS are simply wrong. He makes a judgment at the time not to represent Hanks's character. It is not the same judgment he will make later in the film, after he becomes better informed. Fortunately, he has the open-mindedness to entertain the possibility of representing Hanks's character, that perhaps Hanks's character does have a winnable case, and that perhaps the risks associated with AIDS are not as great as he had at first imagined. He has the inquisitiveness and the truth-seeking to gather more accurate information. And he has the judiciousness to reconsider and to change his mind.

"The expressions "mental disciplines" and "mental virtues" can be used to refer to "habits of mind" as well. The word "disciplines" in a military context and the word "virtues" in an ethical context both suggest something positive. We will use "habits of mind" because the word "habit" is neutral. Some habits are good, others bad. As will become evident, the same can be said with regard to critical thinking habits of mind. Some, like truth-seeking, are positive. Others, like indifference or intellectual dishonesty, are negative."

IS A GOOD CRITICAL THINKER AUTOMATICALLY A GOOD PERSON?

Thinking about Denzel Washington's character in *Philadelphia* raises the natural question about how critical thinking might or might not be connected with being an ethical person. We have been using the expression "strong critical thinker" instead of "good critical thinker" because of the ambiguity of the word "good." We want to praise the person as a critical thinker without necessarily making a judgment about the person's ethics. For example, a person can be adept at developing cogent arguments and very adroit at finding the flaws in other people's reasoning, but then, use these skills unethically to mislead and exploit a gullible person, perpetrate a fraud, or deliberately confuse, confound, and frustrate a project.

A person can be *strong* at critical thinking, meaning that the person can have the appropriate dispositions and be adept using his or her critical thinking skill, but still not be an ethical critical thinker. There have been people with superior thinking skills and strong habits of mind who, unfortunately, have used their talents for ruthless, horrific, and immoral purposes. It would be great if experience, knowledge, mental horsepower, and ethical virtue were all one and the same. But they are not.

> To get some sense of the colossal problems that result from our collective failures to anticipate consequences, watch the documentary film *The Unforeseen* (2007, Directed by Laura Dunn). It is the remarkable story of the loss of quality of life and environmental degradation associated with real estate development in Austin, TX, over the past 50 years.

Critical Thinking Habits of Mind

Positive	Negative
Truth-seeking	Intellectually Dishonest
Open-minded	Intolerant
Analytical	Heedless of Consequences
Systematic	Disorganized
Confident in Reasoning	Hostile toward Reason
Inquisitive	Indifferent
Judicious	Imprudent

Consider, for example, the revelations that Victor Crawford, a tobacco lobbyist, makes in the clip from his *60 Minutes* interview with Leslie Stahl. You can access a transcript of the interview at **www.TheThinkSpot.com**. He admits that he lied, falsified information, and manipulated people in order to advance the interests of the tobacco industry. Ms. Stahl calls him out, saying that he was unethical and despicable to act that way. Crawford admits as much. He used his critical thinking skills to help sell people a product that, if used as intended by its manufacturer, was apt to cause them grave harm. Now, all these years later, he regrets having done that. The interview is part of his effort to make amends for his lies and the harm they may have caused to others.

Building Positive Habits of Mind

Critical thinking skills can be strengthened by exercising them, which is what the examples and the exercises in this book are intended to help you do. Critical thinking habits of mind can be nurtured by internalizing the values that they embody and by reaffirming the intention each day to live by those values.[vi] Here are four specific suggestions about how to go about this.

1 Value Critical Thinking. If we value critical thinking, we desire to be ever more truth-seeking, open-minded, mindful of consequences, systematic, inquisitive, confident in our critical thinking, and mature in our judgment. We will expect to manifest that desire in what we do and in what we say. We will seek to improve our critical thinking skills.

2 Take Stock. It is always good to know where we are in our journey. The "Critical Thinking Disposition Self-Rating Form," presented earlier in this chapter, will give us a rough idea. If we have general positive critical thinking habits of mind, that should show up in the score we give ourselves using this self-rating form.

3 Be Alert for Opportunities. Each day be alert for opportunities to act on our desire by translating it into words and actions. Make a conscious effort each day to be as reflective and thoughtful as possible in addressing at least one of the many problems or decisions of the day.

4 Forgive and Persist. Forgive yourself if you happen to backslide. Pick yourself up and get right back on the path. These are ideals you are striving to achieve. You need discipline, determination, and

The Experts Worried that Schooling Might Be Harmful!

The critical thinking expert panel we talked about in Chapter 1 was absolutely convinced that critical thinking is a pervasive and purposeful human phenomenon. They insisted that strong critical thinkers should be characterized not merely by the cognitive skills they may have, but also by how they approach life and living in general.

This was a bold claim. At that time schooling in most of the world was characterized by the memorization of received truths. In the USA, the "back to basics" mantra echoed the pre-1960s Eisenhower era, when so much of schooling was focused on producing "interchangeable human parts" for an industrial manufacturing economy. Critical thinking that frees the mind to ask any question and evaluate any assumption naturally goes far beyond what the typical classroom was delivering. In fact, many of the experts feared that some of the things people experience in our schools could actually be harmful to the development and cultivation of strong critical thinking.

Critical thinking came before formal schooling was invented. It lies at the very roots of civilization. The experts saw critical thinking as a driving force in the human journey from ignorance, superstition, and savagery toward global

understanding. Consider what life would be like without the things on this list, and you will appreciate why they had such confidence in strong critical thinking. The approaches to life and living which the experts said characterized the strong critical thinker included:

- inquisitiveness and a desire to remain well-informed with regard to a wide range of topics,

- trust in the processes of reasoned inquiry,

- self-confidence in one's own abilities to reason,

- open-mindedness regarding divergent world views,

- flexibility in considering alternatives and opinions,

- understanding of the opinions of other people,

- fair-mindedness in appraising reasoning,

- honesty in facing one's own biases, prejudices, stereotypes, or egocentric tendencies,

- prudence in suspending, making, or altering judgments,

- willingness to reconsider and revise views where honest reflection suggests that change is warranted,

- alertness to opportunities to use critical thinking.

The experts went beyond approaches to life and living in general to emphasize how strong critical thinkers approach specific issues, questions, or problems. The experts said we would find strong critical thinkers striving for

- clarity in stating the question or concern,

- orderliness in working with complexity,

- diligence in seeking relevant information,

- reasonableness in selecting and applying criteria,

- care in focusing attention on the concern at hand,

- persistence though difficulties are encountered,

- precision to the degree permitted by the subject and the circumstances.

Table 5, page 25. American Philosophical Association. 1990, Critical Thinking: An Expert Consensus Statement for Purposes of Educational Assessment and Instruction. ERIC Doc. ED 315 423.

Putting the Positive Critical Thinking Habits of Mind into Practice

Here are a few suggestions about ways to translate each of the seven positive aspects of the disposition toward critical thinking into practical things to do.

Truth-seeking – Ask courageous and probing questions. Think deeply about the reasons and evidence for and against a given decision you must make. Pick one or two of your own most cherished beliefs and ask yourself what reasons and what evidence there are for those beliefs.

Open-mindedness – Listen patiently to someone who is offering opinions with which you do not agree. As you listen, show respect and tolerance toward the person offering the ideas. Show that you understand (not the same as "agree with") the opinions being presented.

Analyticity – Identify an opportunity to consciously pause to ask yourself about all the foreseeable and likely consequences of a decision you are making. Ask yourself what that choice, whether it be large or small, will mean for your future life and behavior.

Systematicity – Focus on getting more organized. Make lists of your most urgent work, family and educational responsibilities, and your assignments. Make lists of the most important priorities and obligations as well. Compare the urgent with the important. Budget time to take a systematic and methodical approach to fulfilling obligations.

Critical Thinking Confidence – Commit to resolve a challenging problem by reasoning it through. Embrace a question, problem or issue that calls for a reasoned decision and begin working on it yourself or in collaboration with others.

Inquisitiveness – Learn something new. Go out and seek information about any topic of interest, but not one that you must learn about for work, and let the world surprise you with its variety and complexity.

Judiciousness – Revisit a decision you made recently and consider whether it is still the right decision. See if any relevant new information has come to light. Ask if the results that had been anticipated are being realized. If warranted, revise the decision to better suit your new understanding of the state of affairs.

---

persistence. There will be missteps along the way, but do not let them deter you. Working with a friend, mentor, or role model might make it easier to be successful, but it is really about what you want for your own thinking process.

Reconnecting Skills and Dispositions

We looked at the skills apart from the habits of mind in Chapter 2, and here in Chapter 3 we looked at the habits of mind apart from the skills. Lest we get the false impression that in real life all these elements function in isolation from each other, we should take care to reconnect the "willing and able" of critical thinking. The skills are the tools we use in making reflective judgments about what to believe or what to do.

Positive critical thinking habits of mind predispose us to approach questions, problems, or issues by using our critical thinking skills. Because there are scientific ways to measure critical thinking skills and critical thinking habits of mind, researchers have explored how they relate by looking at data. The graphs on pages 36 and 37 are representative synopses of massive amounts of data collected over many years on tens of thousands of individuals. For our purposes, however, we can treat each dot on the graphs as if it represents only one person. The dot is located at the intersection of a total score on a standardized critical thinking skills test and a total score on a measure of a critical thinking disposition. The numbers and words along the *x*-axis and the *y*-axis indicate the range of possible scores. If one of our fictional people scored a 29 on the skills test and a 280 on the disposition measure, then we would expect to find the dot representing that person somewhere in the upper right part of the graph.[vii]

The shape of the "cloud" of dots indicates what statisticians would describe as statistically significant positive correlation

> If you feel comfortable with the idea, you may want to ask a close friend or two to rate you using the "Critical Thinking Disposition Self-Rating Form." To do this your friend would substitute replace the words "I" or "my" with references to you. This assessment could provide valuable information about how your critical thinking disposition manifests itself to others.

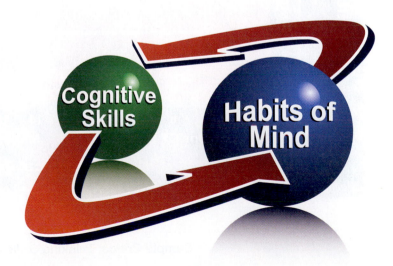

Thinking Critically   Holistic Critical Thinking Scoring Rubric

1 Look at the descriptions of each of the four levels of the "Holistic Critical Thinking Scoring Rubric" on page 10. In each, underline the elements that call out positive or negative critical thinking habits of mind.

2 Go online and locate two editorials from this week's *New York Times* or *Washington Post*. Select any issue or topic you wish. But find something that is controversial enough that the paper published at least one pro and one con editorial. Approach the two editorials with an open mind. Resist forming a judgment about the issue at least until you have read and considered both carefully. Evaluate both using the "Holistic Critical Thinking Scoring Rubric." Explain in detail the reasons for the score you assigned.

between critical thinking skills and critical thinking dispositions. Notice that there are a number of dots in the upper right-hand quadrant signifying strong overall critical thinking skills and a positive disposition to use those skills. There are some dots in the lower left quadrant of the chart that signify poor overall critical thinking skills and an ambivalent or negative disposition with regard to critical thinking. And there are a number dots clustered toward the middle and the upper middle of the chart. These three regions are marked on the next graph with green, red, and blue, respectively. What would you predict would be the challenges and advantages of engaging in joint problem solving and decision making with people in each of these three areas?

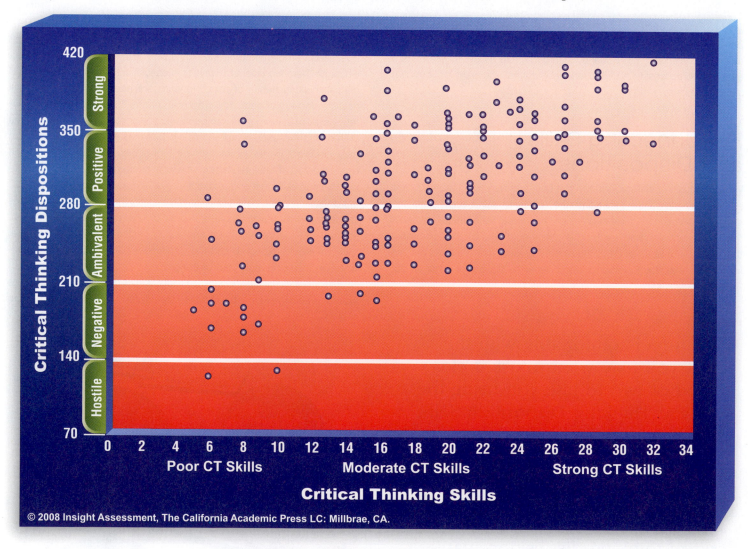

Group Critical Thinking Score Graphs

© 2008 Insight Assessment, The California Academic Press LC: Millbrae, CA.

Sample Critical Thinking Skills and Dispositions Test Scores

Group Critical Thinking Score Graphs

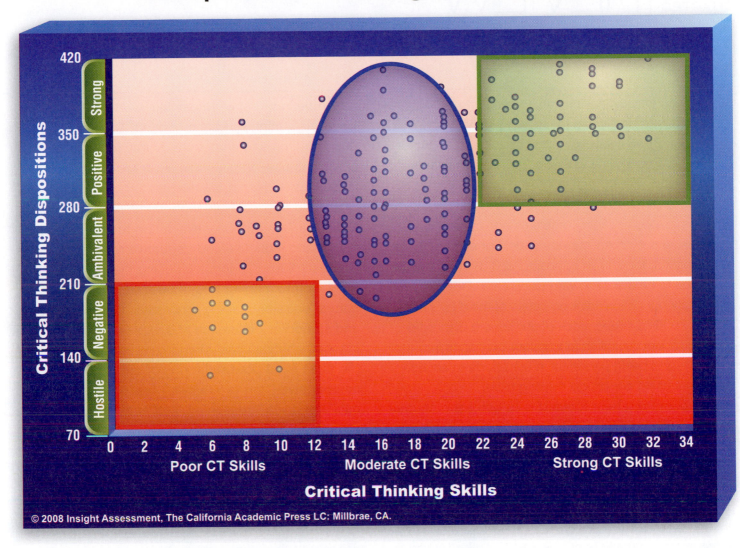

© 2008 Insight Assessment, The California Academic Press LC: Millbrae, CA.

>> Low Score Zone, Moderate Score Zone, High Score Zone.

Thinking Critically

What is Wrong with These Statements?

Each of the following statements contains a mistake. Identify the mistake and edit the statement so that it is more accurate.

1 Having a "critical spirit" means one is a cynic.

2 Critical thinking habits of mind are always positive.

3 If you are open-minded, you must be a truth-seeker. Hint: open-mindedness is passive.

4 Calling on people to be systematic means that everyone must think the same way.

5 If a person is confident in his or her critical thinking, then he or she must have strong critical thinking skills.

6 If a person has strong critical thinking skills, then he or she must be confident in his or her critical thinking.

7 Truth-seeking is fine up to a point, but we have to draw the line. Some questions are too dangerous to be asked.

8 People with strong analyticity are able to foresee the consequences of options and events.

9 If a person can see the value of critical thinking, then the person is disposed toward critical thinking. That's all it takes.

10 People who have not taken a course in critical thinking cannot have strong critical thinking skills.

We defined critical thinking and inquired into its value for ourselves individually and for society in Chapter 1. Then in Chapter 2, we analyzed critical thinking skills, exploring the six core skills and their subskills. This chapter analyzed the "willing" part of "willing and able" to think, describing the seven positive habits of mind that dispose us toward engaging problems and making decisions using our critical thinking skills. For each of these seven habits, there is an opposite habit of mind that disposes us to be averse toward using critical thinking. We can fortify our critical thinking habits of mind by valuing critical thinking, taking stock of our current disposition, looking for opportunities to translate the habits into practice, and being persistent in our efforts to engage problems using our critical thinking skills.

Our plan from here forward is to use each chapter to emphasize different critical thinking skills, always remembering to apply those skills with strong positive critical thinking habits of mind. Chapter 4 uses interpretation and analysis to clarify ideas, and Chapter 5 uses those same skills to map the flow of reasoning evident in arguments and decisions. Chapter 6 applies evaluation to individual claims. Chapters 7 and 8 apply evaluation to arguments, fallacies, and inductive and deductive reasoning. Chapters 9 and 10 focus on using the skill of self-regulation to monitor and, if needed, to correct our natural decision making processes. Chapters 11, 12, and 13 address inference and explanation by exploring the benefits, uses, strengths, and weaknesses of the three most powerful forms of argument making: comparative ("this is like that") reasoning, ideological ("top down") reasoning, and empirical ("bottom up") reasoning.

KEY TERMS

truth-seeking means that a person has intellectual integrity and a courageous desire to actively strive for the best possible knowledge in any given situation. A truth-seeker asks probing questions and follows reasons and evidence wherever they lead, even if the results go against his or her cherished beliefs.   *30*

open-minded means that a person is tolerant of divergent views and sensitive to the possibility of his or her own possible biases. An open-minded person respects the right of others to have different opinions.   *30*

analytical means that a person is habitually alert to potential problems and vigilant in anticipating consequences and trying to foresee short-term and long-term outcomes of events, decisions, and actions.   *30*

systematic means that a person consistently endeavors to take an organized and thorough approach to identifying and resolving problems. A systematic person is orderly, focused, persistent, and diligent in his or her approach to problem solving, learning, and inquiry.   *30*

confident in reasoning means that a person is trustful of his or her own reasoning skills to yield good judgments. A person's or a group's confidence in their own critical thinking may or may not be warranted, which is another matter.   *30*

inquisitive means that a person habitually strives to be well-informed, wants to know how things work, and seeks to learn new things about a wide range of topics, even if the immediate utility of knowing those things is not directly evident. An inquisitive person has a strong sense of intellectual curiosity.   *30*

judicious means that a person approaches problems with a sense that some are ill-structured and some can have more than one plausible solution. A judicious person has the cognitive maturity to realize that many questions and issues are not black and white and that, at times, judgments must be made in contexts of uncertainty.   *30*

FIND IT ON THE THINKSPOT

Dramatic reenactment is not real life, but then neither are so-called "reality" shows. However dramatic reenactments can be very valuable because they often highlight ideas and decision making in tense situations in which uncertainties and risks abound. The clips from *Apollo 13* and *Philadelphia* certainly do that. The transcript of Leslie Stahl's interview with Victor Crawford is dramatic for what it reveals. Access all three of these clips at **www.TheThinkSpot.com**.

• When I reference a video clip in the exercises, as with the "truthiness" clip from Comedy Central's *The Colbert Report*, you can also find it at **www.TheThinkSpot.com**.

Exercises

REFLECTIVE LOG

Mark Twain is reported to have said, "I have never let my schooling interfere with my education."[viii] Connect that sentiment with the information on page 34 in the box, "The Experts Worried that School Might Be Harmful!". What is your reasoned opinion on the matter? If you were critical of schooling, what would you recommend be done to improve it? What evidence do you have that your suggestions would actually work in the real world? Now ask someone who is 10 years younger than you what Mark Twain meant. Note the response in your log. Then ask someone who is at least 20 years older than you what Twain's saying might mean. Log the response. Compare the three opinions: yours, the younger person's, and the older person's. End this notation in your log by reflecting these final questions: Should K-12 schooling be designed to prevent students from learning to think critically for themselves? Why or why not?

GROUP EXERCISE: WHAT WOULD IT BE LIKE?

Our habitual attitudes affect our behavior and the way that we interact with one another. People who are habitually intellectually dishonest, intolerant, or indifferent act differently in household and workplace settings than those who have opposite, positive habits. This exercise invites you to draw on your experience to describe what it would be like to interact regularly with a person with negative critical thinking habits of mind.

Scenario #1. You have a brother, close to your age, who is habitually intellectually dishonest, intolerant, and imprudent in making decisions. He has been like this since junior high school, and he recently enrolled at your college. Now he wants to share your apartment, borrow your car, and get you to help him with his academic assignments. What is it like to have this person as your family member? Given that you have the power to say no to his requests, what are your plans with regard to his requests?

Scenario #2. You have a part-time job in a department store as a clerk. Your old manager used to let your group solve a lot of its own problems, like who is going to cover a shift if someone can't work on a given day. But now you have a new manager. This person makes scheduling decisions arbitrarily, and is disorganized, and this means that your group always seems to be rushing to meet deadlines. She also habitually does not think about the consequences of her actions. What is it like to work for this supervisor? Given that you have the right to complain to management about your new supervisor, is that an option you will pursue? What other plans might you make to help you cope with the approach taken by this new supervisor?

THE COLBERT REPORT

Stephen Colbert, a master of humor and irony, offers "truthiness" as his word of the day. How does "truthiness," as Mr. Colbert defines it, relate to "truth-seeking"? Go to www.TheThinkSpot.com to view the clip.

APOLLO 13 QUESTION

Group or Individual Exercise: The scene in *Apollo 13* when the engineers are put in a room and given a task is a memorable dramatization of a critical thinking challenge. Their task is to engineer something that will reduce the toxicity of the air in the spacecraft (a) as quickly as possible because time is running out, (b) using only the things the astronauts have at their disposal, and (c) using methods that the astronauts can repeat so that they can build the device themselves. Go to www.TheThinkSpot.com, and watch the scene two or three times. The second or third time through, focus on trying to identify evidence of the critical thinking skills and habits of mind. Listen to what the characters say and watch their body language. Discuss the scene in detail, and then prepare a brief description of the scene, like the description that begins this chapter. Your description should highlight those critical thinking skills and habits of mind you noticed the characters displaying either individually or as a group.

"Then you interpret!"

declares Spencer Tracy to Frederic March.

As Spencer Tracy cross examined Fredric March in *Inherit the Wind*, it was the word "day" in the Bible's Genesis that turned out to be the problem. How long is a "day" to the eternal Creator, particularly if the sun had not yet been made? Is it necessarily a 24-hour day, or could it have been much longer, perhaps 10,000 years or 10 million years? "No way to know," muses Spencer Tracy.

Watch the clip from the Academy Award-winning film at **www.TheThinkSpot.com**.

Scientific advances over recent centuries have reshaped our understanding of ourselves, our world, our solar system, and our universe. Without diminishing the value of the biblical book of Genesis, to offer the book as a historical record of actual events occurring within the specific time frames stated there is to invite precisely the kind of exposure that Spencer Tracy delivered. On a literal level, Genesis's obvious contradictions (e.g., light being created before the sun) and vast inconsistencies between that text and all that we have learned scientifically pose too great an intellectual obstacle for reason to vault. But, what if the authors and editors of Genesis had other purposes in mind as they told their marvelous and meaningful stories around the campfires of their nomadic kinsmen?

This chapter is about interpreting the meanings of ideas as they are conveyed in language. Our goal, in the exercise of our critical thinking skill of interpretation, is to achieve as much accuracy and precision as may be required for the purposes and the context at hand.

CLARIFYING IDEAS

CHAPTER 04

Interpretation, Context, and Purpose

The authors and editors of Genesis meant to communicate their faith perspective. By telling of the powerful and awe-inspiring Yahweh, the authors of Genesis wanted to reassure the Israelites that Yahweh was far superior to the pagan gods. The tales of fearsome divine reprisals for straying from the teachings of Yahweh (e.g., death for those who went with the Moabite women to ceremonies honoring the god Baal) were meant to reinforce compliance. Genesis is meant to bind the Israelites as a group by giving them a common religious heritage and identity. To do this, the authors and editors of Genesis used some of the most memorable stories known to man.[i]

We do not expect a scientific publication to be a musical score. And we do not defend it or criticize it using the standards that are meant to be applied to music. The purposes and context of the material determines how it should be interpreted and used. Take the book of Genesis, for example—to interpret it as a scientific work would be a mistake. First, as indicated earlier, it is very probably not an accurate understanding of the purposes of the authors. Second, the historical, social, and cultural contexts within which the work was produced was pre-scientific. The investigatory methodology we know as science was foreign to the authors and the audience of Genesis. Thus, it would be equally wrongheaded either to criticize or to defend that collection of religious stories as if it were astronomical, biological, or geophysical science. As we shall see throughout this chapter, a grasp of context and purpose forms the starting point for interpretation.

HOW PRECISE IS PRECISE ENOUGH?

We apply our core critical thinking skill of interpretation and our habit of judiciousness when endeavoring to determine the meaning and significance of what is being communicated. *The first rule of fair-minded interpretation is to be sensitive to context and purpose.*

From: Mom and Pop
To: Susan, Bill, and Karl

Dear Susan, Bill, and Karl,

You probably never thought you'd see our last will and testament sent by email, but here it is. We know that you are all over 40, but Pop and I still think of you as our kids. We're getting old and we've been thinking a lot lately about passing our belongings on to the three of you. We have no plans to do this in the near or foreseeable future. But, you never know. We have our aches and pains, and we are getting to that point when it is important to be sure that our ideas are known before it gets to be too late.

So, here's what we want. We want all our money to go to each of you equally. Bill, we want you to have our business, which is no prize because it takes a lot of work. But we love it, and it has been good to Pop and me over all these years. Each year it provides us with a little profit, so we can't complain. And you are the only one who ever really took an interest in it. Susan, we want you to have our house in Milwaukee. We had some fun times there when you kids were growing up. Maybe you can sell it if the economy improves. Karl, we want you to have the house here in Lakeland we're living in now. The real estate market is the pits right now. And the house needs a new roof and the plumbing is a mess. But you know all that because you're living here now. So, Karl, it's yours.

Divide up our furniture, pictures, books, and personal things, and give everything you don't want to Goodwill.

The main thing is for you three to <u>divide everything equally</u>. Including whatever might be left in our 401K. Please respect our wishes about not squabbling over what little there will be in our estate.

We love you.

Oh, and Karl, you get our dog, Lobo Loco. Lucky you.

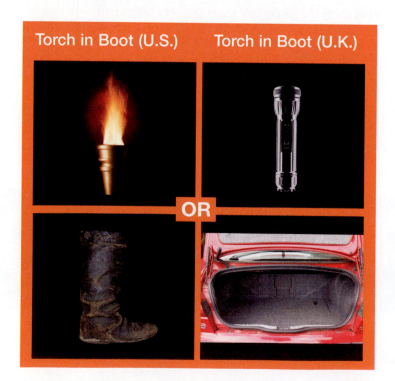

Torch in Boot (U.S.) **Torch in Boot (U.K.)**

OR

To uncover context and purpose, we can use a few basic questions. For example, assume that someone texts this message: "Torch in boot." At first this message appears nonsensical. Here is some context: The message was sent in response to a question, "Do we have a torch?" A Liverpool teenage driver sent this message at night to her dad. The dad's purpose in sending "Torch in boot" was to respond to his daughter's question. OK, now we can make a reasonably accurate interpretation of the message. It means, "Yes, we do have a torch (flashlight). You'll find it in the boot (trunk) of the car you are driving."

Use these questions to initiate the interpretation of written material:

- In what social–cultural–historical context was this written?
- What was the author's purpose in writing it?
- Who was the author's intended audience?
- What does the author believe that the audience already knows?

LANGUAGE AND THOUGHT

Our use of language and our thinking are so closely connected that most of us think in our native language. As children, years before formal schooling, we begin to learn how to express our ideas in words and sentences. As we grow and learn more, our vocabulary expands, as does our ability to express ourselves with greater precision. If we try to learn a new language as an adult, we often find ourselves translating from the new language into English (if English is our native language) and then back into the target language.

Some anthropologists maintain that the capacity to use language gave the young species *Homo sapiens* great advantages over the other hominids, such as Neanderthals, who had greater numbers and greater physical strength.[ii] Using language early human beings were able to coordinate efforts in combat and refine our strategies for acquiring the resources our species needed to survive. Early human language may have included, along with words and pictographs, sounds like clicks and whistles, which we do not use in English. Because communication was almost always face-to-face in the centuries before writing, gestures and movements were also used to facilitate communication. Taken in its broadest sense, language in the earliest millennia of our species was a rich and varied system of gesticulations, sounds, pictures, and symbols.

As human society became more complex and agreements and ideas became so important that they had to be passed down to future generations, written language evolved to capture those ideas and agreements. Whether it was the location of the family plot of land in a river delta that flooded each spring, or the dictates of the monarch, some things needed to be remembered. Written language became our means of commemorating important things like these. Yet words on a page are poor messengers compared to a face-to-face conversation, in which facial expressions, gestures, and body language add so much. When immediate face-to-face communication is reduced to words on a page, we run the risk that vagueness or ambiguity can make accurate interpretation more difficult.

For example, consider the e-mail letter on page 42, written by an older couple, to their adult children. Suppose several years later, the day has come when the three adult children pull out their parents' letter and try to figure out how to honor what it tells them.

Years later, their parents having died, Susan, Bill, and Karl, discuss the letter.

- **Susan:** "Our parents said that their whole idea was to divide everything equally. But the house in Milwaukee is worth only 70% of what the house in Lakeland, Florida, is worth. So, how is that equal?"

- **Bill:** "The business was making money back in the day when Mom and Pop were more active, but the last few years it has been a struggle to break even. These days, it is nothing but headaches. Even if I sold the business I would have almost nothing left after I paid off the loans they needed just to keep operating these past couple of years. How is that equal to a house in Milwaukee or a house in Lakeland?"

- **Karl:** "Look, they didn't want us to fight over things like this. So, why don't we put a value on each house and on the business, then sell everything, and divide the proceeds equally?"

- **Susan:** "Well, that makes financial sense. But would it really be what they wanted? After all, they were very specific about which one of us would receive each of the houses and the business."

As we review the parents' letter, we can see the problems that the three siblings are having. The parents thought that their instructions were clear and precise. But, as it turned out, they were wrong. The instruction to "divide everything equally," is problematic in two ways. First the word "everything" is vague. Did the parents intend that "everything" should include the two houses and the business, or does it apply to all their money and possessions other than the real estate and the business? The siblings need to clarify what's in and what's out so that they can fulfill their parents' intent and divide "everything" equally. The letter is vague. Arguments could be made for both interpretations.

The second problem has to do with the word "equally." Should the siblings interpret that word to mean "financially exactly the same dollar value," or should they interpret "equally" to mean "each gets one major asset, each gets one third of the books, furniture, and personal possessions, and each gets one third of the dollar value remaining in the parents' 401K"? In this second sense of "equally," the result may not be that each person would receive the exact same total dollar value, but each would have been given an equal share of each category of objects in the parents' estate. The letter is ambiguous. Arguments could be made for both interpretations.

In the sections that follow we will first talk about the problem of vagueness and then the problem of ambiguity. The good news is that both kinds of problems can be reasonably resolved through the wise application of our critical thinking skills and habits of mind.

VAGUENESS: "DOES THE TERM INCLUDE THIS CASE OR NOT?"

Common sense tells us that we should not bring animals to the airport. Cows, chickens, cats, goldfish, snakes, and monkeys are not welcome there. Although we all can agree with the general principle, it would still be reasonable to ask, "What about companion animals and assistance animals?" And as soon as the question is asked, we realize that our common sense understanding, while generally correct, is not sufficiently precise enough for practical purposes.

A guide dog is an assistance animal, which we would not *intend* to prohibit from the airport. We can address the uncertainty about whether the term "animal" *in this context* is meant to refer to guide dogs or not by adding a qualification or exception to our initial statement. We could say, as they do in Tampa, "No animals are allowed in the airport terminal except assistance animals."

OK, but now what about "companion animals"? For reasons of psychological health, in some states elderly people and others are permitted to legally register certain animals as "companion animals." Often this registration permits the owner of the companion animal to be granted exceptions to restrictions that generally apply to pets. So, we might want to make a further amendment to our dictate about no animals at airports to permit another exception. In this case, for "registered companion animals." Again, the uncertainty about whether the word "animals" applies *in this context* to companion animals needs to be resolved. Our intent is to permit them to be brought to the airport. So, for our current purposes, a dog that is either an assistance animal or a companion animal is permitted. In real-life situations, we think about our purposes and about the context to decide how to resolve uncertainties just like these.

Notice that we did not ask whether human beings were excluded from airports on the grounds that human beings were animals. In terms of the purpose and context, it simply was not a reasonable question. But in other contexts or for other purposes, it could be, as for example in the question of whether or not a viral strain, say avian flu, can jump animal species. In that situation, human beings are animals, rather than plants.

Consider this question: Given the purposes for not permitting animals at airports, how would you resolve the vagueness in the word "airport" if a child were to ask, "Is it OK if we bring our pet dog with us in the car when we take Grandma to the airport? Please, we are only going to drop Grandma off." Does "airport" in this context and for these purposes include or not include the interior of vehicles that use the departure street outside the terminal building?

Thinking Critically   Interpreting "Dependent"

The term "dependent" in the sentence, "Are you dependent on your parents?" can be interpreted to mean "needy" or "reliant" as contrasted with "independent." But for purposes of filing federal income tax, the term "dependent" has a far more precise meaning that is stipulated in the tax code. For individuals, IRS Publication 17, which is available free from the **www.irs.gov** Web site, is the basic source of information on how to interpret the word "dependent" in the context of our tax rules and for the purpose of correctly filing a federal tax return. The table below is from page 28 of Publication 17. By interpreting the table, answer each of the following questions and write out the explanation for why you believe your answer is correct.

1 Can you claim your child as your dependent if you are claimed as a dependent on your parent's or parents' tax return? _____ Explanation:

2 Is it possible for you to claim a person as a dependent if that person is a resident of another country? _____ Explanation:

3 If you adopt a child and the adoption is finalized by the court on December 10, can you claim that child as your dependent for that year? _____ Explanation:

4 Say you are 22 years old, a full-time student, and you live at home. You pay fair-market rent and provide for more than half of your own support (food, clothing, travel expenses, tuition, books, cell phone, etc.). Can your parents claim you as a dependent on their tax return? _____ Explanation:

5 Say you are divorced and have a multiple-support agreement that awards your ex the right to claim your child as a dependent on his/her tax return, but you actually provide more than half of the child's support.

Can you claim the child as your dependent on your tax return, too? _____ Explanation:

6 Can you claim the child of your step-brother as your dependent? _____ Explanation:

7 Can you claim your grandmother as your dependent if she lives in your home all year, earns less than $7,500, and you provide more than half of her support? _____ Explanation:

8 Can you claim your 10-year-old child as your dependent if your child lives with you all year, receives $50,000 in movie royalties each year that are deposited into a trust fund that cannot be touched until the child is 25 years old, and you provide more than half of the child's support? _____ Explanation:

Table 3-1. Overview of the Rules for Claiming an Exemption for a Dependent

Caution. This table is only an overview of the rules. For details, see the rest of this chapter.

- You cannot claim any dependents if you, or your spouse if filing jointly, could be claimed as a dependent by another taxpayer.
- You cannot claim a married person who files a joint return as a dependent unless that joint return is only a claim for refund and there would be no tax liability for either spouse on separate returns.
- You cannot claim a person as a dependent unless that person is a U.S. citizen, U.S. resident alien, U.S. national, or a resident of Canada or Mexico, for some part of the year.[1]
- You cannot claim a person as a dependent unless that person is your **qualifying child** or **qualifying relative**.

Tests To Be a Qualifying Child

1 The child must be your son, daughter, stepchild, foster child, brother, sister, half brother, half sister, stepbrother, stepsister, or a descendant of any of them.

2 The child must be (a) under age 19 at the end of the year, (b) under age 24 at the end of the year and a full-time student, or (c) any age if permanently and totally disabled.

3 The child must have lived with you for more than half of the year.[2]

4 The child must not have provided more than half of his or her own support for the year.

5 If the child meets the rules to be a qualifying child of more than one person, you must be the person entitled to claim the child as a qualifying child.

Tests To Be a Qualifying Relative

1 The person cannot be your qualifying child or the qualifying child of any other taxpayer.

2 The person either (a) must be related to you in one of the ways listed under _Relatives who do not have to live with you,_ or (b) must live with you all year as a member of your household[2] (and your relationship must not violate local law).

3 The person's gross income for the year must be less than $3,500.[3]

4 You must provide more than half of the person's total support for the year.[4]

[1]There is an exception for certain adopted children.
[2]There are exceptions for temporary absences, children who were born or died during the year, children of divorced or separated parents, and kidnapped children.

[3]There is an exception if the person is disabled and has income from a sheltered workshop.
[4]There are exceptions for multiple support agreements, children of divorced or separated parents, and kidnapped children.

<<< **Do you think this ad hits the "young adult" market?** Will this ad appeal to any other markets as well?

Problematic vagueness is the characteristic of a word or expression as having an imprecise meaning or unclear boundaries in a given context or for a given purpose. However, as the "animal" and "airport" examples illustrate, vagueness is best considered *not as an absolute feature, but as being relative to the context within which and purposes for which the term is being used*.

PROBLEMATIC VAGUENESS

Imagine you work in the marketing department at H&M, and you receive the following brief from corporate for the next campaign: "We want to go after a young adult demographic." Does that mean married yuppies in their mid-20s or urban hipsters? In the sentence, "We have to find those who were responsible for causing this terrible car accident," does the expression "those who were responsible" include only the drivers who were involved, or does it also include any or all of these other persons: the manufacturers of the vehicles involved in the accident, the engineers who designed the street, the city officials who refused to install a stoplight, the people living along the street who never trimmed nor pruned their shrubs and trees, which grow so thick that the vision of the drivers was limited, or the business owner who put up the huge, distracting billboard?

The H&M example does not pose major problems. If married yuppies decide to buy H&M clothing, the corporation will sell them the clothes and take the profit even if the marketing campaign had no particular effect on the yuppies' decision. However, the corporation does care whether the campaign is reaching those who are clearly members of the target audience. Marketing campaigns are expensive. But they're also like shotgun blasts. As long as the campaign hits its main target, it is not a problem if some of the pellets spray raggedly around the edges. Yuppies are probably someplace along the borderline of the marketing campaign's target audience. So, for the purposes of the campaign and in the context of selling clothes, resolving the question of whether "young adults" does or does not refer to yuppies is not going to be a problem that the corporation will worry about.

The car accident example is different. There the vagueness of the expression "those who were responsible" could become the object of highly contentious legal battles. If it is proven that vehicle manufacturers knew of some defect in the braking system of one of the cars but did not recall the vehicle for repairs, then a jury may decide to hold the manufacturer partially responsible for the accident. Similarly, it might be argued that the others listed each knew something, did something, or failed to do something that contributed to the accident. The vagueness of the term "responsible" as it applies to the car accident needs to be resolved for the purposes of determining criminal and financial responsibility. This matter is so problematic and yet so important that our society has instituted a specific methodology for resolving the applicability of the term "responsible" in situations like this. That method almost always involves negotiation between lawyers representing interested parties, and, in the most extreme situations, litigation.

When the use of a term results in imprecision sufficient to cause problems for the interpretation of that term in a given context and for a given purpose, we call that *problematic vagueness*.

AMBIGUITY: "DOES THE TERM MEAN THIS, OR DOES IT MEAN THAT?"

In the movie *My Cousin Vinny*, Ralph Macchio, whose character has been brought in for questioning, tells the Alabama sheriff, "I did it." Watch this clip from *My Cousin Vinny* at **www.TheThinkSpot.com**. Listen carefully to Macchio as he confesses. Macchio's character is referring to his having walked out of the convenience store with a can of tuna fish in his jacket pocket. He forgot it was there, and, so left without paying for it. He is trying to confess to inadvertent shoplifting. The sheriff, on the other hand, is investigating the killing of the cashier at that same convenience store. The sheriff interprets Macchio as having said,"I killed the cashier" when he says, "Sorry, it was a stupid thing to do." The ambiguity of "it" triggers a chain of events that includes Macchio and his traveling companion, played by Mitchell Whitfield, being charged with murder.

the **THINKSPOT**
www.thethinkspot.com

When a word, expression, or statement has more than one meaning, we call it ambiguous. A quick look at the dictionary shows that a great many words have more than one meaning. Why then are we not confused on an almost constant basis? Because, again, knowing the context of the conversation and the purpose of the speaker, we can readily pick out the speaker's intended meaning. "Heads up!" shouted at the people sitting behind first base at a baseball game is not a command to look toward the sky; it is a warning to duck because the batter has just fouled off a pitch. "It's 30 love," at a tennis match is intended to reveal the score, not someone's amorous relationships. "That's sick!" is slang in some high schools for "That's terrific." And, "Baby, you're the greatest!" is Hollywood hyperbole for "You're really quite average."

PROBLEMATIC AMBIGUITY

Macchio's ambiguous confession is problematic because the misunderstanding results in his arrest. Were it not for the stunning defense put on by Joe Pesci, Macchio's character could easily have been convicted of murder and sentenced to the electric chair. The ambiguity of "equal" in the parents' letter about dividing up their estate was problematic because it left the three siblings uncertain how to fulfill their parents' wishes. When ambiguity leads to troublesome misunderstanding or uncertainty about how to proceed, it is **problematic ambiguity**, which is the characteristic of word or expression as referring to more than one object or as having more than one meaning in a given context or for a given purpose.

Resolving Problematic Vagueness and Ambiguity

Resolving problematic vagueness and problematic ambiguity requires us to apply our critical thinking skills and habits of mind. In the case of problematic vagueness, we must make a judgment about where the borderlines of the term are to be located. In the case of problematic ambiguity we must decide which of the possible meanings of the term is the one the author intended. In other words, using thoughtful, reasoned judgment, we must solve the practical problem of what a term or expression means in a given context and for a given purpose.

There are at least five ways to address problematic vagueness or problematic ambiguity:

- Contextualizing
- Clarifying intent
- Negotiating
- Qualifying
- Stipulating

CONTEXTUALIZING

"AAA" can refer to the American Automobile Association, the American Anthropological Association, the American Accounting Association,

Offensive versus Offensive?

OR

These are just two meanings of the word "offensive." Can you think of any other meanings?

the American Academy of Audiology, the Amateur Astronomers Association, the American Association of Anatomists, the American Ambulance Association, the Aikido Association of America, and the Arkansas Activities Association, just to name a few. So, if a person were to say, "I'm joining the AAA," we might find the ambiguity in that statement to be problematic.

Contextualizing resolves problematic ambiguity by reminding us of the topic being discussed or the circumstances within which a statement was made. In the "I'm joining the AAA" example simply noting that the person was an undergraduate physics major talking about her interest in astronomy would clarify which AAA she meant.

Consider another example. "We need to find some more offensive people," can mean one thing in the context of sports and quite another thing spoken as irony after someone has made a particularly rude remark during a meeting. In the first context, the discussion is about building up the team's capacity to score more points by improving its offense. In the second context, the speaker probably intends to express a negative opinion about the behavior of one of the other people at the meeting.

To establish context we ask questions like these:

- Who said it to whom?
- When and where was it said?
- What was the topic of the conversation?
- Was the comment meant to be ironic, hyperbolic, misleading, or deceptive?
- Were technical terms, abbreviations, symbols, slang, code words, double entendre, euphemisms, or acronyms used?

That final question is important because often knowing that the conversation took place among members of a particular interest group or professional group helps us immediately recognize that a given word or expression is used with the special meaning that the given group attaches to that expression. We will talk more about this in the section on language communities later in the chapter.

Words taken out of context can be misleading. Consider, for example, "I smoked 50 years. . . And today I can run a marathon." We might interpret this to be a reasonably unambiguous statement suggesting that smoking is not always physically detrimental. The only clue that there may be more to the story is the three-dot ellipsis. What were the words that the author omitted? The misleading quotation was pulled from the text in the box to the right. Seeing the author's words in context, our interpretation becomes the opposite of what it was. Now we know that the author is advising people not to smoke, instead of saying that it might not be a problem.

Putting an author's words in context not only permits us to make an accurate interpretation, it helps us not be misled by unscrupulous individuals. Intellectual integrity and a strong habit of truthseeking are needed when we synopsize and de-contextualize the words and ideas of others. Accuracy is important, but so is a truthful preservation of the author's original intent. It is too easy to make mistaken interpretations when we do not know the context.

CLARIFYING ORIGINAL INTENT

Because problematic vagueness and ambiguity emerge when we are trying to interpret what someone means, one reasonable way to resolve the vagueness is simply to ask for clarification. Let's go back to the marketing department at H&M. One of the first things we will want to

> I smoked 50 years ago, when I was in high school. But only a few cigarettes just to see what it was like. It was cross-country season, and my coach told me that I was one of the best in the state. He said that if I started smoking, I could kiss the state championship good-bye. So, I quit smoking before I ever really got started and stayed away from cancer sticks ever since. Because I quit smoking and because I've worked out several days a week all of my life, and today I can run a marathon.

do is clarify the target audience that the executives have in mind for the campaign.

We would not want to put all our effort into designing the marketing approach until we were clear whom corporate H&M wants to reach. And our best method for doing this would be to ask the executives, "Can you clarify for us exactly which demographic you have in mind when you say 'young adults'?" We might hear back that we should target single men and women between the ages of 22 and 29 who are college graduates and employed at jobs that pay $35,000 to $60,000 per year. If so, that would add a lot of useful clarification, and we might be able to apply our critical thinking to the question of how best to reach that market segment.

On the other hand, we might hear back from our client that "young adults" is as clear as the client can be at this time about the target audience. In this case, we would probably try to help clarify that problematic vagueness. Given our experience and expertise in producing marketing campaigns, we might explain that the approach we would take to reach a single person who is a college graduate and has a good job is not the same as the approach we would use to market a product to someone who is the same age but married with children, or the same age but not a college graduate, or the same age but not currently employed.

Clarifying the speaker's intent becomes more challenging when multiple alternative wordings are possible and it is not possible to ask the author for clarification. For example, suppose our job was to resolve problematic phrases such as "unreasonable search and seizure," "the right to bear arms," or "freedom of assembly." The framers of the U.S. Constitution and the Bill of Rights are not available, and times and conditions have changed over the centuries. But it is not entirely unrealistic to endeavor to discern the framers' intent. In fact, that is part of the process of interpreting the law, which is essential to our justice system. And, although we do not have benefit of the original authors, we do have a large number of previous rulings that established important precedents.

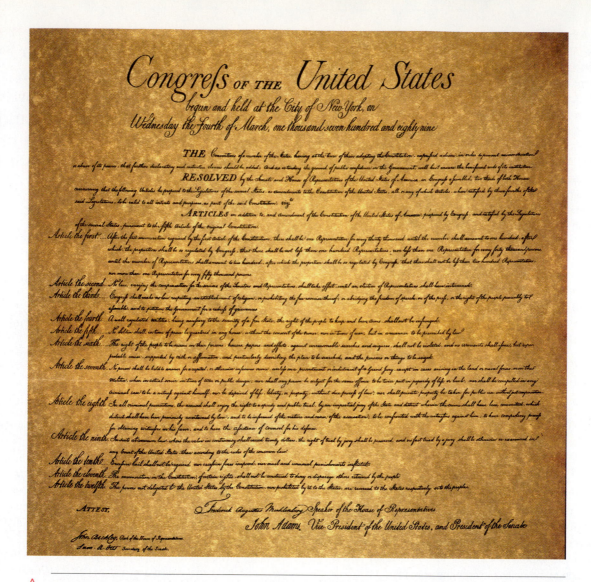

Framers of the U.S. Constitution and the Bill of Rights **were intentionally vague so future generations could interpret these documents** to fit changing times and national circumstances which the Framers themselves wisely knew they could not anticipate.

Fine, but what if the problematic vagueness was intentional? The framers of the U.S. Constitution and the Bill of Rights were wise enough to realize that times and conditions would change and that therefore it would be prudent to write in ways that left room for future generations of Americans to interpret these fundamental documents to fit their times and circumstances. Wise judgment is a very good thing. We want to cultivate that in ourselves and leave room for it to be exercised by others, too, because it is absolutely impossible for any individual or any group to anticipate every kind of problem and every set of circumstances. The habit of judiciousness, which we talked about in Chapter 3, inclines us toward wisdom and prudence in making judgments. It is precisely this virtue that the framers of the Constitution trusted that future generations of Americans would need and would have if the young Republic were going to survive and flourish.

On the other hand, at times intentional vagueness can be frustrating when precise, practical answers are what people desire. Imagine the blustery presidential candidate who pounds the electorate with bromides like these: "I stand with those who want affordable health care reform!"

"Our educational system is such a mess that we need a war on ignorance." "When I'm in office, our nation will never again negotiate from weakness." "Too many hard-working Americans are fed up with Washington politicians who take a business-as-usual approach." As voters, we might do well to demand greater clarity and operational precision, rather than accepting platitudes like those.

NEGOTIATING THE MEANING

Suppose you decide to hire me and we come to a handshake agreement that you will pay me a fair wage. As it turns out, we then discover that it is your position that "fair wage" has an upper limit of $25 per hour and it is my position that "fair wage" means $30 per hour. Because we both want the working relationship to start out being friendly, we decide to try to negotiate away the problematic vagueness by trying to reach a compromise between our two divergent positions. So, for our purposes in this context we can negotiate the mutual agreement that "fair wage" means $27.50 per hour.

Successful negotiation in complex real-world contexts involves much more than the simple compromise this example indicates.[iv] The box "Thinking Critically about Successful Negotiation" on page 50 describes a process for negotiating that is far more satisfying. Strong critical thinking skills are valuable assets in reaching mutually acceptable agreements.

In this example, we have negotiated the meaning of "fair wage" to fit our purposes in the context of a hiring agreement. Must we resolve the meaning of "fair wage" for all the other workers and all the other jobs that there are? No. That would not only be impractical and unlikely to succeed—it may not even be desirable. *There is nothing inherently wrong with vagueness or ambiguity unless it introduces problems in a given real-life context.*

Now that we have agreed that I will work for you, I ask you if there is a dress code of some kind that I should know about. You say, "Why, yes. Glad you asked. We expect everyone who works in our office to wear a shirt with a collar. No T-shirts, tank tops, or V-necks."

I think, "What if we don't mean the same thing by 'shirt with a collar'?" I imagine a golf shirt with a soft collar, a loud Hawaiian shirt with a big collar, and a conservative dress shirt with a button-down collar. The expression "shirt with a collar" is causing problematic ambiguity. So, I ask you to be more specific and you say, "Oh, I meant a dress shirt. You don't have to wear a tie, but we expect everyone to wear a dress shirt to work."

Still some vagueness, I'm thinking. What about colors? Or will only white shirts count as what you mean by "dress shirt"? But I decide not to ask about that because I can just keep my eyes open the first couple of days on the job to see if anyone wears a dress shirt that isn't pure white. I do want to ask one more question–kind of a mini-negotiation. "What about Fridays? Do you have casual Fridays?" And happily you respond, "Of course, we do. You'll see a lot of golf shirts on Fridays at our office."

"Shirt with a collar" as a problematic ambiguity—gone!—for our purposes in this context.

USING QUALIFICATIONS, EXCEPTIONS, OR EXCLUSIONS

One of the most practical ways of resolving problematic vagueness and ambiguity is to introduce qualifications that clarify which cases are included or excluded. Here are some examples of using qualifying expressions to introduce a measure of clarity.

veteran	→	person with prior experience, as contrasted with beginner
veteran athlete	→	player who was with the team last season, as contrasted with rookie
military veteran	→	soldier who has been honorably discharged from service
military veteran	→	soldier who served in combat
cold weather	→	chilly enough to need a jacket
cold weather	→	outdoor air temperatures lower than 45 degrees Fahrenheit
cold weather	→	chill factor the equivalent of 32 degrees Fahrenheit or lower
expensive car	→	more than I want to pay for that car
expensive car	→	more costly than other similar cars
expensive car	→	car that costs more than $100,000
expensive car	→	a new Bentley, Lamborghini, or Bugatti

As the examples above suggest, we can clarify expressions a lot or a little, depending on our purposes, using descriptive phrases, contrasts, technical terminology, and thorough examples.

In the "animals at the airport" example, we clarified the problematic vagueness by making exceptions for two kinds of animals. Our exception allowed us to make a statement that actually appears self-contradictory. "Companion animals are not animals as far as airport policy is concerned." But, in fact, the statement makes good sense given the purpose and context.

If you are getting the sense that critical thinking in real-life contexts requires refining our skill at making good judgments relative to the circumstances and situations at hand, you are correct. The judicious habit of mind impels us to strive to make judgments about what to believe or what to do that are as precise as the subject matter, context, and purposes permit. But no more precise than that. In fact, it would be unwise to strive to be more precise than that. Real-life judgments are often made in contexts in which absolute certitude is not attainable.

Many people see negotiation as the process of trying to find a compromise between conflicting positions. They think of stories about bitter contract negotiations between management and a labor union. Or they remember buying their first condo and finding it stressful because they felt at a disadvantage when bargaining for a good price against the more experienced seller. Negotiating with an insurance company over settlements or negotiating with an ex over child support and visitation rights are more examples of things people would rather avoid. The problem is that when people try to find a compromise between two positions, each party thinks that it is going to be forced to "give up something."

Traditionally, negotiating has been thought of as trying to reach a compromise between two initial positions on the issue. This kind of negotiation, called *positional negotiation*, is often adversarial. The process tends to end up with both sides being dissatisfied with the final outcomes because the process makes them feel forced into making concessions.

Good critical thinkers realize that the methods used to achieve a result and the criteria used to evaluate the result are, themselves, open to review and reconsideration. What if there were a better way to negotiate around problematic vagueness and simply a better method for negotiation period? What if we evaluated the outcome of the process of negotiation as good only if both sides were satisfied, rather than if both sides were dissatisfied? These questions led to the development of an alternative method of negotiation called *interest-based negotiation.*

Instead of competing in an effort not to give up more than the other guy, interest-based negotiation begins with trying to figure out what each party's interests are and then it works to find a way to achieve the interests of both parties. Interest-based negotiation calls for collaboration and creativity. Both parties strive to find a way for their own interest and the interests of the other party to be achieved. Neither party is expected to give up its interest.

Let's revisit the hiring example. Using positional-negotiating, we agreed on $27.50 per hour for 40 hours of work, five days a week. You may have felt that you were paying me too much, and I may have felt that my work was undervalued. There is a reasonable chance that the job will not start on the friendly basis we had hoped.

Using interest-based negotiation, we might have reached a different and far more amiable result. Suppose that we explore why you want to set the limit of "fair wage" at $25 and why I want it to be $30. Your interest is to preserve the pay structure you have for all the workers who are doing the same job as I would be doing. You cannot hire me for more than $25 per hour without creating an unaffordable precedent, from your perspective. You explain that you have done an industry study and the average hourly wage for the kind of work I will be doing for you is actually $23.65. But you pay $25.00 per hour.

For my part, it is not the dollars per hour that concerns me. Rather, my interest is in the total number of dollars I will make in a week and the number of hours I have to be away from my mother because I am her primary caregiver. I explain that I need to make $1,200 per week because I am expecting to pay $250 per week ($50 per day) for her dependent care expenses if I must commute to work five days a week. And I am not happy about the long commute, almost 90 minutes each way. With the commute time added in, I was expecting that my workdays would require me to be away from home for 11 hours each day of the workweek. And I was worried about what that would mean in terms of my mother's care.

Knowing each other's interests permits us to explore more creative resolutions. We might discover, for example, that I would accept $1100 per week if you would permit me to telecommute from home two days a week. Working at home those two days saves me six hours of commuting time per week and $100 of dependent care expenses per week. In return, I guarantee you that I will give you 44 hours of work each week. This agreement permits you to preserve your $25-per-hour pay policy, which is fine with me. Notice too that we have not expanded the meaning of "fair wage" beyond simply dollars per hour. Now it can include telecommuting and a variable number of work hours per week. Our negotiation resolved our problem without promoting greater conflict. In fact, neither of us feels dismayed, disrespected, or dissatisfied with the process or the result.

Tip on negotiating for a job on campus: Most colleges hire large numbers of students part-time. They work as assistants in academic and non-academic departmental offices all over campus, or they work in the library, food services, recreation, and residence life. Colleges often have rigid pay structures that do not permit room for negotiating the hourly wage. It is in the student's interest simply to secure a job, given that pay often cannot be a negotiating point. But the person doing the hiring has other interests: They want to hire students who are flexible about how many hours of work they will do per week and flexible about which hours and which days they will work. (They also want students who are friendly, professional, quick to learn, and show initiative.) So, if it is in your interest to get a job that you might be able to count on for some part-time income not only this year but in future years, and if it is in your interest that the job be close to where you live and go to class (e.g., on campus), then you would want to show that you are willing to be flexible about your work schedule. When you interview you might say that you know how important it is that the supervisor should be able to find students who are flexible about scheduling. Showing you understand the other person's interests is pleasant for the person who is hiring you as it is for you when that person shows that he or she understands your interests.

STIPULATING THE MEANING

When the determination of the exact meaning of a term has major consequences for one or more of the parties involved, then adding qualifications or noting exceptions and exclusions may not be sufficient. This often happens in financial and legal matters, when a word's meaning must be circumscribed as precisely and completely as possible.

We would not want the legal definition of "driving under the influence" to be left to each individual police officer, judge, or prosecuting attorney to define in any way he or she might wish. There would be too much variability in practice. One person might show favoritism to locals, but eagerly arrest folks from out of town. Another person might rely on a person's answer to the question "How many drinks have you had?" Still another might believe that being drunk meant that the driver slurred his words or could not walk a straight line.

It is in the interest of justice and public safety to use a uniform definition of the term "driving under the influence." Ideally, the definition would provide for some objective way of telling which drivers it applied to and which it did not. Knowing exactly how many drinks a person had, for example, will not work. Some drinks have a higher alcohol content than others, some people weigh more than others, and some metabolize alcohol at different rates than others.

As in other states, California lawmakers stipulated the meaning of the expression "driving under the influence." Stipulating meaning is intended to remove problematic vagueness and problematic ambiguity by establishing what a term shall mean for a specific set of purposes. In this case, for legal purposes within the state of California the term "driving under the influence" means exactly what Section 23152 of the state's motor vehicle code says it means. No more. No less.

One way to define "expensive car" is to show what the word refers to—in this case a Bugatti, a Lamborghini, and a Bentley. The base price of a 2009 Bugatti Veyron 16.4 Grand Sport is €1.4 Million, that's about $2,043,000.

Your Language Communities

In this chapter, we have stressed that knowing the context and purpose of a communication provides a vital basis for making an accurate interpretation. As item #18 in the "Resolving Vagueness and Ambiguity" exercise on page 52 suggests, if we know we are talking about psychology then "defensive" means one thing. But if we are talking about sports, it means something else. It is helpful to think of the people who use terms the way psychologists do as members of a community, we might call it the "Psychology Language Community." And, at the same time, those who use terms the way players, coaches, and sportswriters do might be referred to as the "Sports Language Community." It is precisely because we might be members of, or familiar with, both language communities that we are able to appreciate the ambiguity of item #18.

Driving Under Influence of Alcohol or Drugs

California Vehicle Code 23152 states:

(a) It is unlawful for any person who is under the influence of any alcoholic beverage or drug, or under the combined influence of any alcoholic beverage and drug, to drive a vehicle.

(b) It is unlawful for any person who has 0.08 percent or more, by weight, of alcohol in his or her blood to drive a vehicle.

For purposes of this article and Section 34501.16, percent, by weight, of alcohol in a person's blood is based upon grams of alcohol per 100 milliliters of blood or grams of alcohol per 210 liters of breath.

In any prosecution under this subdivision, it is a rebuttable presumption that the person had 0.08 percent or more, by weight, of alcohol in his or her blood at the time of driving the vehicle if the person had 0.08 percent or more, by weight, of alcohol in his or her blood at the time of the performance of a chemical test within three hours after the driving.[v]

Watch Out for Donkey Cart Words

"Donkey cart words" change the meaning of an otherwise perfectly good word. And, at the same time, the use of donkey cart words is designed to make anyone who tries to use that word in the correct way feel a bit humiliated for not knowing the word's "true meaning." The use of donkey cart words is not a sign of wisdom nearly as much as it is a signal that someone is being a bit of a pompous ass.

Authority figures often use donkey cart words to impose on their gullible disciples a way of talking that then becomes immunized against normal criticisms. By talking a special way, they are able to say things that may sound normal to non-initiates, but that have coded meanings for themselves and their followers, thus forming an inner circle of people who know what was meant, while those outside the group only think that they know what was meant. The four most common donkey cart words are:

"True _____", "Real _____,"
"Genuine _____," and "Authentic _____"

"*True freedom* means not choosing to do what you know you cannot do."

"*Real love* requires emptying your identity as a gift for the other."

"*Genuine power* rests only with those who rule by unchallenged will."

"*Authentic human beings* ride their emotions without question."

Although each of these seems like a pearl of wisdom, they are in fact donkey dung. They are nothing more than thinly disguised stipulations, offered without backing of any kind. They are intended to change the meaning of the word that rides in the donkey cart—that is, the word that follows behind "true," "real," "genuine," or "authentic."

The only useful thing about the donkey cart word is that clanging bell that we should hear warning us every time one of these words comes along. We should take note because the speaker is inviting us to depart from the community of those who use these words as they are defined in the dictionary. Instead we are being told that we must venture forth, like the video gamers, into a fictional world where words do not mean what they should mean. The person who drives the donkey cart is the person who controls that fictional world and those of us who would follow that cart.

By learning the "truths" proposed by the donkey cart driver, we are not necessarily gaining new knowledge about the universe or anything else. We are only learning the special vocabulary that the donkey cart driver wants us to use. It is a stinky and manipulative game played with language.

Thinking Critically

Resolving Vagueness and Ambiguity

EXERCISE—Each of the *italicized terms in the statements below introduce a degree of vagueness*. The <u>underlined terms are ambiguous</u>. Use qualifications, exceptions, exclusions, or stipulations to rewrite each statement with sufficient precision to resolve the problematic vagueness or ambiguity.

1 <u>America</u> is *overeating*.

2 *Successful people* should *give back*.

3 In *an emergency*, please *proceed* to the nearest exit.

4 She had the *good judgment* to <u>dump</u> the *creep*.

5 The *tennis star* had to forfeit the <u>match</u> due to *unsportsmanlike conduct*.

6 Kate Winslet was <u>riveting</u> in her portrayal of a *desperate* housewife in "Revolutionary Road."

7 The <u>high schools</u> in our state are a *mess*.

8 <u>We</u> do not <u>negotiate</u> with *terrorists*.

9 The <u>measure</u> of our *greatness* is our ability to *change*.

10 I want to live a <u>meaningful life</u>.

11 Every living breathing *person* has <u>rights</u>.

12 We need to <u>talk</u> *tomorrow*?

13 We never <u>had sex</u>.

14 I was <u>shocked</u> when *she left*.

15 *Usher's lyrics* <u>move me</u>.

16 <u>Direct</u> *inquires* to the <u>front desk</u>.

17 Conan O'Brian is <u>hysterical.</u>

18 He's <u>defensive.</u> [Hint: Soccer vs. Psychology]

19 *The crowd* carried signs that said "*Free* <u>Health Care</u>"

20 *Workers* <u>carried signs downtown</u> that <u>read</u> "Free *Health Care*."

21 In a nonviolent protest, five hundred off-duty firefighters carried signs outside the mayor's office that read "Free Health Care for *Low-Income* Families."

22 *Everything and everyone* <u>has a cause</u>. [Hint: Physics vs. Philanthropy]

23 *Nobody* <u>under 6</u> is permitted in the ER or the ICU. [Hint: Hospitals]

24 | 1 | 2 | 1 |
|---|---|---|
| 2 | 3 | 0 |
[Hint: Hockey vs. Baseball]

25 <u>*For you, connection with all who came before cannot be helped*</u>. [Hint: Horoscope]

NATIONAL AND GLOBAL LANGUAGE COMMUNITIES

Over the millennia our species developed many languages in order to facilitate effective communication between people living in various regions of the world. Sounds became words and took on different meanings within the communities. To preserve ideas, various systems of writing were invented that used symbols, words, and icons that meant specific things to the people of a given tribe, region, or nation. People who shared an understanding of the meanings of the words and icons can be thought of as a community defined in part by its shared language, or a **language community**.

The meanings of the words that form a given language are conventional. The words mean what they mean in a given language by virtue of the tacit mutual agreement of the people who speak that language. Those tens of millions of us who speak English never voted what each English word should mean. We learned our shared language by learning the conventions for how words are used by the English-speaking language community. Dictionaries were invented to record a language community's conventions for what its words shall mean. But, as Mark Twain Prize winner George Carlin illustrates in his bit "I'm a Modern Man," English is

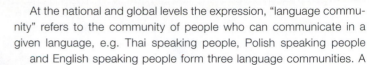

a very dynamic language. New words are invented, and old words take on new meanings. Dictionaries need updates. Access this clip at **www.TheThinkSpot.com**.

At the national and global levels the expression, "language community" refers to the community of people who can communicate in a given language, e.g. Thai speaking people, Polish speaking people and English speaking people form three language communities. A given person may be a member of one or more of these communities, or none of them, but rather be a member of some other language community, such as those who speak Italian, or those who speak Arabic, Bahasa, Dutch, Farsi, Tagalog, Turkish, or Yoruban.

LANGUAGE COMMUNITIES FORMED OF PEOPLE WITH LIKE INTERESTS

Today the idea of a language community has taken on even richer meaning. Those who understand and use the technical vocabulary of a more specialized field of human endeavor can also be called a "language community." For example, there are language communities of musicians, mathematicians, electrical engineers, military officers, bankers, biochemists, health professionals, and model train hobbyists. The words and symbols used within these communities have conventional meanings that are known and used by the members of the community. Look at the "Do You Know Members of Any of These Language Communities?" chart on page 55 to see examples of sets of symbols that are well known to those who are members of specific language communities, but not well known to other people.

A speaker seeking to communicate with a listener whom he or she knows to be a member of the same language community will use the special language and symbols of that community. For example, a hobo

Language Communities Around the World	
English	Love of learning is the first step toward wisdom.
Arabic	حب التعلم هو الخطوة الأولى نحو الحكمة
Chinese (Mandarin)	愛學習的第一步智慧
Greek	Η αγάπη της μάθησης είναι το πρώτο βήμα προς την σοφία.
Italian	Amore di apprendimento è il primo passo verso la saggezza.
Polish	Miłość nauki jest pierwszym krokiem na drodze do mądrości.
Spanish	Amor por el aprendizaje es el primer paso hacia la sabiduría.
Thai	รักของการเรียนรู้เป็นขั้นตอนแรกที่ไปภูมิปัญญา
Vietnamese	Tình yêu và học tập là bước đầu tiên hướng về trí tuệ.

wanting to warn other hobos to beware of the local authorities will use a particular symbol that to the members of the hobo language community has that particular conventional meaning. *To make a correct interpretation, we need to know how words and symbols are used by the members of the language community.*

ACADEMIC DISCIPLINES AS LANGUAGE COMMUNITIES

When we are novices relative to a given area of human endeavor, for example, the subject fields represented by the academic departments of a college or university, we may feel somewhat intimidated by those language communities. We know those who have already been initiated into that community—for example the faculty, graduate students, and undergraduate majors—know vocabulary we do not know. They are able to speak with one another about that subject field in ways that we cannot yet comprehend.

As novices who have yet to learn our way around those language communities, we may not fully understand the textbooks or lectures senior members of that community have prepared for us. One reason is that the terminology differs from one discipline to another. "Freedom," for example, has different meanings depending on whether the discipline is political science, mathematics, economics, philosophy, statistics, or chemistry.

Another reason understanding what is being said can be difficult for novices is because there are different conventions within the different disciplines for how one conducts inquiry and communicates findings. As we shall see in Chapter 13, science proceeds seeking evidence empirically to confirm or disconfirm hypotheses. In science the professional papers that present research findings follow a specific outline in which methods, findings, and results are described separately, data are displayed in charts and graphs, and often statistical analyses are used to establish that the data are not simply the result of random chance.

In contrast, in the humanities, scholars work to refine the meanings of terms and provide textual analyses based on the author's intentions, cultural context, word choice, and historical time and place. We illustrated this briefly at the beginning of this chapter in the Genesis example. Charts and graphs displaying experimental data are almost never found, although scholars in the humanities take due note of evidence, such as historical and cultural facts. Their work is presented in papers that often begin by stating a problem and then proceed by introducing important distinctions and parsing out alternative meanings.

Historians, musicians, accountants, political scientists, poets, nurses, civil engineers, journalists, physicists, social workers, lawyers,

and all the other academic language communities at a university each follow the standards of their professional or academic field for how to conduct inquiry and communicate findings.

CRITICAL THINKING AND COLLEGE INTRODUCTORY COURSES

General studies requirements are intended to introduce students to the array of different academic language communities. To help us understand how a given academic discipline functions, the typical introductory course is designed to explain

- The kinds of questions that the discipline seeks to address
- The evidence the discipline understands to be relevant to resolving its questions
- The concepts, terminology, and basic theories of the discipline
- The methods and techniques of inquiry used in the discipline
- The criteria the discipline applies when evaluating the quality of work produced
- The contexts within which the discipline conducts its work

Notice how well this list matches the list presented by the expert consensus researchers, cited in Chapter 2, as they described critical thinking[vi]: "We understand critical thinking to be purposeful, self-regulatory judgment that results in interpretation, analysis, evaluation, and inference, as well as explanation of the *evidential, conceptual, methodological, criteriological,* or *contextual* considerations upon which that judgment is based."

Critical thinking within a disciplinary language community is like critical thinking within any language community. Different language communities, and in particular different academic disciplines, focus on the specific evidence, concepts, methods, criteria, and context. But the critical thinking skills and habits of mind apply across all language communities. As a result, strengthening our critical thinking skills and habits of mind helps us when we venture into different academic language communities.

Through steady effort, practice and attention to the language conventions of the different communities, we gain warranted confidence in our own ability to speak effectively and interpret accurately. In our introductory college courses, our challenge is to learn the terminology and the way that the discipline conducts its work—its questions, evidence, concepts, methods, criteria, and context of inquiry. By applying our critical thinking skills, and in particular the skill of interpretation, we can begin to take a few successful steps along the path toward fuller membership in these different academic language communities.

<<< **The term "gadget" may mean one thing to you** but something completely different to a member of the military.

Do You Know Members of Any of These Language Communities?

Examples of Special Terms & Symbols	Language Community
LOL, TMI, BFF, BFN, BIOYE, SNAG	Cell phone texters
Pt, Au, Hg, H_2O, CO_2	Chemists
Stet, ^, :/, tr, ?/	Copy editors
SATCOM, SEABEE, UNSC, SOP	Department of Defense employees and contractors
	Electrical engineers
	Hobos
	iPhone owners
3 4 0 = +	Mathematicians
	Military field commanders
	Musicians
	Racist prison gangs
	Workflow planners

55

Clarifying Ideas

In this chapter we applied our critical thinking to the problem of interpreting ideas expressed in language. Knowing the context within which a word or expression is used and the intent of the speaker in using that word or expression is essential to making an accurate interpretation. Vagueness and ambiguity are unproblematic if the context and purpose make the speaker's meaning clear to the listener. But vagueness and ambiguity can be problematic in those contexts in which multiple plausible interpretations are possible. We may not be sure exactly what cases a problematically vague term is intended to include or exclude. We may not be sure which meaning of a problematically ambiguous term the speaker intends.

There are strategies we can use to resolve problematic vagueness and ambiguity. Using our critical thinking skills, we can ask probing questions to contextualize, to clarify intent, to negotiate the meaning, to establish exclusions and exceptions, or to stipulate the meaning for a given purpose.

People with a shared understanding of the meanings of words and icons can be thought of as a language community. Academic language communities, also known as professional fields or academic disciplines, are defined not only by their terminology, but by the sets of questions, kinds of evidence, conceptualizations, methods, and standards of proof that they accept. Critical thinking calls for us to give reasoned consideration to precisely this same list of things when we are making a reflective judgment about what to believe or what to do. The core critical thinking skill of interpretation is vital for this, because using it well enables us to understand what words and symbols mean in a given context and, therefore, what the members of these different language communities are saying.

KEY TERMS

problematic vagueness is the characteristic of a word or expression as having an imprecise meaning or unclear boundaries in a given context or for a given purpose.   *45*

problematic ambiguity is the characteristic of a word or expression as referring to more than one object or as having more than one meaning in a given context or for a given purpose.   *46*

language community is a community in which people share an understanding of the meanings of words and icons. Dictionaries were invented to record a language community's conventions for what its words *shall* mean.   *53*

FIND IT ON THE THINKSPOT

Both *Inherit the Wind* (p. 41) and *My Cousin Vinny* (p. 45) send us to **www.TheThinkSpot. com**. There are so many great scenes in these two wonderful films that it's difficult to know which to offer as examples of strong or weak critical thinking. Both films are courtroom dramas set in Southern states, and both bring to mind the importance of precise language and rigorous thinking.

George Carlin's bit "I'm a Modern Man" (p. 53), found at **www.TheThinkSpot.com**, is not only fun but is also a masterful display of linguistic dexterity. The precision with which Carlin uses language is matched by the troubling sloppiness with which some toss around the word "science." That's why the Small Group Exercise on page 57 invites you to visit the National Science Foundation link at **www.TheThinkSpot.com**.

Exercises

ANALYZE AND INTERPRET

Reword each of the following to expose the problematic ambiguity or vagueness, if any, that each statement contains. Add context as needed. Remember that a given statement might be both ambiguous in some respects and vague in other respects. Mark any that are crystal clear and entirely unproblematic no matter what the context or purpose as "OK AS IS."

1. America is the land of opportunity.
2. If you can't afford food, then you're not free.
3. I love my brother and my wife, but not in the same way.
4. God is love.
5. When in doubt, whistle.
6. Organic foods are healthier.
7. Clean coal is a green business!
8. *Hamlet* contains timeless truths.
9. Music soothes the savage beast in all of us.
10. Ignoring lazy thinking is like snoozing on a railroad crossing—not a problem until it's too late.

SMALL GROUP EXERCISE: INTERPRETING "SCIENCE" AND "PSEUDOSCIENCE"

For many years the National Science Foundation (NSF) has conducted surveys of the public attitudes and understanding about science and scintific knowledge. The results inform policy development, legislation, and funding for scientific research and science education in the nation. NSF reports, "In 2002 the survey showed that belief in pseudoscience was relatively widespread. . . For example 25% of the public believed in astrology. . ., at least half the people believe in the existence of extrasensory perception, . . . 30% believe that some of the UFOs are really space vehicles from other civilizations, . . . half believe in haunted houses and ghosts, faith healing, communication with the dead, and lucky numbers." Form a small working group with one or two others in your class. Do steps 1, 2 and 5 as a group. Divide the work among yourselves for steps 3 and 4.

1. Review the public information on the NSF Web site, particularly the report "Science and Engineering Indicators–2002" Access the NSF report at **www.TheThinkSpot.com**.
2. Define the words "pseudoscience" and "science" in a fair-minded and reasoned way.
3. Survey 10 of your friends and family members about their views on astrology, extrasensory perception, and ghosts. In each case invite them to use their critical thinking skills and explain why they believe what they believe.
4. Objectively summarize the reasons pros and cons for each of the three topics.
5. Using the Holistic Critical Thinking Scoring Rubric in Chapter 1, evaluate the quality of the thinking pros and cons for each of the three topics. Explain your evaluation.

REFLECTIVE LOG

Song lyrics and poetry often contain references to emotions, ideas, issues, persons, or events well known to the members of the language community for whom the song was written. Select a song you particularly enjoy. Write out the lyrics. Research the song and the composer or author in order to learn what you can about the purpose and context of that work. Restate what is being said to explain what the composer or poet is trying to communicate with each verse.

Locate and listen to Bob Dylan's original version of "Forever Young," then listen to Rod Stewart's 1988 version. Compare those interpretations to each other and to Will.i.am's rap rendition, which was used in the 2009 Pepsi Superbowl commercial. Use your critical thinking skills to explain how each artist's interpretation slightly modifies what the song is intended to mean.

Making arguments

and giving reasons to explain the basis for our beliefs and decisions are universal in our species. There is a way to ask "Why?" in every language. For example, were we to ask Karen why she believes pot should be legalized, Karen might say, "Because then the state could get sales tax when people buy pot, just like with alcohol." To the question, "Why did you order a moratorium on Illinois death penalty executions in January 2000?" former Illinois governor George Ryan might have responded, "Because our state's criminal justice system has made mistakes, and innocent people have been wrongly executed. There is no way to undo that kind of a mistake."

Our goal in this chapter is to analyze exactly what people's claims are and the reasons they use to back up those claims. We will use a technique called mapping to help clarify how a person's reasoning flows from initial statements taken as true to the conclusion the person regards as being supported by those statements. Like a Google map showing how to get from point A to point B, the maps we will draw show how people reason from their beliefs and assumptions to reach a particular belief or decision.

USING MAPS TO ANALYZE ARGUMENTS AND DECISIONS

Analyzing and Mapping Arguments

In the *Law & Order: Special Victims Unit* clip that accompanies this chapter, a mother explains why she decided not to vaccinate her son against measles. Access the clip at www.TheThinkSpot.com. Her reason was her worry about the possible risks to her son associated with being vaccinated. She says many other things as well. For example, that as a parent, it's her right to make this decision. She asserts that she is not accountable for the consequences of her decision. And she says that for her child the outcome was exactly as she had hoped. Without incurring the risk she associated with a vaccination, her son got sick with measles and then recovered. In the final analysis, her reason is this: "Measles vaccinations have dangerous side effects. Those risks worry me a lot." In view of this, her decision was not to have her son vaccinated. Independently we know that those risks are exceedingly rare and that the disease itself is a far greater risk to her child and to other children.[i] And so, we may want to evaluate her decision negatively.

But our task in this chapter is not to evaluate. For now, our job is to analyze the person's judgment based on the reasons the person gives. Analysis calls for us to be as accurate and objective as possible, even if we totally disagree with that judgment or personally would have used other reasons. In fact, especially if we disagree. When the time comes for evaluation, we will want to be sure that we are being true to the speaker's position with no alteration or revisions from other sources, including our own. Evaluating an argument (the skill we built in Chapters 7 and 8) requires first having made a thoughtful and insightful analysis.

"ARGUMENT = (REASON + CLAIM)"

Consistent with common usage, we will use the term **argument** to refer to the process of giving a reason in support of a claim.[ii] Here are some examples of arguments:

1 [Reason] Student journalists should have the same rights as professional journalists. [Claim it is intended to support] So, laws that shield professional journalist from imprisonment should apply to student journalists, too.

2 [Reasons] {A journalist's confidential sources of information would be in danger if they were publically identified. To legally require journalists to tell the names of their confidential sources to the police will have the effect of publically identifying those confidential sources. It is never a good thing to put people in danger unnecessarily.} [Claim] Therefore, no, the law should not require journalists to reveal their confidential sources.

3 [Claim] Encephalitis (swelling of the brain) cannot be said to be a side effect of measles vaccination. [Reason] Here's why: "This happens so rarely — less than once in a million shots — that experts can't be sure whether the vaccine is the cause or not."[iii]

4 [Claim] I need to get a better job! [Reason] My boss is a total moron.

4' [Reason] I work for a total moron. [Claim] Man, do I need to get a better job or what?

The term **claim** refers to the statement that the maker of the argument is seeking to show to be true or probably true. We will often refer to an argument's claim as the argument's **conclusion**. The other sentences in the argument, namely those that are used to shows that the claim is true or that it is probably true, constitute the **reason**.

Two Reasons, Two Arguments

It is very common in natural conversation to give more than one reason in support of a claim. We will treat each separate combination of reason-plus-claim as a separate argument. To help see why, consider this: "I should buy the thin crust pizza because it costs less and it tastes better." It is reasonable to analyze that sentence as expressing two arguments:

5 [Reason] Thin crust pizza costs less.
[Claim/Conclusion] I should buy thin crust.

6 [[Reason] Thin crust pizza tastes better.
[Claim/Conclusion] I should buy thin crust.

Now suppose someone tried to argue against that claim that I should buy thin crust this way: "What? You're wrong about the 'tastes better' part. The last time we had thin crust, you said it tasted like cardboard." Let us concede that the person's memory is accurate, and I remember. "Oh, yeah, the last thin crust I had tasted like pavement-baked Wyoming roadkill." And so we all agree that the argument is defeated. Even so, the claim that I should buy thin crust still is being supported by the reason that it costs less.

Two Confusions to Avoid

There are a couple of confusions to avoid. First, by using the word "argument," we do not mean "quarrel" or "disagreement." The discussions that result when making arguments and giving reasons can be civil, constructive, respectful, and collaborative. Second, when using the word "conclusion," we do not mean to suggest that the person's conclusion

Words that Signal Conclusions	Words that Signal Reasons
So . . .	Since . . .
Thus . . .	Given that . . .
Therefore . . .	Whereas . . .
Hence . . .	Because . . .
We can now infer . . .	For the reason that . . .
It follows that . . .	Suppose . . .
This means that . . .	Assume . . .
This implies . . .	Let us take it that . . .
These facts indicate . . .	Let us begin agreeing that . . .
The evidence shows . . .	The evidence is as follows . . .
Let us infer that . . .	We all know that . . .
So it would seem that . . .	In the first place . . .
And so probably . . .	Is supported by . . .
We can deduce . . .	Is implied by . . .
This supports the view that . . .	Is derived from the fact that . . .
You see, therefore, that . . .	For the reason that . . .

must come at the end. Examples 3 and 4 demonstrate that the conclusion, that is, the claim that the speaker intends to support, can be the first statement in the speaker's argument. In natural discourse, it often is.

"Reason" and "Premise"

In example arguments (1), (4), (5), and (6), the reason is expressed in a single statement. In (2) three statements are used together to express the reason. In (3) grammatically only one sentence is used. But when we analyze what that sentence tells us, we see that it expresses two statements[iv]:

- For every 1 million measles vaccinations administered, one case of encephalitis occurs.

- The rate of 1 in 1 million is so rare that experts cannot be sure if the vaccine was the cause or not.

The statement or statements that comprise a reason are commonly referred to as the **premises** of the argument. Here are two examples of arguments that when used in their proper contexts, can afford to leave a premise unexpressed.

7 Optimus Prime and Bumblebee are Transformers. So, obviously they are made of metal.

8 Salerno is south of Napoli. So, it is south of Roma.

The premise missing from (7) is "All Transformers are metal," which is a true statement within the fictional universe of a certain series of action adventure movies. And the implicit premise of (8) is about cities in Italy, "Napoli (Naples) is south of Roma (Rome)."

Distinguishing Reasons from Conclusion

Our language is rich with words we can use to communicate our intentions when it comes to expressing arguments. Some words signal our conclusion, and others signal our reason. The table on page 60 lists some of the most common words and phrases used when we want to be sure people know we are making an argument. Naturally, it would be an error to think that we always are so clear and obvious about our argument making. Context is everything. Miscommunication happens.

The state can get sales tax when people buy pot, just like with alcohol. ⟶ Pot should be legalized.

MAPPING CLAIMS AND REASONS

When we are trying to be precise in our analysis of an argument, especially a complex argument or a conversation in which several arguments are made, many of us find it useful to display the reasoning visually. In effect, we try to map the arguments. Using familiar shapes and connecting lines, we express how we understand the ideas to be related. As analysts, our main responsibility is to develop as accurate an understanding as possible of what the person expressing the argument had in mind. Like the TV show *CSI*, we analyze the evidence and map out our findings. Our aim is to show how that person intended to support the claims being made by the reasons that were used.

Let's map a few simple examples to get started. We will use a **rectangle** to represent the argument's conclusion. Let's use an **oval** to represent the reason. And we will simply draw an **arrow** from the reason to the conclusion to show that the person who made the argument intends to support that claim with that reason. Remember, just because the speaker intends that a given reason should support a given claim, it does not follow that the reason actually does support that claim. Some reasons fail. But, determining whether or not an argument fails is evaluation, and we are only analyzing arguments in this chapter. Now, think back to Karen's argument in the introduction to this chapter. Map 1 shows that argument using our simple oval-arrow-rectangle mapping conventions.

Suppose Karen was to have said, "I think pot should be legalized because, just like alcohol, the state could get sales tax revenues and because people over 21 could buy pot legally. Oh, and another thing, then we could regulate it to assure the pot-buying public gets consistent quality, man." The argument map below shows that Karen offers three separate reasons for believing that pot should be legalized.

MAP > it > OUT 2

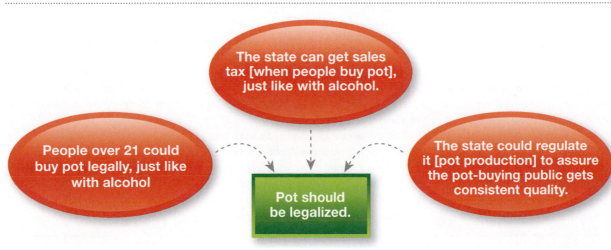

The state can get sales tax [when people buy pot], just like with alcohol.

People over 21 could buy pot legally, just like with alcohol

The state could regulate it [pot production] to assure the pot-buying public gets consistent quality.

Pot should be legalized.

Mapping a Line of Reasoning

There are times when a claim becomes a reason for another claim, thus forming a chain of reasoning. For example, say a person named Sara were to share her reasoning for having rented an apartment on State Street this way: "I wanted a place near the library because I love to study there. It was the closest rental available." Were we to ask Sara why she loves to study in the library, she might give as her reason, "Because it's quiet there." And if we push her to say why quiet is important to her, especially in a world where background music seems to assault us all the time, she might say, "I like my iPod, but I need quiet when I study. Music, or anything that disturbs the quiet, distracts me from my work." The analysis of Sara's reasoning would map out this way:

Sara's line of reasoning begins with a fundamental thing she knows about herself ("anything that disturbs the quiet causes me to be distracted") and concludes with the idea that she should rent an apartment on State Street. If she learns that any of the links along that chain of reasoning is not well connected, then she may well decide to reconsider and rent some place else.

A map like this, which shows a chain of reasoning, suggests that we might want to hold the word "conclusion" for that claim that the speaker is ultimately trying to establish.

MAP > it > OUT 3

- Anything that disturbs the quiet causes me to be distracted.
- It's quiet in the Library.
- I need quiet when I study.
- I love to study in the Library
- I should rent a place near the Library
- [Among the choices I have] the apartment on State Street is the rental closest to the Library.
- So, I should rent the apartment on State Street.

The other claims along the way are intermediate relative to the conclusion. OK, we could do that. But, on the other hand, every additional tweak or restriction on how we will use any given word raises the question Why? Can't we make ourselves understood to more people without that rule?

Mapping Implicit Ideas

In natural conversational contexts when people give their reasons for a claim, they typically offer a specific fact, opinion, observation, or belief. "Thin crust pizza costs less." "It's quiet in the library." "The state can get sales tax." "Optimus Prime and Bumblebee are Transformers." The speaker typically believes that he or she has said enough, given the context, his or her purpose in communicating, and the understandings to be shared with the others in the conversation. That is, unless someone asks for a clarification. In the case of argument (7) about the Transformers, if we did not know the movie reference, we might well ask how the person jumped all the way to "So, Optimus Prime and Bumblebee are made of metal." The response would be to articulate the implicit but unspoken premise, "All transformers are made of metal." But for the most part, most days, in most contexts we get it. Argument making and reason giving are highly efficient processes.

Thinking Critically About Technical Vocabulary

Specialized terminology is valuable because it improves communication among the members of a specific language community. Professional fields, businesses, government agencies, religions, social organizations, clubs, and societies of all kinds inevitably generate specialized vocabulary – words that have special definitions for the members of that language community, definitions that differ from what those words might mean when used by the rest of the people who are not members of that language community. There are many important reasons to generate specialized terminology; often the reasons relate to the activities the language community is engaged in together and the nuanced understandings those activities require. Think of medical or legal terminology as examples.

To become a participating member of that language community, we must learn to use words that have specialized meanings for that community in the same ways that others in the community use those words. We need to internalize the special meanings the group attaches to certain words. The more a language community generates specialized terminology, the less people who are not members of that language community can understand what is being said, even if the words being used are familiar words that have been around for centuries.

In Chapter 4, we said students trying to understand an academic discipline that is new to them need to learn the specialized language of the discipline to be successful. Learning technical terminology means acquiring the facility to use words that have specialized meanings the same way that the other members of the disciplinary language community use those words when conversing with one another.

That said, specialized vocabulary poses major problems for talking with people about their critical thinking. Critical thinking is a pervasive human phenomenon. So, the more

we want to talk with people about how to analyze, evaluate, or explain reasoned judgments about what to believe or what to do, the more important it is for us to use the vocabulary of human thinking in ways that are consistent with the ordinary, everyday meanings of words. We need to be able to talk about these things with people no matter what discipline, profession, political party, religion, business, club, or other language community they may be a member of. If we attach special meanings to common words like "reason," "claim," "analysis," "open-mindedness," etc., we limit the utility of those words to communicate across the greatest possible span of people, topics, and real-life situations. The language community for critical thinking includes everybody. So, the words have to be used in ways that can be understood by everyone . . . even if they were not fortunate enough to have read this book.

So, cutting to the chase, how should we map argument (7) if we want to show both the expressed premise and the implied premise? We can simply put both statements in the oval. To note that the speaker implicitly relied on an idea, but did not actually express that thought, we can use a **cloud shape**, like in a comic strip. The cloud shape is one of the devices we can use to keep track of things we have added to the analysis beyond what the speaker actually said. Looking at the cloud shapes, we will know exactly which ideas we have attributed to the speaker, and we can double-check to see whether our interpretations are reasonable or need to be refined. Here is a map of argument (7) about the two Transformers characters.

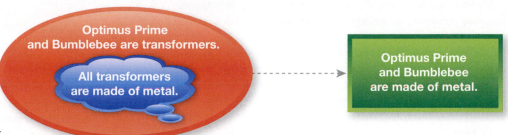

> Students trying to understand an academic discipline that is new to them need to learn the specialized language of the discipline to be successful. "

INTERPRETING UNSPOKEN REASONS AND CLAIMS IN CONTEXT

Teammates are talking about next Saturday's game. One says, "Look, we shut out State last week, and the week before that State buried Western. So, Saturday should be easy." Before we can map this argument, we need to interpret it so that the reasoning is more fully expressed, and we may have to restate it for the sake of clarity.

- Our team defeated State's team last week.
- State's team defeated Western's team the week before that.
- [Our team is scheduled to play Western's team on Saturday.]
- [So, our team will probably defeat Western's team on Saturday.]

How many reasons does the speaker use to support the claim? Only one. The context permitted the speaker to communicate successfully by offering only two facts. Our interpretation of what she said revealed that the team's shared knowledge of their game schedule enabled the speaker to omit the third fact. Here is a map of this argument that includes both of the elements not spoken in the original: a premise and the conclusion itself.

When we give reasons, we naturally assume that the others in our conversation understand us. Much is left unsaid because it very often does not need to be said, given factors like context, shared experiences, common knowledge, and similarities of cultural backgrounds. But, obviously, what we leave unspoken can cause problems. From time to time, we all have experienced such a situation. Either we get someone else's unspoken assumptions wrong, or they are mistaken about our unspoken assumptions. Fortunately, these

problems are easy to spot and easy to fix. Going back to the pot example, clarification could go like this: "Karen, are you saying that the state should raise the sales tax?" "No, I'm saying that an entirely new source of revenue, namely a tax on the sale of pot, will be beneficial to the state budget."

INTERPRETING THE USE OF IRONY, HUMOR, SARCASM, AND MORE

As we saw in Chapter 4, interpretation is an essential critical thinking skill to refine. To understand what people really mean, we cannot always take their words at face value. We spice up our conversations with wit, humor, irony, sarcasm, smack talk, innuendo, double entendre, exaggerations, understatement, slang, imagery, emotion, provocation, and much more. These language tools can give a single word a variety of meanings. For example the words "What a nice tattoo!" can mean that a person thinks your tattoo is awesome, thinks your tattoo is silly, thinks your tattoo should not be showing, thinks your tattoo makes a poignant statement, etc. As we did with the softball team example above, interpretation and restatement are vital preliminary activities to analysis and mapping.

Before mapping an ironic or sarcastic comment, switch the statement from the positive that was spoken to the negative that was intended (or from the negative spoken to the positive that was intended). For example, in one context "He was wonderfully diplomatic" can be meant as sincere praise. In this context it supports the claim, "Let him represent us." But in another context it can be intended sarcastically. There

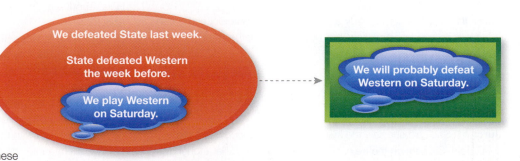

the speaker would be using it to support the opposite claim, "Don't let him represent us." In the latter case, since the correct analysis must reflect the speaker's intent, and we know the speaker was making a negative comment, we would restate the reason as, "He was [not at all] wonderfully diplomatic."

As we have already done a couple of times above, we can use words in **[brackets]** to clarify a statement so that it can be read in the argument map the way the speaker intended it to be understood. We can also use bracketed text to describe the impact on the reasoning process of non-verbal cues. For example, people frown, scoff, cross their arms, or roll their eyes to show that they disagree. Such non-verbal cues can be represented in an argument map in this way: "[Arms are crossed and he's shaking his head – John strongly disagrees with Karen about legalizing pot.]"

Giving Reasons and Making Arguments in Real Life

Asking someone about their reasons and having them share their thinking honestly and fully are complex human social interactions. The context, a gesture, a look, a facial expression, the past history between people, unspoken assumptions, and all kinds of other things can enter into how we interpret what people really mean. As we mature, we gain the skills, knowledge, and experience to understand others and to express ourselves better. As our skills advance, we can handle more challenging arguments, such as the ones in this next section.

THE EL TRAIN ARGUMENT FROM *12 ANGRY MEN*

The clip from *12 Angry Men* used in Chapter 2 offers examples of sarcasm, irony, expressive body language, and raw emotion, all of which may or may not be influencing the thinking of the various members of the jury as they deliberate.[v] Let's apply our argument mapping techniques to the argument Henry Fonda makes in support of the claim that the old man was lying when he testified that he heard the defendant threaten to kill the victim. The part we will focus on runs from 39:30 [minute:second] to 43:00. Go ahead, and watch it again. Access material at **www.TheThinkSpot.com**.

Here is an edited transcript of the things the characters say.

Cobb: (addressing Fonda) You! Down there. The old man who lives upstairs says he heard the kid [accused] yell out "I'm going to kill you." A second later he heard the body hit the floor . . .

Fonda: I was wondering how clearly the old man could have heard the boy's voice trough the ceiling.

Cobb: He didn't hear it through the ceiling. The window was open. So was the one upstairs . . .

Juror #1: Don't forget the lady across the street. She looked right in the open window and saw the boy stab his father [the victim]. I mean, isn't that enough for you?

Fonda: No, it isn't.

Juror #2: (sarcastically) Boy, how do you like this guy? It's like talking into a dead phone. (Turns his back on Fonda and walks away.)

Juror #1: She said she saw the killing through the window of a moving El train. Six cars on the train, she said she saw the killer though the

last two cars. She remembered the most insignificant detail. I don't see how you can argue with that.

Fonda: Has any body here any idea how long it would take an El train . . . to pass a given point?

Juror #3 [After some back and forth time estimates]: All right, say 10 seconds.

Fonda: Let's assume it takes an El train moving at medium speed 10 seconds to pass . . . the open window. It passed so close that you could almost reach out and touch it. Right? Now let me ask you this. Has anyone here ever lived near the El tracks? . . .

Juror #4: I just finished painting an apartment near the tracks. We were there for three days.

Fonda: What was it like?

Juror #4: Noisy. . .

Fonda: I lived in a second floor apartment by the El train once. When the window is open and the train goes by, the noise is almost unbearable.

Cobb: All right, you can't hear yourself think. Will you get to the point?

Fonda: Old man says he heard the body hit the floor one second after he heard through the open window the boy make the threat. Right?

Juror #5: Right.

Fonda: The woman says she saw the murder through the windows of the last two cars of a passing El train. Right. The last two cars?

Fonda: Since the woman saw the murder through the last two cars, we can assume that the body hit the floor just as the train went by.

Fonda: Therefore, the train had been roaring by the old man's window a full 10 seconds before the body hit the floor. [This means] the old man would have had to have heard the boy make his threat with the train roaring past his nose! It's not possible he could have heard what he said he heard!

The edited transcript leaves out things that happened in the film while the argument was unfolding. It leaves out the jurors' playing tic-tac-toe instead of paying attention and the resulting dustup when Fonda stops their game. Even so, many of us still have a difficult time following the twists and turns of a complicated argument like this one when all we have is a page full of text. Argument maps help us organize and display our analyses. And, because the reasoning is presented using simple shapes and arrows, the flow of the thinking quickly becomes apparent. It is easier to collaborate on the analysis of complicated arguments using visuals that can spread across a page in all directions versus a text-based approach, which can only move from left to right and from top to bottom line by line.

Of course, to appreciate the advantages of visual mapping when analyzing more complicated passages, one must understand the mapping process. Practice. That's the ticket. So let's make a map. How about we try to map Fonda's argument from the transcript above?

Here are a few tips. It often works best to begin an argument map by identifying the speaker's final conclusion. In this case, it is easy because the scene has been building up to Fonda's last statement. "It's not possible. . ." Let's put that down first, and then, working backward from the conclusion, let's add the two strands of reasoning, which collide at the point where the old man's testimony about what he says he heard conflicts with the fact of how noisy it is when an El train roars by. The dilemma for the jury is that they either have to reject the facts

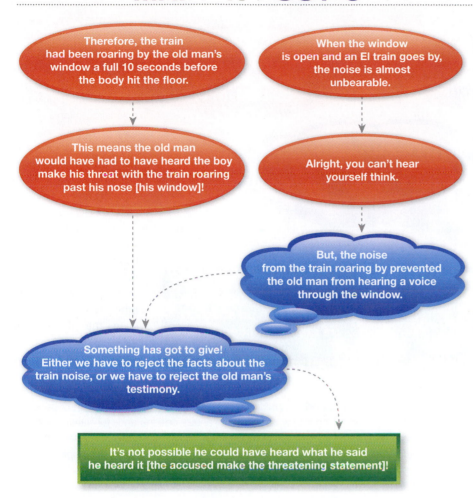

Therefore, the train had been roaring by the old man's window a full 10 seconds before the body hit the floor.

When the window is open and an El train goes by, the noise is almost unbearable.

This means the old man would have had to have heard the boy make his threat with the train roaring past his nose [his window]!

Alright, you can't hear yourself think.

But, the noise from the train roaring by prevented the old man from hearing a voice through the window.

Something has got to give! Either we have to reject the facts about the train noise, or we have to reject the old man's testimony.

It's not possible he could have heard what he said he heard it [the accused make the threatening statement]!

we afford it every protection that would be given to you or me?" Here Jon Stewart interrupts to ask, "Do think that . . . on the side of 'choice' . . . that they do not believe that every human life has value?" By asking this question and by saying that it is unfair to characterize everyone who may be in favor of "choice" as being savagely indifferent to human life, Stewart shows that he believes that people on both sides of this issue can agree that every human life has value. See page 66 for a map of the reasoning evident in their interview so far. It will look somewhat unusual compared to our earlier maps because Huckabee's reasoning is flowing toward his pro-life position. Although he has not yet offered an argument, we might expect that Stewart will head toward the pro-choice conclusion.

In the second half of the interview, Huckabee says, "I believe that life begins at conception. Biologically and scientifically, it is irrefutable; that's when life begins. If you want to argue 'Is it human life?' what else could it be? It's not a dolphin; it's not a stalk of broccoli. It has to be human life because of the cellular structure." As Stewart points out, for Huckabee no other considerations appear to be relevant. As a counterargument to those who would say otherwise, Huckabee argues that their view can result in very undesirable consequences. "If we train a generation [to believe they can] take a human life because that life represents an interference to [their lives], . . .what happens to us when we are old? I do not want to give my kids the opportunity to say, 'Dad, you are an interference. Coming to see you in

about noisy trains or reject the old man's testimony. Map 6 shows that dilemma too.

The map above is not complete. The scene includes arguments that lead to the two ovals with "Therefore, the train..." and "When the window is open..." Try for yourself to map each of those lines of reasoning back to their respective starting points. Expect to do more than one or two drafts before you are satisfied with your analysis. Mapping is like writing. The key to quality comes from drafting and redrafting. Access the clip at **www.TheThinkSpot.com**.

HUCKABEE AND STEWART DISCUSS "THE PRO-LIFE ISSUE—ABORTION"

Let's try another moderately difficult example: On June 18, 2009 the former governor of Arkansas, Mike Huckabee, visited with Jon Stewart on *The Daily Show* specifically to discuss the controversial topic of prolife/abortion. Access this clip at **www .TheThinkSpot.com**.

the THINKSPOT
www.thethinkspot.com

The conversation's first 90 seconds is taken up with humor and conversation about having a conversation about abortion. The next 60 seconds is on point. A transcript of that 60 seconds shows that Governor Huckabee begins saying that the issue for him is about "so much more than abortion." For him, it is about "whether every human life has intrinsic worth and value." He believes that "every life has value." Then he asks, "At what point is it a life, and at what point do

the nursing home is messing up my social life; your long-term care bill is [economically] breaking us' . . ."

Stewart objects, "But you're not at that point living inside your kids." And then he makes a counterargument of his own: "Taking [your view] to its logical conclusion, it [abortion any time after conception] is murder. [So,] you would have to put the woman in jail. The man who got her pregnant would be an accessory." Stewart is intimating that these absurd consequences show there must be something wrong with Huckabee's conclusion.

Although we could use ovals to represent objections and counterarguments, that shape undersells the intended logical force of these elements. Objections and counterarguments are intended to show that some position the speaker does not agree with is seriously flawed. Objections and counterarguments are used to reverse the flow of the reasoning away from the conclusion being rejected and back toward the speaker's position on the issue. They are examples of the use of reasons to disprove, refute, invalidate, or show that a given claim is not true. Let's use a **wide arrow** with words inside to depict objections and counterarguments. The map on page 67 incorporates the arrow device in its analysis. The map includes the elements shown in the first initial map of the Huckabee interview and adds the elements that happened afterward.

It was tough to go through the Huckabee interview in such detail and not evaluate what was being said. So many ideas cried out for clarification, so many distinctions should have been made, so many more considerations should have been brought forward. One lesson, reinforced again and again over the years, is that those with whom we disagree are almost never as evil or as stupid as we imagine. Good critical thinkers know that it is wise not to demonize, underestimate, or disrespect those arguing for a different conclusion.

Analyzing and Mapping Decisions

Argument maps are intended to depict in a helpful way the analysis of the reasons presented in support of a given conclusion. And if our purpose in learning critical thinking was only to be able to present, analyze, and evaluate arguments, then we might be able to end the chapter here and go directly to the exercises. However, as we said in the beginning of the book, critical thinking is extremely practical because it is about judging, in a reasoned and reflective way, what we should actually believe and what we should actually do in real-life situations.

Every human life has intrinsic value.

Every human life deserves the same level of protection accorded to "you and me".

It would not be ethically acceptable to terminate your life or mine intentionally.

From the point at which it becomes a human life, an abortion is not ethically acceptable.

There may be conditions under which an abortion is ethically acceptable.

If the abortion issue were not presented as an abstract debate between two middle-aged men, but rather as the private and highly personal question a woman was trying to think her way through, we would know that she might be wrestling with a myriad of thoughts, feelings, worries, and questions. In her mind she may be able to see several reasons why she should and why she should not have an abortion. In a situation like this, a decision at some point one way or the other is inevitable, for even the decision to delay deciding becomes a decision with very real consequences.

When people are interviewed about difficult decisions they have made, they often talk about how they considered various options and, for various reasons, came to select one rather than any of the others.[vi] In effect, they are describing a series of arguments. *A decision map depicts all the arguments, pro or con, which are used in the decision-making process during the consideration of various options and the selection of the final choice.* Decision maps can be thought of as argument maps used to analyze and depict the deliberations involved in individual or group decision making. To show how to build decision maps, and for more practice mapping critical thinking, consider the following extended example about a spring trip.

"WE SHOULD CANCEL THE SPRING TRIP" #1

The planning committee of a student club called the High Sierra Hikers is talking about a camping trip the club hopes to take during spring break. Eve is the chairperson of the group, Melissa is the treasurer, and James and Felix are the trip coordinators.

Meeting Transcript:

Eve: How are the plans coming for the spring camping trip?

Felix: Bad news. The room rates at the Base Camp Lodge have doubled since last year.

Melissa: Yes, and the money we've set aside for the trip won't cover the difference. Our budget is already a problem because of the all other events we have planned.

Felix: Even if we could get the money, the Lodge has no available rooms during spring break. The only available rooms are during finals week.

James: But wait. We've been planning this trip for almost a year. People are all excited about going. It's going to be a lot of fun.

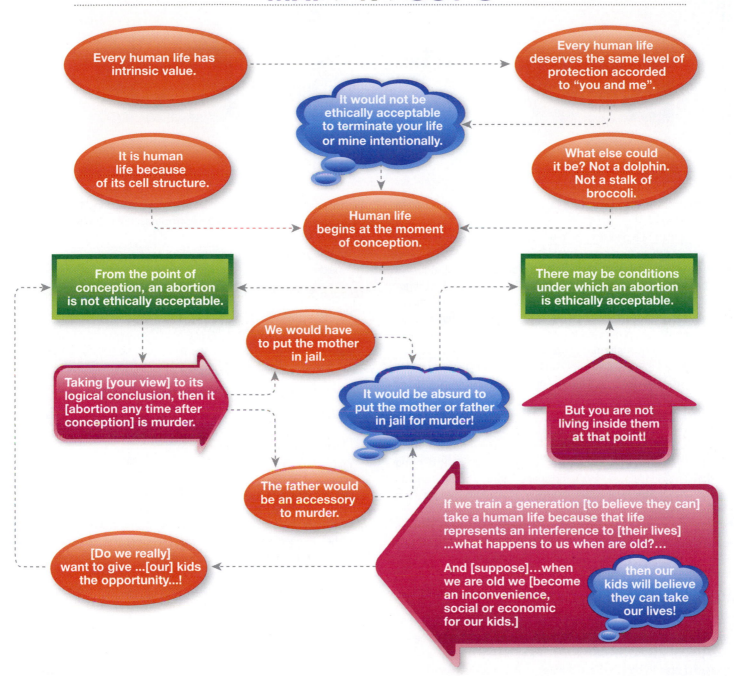

Eve: So, you're saying we have to cancel the trip. What about other places we can stay?

Felix: There aren't enough rooms in any one other place. We'd have to split up our group.

Melissa: It would be a hassle to organize transportation from different sites. And we could use the money for the other events this year.

Eve: OK, we'll cancel. I agree with Melissa, let's use the money we would've spent on the camping trip some other way.

An analysis of this transcript reveals that the planning committee is making a decision between cancelling and not cancelling the trip that the club had planned for spring break. They are alerted to the need to make a decision when Felix responds with, "Bad news" to Eve's question. We can interpret the expression "Bad news" in this context to mean, "There's

a problem about our spring trip." At this early point in the conversation we would not know what that problem might be though. We could use an oval to represent that idea. But, as before, an oval does not seem to suggest enough about the impact of this realization on the reasoning process. Recall Tom Hanks' famous line from *Apollo 13*, "Houston, we have a problem." That was a stunning realization. That declaration alerted everyone that they needed to be thinking about what could possibly be happening.

To capture the sense that some assertions put us on notice that we have to start thinking, although we may not yet know which direction our thinking will go or what the nature of the problem really is, we can opt for a more dramatic shape than the humble oval. Let's use a ***diamond*** to represents that realization that a decision needs to be made or the invitation to deliberate. The content is typically a statement that is neutral relative to the various options and draws attention to the opportunity,

need, or appropriateness of engaging in decision making with regard to the issue at hand.

In the final map of a decision there will be lines of reasoning flowing toward each of the options considered. One of them will end up being the choice that is made, and the others will be options not selected. We already have the rectangle shape for the final conclusion of an argument map, so let's continue to use that shape for each of the options. This gives us the fundamental structure of the decision at hand. Since we know that the group decided to cancel the trip, we can represent the rejected option by a **shaded rectangle**. If the group had considered a couple of other options, we would have put them in as rectangles. The only one we would not have shaded would be the option that the group actually chose.

After we have this, we can add the argument for and against the options. When the reasoning to be mapped is more complex, as it is here, it takes a couple of drafts to design an effective decision map. Redrafting helps refine the analysis and clarify exactly what is being said. Redrafting also lets you move the shapes around on the page so that the flow of the reasoning, as you have analyzed it, can be seen more readily.

Decision map 10 on page 69 emerged after producing two or three earlier versions. Same for the Fonda map and the two Huckabee/Stewart maps; in each case there were two or three preliminary drafts.

"WE SHOULD CANCEL THE SPRING TRIP" #2

Surely, we could make a plausible case not to cancel the trip. Maybe the logistical problems could be overcome, it might not be so bad if the whole group wasn't able to be in the same hotel. Perhaps some money could be shifted from those other events toward this spring trip. But, as decision analysts, it's not our job to solve the problems, but rather to uncover the reasoning process behind them.

Suppose that James, still wanting to go, pushes the group to reconsider.

Meeting Transcript Continued:

James: I know we have to think about the budget. But we could pay for this year's trip using next year's funds.

Melissa: That would be great. Let's just raid the coffers for next year.

Felix: Spoken like a true graduating senior, James!

Eve: Calm down, you guys. Maybe James has a point.

Felix: No, Eve, he doesn't. We can't take the trip during finals week. And we still have problems with where to stay if we go during spring break. It just doesn't make sense.

James: Forget it.

James begins by acknowledging there's a budget problem. From this point of consensus, arguments could flow in either direction, so we can treat it as another invitation to the group to engage in deliberation. We will use the diamond shape for this when we map the group's decision-making process. It opens up the possibility that a new decision can be made. But James's invitation to reconsider is immediately met with a flurry of objections and counterarguments. From the context we can interpret Melissa's "That would be great," as something not meant to be taken literally. Using irony and the slanted and emotionally charged word "raid," she rejects James' proposal. Felix joins in with his contemptuous "graduating senior" remark. Felix is implying that James doesn't care about what future problems he might be making for the club because he will have

Thinking Critically — Interpret with Care and Precision

The first 90 seconds of the Huckabee interview contains so much interpersonal respect and warmth that it invites its own interpretation. Perhaps Jon Stewart and his guest were trying to demonstrate that people who disagree can still treat each other as friends. Knowing the sensitivities of his studio and viewing audience around the abortion issue, Jon Stewart makes it a point to acknowledge that both he and his guest are white men.

Claims like the following can often be heard in a discussion about abortion. With as much truth seeking and open-mindedness as you can muster, do some research first and then develop the strongest reasons for each of the claims. Write out and map the arguments in support of each.

A) A living human embryo is a living human being.

A') A living human embryo is not a person.

B) It is never ethically justifiable to take another person's life intentionally.

B') At times the intentional killing of another person is ethically justifiable.

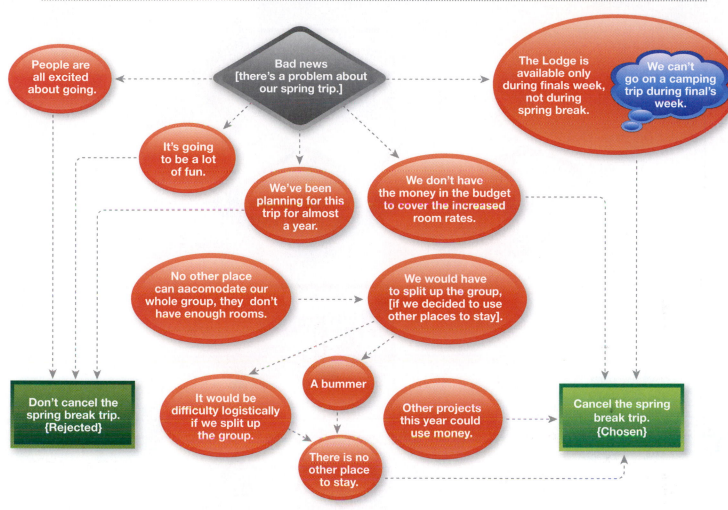

People are all excited about going.

Bad news [there's a problem about our spring trip.]

The Lodge is available only during finals week, not during spring break.

We can't go on a camping trip during final's week.

It's going to be a lot of fun.

We've been planning for this trip for almost a year.

We don't have the money in the budget to cover the increased room rates.

No other place can aacomodate our whole group, they don't have enough rooms.

We would have to split up the group, [if we decided to use other places to stay].

Don't cancel the spring break trip. {Rejected}

It would be difficulty logistically if we split up the group.

A bummer

Other projects this year could use money.

Cancel the spring break trip. {Chosen}

There is no other place to stay.

graduated and left. Eve tries to keep things civil and to reopen the deliberation with a respectfully neutral observation, "Maybe James has a point." But Felix counter's by reminding everyone about the issues James's proposal simply ignored. In the end James abandons the effort to salvage the trip. He's so frustrated he says, "Forget it."

How should we map that remark? "Forget it" is a powerful signal that James is abandoning the effort to salvage the trip. Discontinuing a line of reasoning can be a very important turning point in the decision-making process. We could map it with an oval, but that would not fully convey the force of this element in the group's critical thinking about the trip. Another shape would be better. We will use a **hexagon** for to convey that a line of reasoning has been abandoned. A hexagon marks an ending point of a line of reasoning that otherwise would have eventually connected to a conclusion. See map 11 on page 70.

The hexagon with the word "silence" inside the braces is the analyst's way of showing that the group abandoned the possibility of moving in that direction, toward not cancelling the trip, after Eve's suggestion that James might have a point. To separate any notes or interpretive comments added by the analyst from what the speakers themselves said, simply put the analyst's notations inside {braces}.

MAPPING CONVENTIONS[vii]		
	RECTANGLE	CONCLUSION OR DECISION
	SHADED RECTANGLE	CHOICE NOT SELECTED
	OVAL	REASON SUPPORTING A CLAIM
- - - ▶	CONNECTING LINES WITH ARROW HEADS	INTENDED FLOW OF REASONING FROM REASON TO CLAIM
[....]	BRACKETS	CLARIFICATION OF SPEAKER'S INTENDED MEANING
	CLOUD	IMPLICIT BUT UNSPOKEN ELEMENT
	WIDE ARROW	OBJECTION OR COUNTERARGUMENT
	DIAMOND	RECOGNITION OF THE NEED TO DECIDE INVITATION TO DELIBERATE
	HEXAGON	ABANDONMENT OF A LINE OF REASONING
{....}	BRACES	ANALYST'S NOTE OR INTERPRETIVE COMMENT

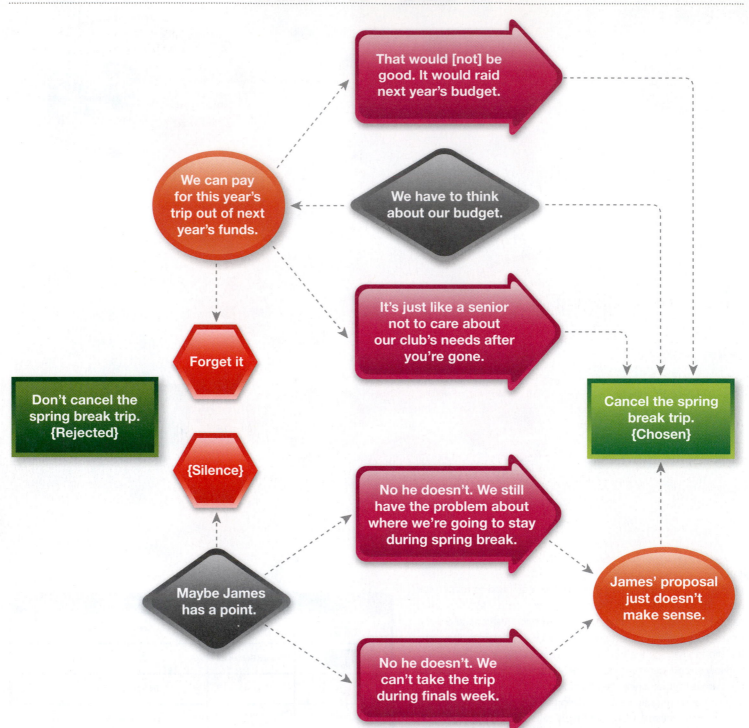

That would [not] be good. It would raid next year's budget.

We can pay for this year's trip out of next year's funds.

We have to think about our budget.

Forget it

It's just like a senior not to care about our club's needs after you're gone.

Don't cancel the spring break trip. {Rejected}

Cancel the spring break trip. {Chosen}

{Silence}

No he doesn't. We still have the problem about where we're going to stay during spring break.

Maybe James has a point.

James' proposal just doesn't make sense.

No he doesn't. We can't take the trip during finals week.

Analyze and Map the Arguments or Decisions in these Quotes

1 "Swimming is a great workout. When you swim you use all your muscles."

2 "It's no use texting her. She lost her cell last week."

3 "If it weren't for how much it costs and how big it is, I'd buy that picture for our bedroom."

4 "When Michael Jackson died last June I was shocked. He wasn't that old! Only 50."

5 "It is right to call Michael Jackson the 'king of pop.' Just look at all that he achieved. He was a pop sensation by the time that he was 11 years old. His album, *Thriller*, was the best-selling album of all time. He started out in show business when he was only five, and he performed for more than 40 years. And he had millions of fans all over the world."

6 "People believe that small class sizes are essential for better learning. I'm not convinced. I say that a good teacher with a large group can be just as effective as a lousy teacher with a small group."

7 "A study in the San Mateo County schools of second grade students' reading and math skills shows that students from classes averaging 15 to 20 students scored significantly higher than students from classes averaging 25 to 35 students. A second study looking at the same test scores for fourth and fifth grade students in the Fresno County schools showed the same results. Kids from the schools with average class sizes around 30 had significantly lower scores, on average, than did kids coming from schools with class sizes around 17. Three other studies, all of them conducted several years ago in Los Angeles, San Diego, and Anaheim, reported similar findings. So, it is reasonable to conclude that average class size makes a difference when it comes to elementary school students' test score results in math and reading."

8 "Whoever loves winter loves cold, snow, and warm sweaters. Uncle Bill loves those things. I guess it's fair to say that he loves winter."

9 "Everyone believes that change is possible. So, change is definitely possible!"

10 "Nobody really believes in global warming. You can tell that by how people act. Political leaders don't pass the legislation needed to change our nation's dependence on coal and oil. Consumers don't install solar heating, and they don't buy electric cars. We keep building hotels and condos along the ocean in places that will flood as the sea levels rise. We pave over our farms to build suburbs. Instead of wearing a sweater, we keep the thermostat too high in the winter. Instead of taking off our suit jackets, we keep our office buildings too cold in the summer."

11 "Many families who have pet dogs also have children. Julio and Teresa have a cute pet dog named Bowser. I know because Teresa was talking about Bowser and how he loves to put his paws on the windowsill and bark at the passing cars. I overheard her telling Arnold about Bowser and the cars last week. So, long story short, Julio and Teresa probably have a couple of kids, too."

12 "I need a break! It's been nothing but nonstop work since last Thursday. I didn't even get a weekend. My parents visited unexpectedly, and that was majorly stressful."

13 "So, let me get this right. You're Harvey's sister's husband. And you're saying that Harvey is actually my uncle. So, this makes his sister my aunt. And, I guess that makes you my uncle, too. Wow."

14 "I think we should have a law to limit salaries for fat-cat CEOs if their companies are receiving government bailout money. That money comes from our taxes. I don't want it going to those same CEOs who screwed up in the first place. Why should we reward them for failing?"

15 The new store manager called the staff together and said, "Looking at our marketing, I think we need to make some changes. First, the display in the store window looks like something out of the 1980s. It's dated and shabby looking. Second, our in-store signage isn't colorful. There are no pictures of happy people. The signs are so small they are hard to read. And they are positioned in places that make them unnecessarily hard for our customers to find. Third, we have to do something about our Web site. When was the last time it was updated—2001? It is clunky, confusing, wordy, and has lots of out-of-date information. Our phone number on the Web site is wrong, for heaven's sake! Finally, our newspaper ads are a total waste of money. Why are we paying graphic designers and printers to produce things nobody pays any attention to? We keep printing 10% coupons in those newspaper ads but we have not had any customers bring in a coupon from one of those ads in over three months."

16 "Everyone has two biological parents. Each of them in turn had two biological parents. So, it must be true that in our grandparents' day there were four times as many people as there are today!"

17 "I was about to register online for music updates, but decided not to. The thing was that if you registered they gave you an e-mail account. You couldn't use any of your existing e-mail accounts. And the last thing I wanted was one more e-mail account. It takes too much of my day to check the three I already have."

18 Analyze and map the argument "sovereignty" which Jon Stewart makes in the extended Huckabee interview: Access the interview at www.TheThinkSpot.com.

the THINK SPOT
www.thethinkspot.com

CHAPTER REVIEW

An argument is a claim plus the reason offered in support of the truth of that claim. We make arguments and offer reasons to explain our decisions and to reason through our problems. Often, we make multiple arguments, pro and con, when we are deliberating. In real life, human communication is highly expeditious. Verbal and non-verbal elements comprise human communication. It is also layered with humor, irony, sarcasm, and, quite often, complex and potentially divergent purposes. In a given context, people often express aloud some, but not all, of the elements of their arguments because so much is implicit and understood by the people with whom we are conversing. But to properly interpret what people mean and to analyze their arguments in an objective and fair-minded way, we must make explicit all the premises contained in a person's reason and all the unspoken assumptions that the person relies upon to support his or her claim.

Mapping is a technique for analyzing arguments and decisions. In mapping a person's reasons and claims, we make explicit and accessible the ideas that the person has advanced for the conclusion he or she has reached or the decision made. The map displays the flow of the person's reasoning from reasons through intermediate claims to the final conclusion. The map of a human decision can display the realization that a decision or deliberation is needed, lines of reasoning pursued, implicit but unspoken ideas relied upon, choices not selected, objections or counterarguments advanced, and lines of reasoning that may have been abandoned. Maps not only aid us in our interpretation and analysis of a person's thinking or a group's thinking, but they permit other people to collaborate with us in making and improving the interpretation and analysis. The goals of this chapter are (1) to strengthen our skills in analyzing people's claims and the reasons accurately and with precision and, (2) to provide a product of our analyses that others can improve and critique. Argument and decision mapping achieve both goals. Applying this technique strengthens our analytical skills. And the product of our analyses, namely the argument and decision maps, are open to others to review, evaluate, and assist us to refine.

KEY TERMS

argument is the process of giving a reason in support of a claim. *60*

claim refers to the statement that the maker of the argument is seeking to show to be true or probably true. *60*

conclusion is another way of referring to an argument's claim. *60*

reason is the basis provided by the argument maker to show that the claim is true or probably true. *60*

premises are the statements, explicitly asserted or contextually assumed and implicit, that comprise an argument's reason. Each reason is a separate set of premises. *61*

FIND IT ON THE THINKSPOT

the THINKSPOT
www.thethinkspot.com

The *Law & Order: Special Victims Unit* clip (p. 60) that opens this chapter follows a mother's decision not to vaccinate her child against measles. The argument is similar to some heard this year as parents weighed the risks of H1N1 vaccination against the risks of the disease itself. Visit **www.TheThinkSpot.com** to view the clip.

- Jon Stewart's interview with Mike Huckabee has been viewed more than 100,000 times online. I reference it on page 65 and again on page 71. You can access it directly from the hotlink at **www.TheThinkSpot.com**. View the entire interview; it's remarkable. And look at the comments too. It was fascinating to see the critical thinking, or lack thereof, displayed on occasion in some of the comments.

- The two Bonus Exercises on page 75 are challenging. Both rely on material you can access at **www.TheThinkSpot.com**. One uses a clip from *The Daily Show* and the other uses an interview with Dennis Miller. They make me wonder about the relationship between critical thinking and the kinds of skills required to be a successful comedian-commentator.

Exercises

REFLECTIVE LOG

In regard to a choice a friend has made, ask, "Why do you decide to do that?" After the friend gives his or her initial response, ask that she or he to elaborate so that you can understand his or her thinking. In your log, explain why you decided to ask that friend about that particular decision, describe the context within which your conversation occurred, and write down the questions you used to get a full and accurate understanding of your friend's reasoning. Then write your friend's response as fully as possible. Capture not only the option chosen, but the other options considered and the reasons leading to rejecting those options and selecting the option chosen. Carefully analyze what your friend said, but do not evaluate. In your log, map the decision your friend made, showing the reasoning process as objectively and fair-mindedly as possible, whether you agree or disagree with it. In fact, go out of your way *not* to reveal your evaluation of your friend's decision – be as analytical as possible

without being evaluative. Share a draft of the map with your friend and explain to your friend how to interpret it. Listen to your friend's comments about the accuracy of your analysis as it is revealed in the draft decision map you made. Note in your log all the amendments or revisions your friend wants to offer. Make another draft of the decision map in your log and compare the two side by side. Reflect on what you learned by allowing your friend to view and comment on your analysis. Did your friend change his or her story, add more reasons in favor of the selected choice, add more reasons opposed to rejected choices, ask you to remove argument strands that looked like weak reasons, or ask you to bolster argument strands that looked flimsy?

Using the Holistic Critical Thinking Scoring Rubric from Chapter 1, add a final part to this section of your reflective log in which you permit yourself a few evaluative comments on your friend's decision making.

THREE-PERSON GROUP

Working in a team with two other students, identify an issue in this week's campus newspaper. Then, go to the office of the faculty members or administrators involved and respectfully ask for 15 or 20 minutes to talk about the issue. Bring a tape recorder and ask permission to tape the person's comments. Be open about this; never secretly tape conversations. Explain that the purpose is so that you can be accurate in your portrayal of the person's point of view. Then interview the person with particular emphasis on questions such as:

- Why did you think that?

- Why did you do that?

- Why is that a problem?

- Why is that a good way to resolve the issue?

After the interview, transcribe the things the person said and number each sentence or statement made so you can refer to that statement more easily in your analysis. Then make a map of the person's reasoning. If the interview transcript is too long, focus instead on shorter segments.

EXPLAIN WHAT IS WRONG

1. A good analyst will fix the obvious mistakes in a person's argument.

2. Every line of reasoning in a map eventually connects to a conclusion.

3. Unless people actually say what's on their minds, we can't tell what they are thinking.

4. Every sentence in an argument gets represented by an oval.

5. Argument maps differ from decision maps because argument maps are used when an individual's reasoning is being displayed, but decision maps are used when a group's reasoning is being displayed.

ANALYZE AND MAP THE FRIENDS' DECISION MAKING

1. Decision to join ROTC

    Ana: Hey, girl! Guess what? I just came from the recruitment office. I think I should join ROTC. I have always been interested in the Army.

    Caroline: It's just . . .

    Ana: What?

    Caroline: I don't know. There is a war going on. You could be sent. Isn't that, like, dangerous?

    Ana: This is the best time to join — when I can make a difference.

    Caroline: I could so totally see you in fatigues, looking cute.

    Ana: Be serious.

    Caroline: I am being serious, at least about the danger part. I'd be afraid.

    Ana: ROTC is a way to pay for my education. By the time I graduate the war will be over anyway.

    Caroline: Whatever. It's not for me. But you'd be great, Lieutenant!

2. Decision to buy a gun

    A young woman who lives alone hears that a neighbor's apartment was broken into. She knows that neighbor. The woman is just like her – single, full-time job, pet cat, part-time student. Not one of those old-white-guy-NRA-gun-nuts by any means. It's terrifying to think that somebody is breaking into apartments in the neighborhood. What does the person want, money? What if it's a rapist? So, the young woman decides to purchase a gun and keep it, loaded, in the top drawer of her nightstand. She thought about moving, but that would have cost her a lot of money, and it would have been really disruptive and time consuming. She thought about getting a watch dog, but then she would have all the responsibilities that go along with having another pet. Dogs are more trouble than cats by a lot. She thought about trying to find a roommate, but she wasn't sure she could find anyone whom she really would want to share her apartment with. And finding someone would take a lot of time and effort, too. Forget that, the burglar-rapist-whatever-jerk is in the neighborhood right now. And she thought about just doing nothing, after all she has a deadbolt on the door and she's on the third floor so sleeping with a window open isn't that much of a risk.

3. Decision not to have heart valve surgery

    An elderly widower sits alone in his silent house. He is short of breath, and sleeping is difficult because aortic heart valve stenosis has caused fluid to accumulate in his chest. The cardiologist he saw earlier in the week recommended surgery. Yes, he knows he must decide whether to have the operation before it is too late. The doctor said in a year or so without an operation his heart will fail completely, and he will die. His children, now all middle-aged and living far away, have phoned to urge him to have the surgery. He knows they are worried about him and that they are trying to talk some sense into him. Ah, but they are young. Is it really worth all the pain and bother of heart surgery just so that afterward he can return to his current life? He'll still be alone most days. He'll still be struggling with the problems of old age. He might not survive the surgery. He thinks not.

4. Decisions to donate a live kidney to a friend.

    "Ah, well, I found that, um, I saw a very dear friend of mine in trouble and, ah . . . I didn't like the uh, the uh, prospects for him if he didn't get a live donor. I didn't like the idea of him being on dialysis or waiting for a kidney for several years. And I love him and I love his wife and his baby daughter. And I felt that I've got two kidneys, I don't need both and it was, it was a decision that I made in about 60 seconds or so. Yeah. . . . So, as soon as I found out from him, . . . He said, "And it looks like I'm going to need a transplant," I thought about it for maybe 60 seconds and said, "Well, count me in as a possible donor if you want to have a test done on me."[viii]

5. Decision to buy the '08 model instead of the 2010

    "You see, I need a car to get to work and school. And I plan to keep it a long time; I'll probably drive it till the wheels come off or I get to 250,000 miles. Beside durability, I'm big on safety. So I visited **www.SaferCar.gov** to see which models had 5-star ratings, and a Honda Civic seemed the best way to go. It was affordable, which is big, and reliable, and it had good safety ratings too. Then I went to **www.Cars.com**, **www.Edmunds.com**, and **www.AutoTrader.com** to find out more about the Civic and a few other makes and models, just to compare prices. I even went to the home pages of Honda, Acura, Nissan, Mazda, Subaru, Ford, Hyundai, Chevrolet, Dodge, and Chrysler. That took a lot of time! I used the "build your own" feature, which they all have, to see what it would cost to get exactly what I was looking for. Long story short, it turns out I'm back looking at Civics. The other makes and models each had some good features, but none that I could find were able to combine price, reliability, trade-in value, safety, size, style, and fuel efficiency the way the Civic did. So I settled on looking at Civics. I liked the Si Coupe, which is very sporty. I found I could get a 2010 for about $25,500, including leather seats and 6-speed manual transmission. That is very fun to drive! There were some new 2009 models available, but the prices were only 1K lower. Then I found this great-looking racing-blue 2008 Civic Si. It's a four door, but that's not a problem. The dealer had used it as a demo model and it was fully loaded with all the accessories. The car had only 100 miles on it, too, which is as good as new as far as mileage goes. The price was $22,500 out the door, and that includes taxes, fees, and destination charges. I figured I could save $3,000 and get a machine that was in every way identical to the 2010. And in a color I like a lot better! So that's how I decided to buy the 2008 for $22,500."

    [Hint: This passage includes a description of a process of fact finding and a series of arguments whereby the speaker narrows the choices until eventually deciding on one in particular. Your challenge is to sort through the passage and find the reasons, the intermediary claims, and the connecting points that show why the one option was selected and all others rejected. This is a challenging passage and your map will probably go through three or four revisions. Although not an easy decision to map, it is authentic. It comes from an interview with a person who spent several days learning the facts and reflecting on options. To that person it was effort well spent because of how much money the car would cost and because of how long the person expected to have the car.]

BONUS EXERCISE #1 THE CRAMER SMACKDOWN

The generally affable host of *The Daily Show*, Jon Stewart, lashes out at his guest, Jim Cramer, calling him a snake oil salesman and accusing him of contributing to the devastation of the financial security of millions of Americans. In the third part of his interview with Jim Cramer, Jon Stewart claims that the financial news industry has certain ethical responsibilities to the viewing public. Here's your challenge: Map Stewart's arguments indicating which elements were actually spoken in the interview and which are unspoken but still functionally part of his thinking as Stewart makes his case. Locate the interview at **www.TheThinkSpot.com**.

By the time Cramer appeared on *The Daily Show*, he and Stewart had already gone back and forth about this. Stewart's stinging criticisms had been leveled against Cramer, and Cramer had responded on his own CNBC show.

To analyze Stewart's arguments, we have to step past his strident angry tone, his puns, his humor, and his sarcasm. We have to dig out his claims and reasons. Stewart's main claim is that Cramer is ethically culpable for having caused great harm. Stewart's argument goes like this: On CNBC, a financial news network, Jim Cramer presents himself as a financial expert and gives his viewers financial advice. Stewart reasons that: If you have a show on a network that portrays itself as providing financial news, and if your job there is to give financial advice, then you have the ethical duty to be honest with your audience. Within this statement is the implication that you have the ethical duty to provide advice in the financial interest *of your audience*. (Not just to get higher Nielsen ratings and to make more money for CNBC.) But, the fact is, John Stewart says, Mr. Cramer, you were not honest. Instead, you knowingly gave misleading information, and you did this consistently over a long period of time. Your viewers trusted you, and you conned them. You should be ashamed of yourself; you are ethically culpable.

Stewart's argument depends heavily on the key assertion that Cramer knowingly gave misleading information. If this step in the argument strand is mistaken, then Stewart's case against Cramer disintegrates. So, Stewart bolsters that intermediary claim with evidence in the form of video clips. These become the reasons Stewart uses to demonstrate that Cramer knew better, but kept on giving bad advice.

BONUS EXERCISE #2 THE DENNIS MILLER CHALLENGE

Known for his caustic wit, expansive vocabulary, and conservative politics, Dennis Miller often entertains on FOX. Access his October 21, 2009 interview with Bill O'Reilly at **www.TheThinkSpot.com**. Listen to Miller's arguments for his claim that Sarah Palin is not going rogue in spite of the title of her recent book. And listen, too, for Miller's arguments accusing Balloon Boy's father of being a horrible parent. Map Miller's arguments, as given in that interview, for those two claims.

WHICH SOURCES SHOULD I TRUST?
WHICH CLAIMS SHOULD I BELIEVE?
HOW CAN I EVALUATE A CLAIM'S TRUTH OR FALSITY FOR MYSELF?

RIP Selma Goncalves,

born April 30, 1988 on Cape Verde, an island off the west coast of Africa. Shot to death January 21, 2009 in Brockton, MA, USA, a victim of hate in America.

On January 21, 2009, Selma Goncalves, age 20, was shot to death as she fled her apartment in Brockton, MA. Inside that apartment her sister lay critically wounded after being raped and shot. The hate-filled killer had driven off in his van in search of other non-whites and had shortly thereafter shot to death a 72-year-old West African man who happened to be out walking. When arrested, the shooter, Keith Luke, age 22, told police that he had gone to the women's apartment intent on murder and rape. He said that he planned later that night "to go to a local synagogue and open fire on bingo players." Having purchased his weapon and ammunition six months earlier, he told authorities that his plan was to "kill as many nonwhites and Jews as possible."[i] At his trial, Luke's defense attorney claimed that Luke, who had a history of mental illness, came to believe that he should kill to "defend the white race." He had apparently developed some of his ideas by repeatedly visiting Web sites that glorified racially motivated murder and lone-wolf domestic terrorism. These white supremacist hate-based Web sites display skin-heads beating and killing nonwhite people and immigrants.[ii] Go to **www.TheThinkSpot.com** and watch the emotionally moving video clip from Selma's funeral.

Tragic events like these are all too frequent. Inevitably, the aftermath produces an outpouring of grief and sympathy as well as soul-searching questions: Are there constitutional ways to prevent people like this killer from acquiring guns and ammunition? How can we protect ourselves from violence and hate crimes committed by our fellow citizens without violating their rights? As repugnant as they may be to most of us, can visiting hatemongering Web sites cause a person to go on a killing rampage? Some people will claim yes, and others no, in response to difficult and yet important questions like these. Some people may give reasons, and some may simply assert their opinions with great conviction.

As critical thinkers, how can we evaluate claims like these, particularly when reasons are not given? Answering this question is the focus of this chapter.

EVALUATING CLAIMS

Assessing the Source— Whom Should I Trust?

As critical thinkers, we are inquisitive truth seekers with a healthy sense of skepticism. Positive critical thinking dispositions incline us not to accept naively every claim someone may happen to make. Strong critical thinkers use their knowledge and skills to assess the credibility of the source and the plausibility of the claim itself.

CLAIMS WITHOUT REASONS

When we talked about analyzing arguments in Chapter 5, we said that an argument was a claim plus the reason given to support that claim. But what if the speaker simply makes the claim and does not give any reasons? Real life affords us plenty of examples.

1. Salesclerk to customer trying on a sports jacket: "That looks great on you."

2. Republican political commentator: "The $787,000,000,000 Obama stimulus package is a flop."

3. Person under arrest to police investigator after hearing that if he implicates others he will receive a lighter sentence: "Well, there was Johnnie; it was his idea in the first place."

4. U.S. top military commander: "It will take another 40,000 troops."

5. Candidate interviewing for a job: "I have a college degree and three years of experience."

6. Best friend: "You really need to do something about how much you drink at parties."

7. Parent to daughter in the eighth grade: "No, it is not a good idea to go out with a high school junior."

8. Co-worker to new employee: "Everybody uses his or her office computer to play fantasy football."

9. Apartment roommate: "The manager was here looking for you."

10. Doctor to patient: "The lab test came back positive."

In cases like this, one question that comes to mind for critical thinkers is, "Can I trust this person to be telling me the truth or even to know the truth?" Looking back over those ten examples, we can think of reasons why we probably can or probably cannot trust the speaker in each case. For example, in #1 maybe the salesclerk's compliment is nothing more than an insincere tactic used in an effort to make the sale. Maybe the clerk would have said the same thing if the jacket looked dreadful. In #2 the commentator, being from the opposition party, may have political reasons to characterized the stimulus package as a flop. In #3, the person who was arrested might say anything that the police would find credible in order to reduce his sentence.

On the other hand, in #7 why shouldn't the daughter trust her parent's judgment in that case? She may not like the advice at all. And she may ignore it. But there is no obvious reason in normal circumstances to think that the parent has some ulterior motive that makes the parent untrustworthy. We could say the same for the doctor example in #10. In normal circumstances, why would the patient not trust the doctor about the lab results? Yes, we can imagine a scenario or two in which a child should not trust her parent and a patient should not trust the doctor. But more likely than not such scenarios would be implausible—interesting as movie scripts, but not likely to happen to most people in real life. When we do not know if a claim is true or false and if we cannot independently evaluate it, then the question becomes one of trust; or more precisely, how can we use our critical thinking skills to figure out whom we should trust and whom we should not?

COGNITIVE DEVELOPMENT AND HEALTHY SKEPTICISM

The issue of trust, in particular trust of authorities, is connected to our maturation. The table "Levels of Thinking and Knowing" on the opposite page describes seven stages of maturation. For children in those early stages, trust in authority figures—primarily their parents and teachers—is a major factor in shaping what young minds believe. Karen Kitchener and Patricia King, on whose work the "Levels of Thinking and Knowing" table on page 79 is primarily based, report that most students entering college are stage 3 or stage 4, what we are calling "Feelers" and "Collectors." Many college students become "Relativists" as their studies progress. And there is still room for growth. Even the "Truth Seeker" stage, which critical thinkers greatly value, is not the highest we can achieve.

Strong critical thinkers cultivate a healthy sense of skepticism. They do not trust the word of authority figures in the same uncritical way that those in the early stages of their cognitive development might. Nor are strong critical thinkers satisfied to merely collect information, even though it is important to be well informed. While valuing context and perspective, strong critical thinkers understand that some reasons, perspectives, and theories are actually superior to others. Strong critical thinking habits of mind—such as truth seeking, inquisitiveness, and judiciousness—impel us to try to apply our critical thinking skills to the question of trustworthiness. We know that there are many reasons why we should not always trust everything that anyone might tell us. Some people lie, some speak about things about which they have no expertise,

"That looks great on you."

"The lab test came back positive."

Levels of Thinking and Knowing

(7) "Sages" – We can seek and discover many truths and we can address ill-structured problems with greater or lesser levels of success. But even what we call "knowledge" inevitably contains elements of uncertainty, for as we build from the known toward the unknown, new ways of organizing knowledge often yield unforeseen conceptual revolutions. Even well-informed opinion is subject to interpretation and reasoned revision. Yet, justifiable claims about the relative merits of alternative arguments can be made. We can assert with justifiable confidence that some judgments are rightly to be regarded as more reasonable, more warranted, more justifiable, more sensible, or wiser than others. We solve problems the way a truth seeker does, but we realize that judgments must often be made in contexts of risk and uncertainty, that some issues admit greater precision than others, that at times we must reconsider our judgments and revise them, and that at other times we must hold firm in our judgments. Wisdom comes as we learn which are which.

(6) "Truth Seekers" – Some claims are true and some are not; some evaluations or approaches are not as good as others. Some reasons, perspectives, and theories are actually superior to others. Information is essential, uncertainty is real, and context is important. But not everything is context bound. We can reasonably and rationally compare evidence, opinions, theories, and arguments across contexts. We solve problems by following the reasons and the evidence with courage wherever they lead, by asking the tough questions, by being inquisitive, by being open-minded and tolerant about a wide range of ideas and possible explanations, by being persistent and systematic in our inquiry, and by not fearing what this process will turn up as possible answers.

(5) "Relativists" – Facts exist, but always and only in context. Everything is relative. There are no absolutes. Ill-structured problems abound. Every theory and every perspective is as good as every other theory or perspective. Proof and evidence are entirely context dependent. Disagreements about basic theories and fundamental principles cannot be resolved by any rational means because the criteria themselves are perpetually contested.

(4) "Collectors" – All knowledge is idiosyncratic—a collection of isolated facts to be memorized for later retrieval if needed. There are many separate databases, e.g., scientific, business, political, and religious. They are not combinable. Information in one of them may or may not be consistent with information in another one of them. Uncertainty is real; external validation is impossible. So-called authorities and experts are just as limited as everyone else. To solve any problem, look for all the information you can find about that topic.

(3) "Feelers" – Authorities know everything that can be known now, but the evidence is incomplete, even to authorities. Some things may never be known because of the limitations of the human mind. Uncertainty is real, so we need to be cautious or we are apt to stray and make mistakes. The best policy is to stick with beliefs that feel right to us because they are familiar, comfortable, and conform to what everyone else in our peer group thinks.

(2) "Trusters" – Truth is knowable. We have absolute confidence in the authorities who share the truth with us. All problems have solutions, and all questions have answers. What we do not know today will someday be known by somebody. Anyone who disagrees with the truth as presented by our authorities must be wrong. To question any element of the truth is to abandon all of it. We must learn to defend ourselves from any person or idea that threatens the truth.

(1) "Touchers" – To touch is to know. Knowledge is nothing but direct personal experience. Facts are absolute, concrete, and readily available. There are no lenses on experience; things are exactly as they appear to be.

some say things under duress that are not true, and some may have been deceived themselves and pass on misinformation unwittingly. We can be skeptical without being cynical. And certainly one good time to keep this in mind is when it comes to evaluating the credibility of sources.

AUTHORITY AND EXPERTISE

We have been using the word "authority" to refer to a person who is potentially a trustworthy source of information and good advice. In the context of cognitive development, the typical examples of authorities for children would be parents, grandparents, teachers, ministers, and police officers. But that is where the word "authority," as we have been using it, begins to reveal its problematic ambiguity and problematic vagueness.

"Authority" can also mean "a person with the rightful power to control the behavior of another." Parents and teachers have authority, in that sense of the word, over children. But as we mature, we realize that a police officer, our boss at work, our landlord, or even a teacher or parent may have the rightful power to control our behavior, but that does not necessarily make the person more knowledgeable than we are on a given topic.

The sense of the word "authority" we are looking for is "person with expertise." To a child, parents, ministers, teachers, and police officers are

authorities in both senses of the term; children perceive them to be experts with the power to control behavior. Okay. But we are not children anymore. The authorities we may wish to trust are those with expertise.

Wikipedia offers a useful discussion of expertise, including this characterization:

> An expert is a person with extensive knowledge or ability in a particular area of study. Experts are called in for advice on their respective subject, but they do not always agree on the particulars of a field of study. An expert can be, by virtue of training, education, profession, publication or experience, believed to have special knowledge of a subject beyond that of the average person, sufficient that others may officially (and legally) rely upon the individual's opinion. Historically, an expert was referred to as a sage. The individual was usually a profound thinker distinguished for wisdom and sound judgment. . . . An expert is someone widely recognized as a reliable source of technique or skill whose faculty for judging or deciding rightly, justly, or wisely is accorded authority and status by professional peers or the public in a specific well distinguished domain. ... Experts have a prolonged or intense experience through practice and education in a particular field.[iv]

Thinking Critically   *Wikipedia!* OMG!

The bitter irony of citing *Wikipedia* in a discussion about the trustworthiness of sources screams out. Why should we trust *Wikipedia*, you may well wonder. *Wikipedia* is not a source; it's a vehicle. Anyone can edit a *Wikipedia* entry. How can we know if what it says is actually true? In fact, that's the same question we have for everything we see on the Internet or in print: Who wrote that, and can we trust that person (or that government agency, corporation, or organization)? These days there is so much untruth, disinformation, propaganda, and out-

right deceit on the Internet that we dare not believe it simply because we see it written there.

Your challenge in this exercise is to fact-check the *Wikipedia* entry on page 79 for its accuracy. I suggest you use three different ways to do this: (1) Go to the entry itself and see if you can tell who wrote it and what references it uses. Fact-check those references and Google the authors using *Google Scholar* to see if they are credible authorities on the topic of expertise. (2) Seek independent confirmation by looking up "expertise" in other, more trusted, sources,

including dictionaries, encyclopedias, and books on expertise. (3) Show the *Wikipedia* characterization of "expertise" to people who have expertise in their various fields, like your professors, and ask them if they would agree with the *Wikipedia* interpretation. If all three ways point to the accuracy of the entry, then good, we'll go with it. If the three ways diverge or contradict each other, we have problems. Use your analytical and interpretive skills to articulate an accurate understanding of "expertise" if the one in *Wikipedia* is defective.

Learned and Experienced

Two things a person must establish in order to be recognized as an expert on a given topic is that he or she is learned with regard to that topic and that he or she has significant relevant experience. The first condition, being learned, can be accomplished through formal education or through training under the guidance of good mentors and coaches. The second condition, having relevant experience, means that the person is not a novice or a beginner when it comes to the activities and practices associated with that topic.

We will use the word "**expert**" to refer to someone who is both experienced and learned in a given subject matter area or professional practice area. Establishing that a person is both learned and experienced is important in the legal context, because that person's expert testimony on matters within the domain of his or her expertise can be relied upon by juries when they deliberate the guilt or innocence of a person accused of a crime. We all have seen courtroom dramas where a pathologist, a fingerprint expert, or a psychiatrist is put on the witness stand to provide expert opinion with regard to the cause of death, the match of the fingerprints found at the scene of the crime and the fingerprints of the accused, or the mental state of the accused at the time of the crime. In standard examples, the people that the defense or the prosecution introduce as expert witnesses are considered to be qualified due to their many years of professional experience, formal education, and relevant state licenses.

As the movie *My Cousin Vinny* so aptly illustrates, on-the-job training and many years of practical experience can qualify a person as an expert in certain domains. Marisa Tomei, who plays a hairdresser and the fiancée of the defense attorney, played by Joe Pesci, is put on the witness stand as an expert in automobiles. The prosecuting attorney tries to discredit her as an expert, but fails. The judge accepts her as an expert on automobiles. Access this clip at **www.TheThinkSpot.com**.

Determining that a person qualifies as an expert witness is a matter of serious concern for strong critical thinkers because the person's expertise, if established, gives us a good reason to consider putting our trust in what the person has to say regarding the area of his or her expertise.

Assuming that a person qualifies as an expert on X by virtue of prolonged, relevant experience, training, or education, what else could go wrong that would lead us not to find the person credible? Lots of things!

- The expert on X may be speaking about some other topic.

- The expert, having qualified long ago, may have failed to stay current on X.

- The expert on X may not be able to articulate exactly how X is done.

- The expert may be biased.

- The expert may lie or mislead.

- The expert may have a conflict of interest.

- The expert may give advice that is not in the interest of his or her client.

- The expert may be under duress, threatened, or constrained in some way.

- The expert may be misinformed about the facts of the specific situation.

- The expert may have become mentally unstable.

On-Topic, Up-to-Date, and Capable of Explaining

Expertise with regard to a topic, X, implies that the expert is knowledgeable about X. But suppose that someone—say, an accomplished musical virtuoso—makes the claim, "The best way to eliminate pesky aphids from a rose garden is by spraying on a mix of water, mineral oil, and Murphy's soap." That concoction might work. But wait—gardening is not the virtuoso's area of expertise. Whatever measure of trust we would reasonably extend to the expert, were she or he speaking about music, does not carry over to claims the expert may make that are off-topic. Regarding gardening, the musical virtuoso is no more nor less of an expert than any other person. To be credible, the expert must be speaking on-topic.

A good friend of mine was an accomplished physician. She retired about fifteen years ago and moved to Sarasota to enjoy her retirement playing golf and bridge. One of her friends asked her the other day about

 What makes a person an expert witness?

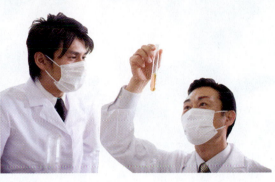

a cancer treatment that another physician had recommended. Unlike traditional chemotherapy, the treatment was one of the newer pharmacological approaches that targets the protein receptors on the cancer cells. My friend rightly declined to offer an expert opinion about the new treatment method. Why? Because she knew that she had not kept up-to-date about advances in cancer treatment since her retirement. Although as a doctor she had the credentials to provide an expert opinion about cancer treatment in general, as a responsible expert she knew that it would be wrong for her friend to rely on her expertise in this case.

We trust experts when they speak within their areas of expertise in part because we assume that, were they challenged, they could explain exactly why their claim is true or their advice is good. The capacity to explain why is a critical component of expertise. The second half of the *My Cousin Vinny* video clip illustrates this. Marisa Tomei offers the expert opinion that the defense's theory of the crime does not hold water. So the defense attorney, Joe Pesci, who had called her as a defense witness, demands that she explain exactly why she thinks that. She draws upon her extensive knowledge and experience as an expert to provide a factual, precise, and cogent explanation. And, in the process, the explanation she offers exonerates the defendants as well.

What if the expert cannot articulate the explanation? For example, a superstar athlete fails as a head coach and we learn afterward that the star was not able to teach others all that he or she knew about the game. The successful head coach turns out, instead, to be a former athlete who was good but not great. Unlike the person blessed with extraordinary natural ability, this person had to think constantly as a player about how to maximize his or her own talents to compete effectively against other, more skilled players. And those years of reflective practice translate later into the ability to teach and coach others.

There are many reasons why experts may fail to provide adequate explanations. Some may never have developed the practice of reflecting on their experiences to explain to themselves why events occurred as they did. Lacking the critical thinking habit of analyticity, they may have failed to analyze the likely effects of decisions and actions. Lacking the critical thinking habit of inquisitiveness, they may have failed to examine the implications of new information for their field of expertise. Experts who have weak skills in self-monitoring and self-correcting may not take the time to be sure that they can explain their current beliefs to themselves. Being unreflective, they may describe their own thinking using expressions like "I go with my gut" or "I just instinctively knew what I had to do." Unfortunately, statements like

those explain nothing and teach nothing.[v] It is difficult to place trust in experts when they cannot explain why they believe what they believe nor why they do what they do. For the same reason, it is challenging to learn from these experts. Although we may be able to copy what they are doing, and it may even work, what we most need for learning is to know why it works. And these experts have a difficult time communicating that.

Consider this example. Suppose it is the first day of class and your Biology professor says, "This course will require more time than most other courses. So if you haven't got a job, don't bother getting one. If you thought you could work and study Biology in my class, think again." Suppose that someone asks the professor to explain the basis for that advice. Here are two possible responses:

Professor #2:
"Working puts great demands on your time. In this course, you have three lecture hours each week plus a required lab each week. I demand experiments in each lab, and the reports from these experiments must be submitted in written form each week. If you do not pass in-class pop quizzes, I require you to attend review sessions. Our goal together is for you to learn biology, and I provide you with every opportunity to be successful. But I will not lower my standards, nor will I accept any excuses about your being too busy with other obligations. I grade on a curve and this course attracts the most serious and academically competitive students in biology. You will have to put a lot of time into this course just to get a passing grade. So I recommend that you not take on other responsibilities, like a job, that will pull you away from your studies."

Professor #1:
"Why did I say that? Because I say it to every class to warn them. I give out F's to people who can't perform in my class.

Professor #1 offered nothing more than a statement of his or her own past practice and a veiled threat. Professor #2 explained why the course would demand a lot of time and why taking on outside responsibilities could become a problem for a student enrolled in this course.

We now have five conditions we can check when we are deciding whether or not a source is credible when that source makes a claim about topic X: Is the source experienced, learned, on-topic, up-to-date, and capable of explaining why his or her opinion on the matter is right?

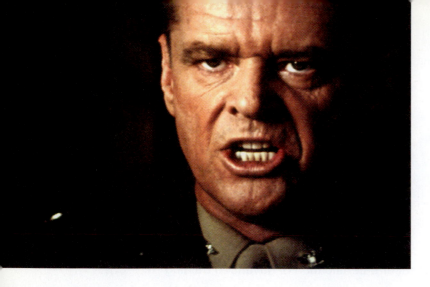

Unbiased and Truthful

Experts are human beings and, like the rest of us, they may have biases. Olympic gymnastics and figure skating judges, every one an expert in his or her sport, are often accused of being biased in favor of athletes from some countries or against athletes from other countries. Or they are accused of showing favoritism toward more experienced athletes and being tougher when evaluating the performances of athletes who may be newer to that high level of competition. Ask anyone who has tried to umpire a baseball game or referee a high school basketball game, and they will tell you that accusations of bias are a regular feature of officiating.

If an expert is called as a witness in a trial and that expert happens to be biased in favor of or against defendants of a certain race or age or socio-economic status, that fact alone should be enough to cause the jury not to trust that expert's testimony. Expert claims are supposed to be grounded in learning and experience, not in prejudices, biases, or favoritism of any kind.

But even unbiased experts may elect not to speak the truth. Recall that great scene in the 1992 film *A Few Good Men* where Jack Nicholson tells Tom Cruise, "You can't handle the truth!" Nicholson's character, a senior military officer and clearly an expert by training and experience, loses his temper. In his outburst, he explains why Tom Cruise, like so many of his complacent countrymen, do not want to know the truth about what, in Nicholson's opinion, the military must do to keep this nation safe and free. In other words, Nicholson's character is condoning the practice of our nation's defense experts practicing misdirection and lying to the American people. Access this clip at **www.TheThinkSpot.com**.

the **THINKSPOT**
www.thethinkspot.com

We can interpret Nicholson's character as practicing the "Noble Lie," as proposed by Plato in *The Republic*.[vi] In Plato's opinion, most people do not recognize their own best interests, nor can they fully comprehend what is in society's

best interests. Plato's recommendation was that well-informed leaders who know the whole truth should guide the rest of us by using, when necessary, the "Noble Lie." That is, Plato proposes that the leaders should flat out lie to the people, having in mind the most beneficent and purest of motives. In other words, the Noble Lie is a lie our leaders tell us because the lie is in our best interests. Not knowing the truth, we would be passive, content, and compliant. Social harmony would be preserved, unrest and discontent prevented. Of course, when the lie is discovered, the people may become more than a little disenchanted with their "benevolent" leaders. The leaders would surely lose all credibility. We should not trust an expert source who believes that lying and misdirecting are acceptable when making expert claims and offering expert opinions.

The Noble Lie! My, how convenient for totalitarian leaders intent above all on maintaining political power for themselves. Surely they would be able to rationalize just about any propaganda they wished to put out as being "in the best interests of the people." A little healthy skepticism would be very useful about here!

Free of Conflicts of Interest, and Acting in the Client's Interest

If an expert's personal interests diverge from the interests of the person he or she is advising, then there is good reason not to trust what that expert may have to say. Suppose you go to a mortgage broker seeking guidance about how to finance a condo you want to buy. The broker offers you three options with three different banks: A, B and C. The broker strongly recommends bank B, saying that in his expert judgment bank B best meets your needs. At this point you may be inclined to accept the broker's expert opinion because mortgages are complicated and difficult for many of us to understand.

What if, unbeknownst to you, bank B has agreed to pay your broker a large fee for bringing his mortgage clients to that bank? And suppose that neither bank A nor bank C will pay the broker nearly as much. This puts the broker in a conflict-of-interest situation. It is in the broker's interest for you to go with bank B because he will get a larger fee. But would the broker have been so enthusiastic about bank B if bank B paid the same fee that banks A and C pay? If the answer is "no," then this broker's conflict of interest has made him an untrustworthy source of advice. Many professionals take it upon themselves, or are required by law, to disclose conflicts of interest to their clients. That way, the client can take that into consideration when evaluating the trustworthiness of the professional whose advice is being sought.

In an effort to protect us from unscrupulous experts who might give us bad advice, there are laws that require that health care professionals, real estate professionals, bankers, lawyers, high-level executives, and members of governing boards act in the interests of their clients or in the interests of their organizations. Under the law, this obligation is called their fiduciary responsibility. The president of the university has a fiduciary responsibility as the institution's chief executive officer to make decisions that are in the best interests of the university. A doctor has a fiduciary responsibility to make medical decisions and offer medical advice that is in the best interests of the patient.

If the university president makes decisions that are not in the university's best interests, but rather are in the best interest of some other organization (e.g., the city, the employees of the institution, the department of athletics, or to some other organization to showcase his own reputation) to the detriment of the university as a whole, then the president has failed to fulfill his or her legal obligations. Having broken trust with the institution by that decision, the president might be fired. If a doctor gives medical advice that is in the best interest of a scientific experiment but not in the best interest of the patient, then the doctor has broken trust. In cases where the expert makes claims or offers opinions that are not in the best interest of the person or organization to which the expert owes a fiduciary responsibility, then the expert cannot be trusted as a reliable source of truthful information or sound advice.

Unconstrained, Informed, and Mentally Stable

Unconstrained: When being tortured, people are apt to say anything to stop the pain. Intelligence services, knowing this, have devised other tactics to extract accurate and useful information. Torture is one form of constraint that can cause an expert to make claims that are not reliable. Also, an expert may be legally constrained from offering advice or information on a given topic. For example, the expert may have signed an agreement with a former employer that prohibits the expert from revealing proprietary business secrets that are the property of the former employer for a certain period of time, typically a year or two. In this case, even if the expert goes to work for a new employer, the expert cannot legally violate the agreement with the previous employer. Under this constraint, the expert's claims will not rely on the expert's full range of knowledge. This is a reason not to fully trust what the expert has to say.

Informed: A friend of mine is a personal trainer with great expertise. People he happens to meet often ask him casually for advice. They want to know which exercises to do in order to gain greater strength, speed, or endurance. He could give them broad general answers, but he declines. Why? Because in these causal encounters, he does not have the opportunity to fully evaluate the person's physical status, so he worries that any advice he may offer or any claims he may make might be wrong for this particular person. As an expert, he realizes that knowing a lot about exercise in general is not always enough to give this particular person the right advice. The expert must also become informed about this particular person's individual circumstances and condition. To use another example, general advice about how to prepare for a job interview may or may not be the right advice to give one particular person who is preparing for one specific interview for one specific job. An expert's claims and advice gain credibility if the expert has taken the time to inform himself or herself about the specific case at hand.

Mentally Stable: We have come quite a long way in developing our list of things to think about when evaluating the credibility of a source. And there is only one more issue to add, and that is that the expert is mentally competent, unimpaired, and, to use a layman's term, "stable." Drugs and alcohol can impair judgment, including expert judgment. Psychosis, severe clinical depression, and recent traumatic experiences can cause people who may ordinarily have good judgment to make mistakes. And, as research with health care providers and pilots shows, long hours in stressful situations and sleep deprivation are associated with increased risk of errors. An expert who is not mentally stable cannot be trusted to provide reliable information or advice.

In summary, when evaluating a **trusted source on topic X**, it would be reasonable for us to trust a person (or the words of a person) who fulfills all twelve of the criteria below.

Twelve Characteristics of a Trustworthy Source

- Learned in topic X
- Experienced in topic X
- Speaking about X
- Up-to-date about X
- Capable of explaining the basis for their claim or their advice about X
- Unbiased
- Truthful
- Free of conflicts of interest
- Acting in accord with our interests
- Unconstrained
- Informed about the specifics of the case at hand
- Mentally stable

This may seem like a formidable list, but asking people who have a healthy skepticism to take one's claims and advice on faith is a sizable request. So it is reasonable that we should have high standards when it comes to establishing and maintaining trust. You may already have noted many of these positive characteristics in people whose advice you trust.

Assessing the Substance— What Should I Believe?

In the previous section, we focused on assessing the credibility of a person who makes an assertion without supplying reasons. Often, the claim stands alone, its source unknown, and no reasons in support of it are supplied. Here are a few examples:

1 "Rumor has it that the dean is going to resign."

2 "I heard that she was so angry with her boyfriend that she keyed his new car."

Thinking Critically Whom Do *You* Trust?

When you think about it, you have known a great many people now and throughout the years, such as family, friends, teachers, co-workers, and classmates. Identify two people you trust. Then review the list of twelve criteria and see how many of the twelve each of the people on your list fulfills. Did either of them do things or say things that lead you to evaluate them highly on one or more of the twelve criteria? Did either ever do anything that would disqualify them from being trusted by you because they missed on one or another of the twelve items? Next, think of two people you do not trust. Identify which of the twelve criteria leads you not to trust each of those people. Has each done something or said something relating to one or more of the twelve critiera that leads you to regard him or her as untrustworthy? What did he or she do and how did you connect that to being untrustworthy? Do you notice that it takes much effort to build trust and little effort to lose it?

3 "An unnamed source close to the police investigation told us that murder indictments were going to be handed down soon for as many as 35 gang members."

4 "According to a high-ranking administration official, the president is not happy with the leadership of his own party."

5 "Wind power generation of electricity will cost so much to implement that reliance on coal is financially a better option."

6 "Wind power has to be in the mix of alternative renewable sources of energy."

7 "The nursing staff knows that what happened today in room 314 was assisted suicide."

8 "The patient in 314 was dying of cancer and had less than a week to live."

9 "Doctors recommend getting your annual flu shot early this year."

10 "A huge killer anaconda lives in the utility tunnels under the main campus quad."

In this section, we will look at ways of evaluating the truth or falsity of assertions in the absence of supporting reasons and in the absence of identifiable sources.

DONKEY DUNG DETECTOR

Except for in two rare situations that we will take up a bit later in this section, there is no reliable way of telling that a claim, standing alone, is true or false. We may have some initial impressions or some common-sense notions, for example, that a claim like #10, about a killer anaconda, is highly unlikely and that a claim like #9, about getting a flu shot early, seems plausible. But initial impressions are not proof, and so-called common sense is not something that a person with a healthy sense of skepticism is going to rely upon. In fact, a healthy sense of skepticism (which is the alternative name for our personal "Donkey Dung Detector") turns out to be our best defense against being deceived by false claims.

A strong critical thinker with a healthy sense of skepticism would probably respond to the ten claims beginning on page 83 by asking a number of probing questions. Here are some examples. Note that some questions focus on trying to identify the source of the claim and that others focus on the plausibility of the claim itself.

1 Who said that about the dean and how would that person know?

2 Who told you that? Did the person actually see her key the car? Are we sure that the car was keyed? If so, might it not have been someone else who vandalized his car?

3 Why would the police leak information like that to anyone? Revealing their plans for a major bust would only cause the suspects to flee, if they knew that they were going to be arrested.

Thinking Critically   Blogs and Web Pages

Web pages and blogs can be posted by reliable and informed experts and by unscrupulous people bent on fraud, hate, or mischief. Truths and falsehoods spread as people cite other Web pages as their sources, as they e-mail URLs to friends, and as they blog, tweet, and comment about things they have seen on the Web. Blogs and Web sites can provide pros and cons for almost any idea. Question: In addition to healthy skepticism, what are the most reasonable, most reliable, and smartest strategies to determine what on the Web can and cannot be trusted?

4 Did anyone else in the president's administration confirm that rumor? Isn't the president the leader of his political party, so you're saying he's unhappy with himself?

5 Can you show me the financial projections that support this?

6 Why? What if wind power turns out to be inefficient and not cost-effective? Let's not just go along with something because nobody seems to be questioning the party line on this.

7 Oh, and how do you know that?

8 Did someone on the hospital staff share information about that patient's diagnosis with you?

9 Which doctors, the ones working for the pharmaceutical company, doctors with independent practices, who? Why do they recommend getting a flu shot? And who should get flu shots? Everyone? What does "early" mean? September? December?

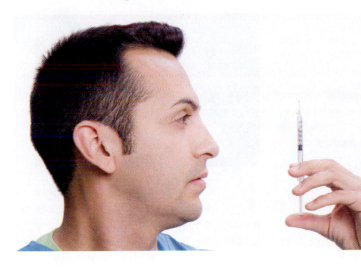

10 Right. And it eats what? Freshmen who happen to go exploring in those tunnels?

Self-Contradictions and Tautologies

We said that there were two rare situations where we actually could know that a given claim was false or was true just by what it says. The first situation is when the claim is self-contradictory, as in these examples:

- No point on the circumference of a circle is the same distance from the center of the circle as any other point on the circumference of the circle.

- The moon orbits the earth and does not orbit the earth.

- Everyone in our club despises our club president, and there are only one or two people who still admire her.

A **self-contradictory statement** cannot be true. The self-contradiction comes about because of the meanings of the words used to form the claim. For example, the definition of the word "circle" is not consistent with the notion that the circumference is variable distances from the

center. Conveniently, self-contradictions, when you stop and think carefully about them, do not make sense. As they stand, they are un-interpretable. In real life, if someone happens to make a self-contradictory claim, strong critical thinkers use their question-asking skills to seek clarification from the speaker.

- If you are talking about a circle, then by definition every point on the circumference is the same distance from the center. Or else you are not talking about a circle. Which is it?

- Which is it, does the moon orbit the earth or not? Pick one. Both can't be true.

- That does not make any sense. You can't say that everyone despises the president but some do not. Can you clarify what you mean?

Some may worry that they will not always be able to identify self-contradictions in real life. But as a practical matter, what is important is that we recognize that a person's claim is not making sense to us for whatever reason. As we saw in Chapter 4, whenever we are trying to interpret a claim correctly, we should be prepared to ask the author respectful but challenging questions about what the author intends to communicate by making the claim that we find to be confusing or self-contradictory.

Just as some claims cannot be true by virtue of what their words mean, other claims cannot be false by virtue of what their words mean. Here are examples:

- Every student enrolled in this university is a student enrolled in this university.

- Two straight lines on a plane that are not parallel to each other intersect at one and only one point.

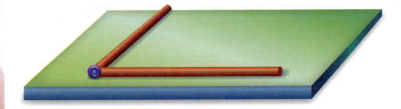

- If God is all-powerful, then there is nothing that God cannot do.

The first example almost sounds as redundant as "if a student is enrolled, then a student is enrolled." The second is a truth of plane geometry. The third is equivalent to saying, "If God is all-powerful, then God is all-powerful" except that a definition for "all-powerful" is used in the predicate. In each of these cases, the statements must be true based simply on what the words mean. A statement that is true entirely because of the meanings of the words it contains is called a **tautology**. Here's one more example:

- You gotta do what you gotta do.

Imagine James Gandolfini playing the character Tony Soprano saying something like this to one of his Mafia lieutenants. Yes, technically he is speaking a tautology. But we might ask ourselves, "Why?" In context, people use statements like these for purposes other than to communicate informational content. Here, the Mafia don may be giving a murderous assignment to that underling, saying, in effect, "This decision to act is absolutely necessary." From the point of view of critical thinking and in order to make a full and accurate interpretation, we still must look to context and purpose, as was emphasized in Chapter 4, rather than only the literal meaning of a claim.

Cultivate a Healthy Sense of Skepticism

Each of the following claims may be true. But as they stand, cut off from their authors and without reasons being supplied, it is difficult to know whether they are true or false. For each claim, write four questions that, if answered, are likely to yield information that would help evaluate the claim's plausibility or implausibility.

1 The composer Richard Wagner (b. 1813) was a racist and anti-Semite whose music Hitler enjoyed and employed to further his Nazi political agenda.

2 Within five weeks after his death, over 10 million recordings and MP3 downloads of Michael Jackson's music were sold worldwide.

3 Your presence will be powerfully felt by your acquaintances and loved ones if you eliminate what does not add value to your life.

4 You can get cash for your old and unwanted gold jewelry from our friendly, professional staff of experienced appraiser-buyers.

5 If you exhume my father's grave and move his casket to another location, he will never rest in peace again.

6 Subscriptions to online pornography Internet sites are more prevalent in states "where surveys indicate conservative positions on religion, gender roles, and sexuality."[xi]

7 For the next couple of years, you will be hearing stories about the huge number of Americans who lost their jobs during this recession and were not able to find work even after the recession ended.

8 The vulnerable workers in Zimbabwe's diamond fields are protected from external violence and lawlessness by the presence of Zimbabwe's military, which has restored order in the Marange district.

9 Because the virus so closely resembles the killer 1918 virus, the H1N1 flu virus will devastate the world's population in much the same way that the world flu pandemic of 1918 did.

10 Shiny striped gym bags and long-sleeve micro-mesh miniskirts are the newest fashions sweeping the nation.

11 More children between the ages of 13 and 17 have been killed playing football in the past 60 years than have been killed by other children with firearms.

12 Teen virginity pledges are effective in reducing the percentage of teens who have sex and in reducing the number of unwanted pregnancies among teenagers.

13 Unaware of how long they have to live and not knowing how chemotherapy will affect their lives, more than 20% of Medicare patients who have advanced cancer start a new chemotherapy regimen two weeks before they die.

14 The tree stump with the image of the Blessed Virgin Mary "is doing no harm and it's bringing people together from young and old to black and white, Protestant and Catholic, to say a few prayers," claims Seamus Hogan of Rathkeale, County Limerick, Ireland.[xii]

15 When choosing colors for your favorite room, remember that "the antidote to fog is color. . . A warmer color temperature in a room is a really good approach, so you don't feel like you're living on a glacier."[xiii]

MARKETING, SPIN, DISINFORMATION, AND PROPAGANDA

Claims without supporting reasons are the stock and trade of people who have ulterior motives. A marketer, wanting us to purchase something, makes claims about the virtues of the product. Extremist organizations eager to discredit someone make claims about the opponent's position on controversial issues. Government officials trying to drum up public opinion in support of their proposals make exaggerated claims about the benefits of those potential programs.

- Over 75% of the cars we make are still on the road.
- Supreme Court Justice Sonia Sotomayor supports Puerto Rican terrorists.
- Just like under Adolf Hitler, government-controlled health care means "death panels" ordering that the infirm be euthanized.

Those with a healthy sense of skepticism are ever on the alert for the donkey dung being distributed by people with ulterior motives. Whether they wrap it in humor, sincerity, or vitriolic rhetoric, it comes to the same thing:

unsubstantiated claims made specifically for the purpose of getting us to do something that we otherwise would not do—such as to buy something we do not really need, to vote for something we don't believe in, or to support a cause we might not otherwise support. Or perhaps it is simply a way of responding to the desire some have to be the center of everyone's attention.

Skepticism is not cynicism. We need to remember that open-mindedness is a positive critical thinking habit of mind. So, when we evaluate the plausibility or implausibility of claims, we must discipline ourselves to be open-minded. Fortum, a Scandinavian energy company, won a Clio Award for its ad that features the following claim:

- "We fill the Fortum brand with positive energy by activating our customers instead of just sending out bills to them."

Is this only a clever marketing gimmick, or might there be something more to the idea? Before you propose an evaluation, you will need to understand how to interpret Fortum's curious claim. Begin by watching the video that won the Clio Award. Access the video at **www.TheThinkSpot.com**.

the THINK SPOT
www.thethinkspot.com

- John is just another overpaid municipal employee working in public safety.
- Basketball combines finesse, grace, power, and skill.
- Basketball combines passing, dribbling, shooting, and defense.
- Basketball combines sweat, aggression, cunning, and brute force.
- Love is you and me together happily forever in each other's arms.
- Love is a strong emotional attachment to another.
- Love is that stupefying feeling you had before you really knew the bastard.

Slanted language and loaded expressions are not always easy to recognize. Certainly if we disagree with a claim we can often pick out the slanted language and loaded expressions. A good percentage of Keith Olbermann's show *Countdown* on MSNBC is devoted each night to pointing out the slanted language, half-truths, exaggerations, and loaded expressions used by those on the extreme right of the American political spectrum. This is not to say that Mr. Olbermann does not also use some of the same tactics to create his humorous retorts.

On the other hand, if we happen to agree with what is being said, it is often quite a bit more difficult to see anything particularly unfair, loaded, or egregious with the claims being made. Everyone likes to think of himself or herself as objective and able to see all sides of an issue. But the psychological fact is that most of us have a difficult time putting ourselves in the minds of people with whom we disagree. Rather, we tend to prefer to make an idiot out of our opposition in our own minds, underestimating the merits of what the person may be saying and overestimating the clarity and strength of our own views. We will learn more about the psychology behind this common human propensity in Chapter 10. That said, evaluating claims that tug at our emotions, either positively or negatively, by virtue of the language those claims employ must be done with care. A strong truth-seeking habit of mind can dispose us to approach this evaluation more objectively.

To sum up this section, we need a healthy skepticism when trying to evaluate claims that stand alone, without their authors and without reasons. Except for self-contradictions and tautologies, it is almost impossible to evaluate the claims by themselves as either true or false. Through tough questioning, we may find some claims more plausible and others less plausible. But even then, other factors, including the ulterior motives of the people who are making the claims and the emotion-laden language which is often used, make it difficult, if not impossible, to evaluate a claim standing alone. Almost, but not entirely impossible. There is another strategy, and that is to take upon ourselves to investigate the claim independently.

Independent Verification

Suppose we encounter a claim on the Internet and we hear it being repeated by friends and talked about in the media. Assume that on its face the claim appears plausible, yet we are skeptical. We know no claim is true simply because it is widely believed and frequently repeated. What can we

Given that consumers can become jaded and skeptical, marketers often try to separate us from our money using humor and entertainment, rather than with extravagant claims. This is particularly true if the product being marketed is something familiar, rather than a new program as in the Fortum example. Many Clio Award quality commercials employ entertainment value and humor. I easily found many great examples by visiting YouTube and searching "Clio Award Commercials." The Guinness "tipping point" ad, Dr. Pepper's take off on the "Hunchback of Notre Dame," and the Skittles "touch" commercial were some of my favorites. Does it make sense that we should be more inclined to purchase a product having seen a funny and entertaining ad? And if so, why? It often takes imagination, good critical thinking, a team of professionals and millions of dollars to produce commercials of this quality. What does it take not to be drawn in by them?

SLANTED LANGUAGE AND LOADED EXPRESSIONS

Often, it is difficult to evaluate claims that use language that carries a positive or negative emotional charge. Some expressions are so loaded down with social and cultural baggage that the very use of them excites strong positive or negative reactions. Here are sets of three statements each. The first in each set is intended to elicit a generally positive response to the topic, the second is neutrally factual, and the third is slanted negatively.

- John is a true American hero.
- John is a New York City firefighter.

Your Best and Worst Commercials

We see or hear dozens of ads and commercials each day on TV, on the radio, on Web pages, in the newspaper, on T-shirts, on billboards, etc. (Have you ever asked yourself why we pay for clothing that sports a logo or promotes a brand name, instead of demanding that the corporation pay us to wear that clothing?) Mark the time. For the next 24 hours, keep track of the ads and commercials you see or hear. Focus on the ones you think are the very best and the ones that are the very worst. Keep two lists and refine the lists by crossing off and adding candidates as you hear or see another that is better or worse. After 24 hours, analyze your top three and your bottom three. What makes them the "best" and the "worst" in your mind? Were they funny, informative, creative, and effective in influencing you to want the product they were promoting? Or were they boring, stupid, confusing, and ineffective?

Independent Verification

do if we need to make a decision and this particular claim, if true, would lead us to make one decision, but, if false, would lead us to make a different decision? Is there any other way to figure out if we should believe the claim or not? Yes. One way to do this is to ask if the claim can be confirmed. The other is to ask if it can be disconfirmed. Let's look briefly at both.

CAN THE CLAIM BE CONFIRMED?

A claim becomes more plausible if we can find confirmatory information or information that is consistent with the claim. For example, suppose someone claims:

- Mother's Day is the most popular holiday celebrated in the United States.

How might we go about finding confirmation for this? First, we would need a measure of "popularity" as applied to holidays. For example, we could use the number of greeting cards sold per holiday, the money spent sending flowers per holiday, restaurant revenues per holiday, telephone calls made per holiday, or an opinion survey with an appropriately structured sample.

Another approach when attempting to confirm a claim is to ask ourselves if the claim in question is consistent with other things we may know. If it is, then the claim takes on more plausibility in our minds. Consider this claim:

- Samuel was the last person to leave this morning, and he forgot to lock the apartment door.

To confirm this claim, we might begin by asking how many people live in Samuel's apartment, and then we might ask each of those people what time he or she left the apartment this morning and whether he or she

noticed who was still there when he or she left. But suppose that this line of questioning results in uncertainty because people can't recall the exact time they left or because they are not sure if others may or may not have been in the apartment when they left. Then we would go to things we know about Samuel, looking for something that may be consistent with the claim being evaluated. For example, we may learn that Samuel is often the last one to leave in the morning because he does not have any early classes. We may learn that in the recent past Samuel admitted to having forgotten to lock the apartment door when he left. And we may learn that Samuel is a generally irresponsible and unreliable person, often neglecting his responsibilities and not keeping his promises. If things should turn out this way upon investigation, then we would have reason to evaluate the claim as highly plausible.

CAN THE CLAIM BE DISCONFIRMED?

An alternative to trying to confirm that the claim is true is setting about trying to establish that it is false. Consider the claim. While the burden of proof would ordinarily be on those seeking to confirm a claim, at times it becomes desirable to try to disconfirm a claim. Consider these two claims:

- You are the person who murdered Mrs. X on Sunday at noon in her home in Boston.
- President Obama does not have a valid U.S. birth certificate.

In the first case, to disconfirm the accusation, the accused would have to establish a solid alibi. For example, "No, sir, I did not kill Mrs. X. I was onstage in Orlando, making a speech to 2000 people exactly on the date and time that the murder occurred in Boston. My proof is the videotape of the speech, which is date stamped, and the testimony of the audience members and technical support staff who were present at the time."

Some claims, like the second example about the president's birth certificate, are more challenging to disconfirm for reasons that go beyond the substance of the claim itself. All that would appear to be required to disconfirm that claim would be presenting for public inspection the president's birth certificate. Although we may not personally be able to access the president's birth records, presumably the president or his attorney can. "Public inspection" in a case like this would then, in ordinary circumstances, be the responsibility of the news media.

Prior to the general election in November 2008, the *Chicago Tribune*'s Washington Bureau did post a story confirming that both presidential candi-

Thinking Critically   Selling Risk

Watch the national news on CBS, NBC, or ABC. Focus on the commercials and make a list of each one and what it is advertising. In each case, the product can benefit people, and yet each comes with a measure of risk. The job of the commercial is to lead us to desire the product in spite of its inherent risks. When a commercial for a drug or medical device comes on, listen very carefully to the list of side effects and cautions. Write down as many as you can for each drug or medical device that is advertised. When a car commercial comes on, note what the manufacturer is using to sell the car, e.g., sex, power, prestige, popularity, comfort, fuel economy, safety, or resale value. When a banking or investment commercial comes on, record the disclaimers, cautions, and exceptions, like "not a guarantee," "read the prospectus care-fully before investing," and "rates and conditions subject to change without notice." After the news broadcast is over, review your lists. Which of the commercials, in your judgment, was the most misleading with regard to the risks associated with the product? Why? Which company provided the least substantive guarantees with regards to the product's expected benefits in its commercial? Explain your choices.

Suppose you see a claim in the campus paper, published on February 10, that says, "Valentine's Day is the most popular holiday on this campus." Develop a strategy by which you can determine which holiday is the most popular among the students enrolled in your university or college. Write up your recommended procedure in draft form. Work with up to two other students to combine the best ideas from your approach and their approaches. Then, develop a final recommendation for how to conduct the investigation.

The critical thinking involved in this strategy includes the question, "What sorts of evidence should we be able to find if we assume that the claim is true?" And our answer to that question in the Mother's Day example was evidence about cards, flowers, phone calls, etc., which would reflect that if people valued this holiday, they would show that in their behavior. The strategy is a good one if cards, flowers, phone calls, etc., are part of other holidays too. As you discovered

in doing the exercise, another aspect of attempting to confirm or disconfirm a claim is to be sure exactly what the claim means. Interpreting the expression "most popular" required finding a way to measure popularity. Interpreting "holiday on this campus" required coming up with a list of holidays, some of which might have been unique to your specific campus, e.g., a "Founders Day" holiday or a religious holiday not celebrated at other colleges or universities.

dates were natural-born U.S. citizens, Obama having been born in the state of Hawaii and McCain at a naval hospital in the then U.S.-controlled Panama Canal Zone.[vii] But then in the summer of 2009 a U.S. Army reserve soldier named Stefan Cook, a birther, refused to be deployed to Afghanistan on the grounds that he was being sent by a commander in chief who was not eligible to be president because he was not a native-born U.S. citizen. It turned out that Mr. Cook was misleading the public, for he had in fact volunteered for the military assignment in Afghanistan. And when he changed his mind about volunteering for military service in that country, his orders to deploy to Afghanistan were revoked, which is standard policy in the case of volunteers. But with the media attention to the initial story, these subsequent facts went relatively unnoticed and the rumors about Obama's birth certificate lived on.

The durability of claims like the one about Obama and his birth certificate is fascinating in its own right. Some claims, call them "urban legends," seem to endure no matter what investigative findings reveal. Even when the claim has been plausibly refuted, there are those who will not accept the evidence. Alex Koppelman offers an interesting analysis of why "conspiracy theorists" will never be satisfied about the validity of the birth certificate or the eligibility of Obama to be president.[viii]

But with due respect to the conspiracy theorists of every stripe, there is a difference between healthy skepticism and stubborn refusal to abandon a discredited position. In fact, the difference is rather profound. The skeptic is asserting that he or she is uncertain what the truth of the matter is. The conspiracy theorist is making a claim, often one that can be neither confirmed nor disconfirmed, that a certain version of events is the truth and that all other versions are false. This puts an enormous burden of proof on the conspiracy theorist, not the skeptic. The conspiracy theorist must do much more than discredit all other known versions of events. The conspiracy theorist must confirm his or her version of events. That is the step that most often is not rigorously fulfilled.

INDEPENDENT INVESTIGATION AND THE Q-RAY BRACELET CASE

The case of the Q-Ray bracelet offers us an excellent example of the value of independent investigation into the veracity of the claims people make to promote products and reap profits at the expense of gullible consumers. Perhaps you have seen the ads for the Q-Ray bracelet. Millions of Q-Ray bracelets have been marketed and sold, at prices ranging from $50.00 to $250.00, to people seeking relief from chronic pain caused by a variety of

illnesses and medical conditions, including pain from chemotherapy. Its inventor, an infomercial entrepreneur, formed a company, QT Inc., to manufacture and sell the Q-Ray bracelets. Initially, the bracelets had been described as having been made from special metals that offer natural and effective pain relief. The fundamental claim made in the promotional infomercials and on the Q-Ray Web site between the years 2000 and 2003 was that an "activated" Q-Ray bracelet relieves pain. Whether or not the Q-Ray works or not turned out to be a multimillion-dollar question because of lawsuits charging that the product was ineffective. In 2002, the Mayo Clinic conducted an independent investigation into the effectiveness of the "ionized" Q-Ray bracelet as to whether it did or did not relieve pain.[ix]

The independent Mayo Clinic researchers set up a clinical trial like the ones used to test the effectiveness of pharmaceuticals and medical devices. Subjects (people with chronic pain) were randomly assigned to two different groups. The first group of subjects was given authentic activated Q-Ray bracelets to wear. The other group was given non-active replicas of Q-Ray bracelets to wear. At the end of the trial, 75 percent of the people in the first group reported experiencing pain relief. None of the subjects knew whether he or she had an "activated" or "non-active" bracelet.

What do you suppose was the percentage of people in the second group, those with the non-active replicas, that reported experiencing pain relief? It turned out to be the same percentage: 75 percent! This investigation established that the Q-Ray bracelet has a placebo effect only. It is the equivalent of taking a sugar pill instead of taking medication that has been demonstrated to be effective. Based on the research at the Mayo Clinic, the judge dealing with the lawsuits ruled that the Q-Ray promoters were guilty of false advertising.[x]

Did this put an end to the sale of Q-Ray bracelets? Hardly. To see for yourself what new claims are being made, visit **www.qray.com**.

Real or Placebo?

SUSPENDING JUDGMENT

Judgments in contexts of uncertainty are unavoidable, given the human condition. The critical thinking habit of judiciousness disposes us toward prudence and caution when deciding what to believe or what to do. Our healthy sense of skepticism tells us that if we can neither confirm nor disconfirm a claim through independent investigation, then the wisest course would be to suspend judgment with regard to that claim. The best judgment about the plausibility or implausibility of some claims may be to make no judgment at all.

In this chapter, we approached the evaluation of claims in three ways. First, we established twelve criteria we could use to evaluate the credibility of the source of the claim. Second, we explored interrogating the plausibility of the claim itself and inquiring into the context within which the claim is positioned and the possible ulterior motives behind the use of the claim. And third, we envisioned conducting an independent investigation seeking either to confirm or to disconfirm the claim. In the next chapter, we reunite claims and the reasons their authors give in support of those claims so that we can explore the application of the critical thinking skill of evaluation to arguments.

KEY TERMS

expert refers to someone who is both experienced and learned in a given subject matter or professional practice area. *80*

trusted source on topic X is a person (or the words of a person) who is learned in X, experienced in X, speaking about X, up-to-date about X, capable of explaining the basis for their claim or their advice about X, unbiased, truthful, free of conflicts of interest, acting in accord with our interests, unconstrained, informed about the specifics of the case at hand, and mentally stable. *83*

self-contradictory statement is a sentence that is false entirely because of the grammatical construction and the meanings of the words used to form the sentence. *85*

tautology is a statement that is necessarily true because of the meanings of the words. *85*

FIND IT ON THE THINKSPOT

The moving story of Selma Goncalves opens this chapter. Visit **www.TheThinkSpot.com** and view the clip there to make this tragedy more real and personal.

In contrast to the sadness of that video we have the delightfully funny "Expert Witness" scene from *My Cousin Vinny* (p. 80). For that clip, and for the memorable "You Can't Handle the Truth" speech by Jack Nicholson in *A Few Good Men* (p. 82), visit **www.TheThinkSpot.com**.

TV commercials provide a rich source of material to analyze. Begin your analysis by asking, "What reasons, if any, am I being given to lead me to want to buy this product?" Often, commercials do not overtly state the reasons; instead, they use music, staging, gestures, and visual cues to subtly suggest the ideas they want us to have. We probably will not find a commercial that comes right out and says that buying someone a bottle of perfume or piece of jewelry will lead to a fulfilling love life, but several holiday commercials certainly intimate as much.

It takes skill, imagination, and a lot of excellent problem solving to produce award-winning commercials. On page 86, I invite you to link through **www.TheThinkSpot.com** to the Fortum commercial and to look for a few other Clio Award winners while you are at it. Can you pick out the implicit and unspoken assumptions that the commercial maker wants you to accept so that you will buy the company's product? Or, if the commercial is not encouraging you to buy a product, then you are being asked to trust a company, appreciate a company's work, contribute to a worthy cause, or join an organization.

Once you start applying your critical thinking skills to TV commercials, you will never passively watch them again. Analyzing them is more fun. This is tough on the advertisers because they want our minds to be on cruise control when we're watching. Commercials are designed so that their messages sneak into our minds under the radar. A lot of commercials do not work at all if the viewing audience actually thinks about what it is seeing!

Exercises

WHAT IS WRONG WITH THESE FALSE STATEMENTS?

For each of the following, explain the mistake that makes it untrue.

1. A statement is a tautology if it is true.

2. A statement that is self-contradictory is seldom true.

3. We can tell if a claim is true or false by looking at what it means.

4. If a claim cannot be confirmed by an independent investigation, then it must be false.

5. If an independent investigation produces evidence that is consistent with a given claim, then the claim must be true.

6. Experts have the rightful authority to impose their beliefs on other people.

7. Relativism is the highest stage of cognitive development college students can achieve.

8. To doubt the truthfulness of a rightful authority means that a person is being disrespectful.

9. If a celebrity endorses a product, you can be sure that the product is of high quality.

10. If we do not believe that a claim is true, then we must believe that the claim is false.

REFLECTIVE LOG: YOUR FAVORITE NUTRITIONAL SUPPLEMENT[xiv]

The ads and testimonials for nutritional supplements are among the most effective marketing tools ever, as is supported by the unprecedented growth in the sales of energy drinks, dietary supplements, vitamin beverages, and stimulants. Select for this exercise one of these products you are already purchasing for your own use or any product of this kind that interests you. Use information provided on the product label and from the product's Web site as needed to respond to these questions in your log:

1. What claims are made about the benefits of the product?

2. What research is cited or what evidence is supplied to support the truth of these claims?

3. Who are the people who have provided testimonials in support of the product?

4. What level of expertise do these individuals have with regard to human nutrition?

5. Were any of these individuals paid to provide their endorsement?

6. What warnings, risks, or potentially harmful side effects are presented?

7. What ingredients does the supplement contain?

8. Biologically and nutritionally, what does each ingredient do? In other words, what is its function?

9. Is the supplement "specially formulated" in any way that is purported to enhance its efficacy?

10. Who are the target consumers of the supplement? Who should use it?

11. What have you been told about the supplement by friends, coaches, and salespeople?

12. Who produces/manufactures the supplement? What is that producer's reputation?

13. Is the supplement approved as "safe and effective" by the federal Food and Drug Administration?

14. In terms of the nutritional benefits and risks, how does the supplement compare to the items on this list: orange juice, milk, coffee, standard multivitamin tablets, carrots, apples, broccoli, ordinary yogurt, cottage cheese, peanut butter, tuna fish, baked turkey breast, and wheat bread?

15. Reflect on your answers to questions 2–14 and then evaluate the claims you wrote down in #1. Are they true, plausible, implausible, or untrue, or should you suspend judgment about those claims?

CHALLENGING CLAIMS WITH TOUGH QUESTIONS

To strengthen the sensitivity of your own personal donkey dung detector, it is a good idea to practice asking tough questions whenever you hear an unsupported claim. As an exercise, review the ten claims listed on page 78 under the heading "Claims Without Reasons." For each of the ten, write two or three questions that either challenge the plausibility of the claim itself or challenge the credibility of the source of the claim.

WHAT PRESUMPTIONS DO WE MAKE WHEN WE OFFER ARGUMENTS TO SUPPORT OUR CLAIMS?

WHAT FOUR TESTS MUST AN ARGUMENT PASS TO BE WORTHY OF ACCEPTANCE?

HOW DO WE APPLY THE FOUR TESTS WHEN EVALUATING ARGUMENTS?

HOW CAN WE RECOGNIZE COMMON REASONING MISTAKES MORE READILY?

"I don't

get why you want to quit," said Malcolm. "You came here to play volleyball. Volleyball is all you ever want to talk about! Now suddenly you want to quit?"

Caitlin looked at Malcolm. He couldn't possibly be this dense. "Look, I explained it all to you already."

"You said that you didn't like Coach Williams. So what? She's your head coach. Nobody likes a head coach. I don't like the marching band director, but you don't see me quitting the band," said Malcolm.

"Coach was screaming at everyone again. She's so negative, always screaming at the players, and that doesn't motivate me to try harder. I just hate all her yelling! Anyway, it's the setter, Jenny; she kept putting the ball too far from the net. It messed up everybody. But coach kept yelling at the rest of us, when it was all Jenny's fault."

"So," said Malcolm, "you're quitting because the coach yells at you? Williams has been a screamer since she took over as head coach two seasons ago. Her yelling never bothered you before. Or is it something else?"

"Yes! No. I don't know," replied Caitlin in exasperation. "Who cares? It's not like I have a future in volleyball after college."

"What does that have to do with anything? You knew a spot on the Olympic team or the AVP beach volleyball pro tour was like a near-impossible long shot before you came here. And another thing: Don't tell me you don't get motivated when the coach is fired up. I've seen you in games. You're angry because you know you can play Jenny's position better than she can. But the coach doesn't let you. So, you're pissed at the coach. It's not about the yelling."

"You're right. Jenny's terrible. I don't understand how she ever made the team."

"But, Caitlin, nobody can spike and defend at the net like you. Coach knows that, and so does everyone else on the team. So, you're going to play the front line. Which is great. I'll bet that Jenny wishes she could play where you play."

"Well, I don't care about any of that anymore. I'm quitting and therefore I'm quitting. End of story. Let's talk about something else. . . . Tell me how your marching band practice was today?"

"Fine, I hear you. You're going to quit. And, yes, we can change the subject. But let me just say for the record that I still don't think you're really being honest about why you're leaving the team and the sport you love. And just saying over and over again that you plan to quit does not explain why you plan to quit."

EVALUATING ARGUMENTS

In the scene that just played out, Caitlin explains her decision to quit the college volleyball team. Her stated reason is that she is not motivated to play harder by the coach's constant criticism. Ergo, she's going to quit the team. That may be a reasonably logical argument, if we also assume that Caitlin is the kind of athlete who does not respond well to that coaching style. But her friend Malcolm knows better. He does not accept her argument because he has seen her respond positively to the coach's style in game situations. The truth is that Caitlin does get motivated to play harder when the coach is fired up. Although Malcolm does not make the point, we might observe that the word "yelling," is negatively slanted. It fits Caitlin's current negative attitude toward the coach. But "yelling" is probably not the best word to use when talking about those times when the coach is successful in motivating Caitlin.

Caitlin offers another argument, saying that she has no future in volleyball. Malcolm points out the irrelevance of that consideration, and then he suggests that her real reason for being upset with her coach has to do with which position she wants to play. Caitlin ends the conversation about volleyball with a definitive and somewhat defensive, "I'm quitting and so I'm quitting." Malcolm makes it clear that her final statement forcefully affirms her intention, but it is not an acceptable answer to the question "Why?"

Throughout their conversation Malcolm has been evaluating his friend Caitlin's arguments. This chapter focuses on building argument evaluation skills. It presents a comprehensive and straightforward evaluative process that we can apply in everyday situations, much in the way that Malcolm did in the opening conversation with Caitlin. The process includes four specific tests. An argument must pass all four tests to be considered worthy of acceptance as proof that its conclusion is true or very probably true. Each of these four criteria is rooted in the natural and universal human practice of making arguments and giving reasons. Because critical thinking requires skill at evaluating arguments in real-life contexts, we begin with the expectations and responsibilities associated with giving reasons and making arguments.

Giving Reasons and Making Arguments

The practice of giving reasons for our claims—that is of making arguments—is part of every human civilization and culture. Every natural human language includes terminology and social conventions for making arguments as well as for evaluating them. But argument making would not

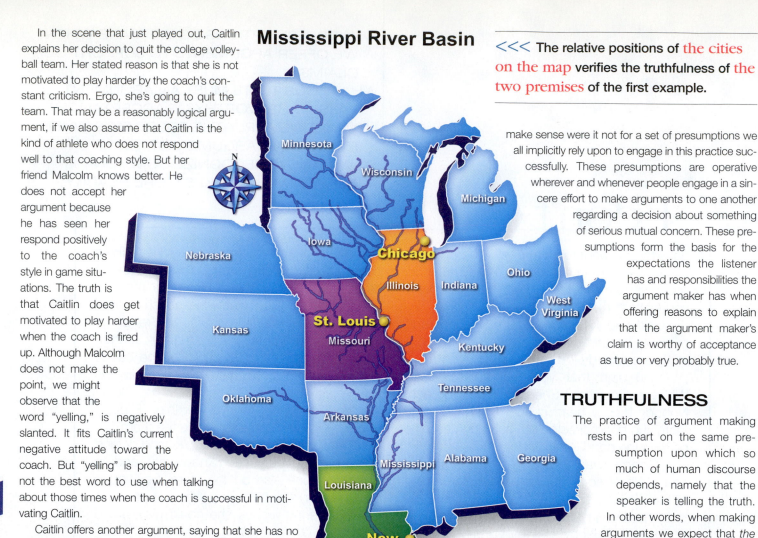

Mississippi River Basin

<<< The relative positions of the cities on the map verifies the truthfulness of the two premises of the first example.

make sense were it not for a set of presumptions we all implicitly rely upon to engage in this practice successfully. These presumptions are operative wherever and whenever people engage in a sincere effort to make arguments to one another regarding a decision about something of serious mutual concern. These presumptions form the basis for the expectations the listener has and responsibilities the argument maker has when offering reasons to explain that the argument maker's claim is worthy of acceptance as true or very probably true.

TRUTHFULNESS

The practice of argument making rests in part on the same presumption upon which so much of human discourse depends, namely that the speaker is telling the truth. In other words, when making arguments we expect that *the statements offered as premises are, in fact, true.* As a rule, people collaborating with one another to think something through do not intentionally use erroneous information or lie to one another. If a disagreement about the truth of any premise arises, then the people involved make a reasonable effort to review the evidence for that premise, or they qualify the force with which they wish to assert and maintain any claims in the line of reasoning that relies on that premise. Of course, people do lie on occasion. And so this presumption often goes unfulfilled.

The assumption that their premises are true provides a reasonable basis for moving to consider whether the premises imply that the conclusion is true or very probably true. But without first considering the truthfulness of the premises, it becomes only an exercise, rather than a matter of practical significance, to consider the argument's logical strength. Here are two arguments with true premises.

- Chicago is north of St. Louis. St. Louis is north of New Orleans. Therefore, Chicago is north of New Orleans.

- There are 325 children registered in grades 1 through 6 at the Carver Elementary School. We have tested 40 percent of these children for reading skills. We also have taken a number of physiological measurements of each of those same children. Our data show that there is a strong positive statistical correlation between the size of a child's feet and the child's reading skill level.

The map verifies that the cities are positioned the way the first example's premises indicate. Regarding the second example, one obvious question is whether the measurements mentioned in the third sentence included foot size. If not, we may want to call into question the truthfulness of what the speaker is saying. If the speaker does not have any information about the children's foot sizes, then the speaker's argument falls apart.

LOGICAL STRENGTH

Consider the following example. In this case, *were we to take the premises to be true*, then its conclusion would have to be taken as true as well.

- We have been keeping track of how often the weekday 6:56 AM Caltrain from San Francisco arrives late at the Millbrae station. We conducted three six-week surveys over the past 12 months. In each survey the weekday train arrived at the Millbrae station late 24 out of 30 times. Therefore, there is an 80 percent probability that the weekday 6:56 AM Caltrain will arrive late at the Millbrae station.

Next we have an example in which all the premises are true as well, but the reasoning is an unacceptable leap from a simple association to an assertion of a causal relationship. The premises of this argument, although in fact true, do not logically justify accepting the truth of the conclusion.

- There are 325 children registered in grades 1 through 6 at the Carver Elementary School. We have tested 40 percent of these children for reading skills, and we have taken a variety of physiological measures as well. Statistically speaking, there is a strong positive correlation between a child's shoe size and the child's reading skill level. Therefore, increased reading ability is caused by increasing the size of the feet.

When someone offers an argument, the speaker's reason is supposed to be the logical basis for the speaker's claim. The point of giving reasons for our claims is that the reasons support the claims. The second presupposition of the practice of argument making is that the speaker's reason, if true, is the logical basis for the speaker's claim. Notice that this is a hypothetical. *Were we to assume that the reason a person gives for his or her claim is true,* that assumption would then imply that the person's claim is probably or necessarily true as well. In the language of logic, this presupposition is expressed this way: The assumed truth of the premises of an argument justifies or implies, either inductively or deductively, that the conclusion of the argument also be taken as true.

RELEVANCE

Because a conclusion might just happen to be true independent of whether the premises are true or whether the premises logically support the conclusion, when we make arguments we also presume that the truth of the reason is relevant to the claim. Consider this example. Here the premises are true and the conclusion is true, but the premises or reason is not relevant to the claim.

- To many around the world, the Statue of Liberty symbolizes the welcome our nation extends to all freedom-loving people. So, as the great Yogi Berra says, "You can observe a lot just by watching."

This argument is so odd that it would get a squawk out of the Aflac duck. But the reason given has no relevance to the truth of the claim. Their only connection is that Yogi Berra happened to be a player for the New York Yankees back in the day and the Statue of Liberty happens to be in New York. For us that is not sufficient to say that the one is relevant to the other. If anyone were to seriously present this reason as the basis for the truth of the conclusion we would say, "That's not

 Shoe size and reading level! How are they related?

relevant!" And this reveals our third presupposition: *the listener takes the reason given by the speaker to be relevant in believing the speaker's claim.*

There is no point to giving reasons if the listener is not going to rely on those reasons in deciding what to believe with regard to the claim. Recall that in our opening example, Caitlin changed her story about why she wanted to quit the volleyball team. At first she talked about how the coach's yelling and berating players was her issue. But then she gave a different reason, saying that she was going to quit because she did not anticipate a future as a professional volleyball player. Malcolm challenged her on that, noting that it was not even relevant, in his view. A future in professional volleyball was never her reason for joining the college team, and the absence of that opportunity is not relevant to why Caitlin now wants to quit the team. Everyone, including Caitlin, may believe that Caitlin wants to quit the volleyball team. But nobody, not even Caitlin, believes that whether or not she has a future in professional volleyball has anything to do with her wanting to quit at this point in time.

NON-CIRCULARITY

Our fourth precondition when we give reasons for our claims is that *the claim must not be part of the basis for believing in the truth of the reason.* Argument making in real life is essentially a one-way street: The reasons are used to establish the acceptability of the claim. But we do not use the claim to explain the reason. We use the premises of the argument to support the

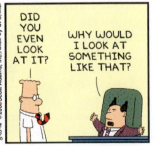

Scott Adams, Inc, United Media/United Feature Syndicate, Inc.

Anyone ever say something circular like this to you **at school, home, or work?**

Four Tests of an Argument's Worthiness

Test Name	Order of Application	Test Condition
Test of Truthfulness of the Premises	First	The reason is true in each of its premises, explicit and implicit.
Test of Logical Strength	Second	If the reason were true, then the conclusion (claim) would be true or very probably true.
Test of Relevance	Third	The truth of the claim depends on the truth of the reason.
Test of Non-Circularity	Fourth	The truth of the reason does not depend on the truth of the claim.

conclusion, not the conclusion to support the premises. In other words, there is a directionality to argument making. The flow of reasoning is from reason toward claim, not the other way around. All the examples of mapped arguments in Chapter 5 show this, because in mapping arguments we used the arrow convention to display the intended directionality of the argument maker's reasoning.

In the example on page 95 Dilbert's boss criticizes Dilbert's presentation for being full of technical words and way too long. We naturally think that the boss came to those conclusions about the presentation by having seen it and evaluated it. But no. The boss then turns around and uses those same two claims as his reasons for not seeing or evaluating the presentation. It makes no sense to give a reason as the basis for one's claim and then to use that claim as the basis for one's reason. In a comic strip circular reasoning is funny, and in real life it can be infuriating.

The Four Tests for Evaluating Arguments

The four presumptions about argument making as an interpersonal human activity form the bases for the four evaluative criteria applicable

to all arguments. In other words, it would be reasonable to accept a person's argument if it met all four of the conditions implied by those presumptions. These are the four conditions:

1 To the best of our knowledge and understanding, the reason is true.

2 The logical relationship between the reason and the claim is such that the claim must be true or very probably true if the reason is taken to be true.

3 The relevance of the reason to the claim is such that the truth of the claim actually depends on the truth of the reason.

4 The truth of the claim must not be used to support the truth of the reason.

An argument that satisfies all four conditions is worthy of our acceptance as a proof that its claim is true or very probably true. We will apply the adjectives "good" and "worthy" to those arguments. A **good argument** or a **worthy argument** is an argument that merits being accepted as a proof that its conclusion is true or very probably true. The four conditions listed define four tests to apply when evaluating arguments. These four conditions are applied in the order given. As soon as an argument fails

Thinking Critically   *The Name of the Rose*

Consider an example from the film adaptation of *The Name of the Rose.* Early in the story the abbot in charge of a 14th-century monastery comes to a visiting Franciscan scholar-detective, played by Sean Connery, to explain why he believes that the recent death was caused by the devil. This attribution of the cause of death to a supernatural intervention occurs about 9 minutes and 15 seconds into the film.

Access the scene at **www.TheThink Spot.com**. Listen carefully to the abbot as he makes his argument. It begins with "We found the body after a hailstorm," and it is only a few lines. Transcribe it so that you can have the language in front of you. Evaluate it for logical strength. Can you think of how the monk might have died other than at the hand of the devil, given the information you have at that point in the story? Is there a set of circumstances so that all the premises of the

abbot's argument could remain true but the claim still be false? How plausible or implausible are those circumstances? [For example, if someone were to answer, "Yes, an alien from another galaxy could have transported into the closed room and killed the monk," we probably would regard that as highly implausible.]

As you watch the film, new information is presented visually. The director gives us a shot looking up a steep ravine at the abbey, which wraps around the crest of the hills above the ravine. There appear to be two towers. Sean Connery's character and the viewer can use that information to show the logical flaw in the abbot's argument about the death being caused by the devil. "No devil needed," says Connery as he completes his alternative explanation to his young apprentice, played by

Christian Slater. The death was natural. Go 6 minutes and 29 seconds further into the movie and view this short scene. Transcribe Connery's alternative explanation. Map it, and after reading this chapter, evaluate it for logical strength.

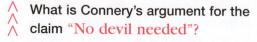
What is Connery's argument for the claim "No devil needed"?

Evaluate each of the following for logical strength by using your imagination to come up with a scenario in which the premises are true and the conclusion false. If there is no possibility of such a scenario, short of changing the meanings of the words themselves, or if every scenario you can think of is highly improbable, then the argument passes the Test of Logical Strength. Otherwise, it does not.

1. If your car is parked in the lot behind the Student Union, it has been ticketed by the campus police. That is where your car is parked. So, it has been ticketed.

2. Either your car is parked behind the Union, or it is parked behind Morrill Hall. It is not parked behind Morrill Hall. So, it is parked behind the Union.

3. People coming into San Francisco on southbound Highway 101 across the Golden Gate Bridge must pay a $4.00 toll. John does not have to pay a $4.00 toll to use the Golden Gate Bridge. So, John must not be coming into San Francisco on southbound Highway 101.

4. On a cold winter night when the sky above Calgary, Canada, is clear and bright with stars, the air temperature can drop below zero. People out on a night like that in Calgary run the risk of frostbite, unless they take precautions. So, you should probably be careful and bundle up if you are going out on a cold winter night in Calgary.

5. Trees are budding, the grass is greening up, song birds are returning, and the days are getting longer. Spring is probably on the way.

---

one of the four, it is no longer eligible to be considered a good or worthy argument. Let's see how to apply each of these four to determine whether or not an argument is worthy of acceptance.

TEST #1: TRUTHFULNESS OF THE PREMISES

In everyday situations and in critical thinking, the truth or falsity of premises is our first concern. If one or more of the premises of an argument is not true, then, for practical purposes, there is little point in moving forward to evaluate other aspects of the argument. If we do not have the best information (actually we have some false information built into our reasoning), our first job is to get our information straight. The critical thinking habit of truth-seeking demands that we courageously endeavor to learn what we can before moving forward with claims and arguments based on incomplete knowledge.

The Test of the Truthfulness of the Premises is a favorite in police dramas. We have all seen the scene in which detectives interrogate someone who gives a lame alibi like this one: "My friends and I were at a movie the night the crime took place." The detectives check the story and discover it is a lie. Having exposed his lack of truthfulness, the detectives no longer accept the person's alibi and may even make the liar their prime suspect.

TEST #2: LOGICAL STRENGTH

One way to apply the Test for Logical Strength is to challenge yourself to imagine a situation, if possible, in which all the premises of an argument are true, but the conclusion is false. If there is no possible scenario in which all the premises of an argument can be true while at the same time its conclusion is false, or if such a scenario is extremely improbable, then the argument passes the Test of Logical Strength. However, to the extent that such a scenario is possible, plausible, likely, or actually true, the argument fails this test.[i] If an argument is deductively valid, then there is no

conceivable counterexample to disprove that argument."[ii] If there is a possible scenario, but it is remote and implausible, perhaps as unlikely as one chance in 20 or one chance in a 1,000, then we can maintain a comparable degree of confidence in the argument's logical strength. Logicians call an argument with true premises that has also passes the Test of Logical Strength a **sound argument**.[iii] "Sound" is used here in the sense of "healthy," meaning that such an argument ordinarily is rather robust and deserves our attention as we deliberate what to do or what to believe.

What if there is more than one reason given to support a claim? Does discovering that one reason has a false premise make the claim unacceptable? Consider this example; here a claim is supported by two reasons.

• "I'm not an alcoholic. Look, I only drink beer. And, in fact, I've never been drunk in my life.

Review Map #1 below to see how we would map these arguments.

Suppose we discover that the speaker is telling the truth when he says that he only drinks beer. However, the implicit but unspoken premise ("Someone who only drinks beer cannot be an alcoholic,") is false. So, the first argument fails the Test of the Truthfulness of the Premises.

MAP > it > OUT 1

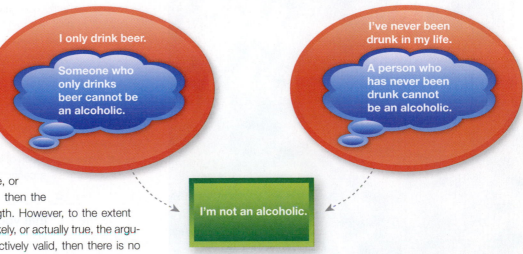

Suppose we then discover that the speaker is also being truthful when he says that he has never been drunk in his life. This, along with the generally accepted truth of the implicit, but unspoken, premise "A person who has never been drunk cannot be an alcoholic," indicates that his second argument passes the Test of Truthfulness of the Premises

That second argument also passes the Test of Logical Strength. It is difficult to imagine a case where a person who has never been drunk is an alcoholic, although it is not impossible to imagine such a case. So, it would seem reasonable to accept that our speaker is not an alcoholic, even though one of his reasons (that he only drinks beer) was poor. His second argument, based on the other reason (he has never been drunk in his life), which is independent of the first, was sound.

People often provide multiple reasons for a given claim and some of those reasons may turn out to be false. One may be inclined to dismiss the claim itself, having heard the speaker present one unsound argument. Dismissing an otherwise-worthy claim simply because one or more of the arguments made on its behalf contains false reasons is one of the most common human reasoning errors. Each reason-claim combination is a separate argument. Thus, before determining that a claim should be rejected, a strong critical thinker would first need to find problems with the soundness of *all* the arguments being advanced.

Because there are so many important varieties of deductive and inductive arguments, which require special attention when testing for logical strength, we will cut this discussion short at this point. We will devote the next chapter to issues of logical strength as they are manifested in deductive reasoning and in inductive reasoning. For the moment, let's complete our review of the four tests of an argument's worthiness to be accepted.

TEST #3: RELEVANCE

The Test of Relevance requires making a reasoned judgment that the truth of the conclusion depends upon the truth of the reason given. If an argument passes the first two tests, then The Test of Relevance is the next in the sequence to apply. Recall that the presumption we are seeking to fulfill is that the author's reason is, in fact, the basis for believing the claim. And the listener must judge if accepting the claim as true depends on support derived from that reason. For example, the following example passes the Test of Relevance.

∧
∧ Is it fair for another driver to expose you to
∧ greater risk just so he or she can text a friend?

• A study from the Harvard Center of Risk Analysis estimates that cell phone use while driving contributes to 6 percent of crashes, which equates to 636,000 crashes, 330,000 injuries, 12,000 serious injuries and 2,600 deaths each year. The study also put the annual financial toll of cell phone-related crashes at $43 billion. The research investigated whether or not a hands-free device was less dangerous. The statistical evidence suggests not. It appears from the data that the fact that the driver was distracted by the conversation was a greater factor than was the type of cell phone technology, hands-free or not, that was being used. The researchers concluded that using cell phone technology of any kind while driving was associated with a greater risk of automobile accidents.[iv]

By contrast, the next argument fails the Test of Relevance.

• Yeah, like I'm really wanting to visit Italy, you know, Old Europe, man. Why is too obvious. See, I've been working part-time at the Golden Gate Park in San Francisco. It's incredible there. Beautiful, open, free. There's this one garden there that kind of reminds me of pictures I've seen of Italy. I love being outside in the spring, the flowers and the fresh air, the smell of fresh-cut grass. And all that makes me think how great it would be to just live slow and relaxed, like they do in Europe, taking life as it comes. You know what I mean?

That the research on car accidents and cell phone usage is relevant to the conclusion in the first example is obvious in the first example. The connection between visiting Italy and working part-time in Golden Gate Park in the second example seems to be tenuous at best, more based on the person's free association of ideas than on any actual evidence. Even if the speaker imagines a connection, the listener can judge that the reason

<<< Is the fact that you like Golden Gate Park relevant to wanting to travel to Europe?

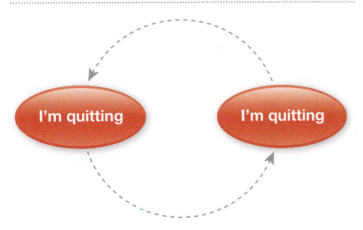

given, even if true, is not a basis for believing that the speaker wants to visit Italy. In fact, if the speaker had simply said, "I want to visit Italy," that might have been more credible than his having come up with the far-fetched and irrelevant dissertation about the glories of a part-time job in a city park—even if it is one of the greatest public parks in this nation.

Applying the Test of Relevance is substantially easier for people with knowledge and experience appropriate to the context and issues under discussion. For example, U.S. laws on discriminating against promotion candidates based on their gender express American society's judgment that a person's gender is not a relevant consideration when deciding whether the person merits a promotion. In another country with a different set of cultural mores, gender-based promotion decisions might be considered both legal and reasonable. The Test of Relevance is important because people often make the argument that they should be excused from responsibility for certain actions. However, as a people, having heard these arguments before, we have come to the judgment that certain reasons are not going to be accepted as relevant. For example:

- Claiming that one was following the direct orders of one's superior is not a relevant defense against charges of war crimes.

- Claiming that one's judgment was impaired by drugs or alcohol is not a relevant defense against charges of vehicular manslaughter resulting from driving while under the influence.

- Claiming that one must protect his or her GPA because one plans to become a doctor is not a relevant defense against charges of academic dishonesty in any course, including general education elective courses.

TEST #4: NON-CIRCULARITY

The fourth and final test of logical acceptability is the Test of Non-Circularity. This test requires that a claim is not being relied upon either implicitly or explicitly as part of a chain of reasoning used to support its own reason. If such a chain looping back on itself is found, then the argument maker is reasoning in a circle. An argument is like a river that flows in one

Circular reasoning, like a moat around a castle, is stagnant thinking.

direction, from reasons and evidence toward the conclusion. A river cannot feed itself and still be described as a river; rather, it becomes a stagnant moat. So it is with good arguments: Claims cannot be the bases for their own reasons. If they were, then the reasoning would simply be stagnant and self-justifying in the most unflattering sense.

The final argument Caitlin made about quitting the volleyball team was "I'm quitting and therefore I'm quitting." Here the circle is so tight that the reason and the claim are identical. If we were to map it, it would look something like Map #2 above.

We can interpret this way of speaking as a way of emphasizing one's claim, but not as a way of proving one's claim. It is like saying "I'm quitting" real loud. But volume is not proof.

Reasoning in a circle results most frequently from the use of multiple arguments in combination with each other. At times people lose track of the reasons for their beliefs, forgetting, for example, that their basis for believing one idea, 'X,' was because they accepted another idea, 'Y,' and that their reason for accepting 'Y' had been their belief in 'X.' The result is that the person has high confidence, although misplaced, in both ideas. However, because

Thinking Critically   Evaluate Argument Worthiness and Explain

Assume that all the premises that are asserted are true. Apply the remaining tests to evaluate each argument to see if it is worthy of acceptance. Remember, if the argument fails a test, you do not have to apply any further tests because at that point the argument is not worthy to be accepted. In each case, give a detailed explanation to support your evaluation. State in your own words why the argument is worthy of acceptance, or why it is not a good argument.[vi]

1 When I stop at a traffic light, I hear this funny rattling sound coming from under my car. It is sort of in the middle or maybe toward the back, but definitely not toward the front. I only hear it when the car is idling, not when I'm driving along at a reasonable speed. My dad said once that the metal baffles inside a muffler can loosen up if the muffler is old and rusty. He said that a loose baffle makes a rattling sound when it vibrates, like when the engine is idling or when the tires are out of alignment. My muffler is at least nine years old. So, I'm thinking that probably the rattling sound is coming from the muffler.

2 Every successful president of the United States was both diplomatic and decisive. General Dwight D. Eisenhower served in WWII as the Commander of the Allied Armies in Europe and then went on to become a successful U.S. president. Therefore, President Eisenhower was decisive and diplomatic.

3 In a perfect world, the government should investigate whether any laws were broken relating to the treatment of wartime detainees. But this is not a perfect world. So, it would be a mistake for the government to engage in such an investigation.

4 Chicago is south of St. Louis. St. Louis is south of New Orleans. Therefore, Chicago is south of New Orleans.

5 The overwhelming majority of Americans believe that health care reform is a top priority for our nation. Therefore, health care reform is a top priority for our nation.

6 Generally, forest fires at this time of the year are caused by careless campers. From where I'm standing I see a column of dark smoke rising out of the forest across the valley. So, some camper must have caused a forest fire.

7 In hot dry regions of the country, new fires can be caused by lightning, arson, or sparks from other nearby fires. Therefore, in the summertime all the fires in states like California, Arizona, and Nevada must be caused by mentally deranged individuals or lightning strikes.

8 If a little child is happy then the child will jump around. Little Marcus is jumping around. So, he must be a happy child.

9 If God intended marriage for the sole purpose of human reproduction, and if same-sex couples are entirely incapable of human reproduction, then it follows that God did not intend marriage for same-sex couples.

10 We interviewed three people and each one was very personable. I think that the first person had the strongest resume. But the second person seemed a lot smarter. I liked the enthusiasm and energy that the third person had, but that person never worked for an organization like ours before. It's a tough choice. But I'm thinking that probably the second person would be the best of the three for us to hire since innovative ideas are more important to us than experience or enthusiasm.

11 Torturing prisoners of war often results in poor quality intelligence. Experience has shown that people in pain will say anything to get the pain to stop. The pain can be either physical or psychological—it does not matter. People crack under the

---

their support for 'X' is 'Y' and their support for 'Y' is 'X,' the reasonable thing would be to have no confidence in either. For example, consider the pair of arguments in this passage:

• I'm sure we can make this marriage work. That's why we're talking through our problems. Which shows that we still care for each other. And that's why I'm sure we can make this marriage work.

The speaker's reason for the claim that the marriage is salvageable is the belief that both parties still care for each other. And the basis for believing that goes back to the idea that the marriage can be saved. If we were to map these arguments, it would look like Map #3 on page 99. This reasoning is as fragile as a house of cards; touch it in the least with an analytical finger and it collapses upon itself.

CONTEXTS FOR ARGUMENT MAKING AND EVALUATIVE TERMS

There is nothing about argument making for purposes of coming to a decision that requires the format to be a debate or in any way an adversarial confrontation. In fact, it does a great disservice to decision making to imagine continually the process as a confrontation of opponents pro and con. In such an adversarial frame, it is too easy to forgo truth-seeking in the false belief that argument making is simply the search for facts that support one's preconceptions. Too often, the courageous desire for best knowledge is trumped by the competitive need to vanquish the opposition. The honest pursuit of reasons and evidence, wherever they may lead, even if the reasons and evidence go against one's preconceptions or interests, is abandoned because intellectual honesty and integrity are not always suitable virtues for warriors who must bring home the victory for their side.

Good arguments—subtle and yet effective as solid proofs that their claims are worthy of being accepted as true—occur within a variety of linguistic behaviors and activities. In natural language contexts, argument making takes many forms. It can be a personable and friendly conversation exploring options and considering ideas. It can be embedded in warnings, recommendations, preambles to policy statements, public addresses, conversations, group meetings, negotiations, monologues, reflections, and even the lyrics of songs.[v]

The vocabulary we use to evaluate arguments must be as flexible as our understanding of the contexts of argument making. A conversation with a colleague about an impending decision can be helpful, even if we would not wish to apply words like "valid," or even "persuasive."

pressure of an experienced interrogator using torture methods. So, we cannot trust the information that comes from that source.

12 Torturing prisoners may be against the Geneva Conventions, but it is a legitimate means of gathering potentially valuable intelligence. There have been cases where the information given to us by prisoners who have been repeatedly water-boarded, for example, has turned out to be correct. Therefore, we are justified in using torture on prisoners even if our laws explicitly prohibit such methods.

13 Assume that 'a,' 'b,' and 'c' are any three numbers. Where 'w' and 'y' are numbers, assume that 'f' is a mathematical function such that 'fwy' yields 'z' where 'z' is the number that is the product of 'w' multiplied by 'y.' It follows deductively then that '($fa(fbc)$)' yields to the product of 'a' multiplied by the product of 'b' multiplied by 'c.'

14 In the past whenever the TV news programs in Chicago ran headline stories featuring a sketch artist's drawing of a fugitive, the Chicago Police Department hotline received over 200 phone calls from people all over the city who said that they spotted the person. Tonight the Chicago TV news programs are going to feature a sketch artist's drawing of a fugitive whom the police are trying to locate. This will probably yield hundreds of calls on the CPD hotline.

15 Suppose we imagine electricity flowing through wires in the way that water flows through pipes. With this analogy in mind, it would be reasonable to infer that wires that are larger in circumference should be capable of carrying greater electrical loads.

16 James Harris: "I made a commitment, threw balls 'til my arm got sore. They always talked about the down-and-out in the NFL, so I went to the park—nobody there but me—to test myself. I was going to throw at this tree blindfolded. I figured if I hit the tree, I'm ready. If I miss the tree, I've got to walk and get the ball. The first time I tried, I missed. The ball was way downfield. I debated about trying it again. I dropped back and threw, heard the ball hit, and something went through me—gave me all the confidence in the world."[vii]

17 The novice pointed eagerly in the direction of the pier and said, "There, do you see them? What fine specimens of brown pelicans." His instructor asked, "Why do you think that they are brown pelicans." "Because," answered the novice, "they look just like the brown pelicans in this picture that I just took with my phone. It's really a great shot. Come and see."

18 As you all know, there has been a successful Chinese experiment that used a single cell from a laboratory rat to generate a living chimera of that rat. In the chimera, which lived to adulthood, 95 percent of its genetic material was identical to the donor rat. Noted cell biologist, Dr. Kastenzakis, believes tinkering with nature is just what scientists do. Therefore the Chinese experiment raises no ethical questions and poses no ethical risks.

19 My client did not intend to use the weapon, and so he is not guilty of armed robbery. Yes, we agree with the prosecution that he committed the robbery. And, yes, we agree that he was carrying a weapon and that he brandished the weapon to intimidate the store clerk and the customers. We agree that the law reads, "Anyone who carries a weapon in the commission of a robbery shall be guilty of armed robbery." And, yes we admit that he shouted, "Everyone down on the floor or I'll shoot." But, and here is the key fact, the weapon was not loaded. He did not have ammunition anyplace on his person or in his possessions. He never intended to use that weapon. And, therefore, the crime that he is guilty of is robbery, but not armed robbery.

20 Not every argument is of equal quality. Therefore, at least one argument is better than at least one other argument.

Natural language offers such richness in its evaluative repertoire that it seems wise, at least at this early point, not to close our options by prematurely stipulating a set of evaluative categories. Thus, with the understanding that these terms are not meant to be interpreted rigidly or in some special technical way, let us simply go forward with our eval-uation of arguments using common language. The table "Evaluative Adjectives for Arguments and Their Elements" below offers some sug-gestions regarding the range of evaluative adjectives that might reason-ably be applied when evaluating the different elements of major con-cern, data, warrants, claims, and arguments.

Evaluative Adjectives for Arguments and Their Elements		
PREMISES	POSITIVE	True, Possible, Probable, Verifiable, Believable, Precise, Clear, Accurate, Factual, etc.
	NEGATIVE	False, Improbable, Self-Contradictory, Fanciful, Fabricated, Vague, Ambiguous, Unknowable, etc.
REASONS	POSITIVE	Certain, True, Probable, Verifiable, Relevant, Wise, Sensible, Well-Applied, Plausible, Believable, etc.
	NEGATIVE	False, Improbable, Self-Contradictory, Poorly Applied, Irrelevant, Foolish, Irrational, Fanciful, Unknowable, Vague, Equivocal, Ill-Conceived, Circular, etc.
CLAIMS	POSITIVE	Well-Documented, Strongly Supported, Well-Argued, Certain, True, Reasonable, Plausible, Probable, etc.
CONCLUSIONS	NEGATIVE	Improbable, Poorly Supported, Unfounded, Self-Contradictory, Uncertain, False, Biased, Preposterous, Implausible, etc.
ARGUMENTS	POSITIVE	Worthy, Good, Acceptable, Sound, Valid, Logical, Strong, Persuasive, Reasonable, etc.
	NEGATIVE	Unworthy, Poor, Unacceptable, Unsound, Fallacious, Illogical, Incomplete, Unreasonable, Bad, Trivial, etc.

Common Reasoning Errors

Humans learn from their mistakes. We can capitalize on that truism to strengthen our skill in evaluating arguments by studying those errors of reasoning that have over the centuries earned themselves a reputation as alluringly deceptive and misleading. As a group they are called "fallacies." **Fallacies** are deceptive arguments that appear logical and seem at times to be persuasive, but, upon closer analysis, fail to demonstrate their conclusions. Many types of fallacies have their own name, as we shall see.

Learning to recognize common fallacies and learning how to explain in ordinary, non-technical terms the mistaken reasoning they contain is a great aid to evaluating arguments. The fallacies of relevance described on pages 102–105, for example, are types of arguments that will fail the Test of Relevance. Those described in this chapter are only a few of the more common types of fallacies. In the next chapter, to help with the application of the Test of Logical Strength, we will expand the list of fallacies to include several that masquerade as logically strong inductive or deductive arguments.[viii]

FALLACIES OF RELEVANCE

For centuries logicians have supplied lists of the kinds of deceptive arguments that people have tended to find persuasive.[ix] When it comes to being deceived by the rhetoric of gifted speakers, eloquent writers, or clever advertisements, many of us are no wiser or more sophisticated than people were in Aristotle's time. Yet in our effort to make an honest argument to another person about what to believe or what to do, we are asking that person to accept the truth of the claim *because of the reason given*. This expectation of relevance at times goes unfilled. Instead we provide a reason that is not relevant. Creative questioning is a powerful tool for uncovering the false assumptions that lie at the core of fallacies of relevance. Whatever the specific application of the question, the fundamental issue is "What does the reason actually have to do with the claim?" From this fundamental concern we can derive a number of specific queries.

There are so many ways that a reason might be irrelevant to the claim being made that it is impossible to list them all. Some arguments appeal to tradition, others, particularly in marketing, try to sell us something simply because it is new. Some use emotions such as fear to move us to accept the claim being made. Others try flattery, praise, trust, or affection to move us to accept a claim that we otherwise would not believe.

- We've always done it this way. I don't want to change our policy.

- Try Sudsy Detergent in your dishwasher. It's new!

- It would be a grave mistake to think that there is no Hell. In fact, an eternal error.

- Hey, trust me. Would I lie to you, baby?

Use Creative Questioning to Challenge the Relevance of Reason to Claim

	Here are six examples of arguments we might hear in everyday situations. In each case the reason offered may in fact be true, and the claim might be true in a few cases as well. But the reason given is not relevant to the claim being asserted.	By applying the fundamental concern, "What does the reason actually have to do with the claim?" to the six examples, we can focus the issue of relevance in each case.
1	John, a world-famous violin virtuoso, endorses Brand XYZ motor oil. So, Brand XYZ motor oil is an excellent product.	What about being a great violinist qualifies one as an expert on motor oil?
2	On the Internet I saw that lots of students said they liked Professor Smith's classes. She's really popular. So, Professor Smith must do an excellent job getting her students to learn the material.	What about being popular implies that a professor is effective in getting students to learn? What if the professor was just an easy grader or funny or likable, but actually a lousy teacher?
3	I can't think of any practical alternatives to gasoline as a vehicle fuel. So, there is no practical alternative automotive fuel.	Are the limits of the possibilities for alternative fuels to be equated with the limits of my imagination?
4	Yesterday in class when we were working on our project, you didn't say a word. So, you must not know anything about the topic.	Could there not have been many reasons, other than ignorance of the topic, why a person does not speak up during group project time in class?
5	If we look around us, we see that people everywhere value human life. So, it is right that we should defend this value over all others.	Why does the fact that many people value something make it imperative that it be regarded as the highest of all possible values? Would we say the same for other things people everywhere value, such as a true friend, a respectful and appreciative supervisor, or satisfying dinner followed by delightful entertainment and a good night's sleep?
6	We chose to go to the moon not because it is easy, but because it is hard.	Just because something is difficult should we now choose to do that thing? Yes it was difficult, but that was not the basis for our decision to choose to go to the moon.

Many fallacies based on irrelevant appeals have earned their own name, which is helpful to remembering the type of mistaken assumption being made.

Appeals to Ignorance

It is false to assume that the mere absence of a reason for (or against) an idea should itself count as a reason against (or for) the idea. Consider these examples:

- We know we have a corporate spy someplace in the organization, probably on the management team itself. There is no evidence that it is Francesca. In fact, she's too clean, if you know what I mean. We should fire Francesca; she's the spy.

- Someone here took my computer and I need it back. Who was it, John? Was it you? No, you say. Well prove it! Aha, you have no proof to offer. Well then, John, it was you. And I want it back now!

- Impressionism, and especially French Impressionism, is the best form of art. You can't name any other form that has been proven to be more beautiful. Can you?

Appeals to the Mob

It is false to assume that because a large group of people believes something or does something that their opinion or their behavior is necessarily correct or appropriate. Here are two examples of the Fallacy of Appeal to the Mob, also known as the "Bandwagon Fallacy."

- Everyone knows that a black quarterback will not be able to lead an all-white team. So we will not put Doug Williams at the quarterback position.ˣ

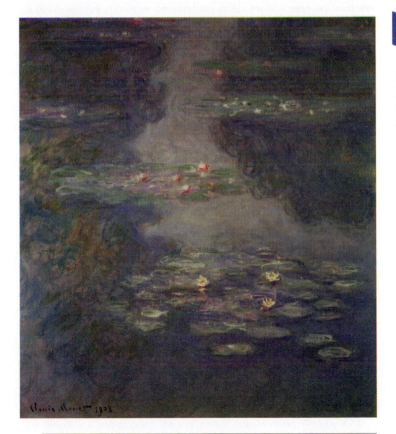

∧
∧ **If you cannot name a superior art form,** does that
∧ imply that French Impressionism **is the best**
art form?

Thinking Critically — Should DUI Homicide be Prosecuted as Murder?

A prosecuting attorney in New York is bringing charges of murder against individuals who have killed other people while driving under the influence. The attorney argues that everyone understands that driving while under the influence poses risks for the driver and for other people, including the risk of a fatal accident. The statutes provide for charges of "depraved indifference" when one's behavior results in the unintended but foreseeable death of another human being. Defense attorneys argue, among other things, that the laws pertaining to murder

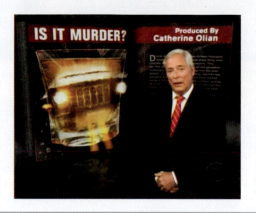

were never intended to be applied in this way. The debate was captured by CBS's *60 Minutes* in a segment that aired on August 2, 2009. Review that segment and map out the reasoning for both sides of this debate. Evaluate the reasoning using the four tests for evaluating arguments. After completing your evaluation, present your own reasoned views on the matter. Access this segment at **www.TheThinkSpot.com**.

- All the kids at school are getting tattoos. Every one of my friends has one, and some have two. I see adult men and women with tattoos. So, I'm thinking that it's about time that I get a tattoo.

Appeals to Emotion

It is false to assume that our initial emotional response to an idea, event, story, person, image, or proposal is necessarily the best guide for forming reflective fair-minded judgments. Chapter 9 discusses this in greater detail, because the relationship between our emotional responses and our decisions about what to believe and what to do are complex. Because gut reaction and reasoned reflection are both real factors in human decision making, strong critical thinkers learn to draw on both of those resources. But, at times, people offer fallacious arguments that provide nothing more by way of a reason than an appeal to one's unreflective emotional response. Here are some examples of the Appeal to Emotion fallacy, which tends to rely on emotionally loaded words and expressions.

- I love you like the son I never had, and because of that I believe you. No, I must believe you. Love leaves no other option.

- He's a lousy, rotten terrorist. One of those people. He deserves to die.

- Watch out—the political right is populated by a dangerous pack of hatemongering jackals. They will destroy this nation because they have no respect for the truth or common decency. You can't believe anything they say.

- Watch out—the political left is a goose-stepping gaggle of dangerous tax-and-spend liberals. They will destroy America with bloated, ineffective social programs we hardworking middle-class taxpayers can't afford. You can't believe anything they say.

- I know you have your heart set on going to Stanford; it's something you talked about since you were in the ninth grade. You kept up your grades, aced the SATs and did everything you could to be admitted. And, I'm so proud of you, you did it. Everyone is. And you know what, I don't care what it takes or what the family has to do, we'll mortgage the house, get another job, anything. But somehow some way, whatever it takes and whatever the consequences for me or for your younger brothers and sisters, we are going to find the money so you can go to Stanford. I've made up my mind. That's what we'll do!

Ad Hominem Attacks

It is false to assume that because the person making the argument is deficient in some real or imagined way, the person's argument, work product,

or views should not be accepted on their own merits. *Ad hominem* is Latin for "against the person" and it expresses the error this fallacy makes, which is to claim that a person's ideas must be tainted because the person has some vice or flaw. The opposite would be equally fallacious, which is to assume that because the person making the argument is virtuous the argument must be a good, too. Here are some examples.

- I don't trust you because of what you did last week at the party. Don't bother trying to explain yourself. As far as I'm concerned, anything you say is a lie.

- He worked for Clinton and Carter. How can we believe that the legislation he's proposing will do anything but ruin this country?

- The Governor was spotted drunk in a Brazilian bordello. There are pictures on the Web already. So we can't believe anything he says about environmental problems or clean energy solutions.

- You have nothing of value to contribute to this conversation about minority race relations. You're not Black, Latino, Asian, Native American, or anything. You're White.

- I'm sorry, but I don't find his income and expenses projections credible. I don't see how he could have done those numbers correctly. After all, we know he's looking for another job. He has no company loyalty.

Straw Man Fallacy

This fallacy relies on the false assumption that, by refuting a weaker argument among several reasons given in support of claim, one has successfully refuted all the reasons for that claim. For example:

- Look, we can't approve your request for additional advertising funds. You said that one of the four marketing options you were reviewing was Web page design. But we have a policy not to support any further Web-based development.

- You said in Chapter 1 that legalizing drugs was a good idea because then they could be regulated for quality and taxed. And you said it would permit us to shift law enforcement resources toward preventing other more harmful criminal behaviors. But I'm opposed to new taxes of any kind. So, I cannot agree with you about legalizing drugs.

A variation on the theme, also called the Straw Man Fallacy, is the pernicious practice of attributing to the opposition an argument that is not theirs, and then demolishing that argument. The misattribution may be mistaken, or worse, intentional. From this the person committing the fallacy misleadingly then argues that he or she has destroyed the opposition's position entirely. Besides being intellectually dishonest and inconsistent with the critical thinking virtue of truth-seeking, this practice violates the values of objectivity and fair-mindedness. And, adopting the strategy of trying to make an idiot out of the opposition can be risky, too. To use straw men and misrepresentations when presenting the opposition's arguments can lead one's listeners, and at times one's self, in the mistaken belief that there is little or no merit to the opposition's view. In the health care reform debates during the summer of 2009, those opposed to "death panels" demonized the proposed legislation for a provision that, as it turned out, was already part of existing Medicare law. The actual provision to which they objected provided for reimbursement to health care providers if patients voluntarily sought end-of-life counseling about such matters as living wills, power of attorney, DNR orders, or hospice care. When the dust settled, even some who had raised the specter of government death panels backed away from that overly dramatic straw man criticism. Others, however, continued to believe that the proposed legislation would mandate euthanasia.

Underestimating one's opponent in a debate or dispute can backfire. One reason is that listeners can be alienated when they realize that we have not been fair or objective. A second reason is that we may become overconfident. Strong critical thinkers try not to mislead themselves. They school themselves to follow the political adage, "Never believe your own press releases." In so doing, strong critical thinkers try not to confuse defeating a straw man argument with giving due consideration to the opposition's arsenal of worthy arguments.

Playing with Words

In Chapter 4 we saw how vagueness and ambiguity can be problematic in certain contexts. The Playing with Words fallacy exploits stereotyping, problematic vagueness, problematic ambiguity, donkey cart expressions, or slanted language in attempting to support a claim. Because Playing with Words fallacies are so varied and so vexing, we devoted that chapter to learning how to apply our critical thinking skills to resolve those problems. Here are three more quick examples of arguments that are fallacious because they exploit problematic uses of key terminology.

- Everyone who is in prison can still be free, for true freedom is the knowledge of one's situation. The more one knows about one's self, the more one is truly free.

- I'm selfish, you're selfish. When you really look at it, everybody is selfish. So, we are wrong to be so harsh on a guy just because he spends all his money on nice clothes and fine food for himself while letting his children run around hungry and in rags.

- We cannot know that others experience the world as we do. To truly know is to be inside the minds of others. And that is simply not possible.

Misuse of Authority

One version of Misuse of Authority relies on the false assumption that if a powerful or popular person makes a claim, then the claim must be true. In addition to this error, there are other ways that expertise can be misrepresented and misused, as we saw in Chapter 6. In that chapter we talked about the many characteristics of an authority whose word should, in all probability, be accepted. Because reliance on the word of another is such an important part of how people decide what to do or what to believe, critical thinkers are alert to the fallacies of Misuse of Authority. In addition to the many given in Chapter 6, here are a couple more examples:

- When asked why the curriculum had been changed, the Superintendent of Schools replied that the city's Chamber of Commerce had advised that the students in the Junior High School would be educationally better served if all teachers spent more time during class preparing the students to take standardized math tests and less time on American History, Creative Writing, Social Studies, Art, Leisure Reading, or Health Education.

- In the annual NCAA March Madness office pool, the boss picked North Carolina State to win it all. I'm going to pick the same team she picked. After all, she's the boss.

The written historical record shows that the question of how to evaluate arguments goes back at least 2500 years to the birth of the field study today known as logic. Logic, with its historical roots in rhetoric and argumentation, explores the question of how to decide whether or not the claims based on various kinds of arguments should be accepted. More specifically, it focuses on one of the presumptions of the practice of argument making: If the premises of an argument are taken to be true, that implies that the argument's conclusion is probably or necessarily true as well.[xi] The wisdom and intellectual treasures of many of the world's great cultures and civilizations are evident in the rich history of logic. Fortunately, there are many important and enduring lessons that critical thinking can draw from the study of logic with regard to testing the logical strength of different kinds of arguments, recognizing common fallacies, and understanding the conditions for using inductive and deductive reasoning methods correctly. Drawing on those enduring lessons, we have begun to assemble our tool kit for evaluating arguments in this chapter. We will add some precision tools for the evaluation of arguments in the next chapter.

Analyze and Explain

Here and in the next chapter we introduce a great many names traditionally used to categorize reliable argument patterns and unreliable fallacious varieties of arguments. The terminology of logicians and other scholars who study arguments is valuable to the extent that it helps us remember the underlying ideas. People with strong critical thinking skills are good at evaluating arguments because they can recognize logically correct forms of arguments as well as common mistakes that make an argument invalid, unjustified or fallacious. And, they can explain in their own words why one form is reliable and another is fallacious. All around the planet, there are people who are skilled at evaluating arguments, but who may never have learned the academic terminology to classify arguments. Unfortunately, there are others who can recite the textbook definitions of the terms but yet, in practice, lack skill at evaluating arguments.

Being able to explain why an argument is not acceptable is a stronger demonstration of one's critical thinking skills than being able to remember the names of the different types of fallacies. Exercising one's skills in analysis and explanation leads to stronger critical thinking and better communication of one's thinking in daily life. Rote memorization, which is valuable for other things, is not a critical thinking skill.

REVIEW

The natural human practice of reasoning with a friend or colleague to seek the truth reveals how in argument making and reason giving, four important presumptions support the expectations and responsibilities that make that practice work in real life. The reasons we give should be true. The arguments we use should be logical. The reason given should be the relevant basis for accepting the truth of the claim. And the claim should not be used to lend support or credence to the reason. These four conditions ground the application of four straightforward tests to determine whether an argument is worthy of being accepted. The four are the Test of Truthfulness, Test of Logical Strength, Test of Relevance, and Test of Non-Circularity. The tests, which are to be applied in a particular order, must all

be passed if an argument is to be worthy of acceptance as a demonstration that its conclusion is true or is very probably true.

To help with the application of the Test of Relevance, we examined seven common fallacies of relevance. Arguments that manifest these fallacious approaches to presenting reasons and claims often beguile and mislead us. In the next chapter we will explore in greater detail the application of the Test of Logical Strength with special attention to deductive reasoning and inductive reasoning. There we will expand the discussion of fallacies as well, for there are some that masquerade as valid deductive arguments and others that masquerade as strong inductive arguments.

KEY TERMS

good argument (or **worthy argument**) is an argument that merits being accepted as a proof that its conclusion is true or very probably true.   96

sound argument is an argument with true premises that also passes the Test of Logical Strength.   97

fallacies are deceptive arguments that appear logical, but upon closer analysis, fail to demonstrate their conclusions.   102

FIND IT ON THE THINKSPOT

In this chapter I invited you to work three exercises using video clips you could access at **www.TheThinkSpot.com**.

On page 96 we used the argument that the monk was not killed by the devil in *The Name of the Rose*. Later in the story, the real killer is identified. Watch the film in its entirety and then map out the reasoning Sean Connery's character uses to solve this captivating murder mystery.

On page 102 we used an episode of *The Practice*, and our focus was on the arguments

the defense attorney made. The jury ended up agreeing with the defense in that story. View that episode again and this time focus on the arguments the plaintiff's lawyer made. Evaluate those arguments using the four criteria presented in this chapter. The case in favor of the plaintiff's claim of wrongful termination appears strong. Why were those arguments less effective with the jury?

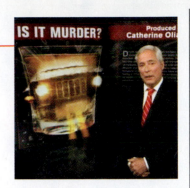

On page 104 we discussed the *60 Minutes* report on prosecuting homicide by drunk driving as murder. What about the person who sold the driver alcoholic drinks in a bar or restaurant just prior to the fatal accident? If that bartender suspected that the driver was having too much to safely operate the car, should he or she have refused service? Did the person have an affirmative obligation to call a taxi or to take away the driver's car keys? If so, then should the person who sold the drinks be prosecuted too as an accessory or an accomplice to the murder? When making your arguments, be sure to present them in ways that will satisfy all four tests for the worthiness of arguments that we learned in this chapter.

Exercises

REFLECTIVE LOG: THE ETHICS OF FALLACIOUS ARGUMENTATION

What if we discovered that we could manipulate the voting public more effectively by the use of fallacious arguments than by the use of worthy arguments? Consider the political impact of the "death panels" issue described under the Straw Man Fallacy on pages 104–105. The entire episode generated more heat than light. And, yet, it may have achieved its political purpose. Many who heard and believed that the proposed legislation envisioned a eugenics program akin to that advanced by Nazi Germany, showed up at town meetings to vent their anger and voice their objections. If the goal was to delay or derail the Democratic legislative agenda, then the strategy succeeded. This is only one example of using one's skills at argument making to achieve one's goals. Defense attorneys who get juries to acquit criminals is another, as are prosecuting attorneys who get juries to convict innocent people accused of crimes. The ethical question for all critical thinkers is: To what purposes ought I to put my powerful critical thinking skills? This question is analogous to the question: to what purposes ought I to put my college education? These are in part ethical questions and in part questions about one's sense of how to make the meaning of one's life. And what are your answers? Why?

FIVE-PERSON GROUP PROJECT: WHAT DO OTHERS THINK?

Each member of the group, having seen the *60 Minutes* video and worked on the exercise on page 104, will have thoroughly considered the issue of homicidal DUI as murder. But for this project, you must first set aside your own individual opinions on this matter. This project involves interviewing people for whom this issue is much more than a textbook's abstraction. So you and the other members of your group need to focus on what you hear in the interviews without letting your personal opinions get in the way.

Your group will conduct four sets of interviews. You must always have at least two members of your group participate in each interview. This is so that you can help each other remember what the person being interviewed said.

First set of interviews: Locate at least one person—two or three if possible—who has been arrested for DUI, even if not for homicide while under the influence of alcohol or drugs. Find out what that person or those people think. Listen to their arguments, and then write them down and evaluate those arguments. Be objective and fair-minded in your evaluation, regardless of whether you agree or disagree with the person's position.

Second set of interviews: Locate at least one person who is a former drinker but who no longer drinks. Perhaps you can find someone who will talk with you by contacting AA. Interview that person the same way. Get his or her views on the matter, write down the person's arguments, and evaluate those arguments objectively and fair-mindedly.

Next, contact MADD or some other volunteer organization that is known for its stance on issues relating to drunk driving. Follow the same drill. Get that organization's arguments down and evaluate them.

Finally, contact the office of your local prosecuting attorney, or the state police and, again, conduct your interview and evaluate the arguments you hear.

Having talked directly with people who are close to this issue, your group must now assemble all the arguments that came forward in the various interviews. In light of these perspectives, take a stance individually and as a group on whether or not homicide by DUI should be prosecuted as murder. Write out the group's opinion and give the reasons. Write out your individual opinion, if you disagree, and give your reasons. Whatever you finally decide, use strong critical thinking and sound reasons.

The distressing dilemma below follows Thomas Barton, a fictional **pilot of the emergency dispatch ship in the 1954 sci-fi classic "The Cold Equations," by Tom Godwin. The story was later made** v
v into an episode of the CBS television
v series *The New Twilight Zone.*

Why should

she have to die? All she wanted was to surprise her brother.

There is precious little margin for error on the boundless emptiness of outer space as Thomas Barton, pilot of the tiny emergency dispatch ship, discovers. Thinking he was on a rescue mission to deliver vitally needed vaccine to an outpost colony, he soon finds he must decide who will live and who will die.[i]

Unless the vaccine reaches the colony in time, everyone at the outpost will surely die. Barton's little craft must get through. No other emergency dispatch vessel can reach the colony in time. A young woman, upon learning that Barton's ship was headed for the distant colony, stowed away aboard his ship. She thought maybe she would have to pay a small fine. But it would be worth it to be able to visit her brother who is stationed at the outpost. When the ship's computer detects the additional weight of her body, Barton is able to locate the young stowaway. Her hopes turn to dust when she learns that standing military orders require stowaways aboard emergency dispatch ships to be summarily executed.

Barton does not want to execute the young woman. But the computer says that the craft does not have sufficient fuel to land safely with her aboard. The immutable physics of mass and velocity require that 120 pounds must be jettisoned into space. Desperately, Barton and the young woman pile everything that is not welded down into the airlock. Binders, tools, eating utensils and everything else they find is jettisoned into space to lighten the load. But it is not enough. With nothing else left to jettison, except one of the two of them, the cold equations become all too real.

The mission will fail, the colonists will all die, and so will Barton and the young woman unless the excess weight is shed before the craft enters the atmosphere. Barton considers sacrificing himself. But that will not work. The young woman cannot possibly land the craft safely. If Barton sacrifices himself, he will guarantee that she and all the colonists will die.

The logic of the situation makes Barton's dilemma inescapable. No matter what choice he makes, someone must die. Deciding not to decide is the equivalent of deciding that everyone should die. All the options are bad. The story draws to a close with the young woman stepping into the airlock. The hatch is sealed. Barton reaches for the red handle that will jettison her into space. Cold as this logic may be, only with her death can others live.

109

EVALUATING DEDUCTIVE AND INDUCTIVE REASONING

CHAPTER 08

Although at times we all have wished otherwise, none of us can suspend the laws of nature or the laws of logic. In business, a company that is losing money may have no choice but to lay off good employees. In a medical emergency, health care professionals have to triage those needing care. Military leaders have to send good soldiers into combat knowing that some will not return. Regardless of our feelings in the matter, there are times in our lives when the facts and the logic of a given situation force us to entertain options we had hoped never to face. In those situations we cannot afford to be wrong about the facts or about the logical strength of our reasoning.

In this chapter we drill into the Test of Logical Strength more deeply than in the previous chapter. We will focus on evaluating the logical strength of deductive arguments and inductive arguments. Recall that earlier in the book we characterized the distinction between deductive arguments and inductive arguments this way: Deductive arguments present their conclusions as necessarily true, if all the premises are true. By contrast, inductive arguments present their conclusion as probabilistic, given the truth of the premises. Within each of the two broad classifications of arguments, we will find many varieties. So, to extend our skill of argument evaluation, we will explore these different kinds of deductive arguments and inductive arguments more deeply.

Because this chapter focuses on the second of the four tests for evaluating arguments, the Test of Logical Strength, we are going to assume that the examples used here have already passed the first test, the Test of the Truthfulness of the Premises. We are going to assume that the premises of the example arguments are true. This will be a lot to swallow, because some of the premises are patently false. But, for the purposes of focusing on the logic of the arguments, let us entertain the fiction within the context of this chapter. The chapter begins with positive examples of logically correct forms of deductive arguments and then continues with fallacies that masquerade as deductive arguments, but are not logically correct. We then do the same with inductive arguments. We first examine the positive examples and then the misleading fallacies that mimic those more reliable inductive reasoning strategies.

Deductive Validity and Language

For an argument to be evaluated as a **deductively valid argument**, it must be impossible for the premises all to be true and the conclusion false. In other words, an argument is deductively valid if there is no possibility, real or imaginable, short of changing the very meanings of the terms and the rules of grammar, that will make the premises all true and the conclusion false. Deductively valid arguments satisfy the Test of Logical Strength.

Certain configurations of language form deductively valid argument templates. By their very form and structure these argument templates reliably generate valid, deductive arguments as long as we do not change

the meanings of the words or the rules of grammar. This is why the premises of a valid deductive argument are said to make the truth of the conclusion necessary. Without violating the meanings of the words or the grammatical rules of the language, there is no possible way for the premises all to be true and the conclusion false.

REASONING DEDUCTIVELY ABOUT DECLARATIVE STATEMENTS

This first group of valid deductive argument templates we will consider include those that derive their valid structures from the way simple statements interact grammatically when we use prepositions or adverbs that have logical force. These include the words "and," "or," "not," and "if . . .then. . ."

Denying the Consequent[ii]

One valid deductive argument template we rely on regularly produces arguments structured like this:

Premise #1:   If **A**, then **B**.
Premise #2:   Not **B**,
Conclusion: Therefore, not **A**.[iii]

The argument template uses the capital letters "A" and "B" to stand for simple positive declarative statements, like "**A**" = "**The Nissan Titan gets good gas mileage**." And "**B**" = "**The Dodge Ram 3500 gets outstanding mileage**." Substituting those two statements in the template for "**A**" and for "**B**" produces this argument:

- Premise #1: If the **Nissan Titan gets good gas mileage**, then **the Dodge Ram 3500 gets outstanding mileage**.
- Premise #2: It is not the case that the **Dodge Ram 3500 gets outstanding mileage**.

Conclusion: Therefore, the **Nissan Titan does** not **get good gas mileage**.

In each of the examples below, the **blue statement is "A"** and the orange statement is "B." Here are three more examples of valid deductive arguments built by substituting declarative statements into the "denying the consequent" argument template.

- If **Richard graduated with honors,** then Richard maintained a GPA of 3.2 or higher.
  It is not the case that Richard maintained a GPA of 3.2 or higher.
  Therefore, **Richard did** not **graduate with honors.**

- If **you have been promoted to the rank of captain,** then you have served for at least a year.
  You have not served for at least a year.
  It follows then that **you have** not **been promoted to the rank of captain.**

- If the **sun shines on the far side of the moon,** then red roses grow inside the barns in Iowa.
  It is not true that red roses grow inside the barns in Iowa.
  So, it is not true that **the sun shines on the far side of the moon.**

This last example is curious because it is structurally valid, but in fact we would not rely on it as a proof that the sun does not shine on the far side of the moon. The argument is not acceptable because even if the second premise were true, which is highly doubtful, the first premise is not. This example is a quick reminder that logical strength, while essential, is not the only consideration that strong critical thinkers have in mind when evaluating arguments in real life. Again, in all the examples here and to follow we are maintaining our focus on the logic while assuming that all the premises are true.

Fill in the argument template to create two deductively valid examples of your own

If _____, then _____.
It is not the case that _____.
Therefore, it is not the case that _____.

If _____, then _____.
It is not the case that _____.
Therefore, it is not the case that _____.

Affirming the Antecedent

A second very commonly used deductive argument template also relies on the meaning and grammatical power of "if ___, then ____" expressions. In this case, however, the second premise affirms that the "if ___" part is true.

Premise #1:   If **A**, then **B**.
Premise #2:   **A**.
Conclusion: Therefore, **B**.[iv]

Here are three examples of arguments that are valid on the basis of affirming the antecedent deductive argument template.

- If the **price quote from College Insignias is lower than the price quote from University Logos,** then **we will get the T-shirts for our AIDS walk team printed at College Insignias. The price quote from College Insignias is lower than the price quote from University Logos.** Therefore, **we will get the T-shirts for our AIDS walk team printed at College Insignias.**

- If **you are eligible to graduate with honors,** then **you will receive notification from the Registrar. You are eligible to graduate with honors.** So, it follows that **you will receive notification from the Registrar.**

- If the **sun shines on the far side of the moon,** then **yellow roses grow inside the barns in Missouri. The sun shines on the far side of the moon.** So, **yellow roses grow inside the barns in Missouri.**

As with pre-algebra, we are substituting values for the variables in the formula. In pre-algebra the result was an equation, here the result is a valid argument. Fill in the "affirming the antecedent" argument template to create two deductively valid examples of your own

If _____, then _____.
_____.
Therefore, _____.

If _____, then _____.
_____.
Therefore, _____.

Disjunctive Syllogism

When we are presented with various alternatives and then learn that one or more of those alternatives will not work, it is logical to reduce our options. The argument template for this deductively valid structure produces arguments with this pattern:

Premise #1:   Either **A** or **B**.
Premise #2:   Not **A**.
Conclusion: Therefore, **B**.

Here are two examples of arguments that are valid by virtue of the "disjunctive syllogism" argument template.

- Either **we'll go to Mexico for spring break,** or **we will go to San Diego. We are not going to Mexico for spring break.** So, **we will go to San Diego.**

- Either **I'll take organic chemistry over the summer,** or **I'll register for that course next fall. No way will I be able to take organic chemistry over the summer.** So, **I'll register for that course next fall.**

The next example is a variation on the second. Instead of the first alternative being eliminated so that the second emerges as the only remaining

Grammatically Equivalent Structures

These pairs of logically equivalent grammatical structures . . .		. . . give us two ways to say the same thing.	
A unless B	A or B	The dishwasher is still full unless you emptied it.	Either the dishwasher is still full or you emptied it.
Not A unless B	If A then B	The table is not set unless Grandma set it.	If the table is set, then Grandma set it.
A only if B	If A then B	The table is set only if Grandma set it.	If the table is set, then Grandma set it.
If A then B	Either A or not B	If the table is set, then Grandma set it.	Either the table is set or Grandma did not set it.
Neither A nor B	Not A and not B	Neither Bill nor Sue likes singing.	Bill does not like singing and Sue does not like singing.
Not both A and B	Either not A or not B	We cannot buy both a car and a boat.	Either we cannot buy a car or we cannot buy a boat.
A if and only if B	If A then B, and if B then A	We will rent a cottage if and only if our vacations coincide.	If we will rent a cottage, then our vacations coincide, and if our vacations coincide we will rent a cottage.
If A then not B	If B then not A	If the rent is due then we cannot afford to go out to dinner.	If we can afford to go out to dinner, then the rent is not due.

There are other terms that, when used correctly, can be used in valid deductive argument templates. Create 10 arguments by first filling in the templates using the 3 declarative statements provided.

Statement A: The Republicans will gain congressional seats in the next election.

Statement B: The President's overall job approval rating remains above 55 percent.

Statement C: The Democrats might delay vital legislation by fighting among themselves.

1 Either A, B, or C. Not B or C. So, A.

2 It is not the case that both A and B are true. So, either A is not true or B is not true.

3 Neither B nor C is true. So, B is false.

4 A unless B. Not B. So, A.

5 A only if B. A. Therefore, B.

6 Not A unless C. Not C. Therefore, not A.

7 If A then C. If B then C. Either A or B. So, C.

8 It is not the case that if B then C. Therefore, B, but not C.

9 It is not possible that not B. Therefore, B.

10 A if and only if B. Not B. So, not A.

On some topic of your own choosing, write 3 declarative statements. Fill in the 10 templates using your statements. Now evaluate each of the arguments created by the first 10 fill-ins and the second 10 fill-ins. Is it possible in any of those cases that the argument's conclusion could be false if you assume that all argument's premises are true? The answer should be "no" in all 20 cases.

option, in this case the second alternative was eliminated so that the first emerged logically as the only remaining options. The template for this is:

Premise #1:   Either **A** or **B**.
Premise #2:   Not **B**.
Conclusion: Therefore, **A**.

- Either **I'll take organic chemistry over the summer,** or **I'll register for that course next fall.**
No way can I take organic chemistry next fall.
So, **I'll take that course over the summer.**

In context "that course" refers to organic chemistry. In actual practice, when we make arguments, we seldom repeat statements verbatim. Instead, we use internal references that are contextually unproblematic.

REASONING DEDUCTIVELY ABOUT CLASSES OF OBJECTS

Other deductive arguments derive their valid structures from the meanings of words in the language used to show the interaction of groups of objects. Words like "some" and "all" are used to express our ideas about how individual objects and groups of objects relate.

Applying a Generalization

Consider this example of reasoning about individual objects and groups of objects:

- All the books by Michael Connelly feature his fictional hard-boiled LAPD detective, Hieronymous Bosch. *Echo Park* is a book by Michael Connelly. So, *Echo Park* features Detective Bosch.

    In this example the first premise states every member of a class of objects (books by Connelly) has a specific attribute (features

Detective Bosch). The second premise identifies a specific member of that class (*Echo Park*). And the conclusion that follows necessarily from those two premises is that *Echo Park* features Detective Bosch. Whenever we have a generalization that asserts that a given characteristic applies to each of the members of a class of objects, we can logically assert that a given individual or subgroup of individuals that are members of that class has that characteristic. For example:

- Everyone who installs attic insulation runs the risk of inhaling potentially harmful dust and fiberglass particles. Angela and Jennifer install attic insulation. This means that both of them run that risk.

- Anyone who plays in a rock band knows that after you play a set lasting 40 minutes, you need a short break. Angela plays drums and Jennifer plays bass guitar in the Blazing Sunsets, a rock band at our college. So Angela and Jennifer know that after playing a set lasting 40 minutes, they need a short break.

If "F" and "G" stand for classes of objects, and if "X" stands for an individual object, then the argument template for "applying a generalization" would be this:

Premise #1:   Every member of F is a member of G.
Premise #2:   Individual object X is a member of F.
Conclusion: So, X is a member of G.

The figure to the left illustrates this argument structure. The oval represents all the things that are F. The circle represents all the things that are G. The red area of F that is outside of circle G is empty, because premise #1 states if anything is an F then it is also a G. As premise #2 says, X is the member of F. So, the only place we can put X is in the region where F and G overlap. This establishes pictorially that the conclusion cannot be false. Any other placement of X would violate what the premises state.

G   F   X

Applying an Exception

If we know that every member of a given class of objects has a certain characteristic, and we also know that one or more specific objects do not have that characteristic, we can logically infer that they are not members of that class. For example:

- Everyone who waits table has experienced the challenge of trying to be respectful to a rude customer. Alexander has never experienced that challenge. That implies that Alexander has never worked as a waiter.

- Everyone who installs attic insulation runs the risk of inhaling potentially harmful dust and fiberglass particles. Angela and Jennifer have jobs that do not put them at risk for inhaling anything that is potentially harmful. So, Jennifer and Angela do not install attic insulation.

- The numbers 5, 7, 13, and 37 are not divisible by 2 without a remainder. Every even number is divisible by 2 with no remainder. So, 5, 7, 13, and 37 are not even numbers.

The argument template for "applying an exception" looks like this:

Premise #1:   Every F is a G.
Premise #2:   The object X is not a G.
Conclusion: So, X is not an F.

In the figure below, premise #1 assures us that the red area of F that is outside of the circle G is empty. If there are any members of F, then they will all be inside circle G. But, because of premise #2, the only place to put X is outside of G. This establishes pictorially that the conclusion must be true. We cannot locate X in any place inside oval F without violating one or the other of the premises.

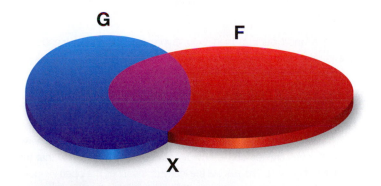

The Power of "Only"

One of the most interesting words in the language, "only" has the power to change the meaning of a sentence depending on where it is placed. Consider this example. Here is a simple sentence.

- Some objected to being forced to attend.

Now watch how the meanings change depending on where "only" is positioned.

Location of "Only" to Change Meaning	Interpretation of New Statement
Only some objected to being forced to attend.	Others did not object.
Some **only** objected to being forced to attend.	They did not quit, go on strike, or boycott.
Some objected **only** to being forced to attend.	They would have preferred to have been asked or invited to attend voluntarily.
Some objected to being forced **only** to attend.	They wanted to do more than attend; they wanted to participate actively.

Here is another example, but this time you fill in the left-hand side of the table showing where the word "only" would be located to enable the interpretation on the right.

- Some who are students pursue excellence.

Location of "Only" to Change Meaning	Interpretation of New Statement
some who are students pursue excellence.	They do nothing but pursue.
some who are students pursue excellence.	The one thing they pursue is excellence.
some who are students pursue excellence.	Some students do not pursue excellence.
some who are students pursue excellence.	They have no other identity besides being students.

Thinking Critically

Classes and Objects

Let "F" be fun-loving people.
Let "G" be college graduates.
Let "H" be high-paid professionals.
Let "X" stand for Xavier.
Let "Y" stand for Yolanda.

Create arguments using each of these templates. Some of the arguments will turn out to be valid, and others will not. Evaluate each using the Test for Logical Strength to determine which are not valid deductive arguments. If you can think of a counterexample, then the argument is not deductively valid.

1. If anyone is an F, then that person is a G. Both X and Y are G. So, X is an F, and Y is also.

2. Some who are F are also G. Some who are G are also H. So, some who are F are H.

3. If X is an F and a G, then X is an H. As it turns out, X is an F but not a G. So, X is not an H.

4. Few H are F. But Y is an H and a G. If anyone is a G, then he or she is an F. So, Y is an F.

5. All F are H. All G are H. So, all F are G.

6. No F are H. No G are F. So, no F are G.

7. Some H are not G. All G are F. So, some H are not F.

8. Only some F are H. So, some F are not H.

9. Not all F are H. So, at least one F is not an H.

10. Only some F are not H. So, some F are H.

REASONING DEDUCTIVELY ABOUT RELATIONSHIPS

Natural languages are rich with terms that describe relationships. We use our understanding of the meanings of these terms to make deductive inferences about the objects to which the terms apply. For example, the arguments below are deductively valid because of the meanings of the relational terms like "sibling," "brother," "sister," "shorter than," "older than," "taller than," "younger than," "greater than," or "equals." Notice that in ordinary discourse it is not necessary to specify generalizations like "Anyone who is a person's brother is that person's sibling," because those relationships are part of the meanings of the terms. Our understanding of the logical implications of relational terms is part our comprehension of language. We seldom, if ever, attend to the deductive logical complexity embedded in natural language. Here are some examples of valid deductive arguments built on the meanings of the relational terms these arguments use.

- John is Susan's younger brother. So, they must have the same mother or the same father.
- Fresno is north of Bakersfield. Bakersfield is west of Phoenix. So, Phoenix is southeast of Fresno.
- Six is greater than five. Five is greater than four. Therefore, six is greater than four.
- $(4 + 6) = 10$. $(2 \times 5) = 10$. Therefore, $(4 + 6) = (2 \times 5)$.

Transitivity, Reflexivity, and Identity

Three relational characteristics we rely upon regularly when using deductive reasoning are named Identity, Reflexivity, and Transitivity. Here are two examples of valid deductive arguments based on each, beginning with two examples of transitivity:

- Tomas is taller than Jose. Jose is taller than Miguel. So, Tomas is taller than Miguel.
- Susan is Joan's ancestor. Joan is Philip's ancestor. So, Susan is Philip's ancestor.

Transitivity Relationship = *If x has a transitive relationship to y, and y has the same transitive relationship to z, then x has the same transitive relationship to z.*

- David is Stanley's neighbor. So, Stanley is David's neighbor.
- Sara is Helena's roommate. So, Helena is Sara's roommate.

Reflexivity Relationship = *If x has a reflexive relationship to y, then y has the same reflexive relationship to x.*

- The actress who played Julia Child is Meryl Streep. The actress who played Julia Child should get an Oscar nomination for her performance in that film. So, Meryl Streep should get an Oscar nomination for her performance in that film.
- The President of the United States was assassinated in 1963. People still remember where they were and what they were doing when they heard that shocking news. John F. Kennedy was the President who was killed that November day in Dallas. So, people still remember where they were and what they were doing the day they heard that Kennedy had been assassinated.

Identity Relationship = *If x is y, then y is x.*

FALLACIES MASQUERADING AS VALID DEDUCTIVE ARGUMENTS

Just as there are valid argument templates, there are fallacious argument templates. In every case, an analysis of the meanings of the terms used and the grammatical rules of the language reveal the source of the error. Precision of thought and expression is the key to avoiding these mistakes in our own argument making and also in our evaluation of the arguments offered to us. Often, a counterexample that mirrors the fallacious argument template will have the power to reveal the illogical structure, expose the fallacy, and squelch the argument's apparent persuasiveness. As before, in this section please assume that the premises of the example arguments are all true, so that we can focus on their logical flaws rather than their factual inaccuracies.

Affirming the Consequent

Suppose it is true that "If the river continues to rise, then the carpet will get wet." And suppose that we observe that the carpet is wet. It does not follow that the water that wet the carpet came from the river. The wetness may have come from an entirely different source, for example, the dishwasher overflowing, a pitcher of water being spilled, rain coming in an open window, or even old and sadly confused Uncle Joe bringing in the garden hose yet again to water the sofa with flower pattern upholstery.

The fallacy of Affirming the Consequent follows this invalid pattern:

Premise #1:   If **A**, then **B**.
Premise #2:   **B**.
Conclusion: Therefore, **A**.

But **A** may not be the only condition that brings about **B**. So, it does not make logical sense to believe that **A** must be true simply because **B** is true. Here are more examples of the fallacy of Affirming the Consequent.

- If we put an American on Mars before the end of the 20th century, then we have a successful space program. We do have a successful space program. So, we put an American on Mars before the end of the 20th century.

- If I am a good person, then God favors me with good friends, wealth, and fame. God has favored me with good friends, wealth, and fame. Therefore, I must be a good person.

Denying the Antecedent

Suppose the same hypothetical as before: "If the river continues to rise, then the carpet will get wet." And suppose that we receive the good news that the river has crested and is now receding. It does not follow that the carpet will not get wet. There is still the leaky dishwasher, the open window, and dear old Uncle Joe to contend with.

The fallacy of Denying the Antecedent follows this invalid pattern:

Premise #1:   If **A**, then **B**.
Premise #2:   Not **A**.
Conclusion: Therefore not **B**.

As before, **A** may not be the only condition that brings about **B**. So, it does not make logical sense to think that just because **A** does not happen, **B** cannot happen. Here are two more examples of the fallacy of Denying the Antecedent.

- If everyone east of the Mississippi drank red wine daily, then the industry would be booming. The industry is booming. So, everyone east of the Mississippi is drinking red wine daily.

- If we see a light in the window, we know that there is someone at home. But we do not see a light in the window. So, no one is home.

Thinking Critically — Therefore . . .

Complete each argument below by using your deductive reasoning skills to draw a logically correct conclusion from the premises given.

1 If I put sugar in my coffee, then I enjoy it more. I put sugar in my coffee. Therefore _____ .

2 David and Sharon both love cats. Anyone who loves cats is a friend of mine. Therefore _____ .

3 Barbara and Bill are planning to marry. No couples planning to marry want to live in poverty and squalor. Therefore _____ .

4 Alex is William's father. William is Kirk's father. And Kirk is Patricia's father. Therefore, Alex is Kirk's _____ and Patricia's _____ .

5 Apartment vacancy rates in town exceed 15 percent. Every time the rate exceeds 12 percent, you can be certain that there are some great deals on rentals near campus. Therefore _____ .

6 Triangle ABC is congruent to triangle XYZ. Triangle XYZ is congruent to triangle PQR. Therefore _____ is congruent to _____ .

7 Mary's sister's mother is Genevieve's aunt. Therefore, Genevieve and Mary are _____ .

8 Harry bought a used car at Sam's Used Cars. All the cars ever sold at Sam's Used Cars are junk on wheels. Therefore _____ .

9 Among Women's National Basketball Association (WNBA) Western Division teams, the Phoenix Mercury are better than the Minnesota Lynx. And the Minnesota Lynx are better than the San Antonio Silverstars. Therefore _____ .

10 In the Eastern Division of the WNBA the Connecticut Sun, the Washington Mystics, and the Chicago Sky are very competitive with one another. The Atlanta Dream is very competitive with the Connecticut Sun. Therefore the Atlanta Dream is _____ .

False Classification

Suppose "Criminals enjoy mafia movies" and "Cassandra enjoys mafia movies" are both true. It does not follow that Cassandra is a criminal. The same feature or attribute can be true of two groups or two individuals without requiring that one group can be classified as part of the other group or that the two individuals can be classified as the same person. The facts that Emile attended the campus concert and so did 50 students from the local high school does not make Emile a high school student.

Yet examples of False Classification seem remarkably abundant. Here are more examples of this fallacy.

- A good number of residents of Utah enjoy reading popular fiction. Some who enjoy popular fiction also enjoy windsurfing. So, a good number of residents of Utah enjoy windsurfing.

- The police profiler said that the rapist was a white male, age 25–35, and aggressive. The suspect is a white male, 28 years old, and aggressive. This establishes that the suspect is the rapist.

- There are ways of telling whether or not she is a witch. Wood burns and so do witches burn. So how do we tell if she is made of wood? Well, wood floats. And ducks float. So, if she floats, then she weighs the same as a duck and therefore she is made of wood. And therefore . . ., she is a witch! (Condensed from *Monty Python and the Holy Grail* Scene 5: "She's a Witch," 1975.)

Millions have enjoyed the humor that Monty Python created out of this fallacy in the famous "She's a Witch" scene from *Monty Python and the Holy Grail*. Go to **www.TheThinkSpot.com** to access the clip.

The knight's deductive reasoning implies certain death for the poor woman accused of witchcraft, but only if all three premises are true.

Premise #1. If she floats she is a witch and we shall burn her.

Premise #2. If she does not float, she'll drown.

Premise #3. Either she will float or she will not float. [Unspoken.]

Conclusion. Ergo, she dies.

Fallacies of Composition and Division

Reasoning about the relationships of parts and wholes can appear to be deductively valid, but fail because the attribute that applies to the parts may not apply to the whole, or visa versa. Here are some examples.

- It is in each person's financial interest to cheat a little on his or her income tax return. So, it is financially good for the nation if people cheat on their taxes.

- No muscle or joint or organ or cell in your body has the right to give its individual informed consent to a medical procedure. So, why should you, who are composed entirely of those many parts, have such a right?

In the first example, an attribute of individual people who pay taxes is being illogically attributed to the class of objects ("the nation"). The good

Evaluate Argument Worthiness and Explain

Assume that all the premises that are asserted in the arguments below are true. Apply the remaining tests to evaluate each argument to determine which are worthy of acceptance. Begin with the Test of Logical Strength. Remember, if the argument fails a test you do not have to apply any further tests because, at that point, the argument has been found to be unworthy of acceptance. In each case, give a detailed explanation to support your evaluation. State in your own words why each argument is worthy or unworthy of acceptance. Hint: Be prepared to add implicit but unspoken premises and assumptions. After finishing the chapter, see if you want to amend any of your answers.

1 Anthony was at risk of dying from the severe fall that he took when he was climbing. Many who had the same near-fatal experience become averse to climbing afterward. So, Anthony will become averse to climbing after his fall.

2 Susan is John's younger sister. Linda is John's elder sister. So, Linda is Susan's elder sister.

3 I want to buy a boat and you want to buy a car. If we buy a car we can't use it for fishing or to go tubing. But if we buy a boat we can't use it in the city or anywhere else but at the lake. Either way we're stuck.

4 Blood samples taken from the crime scene were type AB. The accused person's blood is type AB. Therefore, the accused was at the scene of the crime.

5 Either we'll study together tonight for tomorrow's exam, or we will both blow it off. I'm too tired to study tonight. So, we're going to blow it off.

6 Whenever I play the lottery, the number I put in is my birthday. If that's not my lucky number, then I don't have one.

7 Randolph knows that John Glenn was a senator. John Glenn was an astronaut. Therefore Randolph knows that John Glenn was an astronaut.

8 Every member of the House of Representatives is under the age of 90. Therefore, the House of Representatives is an organ of government that was created less than 90 years ago.

9 73 percent of the people surveyed said that they wanted universal health care coverage. 54 percent said that they were worried about the cost of the program or the quality of the care that would be provided. Therefore, the American people are opposed to the President's health care reform legislation.

10 Obama has been president for six months, and the economic recession has not gone away. He needs to take full responsibility for the sorry state of the economy.

11 My dear old Uncle Joe has a statue of the Red Faced Warrior on his kitchen table. It faces the side door, and he says that it keeps bad people from coming into his house. He also has a picture of St. Christopher taped to the dashboard of his old Buick and a rosary draped over the rearview mirror. More protection he claims. On the other hand, he never locks his house, and he needs to get his eyes checked!

12 But if we don't study together, then I'm not going to get through the course. And if I don't get through the course, then I'm going to ruin by GPA and lose my financial aid. So if we don't study together tonight, then I'm going to lose my financial aid.

13 We've lost six games in a row; our luck has to change today.

14 We didn't know what to do to improve sales. So, we all started wearing bow ties and navy blue sweaters to work. And look, three weeks later sales are way up. I'm sure it's our new office dress code.

15 "It's January tenth and already six people have ordered new glasses with plastic frames. Last year only four people had ordered plastic frames by this date. That's an increase of 50 percent. We had better stock up. It's going to be a busy year."

16 Everyone loves ice cream. Children love ice cream. So, everyone's a child.

17 Water is our most precious resource. So, a towel on the rack means "I'll use it again" and a towel on the floor means, "Please replace."

of each is not necessarily the good of all. The second attempts to withhold from individuals the right to give informed consent because none of our body parts have that right. These examples of the Fallacy of Composition, so called because these fallacious arguments err by reasoning that a group has exactly the same attributes that each of its members have. "I don't know, Bill. Everyone on the Budget Committee is really smart. But, wow that Committee makes stupid decisions. How can that be?" Simple. What is true of individuals is necessarily true of groups, including how well the group performs. Now consider these three examples:

- The president of the large corporation sent a memo to every vice president, director, manager, and supervisor saying, "In corporations of our size with hundreds of employees we can be certain that 10 percent of our total workforce is performing at a substandard level. Therefore, I am directing everyone in charge of a unit of 10 or more people to immediately terminate one person of every ten in the unit. Forward the names of your substandard employee to Human Resources by 5:00 PM tomorrow."

- Fetal stem cell research should be banned because every single human cell is a human being, and human beings should not be used for medical research without their informed consent.

- The average class size at the university is 35 people. Therefore, every class you are taking this term must have 34 other people enrolled in it.

These three examples illustrate the Fallacy of Division, which is the same err, but committed in the opposite direction. Fallacies of Division attribute to each individual member of a group a characteristic that is true of the group as a whole. In the first, an attribute of the class of objects known as the corporation's total workforce is being illogically attributed to each individual small department or unit. In the second, an attribute of human beings—the right to informed consent—is being attributed to each individual part of a human being, each cell. In the third, the average class size, which is an attribute of the university, is illogically attributed to each and every class being offered, as if small seminars and large lectures did not exist.

An Act of Mercy?

Any sparks of humor we might find in the Monty Python silliness are quickly extinguished by the realization that witch burning really happened. Innocent women suspected of witchcraft were interrogated to the point of exhaustion. Misfortunes that may have befallen others in their community were interpreted as evidence that the accused had put a witch's evil spell on that unfortunate person. Any blemish on the accused woman's body—a bruise, a birthmark, or a scar from an old wound or burn—could be interpreted as the "mark of Satan," for further confirmation of her guilt.

As the video clip from *The Day the Universe Changed* illustrates, given our 21st-century worldview, the burning of a woman alive is a horrific killing of an innocent person. But, given their 17th-century worldview, the people living in Scotland only four centuries ago interpreted the very same event as an act of mercy. The laws of logic are the same here and now as they were then and there. What has changed? The differences in how the event is seen result from the vastly divergent set of implicit unspoken assumptions that constitute the two world-views. It is within the context of our "truths" about the world that the laws of logic function. Today in parts of the world where a non-scientific worldview prevails, beliefs in voodoo and magic have a very real influence over the lives and decisions people make. In those communities, it would be "common sense" to fear that some might have the power to cause harm or misfortune simply by thinking evil thoughts and incanting spells.

Learning to make logical inferences is vital. But logic alone is not enough. Strong critical thinking requires more than skillful inference, analysis, explanation, and interpretation. It requires courageous truth-seeking and the intellectual honesty to reflect from time to time on our own most cherished beliefs and unspoken assumptions. Which of our 21st-century practices that we see as righteous and sensible will the people in the 24th century look back on in horror? Access the video clip at **www.TheThinkSpot.com**. Be advised that the images in this clip may be disturbing.

False Reference

Suppose that "The dean knows that this year the School of Engineering award for Best Senior Project should go to Team Steelheads." And suppose that "The four members of the team are Karen, Anna, Dwight, and Angela" is true. It does not follow that the dean knows that Karen, Anna, Dwight, and Angela are winners of this year's award. Why? Because the dean may not know that they are the members of Team Steelhead. Knowing, believing, wanting, or intending something when it is described or named in one way does not imply that the person necessarily knows, believes, wants, or intends that very same thing as described or named in another way. That is, unless we add that the person is aware that the two descriptions actually refer to the same thing. Here are two more examples of the fallacy of False Reference.

- Tyler, who is ten, has often told his parents that in college he wants to learn how big buildings and bridges are built. These are subjects addressed in civil engineering. Therefore, Tyler has said that he wants to study civil engineering in college.

- Anthony heard that the winner of the Tour de France used banned performance-enhancing substances. Spanish rider, Alberto Contador, won the Tour de France. Therefore, Anthony heard that Alberto Contador used banned performance-enhancing substances.

Inductions and the Evidence at Hand

In contrast to the structural necessity of valid deductive reasoning, inductive reasoning is probabilistic. An **inductively justified** (or "warranted") **argument** is an argument such that were all of its premises true then its conclusion would most likely or very probably also be true. Here is an example, based on a story from the CBS series *CSI*.[v]

- A man is found dead of a gunshot wound to the stomach, his body in a seated position at the base of a tree in a forest. It is deer hunting season. Except for not wearing an orange safety vest, he is dressed like a hunter. His hunting rifle, never having been fired, lies on the ground at his side. The evidence strongly suggests that his death resulted from a hunting accident. The investigator infers by inductive reasoning that had the man been wearing his orange safety vest, he probably would be alive today.

The investigator's inductive inference is plausible. Although we can imagine alternative scenarios, in the absence of any further information, we have no basis for evaluating the investigator's induction as other than warranted.

In contrast to deductions, which depend on the meanings of words and rules of grammar, inductive reasoning depends on the evidence at hand.

Thinking Critically — Create Your Own Examples Part 1

Write two valid arguments based on each of these deductive templates:

Denying the Consequent
Affirming the Antecedent
Disjunctive Syllogism
Applying a Generalization
Applying an Exception
Transitivity Relationship
Reflexivity Relationship
Identity Relationship

Write two fallacious arguments exemplifying each of these errors:

The Fallacy of Affirming the Consequent
The Fallacy of Denying the Antecedent
The Fallacy of False Classification
The Fallacy of Composition
The Fallacy of Division
The Fallacy of False Reference

New information can lead us to revise conclusions reached using inductive inferences. Take the *CSI* story described on page 117, for example. Suppose we come to learn the following additional facts:

- The time of death was mid-afternoon, a time when deer are not hunted. Deer are hunted at dawn and at dusk. The dead man had not purchased a hunting license. There was gunshot residue on the man's clothing, which indicates that he was shot at very close range. The gun that shot him could not have been more than a foot or two from his body. A $1,000,000 insurance policy had been purchased on his life only two weeks prior to his death. The policy had been paid for with his wife's credit card. The wife is the beneficiary who would receive the money if he should die by illness or by accident.

The initial inductive conclusion, death by accident, looks mistaken in the light of this new information. Now a more plausible conclusion would be that the man had been murdered by his wife or perhaps by someone she hired. Her motive, of course, would be the insurance money.

Conclusions accepted on the basis of justified inductive arguments remain subject to revision or possible rejection based on new information. The *CSI* example is fiction, of course. But there are real-life examples, too. A person may be found guilty beyond a reasonable doubt based on the circumstantial evidence presented to the jury at the time of the trial. A great many people who are found guilty really are guilty. Even so, new information may come to light years later that demonstrates that, in some cases, the guilty verdict was mistaken. The Innocence Project, which has exonerated hundreds of innocent people wrongly convicted, is a sobering reminder to us all about how difficult and yet how important it is to evaluate the logical strength of inductive arguments carefully.

∧
∧   How does the Innocence Project use
∧   critical thinking to free dead men
walking who are innocent?

tested positive. Based on the data from these inspections, we estimate that **73 percent of the hotel room beds in this city are infested with bedbugs.**

3 I have visited San Francisco maybe seven times over the past 25 years. It is one of my favorite vacation cities. I've gone in the summer and in the winter. And I can tell you one thing, bring a coat because **it's probably going to be cloudy and cold in San Francisco if you go in August.**

It is easy to imagine scenarios in which the information in the premises is true but the conclusion may not apply. We can conjure the possibility that someone over 60 does not like oldies. We can imagine that there may be one hotel in the city where most of the beds are not infested. It is no problem to think of the possibility that there should be at least one warm sunny August day in San Francisco. But, developing a possible counterexample does not necessarily diminish the logical strength of an inductive argument. A single counterexample is sufficient to invalidate a deductive argument, but not an inductive argument generalization. In the first example we have a somewhat modest assertion about what people over the age of 60 "tend to" prefer. The second says that it applies to 73 percent of the hotel beds, but not that the infected beds are evenly distributed among the city's 50 hotels. And the third says that it is "probably" going to be cold in San Francisco in August.

To evaluate the logical strength of inductive generalizations, we need to do more than find a single counterexample. We must, instead, examine whether the sampling of cases reported in the premises is adequate to support the probabilistic inferences that are drawn. This means asking four questions and finding satisfactory answers to each of them.

Was the correct group sampled?

Were the data obtained in an effective way?

Were enough cases considered?

Was the sample representatively structured?

EVALUATING GENERALIZATIONS

A generalization may be based on data gathered systematically or unsystematically. We would be wise to place greater confidence in the claim if it were supported by data gathered more systematically, rather than on simply one or two happenstance personal observations. Consider the following three inductive generalizations. The claims, which are bolded, are supported by premises that report personal experiences, conversations focused on these topics, or information derived from historical records or opinion surveys.

1 **People over the age of 60 tend to prefer to listen to oldies**. This claim is based on the data gathered in telephone surveys of persons between the ages of 60 and 90, which were conducted in Florida, Arizona, Ohio, and Connecticut. In all, 435 interviews were conducted. Participants were asked to identify which type of music they preferred to listen to most. They were given eight choices: Classical, Pop, R&B, Country, Oldies, Broadway, Religious, and Top 40.

2 In May, inspectors from the city sanitation department made unannounced visits to all 20 hotels in the downtown area and to 10 of the other 30 hotels within the city limits. The 10 were representative of the type and quality ratings of those other 30 hotels. The inspectors by law could demand access to any room in the hotel to look for pests and to evaluate cleanliness. Careful records were kept of each room inspected. In all, 2,000 beds were examined for bedbugs. 1,460 beds

Was the Correct Group Sampled?

The first example makes a claim about people over the age of 60. The premises tell us that adults between the ages of 60 and 90 were sampled. That is the correct group to sample if one wishes to make generalizations about persons in that age range. It would not do, obviously, to sample people under the age of 60 and then present those data as a basis for a claim about people over that age. One would think that sampling the wrong population would not be a mistake commonly made. But for years, pharmaceutical companies made inferences about children's drug dosages and the effects of various medications on women based largely on studies conducted on adult males. More recently, we have learned that there are genetic factors that affect the rate at which common pain relievers, like the ibuprofen in Motrin, are metabolized. This new finding should influence dosage recommendations for those who are poor metabolizers (e.g., six to ten percent of Caucasians).[vi]

Were the Data Obtained in an Effective Way?

In our example about the music listening preferences of adults over 60, we see that the data were obtained via telephone surveys. We might think that a telephone survey may not be as efficient as using a Web-based survey, which would reach many more people and be much more cost-effective. But, upon reflection, it does not seem unreasonable to use the telephone to reach older adults, many of whom may not be comfortable with the use of computers and Web-based survey tools. Finding an effective method to

<<< If one counterexample invalidates a deductive argument, can one bed bug or one sunny day invalidate example 2 or 3 from page 118?

gather data from the sample is often a major challenge for researchers.[vii] For example, consider how difficult it is to gather high-quality data about the state of mind of combat veterans in the year after their return from a war zone.

Were Enough Cases Considered?

In general, the more cases the better. But there comes a point of diminishing returns. If we are trying to make a reasonable generalization about millions of people who live in major metropolitan areas like Boston, New York, Chicago, or Los Angeles, it is neither necessary nor cost-effective to survey even one percent of a group so large. At some point the distribution of responses simply adds numbers, but the proportions of responses selecting each possible answer do not change significantly. Social scientists have worked out sophisticated statistical methods to provide a precise answer to the question of sample size. The answer establishes a minimum necessary depending on the kinds of statistical analysis to be conducted and the degree of accuracy needed for the question at hand. For example, to keep us up to date on the likely voting patterns in a forthcoming election, it is sufficient to track what likely voters are going to do within a margin of error of plus or minus two percent. Called a "power analysis," the calculations social scientists make begin with a projection of the number of cases expected to fall randomly into each possible category. Scientists can then determine whether the observed distribution varies significant from the expected random distribution.[viii] As a rough rule of thumb, they would want at least 25 cases per possible response category. In our "Oldies" example there are eight categories of music. So, we would need a sample of at least 400 individuals. We have 435, so the sample size is adequate. But we do not have a claim that reports a percentage. In our example the claim reports a *tendency*. Social scientists would not regard a tendency as being a strong enough deviation from random to be called "statistically significant."

Was the Sample Representatively Structured?

We said that 435 was an adequate sample size for our example, but were the 435 representative of the population being talked about in the claim? The claim talks about everyone over the age of 60. Because more than half of the people between 60 and 90 are women, and because women might have different preferences with regard to the music they like to listen to, we would need to be satisfied that the 435 reflected the actual ratio of women and men in that age group. We do not know that from the information given. If we hypothesize that music-listening preferences might be related to educational background, race, ethnicity or socioeconomic status, then we would want to assure ourselves that the 435 was representative of the distribution of those factors among the target population. Because we do not know if 435 is a representative sample, we cannot answer this fourth question in the affirmative. And, as a result, example #1 on page 118 is not logically strong.

COINCIDENCES, CORRELATIONS, AND CAUSES

Decades ago scientists first observed that there were a number of cases of heart disease where, coincidentally, the person was a smoker. Further systematic research demonstrated a strong positive correlation between smoking and heart disease. Scientists hypothesized that perhaps smoking was a contributing factor. However, before making a defensible argument that quitting smoking would reduce a person's chances of heart disease, researchers had to explain scientifically how smoking caused heart disease. Researchers demonstrated scientifically that nicotine constricts blood vessels in the heart, which reduces blood flow to the heart muscle, thus causing heart attacks.

The progression from coincidence to correlation to causal explanations marks our progress in being able to explain and to predict events. At first we may observe two events and think that their occurrence is a chance coincidence. Then, as more data are systematically gathered and analyzed, we may discover that the two events are statistically correlated. And, with further experimental investigation, we may learn that in fact what had at first seemed like only a coincidence actually occurs because of important causal factors. When and if we reach that stage we will have generated a causal explanation.

Coincidences

If two events happen to occur together by chance, we call that a coincidence. For example, annually in the United States on average 90 people are

Thinking Critically   Hotel Bedbugs and August Cold

Evaluate the bedbug example and the San Francisco in August weather example. In each case ask:

Was the correct group sampled?
Were the data obtained in an effective way?
Were enough cases considered?
Was the sample representatively structured?

When the premises do not provide enough information for a satisfactory answer, explain what information one would have to find, as we did when we noted what would be needed for the sample of 435 to be considered representative of the population of people over the age of 60.

Thinking Critically — Grading Written Submissions

If the purpose of grading is to identify which essays fall into which broad groups, e.g., "Fail, Pass, High Pass" or "F, D, C, B, A," and if a computer can manage this faster, with greater consistency, and with an accuracy that matches a well-trained human reader, it seems reasonable to use the computer.

If, on the other hand, the purpose of grading is to advance learning through commenting on the content and presentation of the student's written work, then automated grading does not seem to be a feasible nor desirable alternative. To provide useful feedback, the grader must understand the content being presented, follow the reasoning and the evidence presented, and be able to interpret, evaluate, and comment accurately and usefully.

Well-programmed computers and well-trained graders may assign different grades under certain conditions. These represent threats to the validity of the assigned grade. For example, essays that use information that is not factual may receive higher grades from the computer than human readers who recognized those factual errors. Essays that rely on irony, hyperbole, sarcasm, and humor may receive very different grades from humans and from machines, which presumably would neither recognize nor attend to those stylistic differences. Essays that use plagiarized material might receive a lower grade from the computer, because it can check for the replication of text published elsewhere, than from a human grader who may not recognize the plagiarized material.

There are threats to the reliability of human graders because humans can become fatigued and less attentive as they grade written submissions for long periods of time. Different human graders may give the same essay different grades because they disagree on the relative importance of various elements in the essay. Humans may be influenced by their own personal beliefs, tending to give somewhat higher grades to essays that reflect their point of view. Computers do not suffer from these problems.

If the purpose of grading written submissions is to determine which candidates shall be admitted to highly competitive programs and which shall be excluded, then the threats to validity identified here may lead to unfortunate mistakes. If the purpose of grading written submissions is to determine who shall receive honors, awards, financial support, grant funding, publication, or special privileges, then categorizing essays into broad groups must be refined so that the most meritorious can be validly and reliably identified.

No one would want to be denied admission, funding or the honor she or he was due because the grader (computer or human) failed to give a written submission its true score.

---

killed by lightning. That comes to one death for every 345,000 flashes in the United States.[ix] What are the chances that a given individual will be killed by lightning in a given year in the United States, given that the population is roughly 306,000,000? That coincidence has roughly one chance in 3,400,000 of occurring, all else being equal. The qualifier "all else being equal" means that the individual does not do something to increase or decrease his or her chances of being killed by lightning in the United States, such as becoming a permanent resident of some other country or standing in an open field holding aluminum rods in the air during a lightning storm. But, all things being equal, we can use inductive reasoning and statistical facts to calculate the probabilities that a given coincidence might occur.

Although we cannot predict with certainty that the next time you flip a coin it will come up heads, we can predict with a high level of confidence what will happen 50 percent of the time in the long run. We know how to calculate mathematical probabilities for events such as these because we know that each individual outcome occurs randomly with equal frequency. If we roll two regular dice, the result will be two sixes 1 time out of 36 rolls over the long haul. We calculate that by multiplying the chance of rolling a six on die #1, which is 1 out of 6, times the chance of rolling a six on die #2, which is also 1 out of 6. Then we multiply those odds to get the mathematical probability of both outcomes happening together—the product is 1 out of 36.

The lavish luxury hotels in Las Vegas and other gambling hubs are monuments to the reliability, over the long run, of these calculated coincidences. If 98 percent of the money bet in a casino on any given day goes back to the players as winnings that day, then on an average day the casino can be very confident of retaining 2 percent of every dollar bet. The more money bet, the more dollars that 2 percent represents. Unless more than 100 percent of the money bet is returned to the bettors as winnings, we can be sure that over the long run the bettors go home losers, not winners and not "breaking even." An individual person winning a specific bet is, considered in itself, a random coincidence. The totality of all those coincidences can be aggregated into a large and highly predictable profit margin for the casino. The best generalization to infer is that, in the end, the casino will very likely separate the chronic gambler from more and more of his or her money.

Correlations

As in the smoking and heart attack example on page 119, when the same coincidence is observed over and over again, people begin to suspect that the events may be related by something more than pure random chance. Even before knowing that one event may be the cause of another, we can determine whether the two are correlated. Correlations, calculated using statistical analyses, describe the degree to which two different sets of events are aligned. For example, scores on critical thinking skills tests are positively correlated with student success on state licensure exams in a number of health sciences professions.[x] We might wish to speculate about the possible causal relationships of critical thinking skill to academic or professional success. But simply having the correlation in hand can be valuable to those professional programs that have more applicants than can be accepted. The admissions committees can use an applicant's critical thinking skills test score in the way that it uses GPAs or letters of reference, namely as another valuable data point to consider when making its decision to admit or not to admit an applicant.[xi]

When a research project reports that a statistically significant correlation has been found between events of kind #1 (scores on a critical thinking skills test) and events of kind #2 (scores on a state's professional licensure examination), that means that the relationship between the two kinds of events is viewed as not likely to be happenstance or chance. Of course, there could be an error in this estimate, but the minimum threshold for this error is 5 percent. So, we can be 95 percent confident that the two events are really correlated. Even greater confidence that the events reported did not happen by mere chance can be found in many fields of research in which statistical significance is reported with 99 percent confidence, at 1 percent or even less (0.001) chance of error. Even so, we remain in the realm of inductive reasoning because the inference, which is logically very strong, holds open the possibility that the findings reported may have happened by mere chance. The odds are very definitely against that possibility, however. If the 0.001 confidence level is reached, then the odds that the conclusion is mistaken one in 1,000.

Well-researched correlations can be powerful tools. Consider this possibility. Suppose that writing assignments, which employ grammatically complex constructions, use expected words and expressions, include sentences with greater average word counts, and include fewer spelling mistakes are statistically significantly correlated with higher grades on those assignments. Based on this, we can design computer programs that assign grades by parsing grammar and counting words.[xii] The computer does not need to understand the meaning of the essay nor does it have to evaluate the quality of arguments used. The grades assigned by computers can then be checked against the grades that human evaluators assign to those same essays. Refinements can then be made in the computer program's grading algorithms to achieve ever closer approximation to the results human beings would have produced. When the computer program is refined to the extent that it assigns the same grades as well-qualified human beings to 99.9 percent of the essays, then essay grading can be automated. To assign you the grade your professor would have assigned, the computer never needs to understand what you wrote. This is not science fiction. Automated grading is used by the Educational Testing Service.[xiii]

Causes

Documenting that a causal relationship exists between events requires more than demonstrating a strong correlation. The intellectual challenges of designing research capable of revealing the causal mechanisms at work in nature is important and interesting work. Perhaps this is why many strong critical thinkers find careers in scientific and technical fields attractive. Causal explanations are desirable because they enable us to explain, predict, and control parts of the natural world. In Chapter 13 we will explore the investigatory methods used by scientists to achieve causal explanations.

It is not always possible to move all the way from coincidence to correlation to causal explanation in every field of inquiry. For example, predicting the behavior of the stock market remains a hazardous and uncertain adventure. Because we do not really know how all the factors that influence the market interact, we are not able to predict with high levels of confidence what the market will do on any given day. Some financial analysts turn out to be right, while others are wrong. Often, it seems as though the analysts announce why the market reacted as it did on a given day only after the day's trading is completed. Then, we hear that the market responded to changes in the jobless rate, the prime interest rate, consumer confidence level, or something else. But those same analysts are not able to use those same factors to predict accurately what the market will do in the future. If their explanations of the past behavior of the market were correct, one would expect that they would be able to make reliable predictions about the market's future behavior. That we are not able, yet, to make good predictions about the future leads us to suspect that we do not yet know, beyond the level of coincidences and correlations, what causal factors, individually or in combination with other

Is it only luck that generated the funding to build these lavish hotels?

causal factors, are relevant to explaining the behavior of the stock market. One can only wonder how relevant the factors those prognosticators identify as causes really are.

FALLACIES MASQUERADING AS STRONG INDUCTIVE ARGUMENTS

Just as some fallacies are presented as valid deductive arguments, others are presented as justified inductive arguments. They draw their power to deceive and persuade from how closely they resemble the genuine article. A closer analysis often helps us avoid being misled by the following fallacies.

Erroneous Generalization

Generalizations, even those based on solid evidence, can be deceptively fallacious, too. At times, we generalize from too little information, exaggerating

Thinking Critically — Group Project Challenge: The U.S. Census

There are two ways to conduct a census. Contact everyone and gather the data being sought, or generalize from well-structured representative samples. This group project invites you to evaluate the methodology used by the U.S. government and make recommendations for improving that methodology. Begin your investigation here: **http://www.census.gov/popest/topics/methodology/**.

To fully evaluate the methodology and make reasonable recommendations, your group will want to consider first and foremost the logical strength of the two alternatives (100% count vs. estimates based on

samples.) When considering the sampling alternative, keep in mind the importance of sample size and representative structure. For both alternatives, keep in mind the question of the method of gathering data. For example, going door to door will assure that homeless Americans are systematically excluded.

Other considerations that may weigh on your ultimate recommendations may include the cost (money and time) of the two alternatives, the political consequences of each, and the social value associated with enlisting volunteers in an effort of national scope.

the claim beyond what the data support. At other times, the exaggeration results from sampling errors. Consider these examples:

- The paper showed a picture of the CEO in chains doing the perp walk as he was being led off to jail. Another middle-aged white guy with a $400 haircut! Same as Bernard Madoff, the guy who swindled 170 million dollars out of rich people with his phony investment Ponzi scheme. All those corporate thieves are overpaid white guys.

- Many medical professionals recommend taking baby aspirin to control blood pressure. More is always better, right? Well, if one aspirin a day is good for you, then two have to be even better.

- Seventy-one percent of the students enrolled in my educational methods course are women. So, women really like my courses.

In each of these cases, even if the premises were true, the conclusion goes unjustifiably beyond what those premises could support. Review each of these three examples and amend them by refining the conclusion so that it is logically justified by the premises given.

Playing with Numbers

Arguments, which use raw numbers when percentages would present a more fair-minded description, or use percentages when the raw numbers would present the more fair-minded description, can be evaluated as fallacies of Playing with Numbers. Arguments that cite statistics or numbers but do not provide sufficient information to make a good judgment about the significance of those numerical data are species of the Playing with Numbers Fallacy as well. For example:

- Six hundred people are affected by the decision you made prohibiting pythons as pets in this apartment complex. I want you to know that 80 percent of the people surveyed said that they wanted you to reconsider your decision. How many people was that, you ask? Well, I personally talked to my four roommates and three agreed with me, which makes 80 percent.

- The average salary for postal workers is 5.6 percent higher than the average salary for the employees of the Transportation Safety Administration. This establishes that postal workers are overpaid.

- The National Highway Traffic Safety Administration reports that there were 26,689 automobile fatalities in 2008. That same year there were 5,290 motorcyclists' fatalities. This means that driving or riding in a car is five times more dangerous than riding a motorcycle.

Review these examples and add premises or restate the conclusion, or do both in order to transform each into an inductive argument that gives reasonable justification for believing that the claim—as you may have restated it—is now very probably true.

False Dilemma

A real dilemma is a situation in which all our choices are bad. In the story, "The Cold Equations," which opened this chapter, Thomas Barton faced a real dilemma. Every option was undesirable; no matter what he decided, someone would have to die. But, at times we may think we are facing a dilemma when we are not. The world often offers more options than we may perceive at first. At times, the consequences of one or another of our options may not be nearly as dreadful as we initially imagine them to be. As the following examples indicate, at times what appears to be a real dilemma turns out upon closer analysis to be a false dilemma.

- The kidnappers have taken eight people hostage and are holding them at a farmhouse just outside town. If the SWAT team assaults the farmhouse, the hostages could be killed. But if we give into the kidnappers' demands for ransom and safe passage out of the country, we'll only be encouraging more kidnappings of innocent people. What can we do? There are no good alternatives.

- If I go to the job interview laid-back and unprepared, I'll blow it. But if I prepare for the interview I could overdo it and be so nervous that I'll blow it anyway. I'm a mess. There's no way to get ready for this interview.

As these examples show, another good name for this fallacy is "The Either/Or Fallacy" because the situations often appear to be limited to one option or another, but on further examination, additional options emerge. This is true of the first example. Assaulting the farmhouse and giving in are not the only possible options. Negotiating for the release of some or all of the hostages is an option. Waiting until those inside the farmhouse run out of food or water is another option. Blasting the farmhouse with mega decibels of sound and shooting teargas in through the windows might force the occupants out. In other words, a little creativity can often reveal a way out of a false dilemma.

The Gambler's Fallacy

Random events, by definition, are not causally connected. But, at times, we make arguments that wrongly assume that what happens by chance is somehow connected or correlated with things we can control. We can use "Gambler's Fallacy" as an umbrella term to remind ourselves that random events are, in fact, random and that drawing inferences based on the assumption that they are correlated or causally connected is a mistake. Here are some examples of fallacious inferences that attribute more to mere coincidences than strong inductive reasoning would warrant.

- If we're going to Vegas, I'm going to bring my blue socks and I'm going to wear them in the casino. They're my lucky socks. Although I've lost money plenty of times wearing them, I've never won at slots without those blue socks on. So, I won't win a dime from the slots if I don't wear those socks!

- Whenever I leave the apartment, I rub the tummy of the little statue of Buddha we have on the table near the door. It makes me happy to do that because I know that it brings me good karma.

- I just flipped a coin twice and it came up heads both times. So, the next two times I flip it, the coin will come up tails because the chances are 50/50.

- Ramirez is batting for the Los Angeles Dodgers. Manny's batting average this year is .333. This is his third trip to the plate this game. He grounded into a double play his first trip and struck out his second time. So, he's going to get a hit this time.

<<< Statistically, who is more at risk, car drivers or motorcyclists?

Write three fallacious arguments exemplifying each of these errors:

The Erroneous Generalization Fallacy

The Playing with Numbers Fallacy

The False Dilemma Fallacy

The Gambler's Fallacy

The False Cause Fallacy

The Slippery Slope Fallacy

False Cause

When two events occur one right after the other, we may mistakenly infer that the first is the cause of the second.

- Look, I put the CD into the player and the windshield wipers wouldn't turn on. It has to be that the problem with the wipers is somehow connected to the CD player.

- It's hard to know exactly what made her so angry. She seemed fine when we were talking earlier about what a jerk her former boyfriend was. Then you came in and boom! She exploded. I think it's your fault.

Called "Post hoc, propter hoc" ["After this, because of this"], confusing temporal proximity with causality is one of several mistakes grouped together under the heading of False Cause Fallacies. Another mistake is to confuse a correlation with a cause.

- Our information shows that in times of economic growth, the hemlines on women's skirts go from below the knee to above the knee. And in times of a bear market when the economy slows down, the hemlines that are considered stylish go down below the knee, at times to mid-calf or even ankle height. I know how we can cure the current recession! All we need to do to pull out of the current recession is to make the fashion designers raise hemlines.

Other mistakes often grouped under the broad heading of False Cause Fallacies result from confusing symptoms, outcomes, or intentions with causes. Here are examples:

- The pressure was intense that day. I had to get from the university to my job, a drive that normally took 25 minutes. But the professor kept us late and then my car wouldn't start. You know there had to be a traffic jam on the freeway that day. And I needed to get to work because I had to make this major presentation. My head was aching and my heart was beating so fast. I felt all sweaty and it was getting harder and harder to breathe. I think that it was all because I couldn't get any air. That's where the pressure was coming from. No air.

- Three years ago we instituted a policy of Zero Tolerance for binge drinking in campus-controlled housing units. Simultaneously, we instituted a nonpunitive program of substance abuse counseling. Today we have been honored by the state legislature because the reported incidents of binge drinking have dropped 32 percent compared to numbers from three years ago. The counseling program is why. That program has greatly reduced the number of incidents of binge drinking in campus-controlled housing.

- We wanted it more than they did! And that's why we won.

Slippery Slope

Everyone knows that simply beginning something is no assurance that it will be completed. For a variety of reasons, too many good students never finish their degree programs. Not everyone who takes a drink becomes an alcoholic. Not everyone who buys a gun becomes a killer. The Slippery Slope Fallacy makes the false assumption that discrete events are linked together so that the first step in the process necessarily results in some significant, usually bad, result way down the road somewhere. The image conjured by this fallacy is of walking along the edge of a muddy wet ridge. One step over that edge and we slide on our butts all the way to the bottom. Another image associated with this fallacy is the "camel's nose under the tent" image. Once the camel gets its nose under the tent, there is no way to prevent the whole, huge clumsy animal from entering one's well-ordered abode.

- If you ever smoke a joint, then you are on the path to perdition. One puff and there is no stopping the inevitable fall. Next it will be snorting coke, then shooting up heroin, leading to addiction with track marks in your arms and hepatitis or worse from contaminated needles.

- I warn you, you had better come to every training session. We start lessons Monday. If you miss the first day, then you'll be behind and you will never catch up.

A person can make a mistake and recover from it. And some of the initial stages that are alleged to be dreadful turn out not to be problems at all. And the middle ground is a very good place to make one's stand. To quote Terence of ancient Rome, "Moderation in all things."

Fallacies—Common Yet Misleading Errors of Reasoning (Chapters 7 & 8 Combined)			
Arguments that Fail the Test of Relevance	**Fallacies of Relevance**	Appeals to Ignorance Appeals to the Mob Appeals to Emotion Ad Hominem Attacks	The Straw Man Fallacy Playing with Words Misuse of Authority
Arguments that Fail the Test of Logical Strength	**Fallacies Masquerading as Valid Deductive Arguments**	Affirming the Consequent Denying the Antecedent False Classification	Fallacy of Composition Fallacy of Division False Reference
	Fallacies Masquerading as Warranted Inductive Arguments	Erroneous Generalization Playing with Numbers False Dilemma	Gambler's Fallacy False Cause Slippery Slope
Fail the Test of Non-Circularity		Circular Reasoning	

The evaluation of inductive and deductive reasoning is a ubiquitous part of everyday life. We evaluate inferences when talking with friends, working on projects, enduring television commercials, or reasoning through a decision. In this chapter we worked to strengthen our critical thinking skill of evaluation of arguments in several ways: We examined a number of deductive reasoning patterns that derive their validity from the meanings of terms and the grammar of our shared language. We then considered inductive arguments that offer to generalize from a limited number of experiences and samplings of data to reach justified claims about the characteristics of larger populations. We reviewed the roster of fallacies that masquerade as valid deductive arguments or as justified inductive arguments to arm ourselves against their tempting deceits.

Arguments guide us toward an option or away from an option, but, as we shall see in the next two chapters, many of us do not make our decision based exclusively by reflection on worthy arguments. In fact, the empirical research that we shall review will show that we often make important decisions about what to believe or what to do without reflection and despite the arguments. Next we will explore why we humans beings do this, and, more importantly, how we can use critical thinking to help ourselves individually and in groups to be more reflective and more attuned to the power of worthy arguments as we make important decisions.

KEY TERMS

deductively valid argument is an argument such that it is impossible for all of its premises to be true and its conclusion to be false. *110*

inductively justified (or "warranted") **argument** is an argument such that were all of its premises true then its conclusion would most likely or very probably also be true. *117*

FIND IT ON THE THINKSPOT

- Evaluating arguments made in real life introduces the added elements of context, purpose, social customs, and all the unspoken implicit assumptions that constitute our view of the world. The witch-burning scene from *The Day the Universe Changed* (p. 117) brings this home for me every time I see it. That's why I included it for you at **www.TheThinkSpot.com**.

I love Monty Python's humor too. But that "She's a Witch!" clip (p. 115), also found at **www.TheThinkSpot.com**, needed to be put into perspective. We humans often do such violence to each other, fully confident in our beliefs.

- The grittiness of real-life critical thinking about issues affecting millions of people comes out again in the two exercises on the opposite page. When we apply our critical thinking to evaluating the arguments, we should come out with very similar assessments if we are working from the same set of assumptions and premises. I invite you to engage these urgent and difficult issues through the *To Kill a Mockingbird* clip (p. 125) and the *Real Time with Bill Maher* "New Rules" transcript (p. 125) at **www.TheThinkSpot.com**.

Exercises

REFLECTIVE LOG: *TO KILL A MOCKINGBIRD*

Gregory Peck plays the defense attorney, Atticus Finch, in the film *To Kill a Mockingbird.* The story is about a young man accused of rape. In this clip, Atticus Finch is giving his summation to the jury. He must be careful not to alienate the members of the jury, whom he regards as potentially biased against the defendant. Atticus first argues that the prosecution has not proved that a crime was actually committed. He then claims that the accused, Tom Robinson, could not physically have done the things that the prosecution claims. Atticus, believing that he must do more than make claims and logical arguments establishing reasonable doubt, then addresses a key question. Why would the accuser have lied about being raped by the accused? Atticus says

he has pity for the victim and then he argues that by accusing Tom Robinson, she was attempting to rid herself of her own guilt. The defense then attempts to challenge the prejudicial assumption: All Negros are to be distrusted. Listen carefully to the claims and arguments made by Atticus Finch. Transcribe them, use the techniques in Chapter 5 to analyze and map them and, using what you learned in Chapters 7 and 8, evaluate them. Explain your analysis and your evaluation. Would you have made the summation differently? If so, how? Access the video at **www.TheThinkSpot.com**.

GROUP EXERCISE: *REAL TIME WITH BILL MAHER*

At the end of the July 24, 2009, episode of HBO's *Real Time with Bill Maher*, Maher argues in support of the "public option" within the proposed health care reform legislation. The "public option" provision would assure the tens of millions of uninsured and underinsured Americans the option of purchasing health care insurance at an affordable price. Either the government would provide the program through a not-for-profit agency, or the legislation would permit the establishing of co-ops. Maher's barbed statements included these: "If conservatives get to call universal health care 'socialized medicine,' I get to call private, for-profit healthcare 'soulless, vampire bastards making money off human pain." "I would love to have some journalist ask a Republican who talks about socialized medicine: If it's so awful, how come it's what we have for our veterans?"

Using these quotes and other Bill Maher quotes you can locate in episode 161 at **www.TheThinkSpot.com**, present, in as fair-minded and non-incendiary a way as possible, his main reasons, as revealed by the quotes, for supporting the "public option" provision. Map his reasons using the techniques presented in Chapter 5. Then evaluate each of his arguments for using the four-tests process. Remain objective. Resist permitting your personal views on the subject to interfere with the objectivity of your analysis of his views or your evaluation of his arguments.

Many good

judgments we make every day are automatic or reactive, rather than reflective. Well-trained pilots can fly complicated machines and take millions of us to our destinations every day. Through training and repetition, veteran pilots have internalized and made automatic a series of complex analyses, inferences, and quick effective judgments that novice pilots often find mentally all-consuming. Automatic reactions are also seen in more "grounded" drivers and in other situations. For example, bike riders often pedal along, paying more attention to the beauty of the surrounding fields, trees, and streams than on trying to maintain their balance. The process of e-mailing friends is another example. Our fingers tap the keys, but our minds are focused on composing our messages, not on locating the letters on the keyboards. Human beings do not make all their decisions using only their capacity for deliberative reflective thought. Human decision making is more complex.[i] Some judgments, including many good ones, are quick and reactive, not deliberative or reflective. Although some judgments are best made more automatically or reactively, some are best made reflectively.[ii] Our real-life critical thinking question is "Which of our reactive judgments ought we to make reflectively?"

For you or me to maximize our personal potential for developing and applying critical thinking to real-life decision making, we first must understand how human problem solving and decision making function in real life. We know that critical thinking, or reflective purposeful judgment, can and ought to be applied to a very large array of vital issues and important decisions. And we know from our experience that we do not always use critical thinking. The fact that we *do* not use critical thinking does not imply that we *ought* not to be using critical thinking.

This chapter and the next chapter focus on the skill of self-regulation, because monitoring our own decision making and correcting our own decision making turn out to be the key skill. Taking a moment to "stop and think" is excellent advice for every one of us, myself included. We begin this chapter with a brief synopsis of the cognitive science research on decision making so that we can position critical thinking, and in particular the skill of self-regulation, within that context. We will learn that many reactive judgments are good judgments. But, in some circumstances, reactive judgments can lead to unnecessary risks and mistaken biases. Our work in this chapter is to use self-regulation to become more aware of those circumstances so we can correct ourselves reflectively, using critical thinking, before we make a mistake.

SNAP JUDGMENTS: HEURISTIC THINKING

CHAPTER 09

Human Decision-Making Systems

Human decision making emerges from the interplay of two cognitive drivers. One is our human propensity toward self-explanation known as argument making. The other driver is the influence on our decision making of mental "shortcuts" known as cognitive heuristics. *Argument making*, as we saw in the previous chapters, is the effort to be logical; that is, to rely on the relevant reasons and facts as we see them when making our decisions. In general, humans value making important decisions as rationally as the circumstances, significance, and content of their judgments permit. This is not to say that we are always successful in this effort. In fact, we often are not. And yet we explain our choices and judgments to ourselves, if not to others, in terms of the relevant reasons and facts—again, as we see them. For example, you ask me why I stayed overnight at a friend's house in another city instead of driving home. I reply that it was late and I was very tired, too tired to drive.

Heuristic thinking is the tendency, which is at times quite useful, of relying on highly efficient and generally reliable cognitive shortcuts when reaching a decision. In the research literature, these mental shortcuts are known as cognitive heuristics. These mental maneuvers are as much a part of the human reasoning process as argument making. Cognitive heuristics often enable us to make judgments and decisions more expeditiously and efficiently. Their influences, while often positive, can introduce errors and biases into human decision making.

THE "TWO-SYSTEMS" APPROACH TO HUMAN DECISION MAKING

Research on human decisions made in naturalistic, everyday contexts, describes the interaction of two overlapping decision-making systems.[iii] One is reactive, instinctive, quick, and holistic (System-1). The other is reflective, deliberative, analytical, and procedural (System-2). Both valuable systems function simultaneously, often checking and balancing each other.

Reactive (System-1) Thinking

System-1 thinking relies heavily on situational cues, salient memories, and heuristic thinking to arrive quickly and confidently at judgments, particularly when situations are familiar and immediate action is required. Many freeway accidents are avoided because drivers are able to see and react to dangerous situations quickly. Good decisions emerging from System-1 thinking often feel intuitive.[iv] Decisions good drivers make in those moments of crisis, just like the decisions practiced athletes make in the flow of a game or the decisions that a gifted teacher makes while interacting with students, are born of expertise, training, and practice. Often we decide first, quickly, and reactively and then, if asked about our decisions, we explain how we analyzed the situation and we provide the reasons and arguments to explain those snap judgments, which are System-1 decisions. Overt explanations using argument making in the case of System-1 decisions are retrospective. We look back at the decision and explain the inferences we made at the spur of the moment.

Reflective (System-2) Thinking

System-2 thinking is useful for judgments in unfamiliar situations, for processing abstract concepts, and for deliberating when there is time for planning and more comprehensive consideration. Humans use heuristic maneuvers in System-2 thinking as well, often integrated as components of their logical arguments. Argument making is often part of the inference and deliberation process when making System-2 decisions. And, of course, explanations involve making arguments and giving the reasons we used during our deliberations. When we share our reflective interpretations, analyses, evaluations, and inferences, we are offering explanations. Because of this, critical thinking is self-regulated System-2 thinking. Critical thinking is System-2 thinking focused on resolving the problem at hand and at the same time monitoring and self-correcting one's own process of thinking about that problem.

As you think about the "two-systems" approach, please avoid all the harsh, rigid, stereotypic, divisive, commercialized oppositional, oversimplified, pop culture dichotomies. We are not characterizing human decision making by expressions and false dichotomies such as "emotion vs. reason," "head vs. heart," "feeling vs. judgment," "intuitive vs. logical," "expansive vs. linear," "creative vs. critical," "right brained vs. left brained," "warm vs. cold," "from Venus vs. from Mars," or "blink vs. wide-eyed." Human decision making is neither this superficial nor this simplistic. We are not saying that normal human thinking is schizophrenic or psychologically disordered in any way. We are not suggesting that some people are only System-1 thinkers while others are only System-2 thinkers.

Normal human beings have and use both systems in problem solving and decision making every day. One advantage of the two-systems approach to understanding human decision making is that it reflects more completely the pushes and pulls that normal human beings often describe as part of their decision making. Second, this approach accounts for the rapid-fire decision making we experience on some occasions and the more reflective decision making at other times that all normal human beings experience.

Because it is considered more useful for addressing novel and complex problems in a reflective and methodical way, System-2 is the mode of broad and informed problem solving and good decision making more often addressed by the liberal education goal of one's undergraduate studies. System-2 is also the mode addressed by the evidence-based practice and research methods components of one's professional or graduate studies. Education aimed at improving one's critical thinking—improving one's skills and dispositions to engage successfully in purposeful reflective judgment—is education focused directly on strengthening System-2 problem solving and decision making.

THE VALUE OF EACH SYSTEM

System-1 and System-2 are vital decision-making tools, particularly when stakes are high and uncertainty is an issue. We can often rely on System-1 to get us through the day-to-day while engaging System-2 on some other topic of concern. People report they can drive from home to work without remembering any of the hundreds of routine automobile operating decisions necessary to make the trip. Others report being able to drink a cup of coffee and finish a bowl of breakfast cereal almost without noticing because they are so engrossed in the morning newspaper. Have you ever had any of these kinds of experiences in your life—experiences where you did something "without really thinking about it" while your mind was preoccupied with a completely different problem or issue?

We do not store the memories of our System-1 guided actions if we are simultaneously engaged in deliberating about something using System-2 to think about something else, like a work assignment, a relationship issue, or a financial problem. Our mental focus is on the System-2 work, and, during those times, System-1 operates in the background. This is why we may not remember routine System-1 judgments, like why we've walked into a room, whether we've already passed our freeway exit, or if we've already added salt to the spaghetti sauce.

System-1 functions in the background or "behind the scenes" more than System-2, but both systems are capable of overriding the other. Conflicted decision-making contexts have, through the ages, been described in different ways—"temptation" being only one example. We are drawn one way, but at the same time, pulled the other way. Although we do not accept the implication that the colloquial expressions are scientifically accurate, we can spot oblique references to the behind-the-scenes pushes and pulls of the two systems in the way people ordinarily talk about their decision making. We have all heard people say things like "My gut says to do X, but my brain says to do Y"; "We looked at all the evidence and all the options and yet we don't feel comfortable with where the deliberations are heading"; or "Emotionally I want to do this, but rationally I think I should do that." Some theorists suggest these common ways of talking are evidence that, in certain kinds of ambiguous or complex situations, the two systems might conflict, drawing the decision maker in different directions. In general, this is thought to be an advantage that reduces the chance of making poor, suboptimal, or even dangerous errors in judgment—a natural system of checks and balances, as it were.

Model of Two-System Human Decision Making

Range of potential factors and inputs:
beliefs, aspirations, observations, experiences, attitudes, aptitudes, interpersonal dynamics, emotions, education, knowledge, health, energy level, distractions, disabilities, goals, interests, etc., which constitute the circumstances, context, and parameters of the specific decision or judgment to be made by this decision maker at this time.

Rote Training and Practice

Cognitive Heuristics

Critical Thinking

System-1:
Reactive
Instinctive
Quick
Holistic

System-2:
Reflective
Deliberative
Analytical
Procedural

Resulting decision or judgment about what to believe or what to do.

Prospective or retrospective articulation of decision or judgment in terms of reasons, options, and whatever the person considers to be a relevant consideration.

Perhaps not the most honorific descriptions, yet humbling and useful reminders that there are times when we base our judgments on unfounded assumptions and fallacious reasoning. The long list of argument fallacies in the table at the end of Chapter 8 does not include all the ways that our decision making can go astray. In this chapter we consider a whole new set of biases and errors emerging from the *misapplication* of those ordinarily reliable reasoning maneuvers known as "heuristics." Given the natural limitations of human rationality, it turns out that errors in heuristic thinking can result in serious problems when the risks are great and the stakes are high.

The correct application of cognitive heuristics is absolutely essential for day-to-day living. We would exhaust ourselves mentally and accomplish very little if every single judgment was a full-blown reflective decision. We get through the routine parts of our day making quick, automatic reactive heuristic judgments. We rely on these snap judgments because (a) most of the time they are good enough for the purpose at hand; (b) we need to conserve our mental energy for bigger, more important, and less familiar problems that life throws our way; and (c) often, we have no time for reflective thought. This will be clearer as you review the exam-

Even a good thinker makes both System-1 and System-2 errors from time to time. We misinterpret things, overestimate or underestimate our chances of succeeding, rely on mistaken analogies, reject options out of hand, trust feelings and hunches, judge things credible when they are not, etc. Often biases like these are directly related to the influences and mis-applications of cognitive heuristics. We all share the propensity to use these heuristics as we make decisions, because at times the heuristics seem to be hardwired into our species. Since the critical thinking skill of self-regulation can help us avoid some of these errors if we become more familiar with how they look in practice, let's examine several in closer detail.

Heuristics: Their Benefits and Risks

Shakespeare called humans the paragon of animals. Aristotle said "rational animals." For Plato, "featherless bipeds" was good enough.

ples and do the exercises in conjunction with each of the following heuristics.

INDIVIDUAL COGNITIVE HEURISTICS

Cognitive heuristics are natural human decision-making shortcuts we all rely upon in real life to expedite our judgments about what to believe or what to do. There are potentially beneficial consequences associated with relying on the cognitive shortcuts we'll discuss. In each case we examine the heuristic shortcut or maneuver itself and note potential advantages and disadvantages of relying on the heuristic. A brief, true-to-life vignette and other examples illustrate how that heuristic looks in real life. In most cases a short exercise invites you to apply your critical thinking, and in particular your skill at reflective self-regulation, to occasions in your own life when reliance on that particular heuristic may have resulted in outcomes that were less successful than you had hoped. There are 17 common heuristics described in this chapter. Each is likely quite familiar.

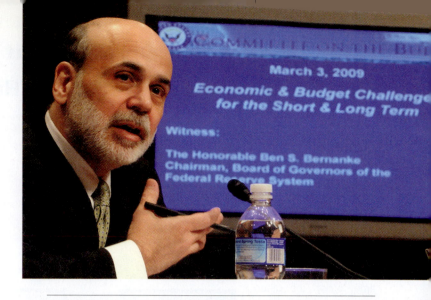

∧∧∧ **System-1:** A soldier reacting under fire based on sound training.

∧∧∧ **System-2:** Experienced policy makers considering possible responses to budget challenges.

1. Satisficing and 2. Temporizing

"The first time he was at the beach, my three-year-old grandson darted down to the wet sand and watched as a small wave washed up toward him. A wave came in and lapped at his toes and ankles, the chilly wet water sending him scurrying up the sand. He turned and cautiously approached the water a second time. Again he got close enough to just let the water touch the tips of his toes, and scooted up the sand. But not nearly as far as the first time. The third time he approached the surf he anticipated the wave as it approached and, instead of turning to run, he back peddled a few steps. Just far enough not to be hit by the salty bubbles. He went just far enough! The kid satisficed, I thought, and, more interestingly, nobody taught him how."

The **Satisficing Heuristic**: Having found an option that is good enough, we take it. We human beings typically do only what must be done to achieve our purposes. In day-to-day living, when faced with choices, instead of expending the resources necessary to identify and then attain the maximally optimal alternative, we decide in favor of an alternative we deem satisfactory.[v] How many times have we read the whole menu in a restaurant compared to reading along only until we spot an entrée that strikes our fancy? We tend to divide the world into "good enough" and "not good enough" and search for a solution until a solution is found

∧∧∧ To the child, the water is captivating, inviting and yet dangerous? **How far away from danger is "far enough" in our own lives?**

that is good enough to attain the desired outcome. Truisms like "If it isn't broken, don't fix it," and "Perfect is the enemy of good" reflect the satisficing cognitive maneuver.

• Example (System-1): Being thirsty, how much water would we drink? Only enough to slake our thirst.

• Example (System-2): Seeking a new job, how hard would we look? Hard enough to find one that meets whatever are our basic criteria for pay, proximity to home, nature of the work, etc.?

• Example (System-2): Having arrested a suspect who had the means, motive, and opportunity to commit the crime, how hard can we expect police detectives to strive to locate other suspects? Satisficing suggests hardly at all. The question of the actual guilt or innocence of the subject becomes the concern of the prosecuting attorney and the courts.

The **Temporizing Heuristic**: Deciding that a given option is "good enough for now," or temporizing is satisficing's running mate. We often move through life satisficing and temporizing. At times, we look back on our situations and wonder why it is that we have settled for far less than we might have. If we had only studied harder, worked out a little more, or taken better care of our relationships and ourselves, perhaps we would not be living as we are now. But at the time, each of the decisions along the way was "good enough for the time being."

We must not overlook the important potential advantages to satisficing. These include conserving time, money, and energy.[vi] If you have to put in 10 percent more effort and time to gain only 1 percent more value, your return on that investment of effort may not be worth the cost. The main disadvantage of satisficing is that we may be mistaken in our estimation of how much is "good enough." Why did the better team lose the game? Because, in underestimating its opponent, the team failed to play up to its own potential. Why did we have trouble on the exam? Because we did not do the homework exercises and study hard enough. Why did my boss not give me a better evaluation compared to my peers? Because I was not productive enough, even though I had thought all along that I was doing just fine. Using our critical thinking in real time, we should take a moment in key situations to be sure our heuristic estimate of "good enough" is really accurate. To achieve greater success we will have to self-correct and recalibrate our sense of how much is enough.

3. Affect: "Go with your Gut"

"I proposed on our first date. She said no. But somehow we both knew that her response was not going to be her final answer. A few months later we were engaged. More than 40 wedding anniversaries later, we are still in love. Perhaps we have been lucky; our marriage could have been a disaster. Whatever was reflective and rational about that decision—as I recall trying to explain it to her folks and mine—had to have been an effort to build a case for a decision we had already made."

The *Affect Heuristic*: Making a decision based on your initial affective ("gut") response.[vii] There is no question that many different kinds of experiences can cause us to respond with joy or sorrow, with desire or revulsion, with enthusiasm or dread. A "gut reaction," that is, an affective response, is a strong System-1 impetus, either positively or negatively, toward the object.[viii] It is natural to have the response.[ix] That response may be the "first word" on the matter, but System-2 self-regulation demands that we ask ourselves whether that should necessarily be the final word on the matter.

- Example: "Oh, I like those shoes. . . . You know, they would look great with the blue jacket I bought."

- Example: "Did you see his eyes? Pure evil! Made my blood run cold. Believe me, a guy like that, no way should you trust him."

- Example: "Forget it. I don't want to hear about how you think we can balance the budget. You said the 'T' word and I won't have anything to do with that. Read my lips, 'No new taxes!' We all pay too much in taxes as it is."

Our natural, initial affective response to ideas, questions, images, people, events, etc., can have obvious advantages and disadvantages. Research on the relationship between facial and body symmetry, perceived attractiveness, and physical health suggests that first affective impressions we have about another human being as a possible mate is evolutionarily selected for and contributes to the survival of the species. Our System-1 affective reaction can influence us toward embracing a choice that "just feels right" or away from an option that appears frightening or repugnant when our System-2 decision making gets bogged down with too many factors to consider, too many divergent criteria, and too much uncertainty. Were it not for this, some of us might never get unstuck and make a decision when one is needed.

But, what if that initially frightening option is actually the best and most reasonable? For example, what if our fear of the anticipated consequences of radiation or chemotherapy influenced us to reject those options when one or both of them were are the best possible cancer treatment options? It may take significant amounts of reflective System-2 reasoning to overcome a powerful System-1 affective response to an idea, but it can be done. And at times it should happen, because there is no guarantee that our affective responses are necessarily always true. Strong critical thinking demands that we check our affective responses. Simply having them is not nearly enough for wise, reflective decision making.

The affect heuristic influences us to make judgments and decisions based on our initial impulsive and subliminal responses. Knowing this, marketing experts coined the expression, "The package is the product," to indicate how important the wrapping, the container, and the initial appearance of a product are to making the sale.[x] Certainly a broken residence hall window and an unkempt campus lawn are not necessarily indicative of an academically substandard college. But college recruiters know that these things had better be fixed before prospective students show up for the campus tour. And on reflection, no one would argue that a cabernet in an attractively designed bottle with a classy label is necessarily superior to a cabernet in a generic bottle with a plain looking label.[xi] There is no question that first impressions count when choosing a college, choosing a wine, or choosing a mate.

4. Simulation

"I was in center field, my favorite position, and the runner at third was itching to tag up and dash for home if the batter hit a fly ball. I imagined what I would do if it was hit to me, how I would run in, position my body, make the catch and fire the ball to the plate on one hop so the catcher could handle the throw easily and tag out the runner. The odds were overwhelming that the batter would hit the ball someplace else. But no!

>>> **Based on your reaction when you first see these two dorm rooms, which residence hall would you prefer?** Did you ever make a mistake by trusting your first reaction?

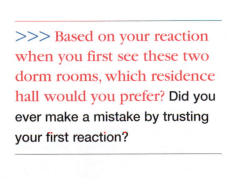

Think of two recent occasions when you had a strong initial affective response to an idea, proposal, opportunity, person, or event. Find one that was positive and one that was negative. Did you reflect on that response, evaluate it, and verify that it was the correct response? If not, this exercise provides the opportunity. Apply your System-2 reflective critical thinking skills to both of those responses. Gather needed information and analyze your response in the light of that new information. Call on your habits of truth-seeking and open-mindedness to support your effort to be as objective as possible in evaluating your initial responses.

The ball was in the air arcing over the infield and sailing out toward center. I darted to my right, took the fly out of the air with my gloved left hand and made my throw toward the plate. The runner had tagged, leaving early I think. But he didn't have a chance. My throw, just up the third base line from home, was on target and on time. The catcher put the tag on the runner for the third out. It was like I had made a movie, watched the movie, and then lived the scene almost exactly."

The *Simulation Heuristic*: Estimating the likelihood of a given outcome based on how easy it is to imagine that outcome.[xii] Simulation is a mental process of imagining ourselves doing something successfully or unsuccessfully. Before giving a speech we might "see ourselves" at the podium talking to the audience with confidence, making our point, and delivering our message effectively. Or we may simulate the opposite, seeing ourselves messing up, getting flustered, and forgetting to say things we had wanted to say. If we experience ease in processing a simulation, this influences us to believe that achieving the anticipated outcome is more likely.[xiii] A person choosing among several options might simulate what it would be like to select an option and then, like making a movie in his or her mind, imagine what life would be like having selected that option. Unless we are being reflective about the actual probabilities that what we picture will actually happen, the simulation heuristic can influence us to select an option that plays out in our minds as the one offering the most desirable result. This might be called "wishful thinking," but whatever it is called, it is not a reflective and well-informed System-2 decision about the actual probability. The same would be true of pessimistically overestimating the likelihood of a bad outcome.

- Example: "You know, I didn't go there to buy a car. But when I was on the lot looking, this salesman came up to me and invited me to sit behind the wheel. Then we went on a test drive, and I could really see myself tooling along I-70 in this baby. So, here it is. My new set of wheels."

- Example: "I don't know what happened, sir!" said the sales representative to the manager after the failed presentation. "Yesterday I could see myself closing that deal."

- Example: "Day trading. I took it up for a while. Lost a lot of money, too. You know it just seemed like it was going to be so easy. All I had to do was invest in some stocks in the morning and watch them increase in value as the day went along. Then sell them just before the market did its typical end-of-day little dip. Well. Things didn't turn out that way at all. I think the only people who made money on my day trading were the guys who work at the brokerage house."

Psychologist Albert Bandura's research on social learning demonstrates the value and power of simulation to increase attitudes of self-efficacy.[xiv] Mentors and coaches use simulation as a technique to improve performance and to help people anticipate being able to succeed at challenging things. Successful advertising often depends on stimulating simulation. Car ads, for example, often show someone with demograph-ics just like the intended buyers taking great pleasure in driving the model of car the ad is promoting. The idea is that if you match those demographics, you would then be led to see yourself in that car and then want to buy it. The process of simulation is quick, easy, and need not be reflective. In fact, it might be better for the advertiser if you do not reflect too much on the actual costs and benefits of buying that new car. The obvious disadvantage of simulation is the potential to err in estimating the likelihood of the imagined outcomes. This can result in misplaced confidence and unwarranted optimism.

Everyone knows that simulating academic success is not a replacement for actually studying, doing the assignments, and doing well on exams. But along with those things, simulation can be very helpful. Take a moment and see yourself being a successful student by simulating how you will structure your time so that you can read the textbook and do all the exercises and assignments. Simulate how you will be organized, focused, and highly efficient in your use of that study time. See yourself going to class or taking tests justifiably confident in what you have learned, well prepared and ready to demonstrate your knowledge on exams and assignments. Oh, yes, and the critical thinking skill of self-regulation requires that we remind ourselves that we have to carry out the study plans that we have simulated if we are to have a reasonable shot at achieving the learning and enjoying the success we anticipate.

5. Availability

"I was doing 75+ heading eastbound on I-96 from Michigan State back home to Detroit, alone, late at night. Darkness had engulfed the rural stretch of interstate. Occasionally, a car heading west passed by on the other side of the wide grassy median. Eastbound was two lanes, and I liked driving in the left lane because it was smoother since the heavy 18-wheelers had not furrowed and gnawed the pavement. But for reasons I'll never know, I decided that night to do the right thing, the thing I'd been taught in driver's education back in high school, and I moved back into the right-hand lane. Then, ahead, just over a slight rise in the interstate, I saw the glare of an approaching vehicle's high beam headlights. It didn't make sense—there shouldn't be any traffic heading west directly in front of me. I sped on, never reducing my speed. The lights grew brighter and brighter. I reached the crest of the rise in the freeway just as the other vehicle did. In a shocking blur it roared by, easily doing 75+. Heading west. On the eastbound side of I-96. And, thank God, he was in his right lane too. Moral of the story. Stay to the right, son, or you'll never know what hit you."

The *Availability Heuristic*: Estimating the likelihood of future events based on a vivid memory of a past experience that leaps easily to mind. Let's experiment with a memory. Imagine a conversation you may have had about foods you can't stand. Does a particularly awful experience with that food leap to mind? For example: "I hate mushrooms. Once when I was a kid I got sick on mushrooms at a restaurant." That quick, automatic connection is a manifestation of the availability heuristic. "No mushrooms on my pizza! Please." This heuristic leads us to estimate the likelihood of a future event based on the vividness or ease of recalling a similar past

Simulate yourself hang gliding off the wind-swept cliffs along the Pacific Ocean. First, see yourself gliding up into the beautiful blue sky, enjoying the grand vistas and the glorious ocean, smelling the salty warmth of the sea air, swooping with silent grace toward the surf, and then lifting effortlessly and joyously on a vector of warm wind with the gulls and pelicans. Take your time. Enjoy the flight. Then when you are ready, ease yourself toward the soft sand and glide slowly to a perfect landing and the admiring approval of your friends. On a scale of 1 to 10, with 10 being "Yes, absolutely," how much did playing that movie in your mind incline you toward wanting to try hang gliding? On a scale of 1 to 10, with 10 being "easy," how easy would hang gliding be?

Now envision a second scenario. See yourself blown along, out of control, harnessed below a tissue-thick nylon wing attached to a flimsy aluminum frame, mentally on the edge of panic, your arms aching, and your back muscles knotted with tension.

You are disoriented, high above the jagged rocks and treacherous waves, trying to dodge other hang gliders. Suddenly, you are distracted by the flock of gulls heading your way. You hear the shouts of people below, but are not able to understand what they are saying. You are uncertain about how to land this contraption without breaking both legs. On a scale of 1 to 10, with 10 being "Yes, absolutely," how much did playing that movie in your mind incline you toward wanting to try hang gliding? On a scale of 1 to 10 with 10, being "easy," how easy would hang gliding be?

Notice that neither simulation supplied any concrete information about hang gliding. Neither detailed the actual risks associated with the sport. Neither explained how one learns to hang glide, whether there are safer or more dangerous places to hang glide, or anything else that would have enabled one to make a reasoned and reflective System-2 analysis and evaluation in response to the question about how easy or difficult it would be.

event.[xv] Because a past experience leaps vividly to mind or because it was so important, we overestimate the probability that future outcomes will be the same as they were back then. People tell stories of things that happened to them or their friends all the time as a way of explaining their own decisions and warning or advising their friends and family about the future. Often these are helpful because they vicariously increase our own range of experiences. The use of stories makes it much easier for us to remember their lesson or moral. Aesop's fables have more than entertainment value—they remind us not to "cry wolf," not to devalue what we have by coveting something we cannot get (as did the fox with the grapes), and many other solid bits of wisdom. On the other hand, there is always the risk that in the retelling, the actual events may be mistakenly remembered, misunderstood, or misinterpreted. Whether accurate or not, stories have an unwarranted amount of influence on decisions about what to expect, what to believe, and what to do.

Availability sells. The news media, knowing the power of a compelling narrative, regularly "put a human face" on news reports. They know it is boring to hear newscasters drone on about statistics and abstractions, for example, about how many homes were damaged by a tornado or how many families lost electric power due to the storm. So instead, the news crew will interview an emotionally distraught person. They will take pictures or video of the person, the damaged home and felled trees in the background, looking lost among the scatterings of furniture and the family's ruined and irreplaceable mementoes. This makes the abstraction "terrible tornado" vividly available to us. And because of the availability heuristic, we, unreflectively, jack up our estimate of the chances that we too might

become a hapless storm victim—just like that sad person we're seeing in the news report.

So vivid were the images of the collapsing towers of NYC's World Trade Center, and so deep was the trauma to the nation's psyche in the days, weeks, and months immediately following September 11th that estimates of imminent terrorist attacks skyrocketed. And not only in places that, upon reflection, one would consider high-threat targets, like transportation hubs in major metropolitan areas. So high were the estimates that all across the nation in tiny towns and villages where the actual chance of a terrorist attack was substantially lower than any of hundreds of other dangers—like storms, floods, epidemics, food contamination, drunk driving, loaded guns kept in unlocked drawers where children can get them—that were being ignored on a regular basis, Americans gave serious thought to the possibility of terrorist attacks and spent time and money to protect themselves

>>> But, on reflection, are we really more likely to become tornado victims simply because we see how a twister demolished this man's home?

against that extremely unlikely eventuality. I would submit that at the time we were making decisions about this possibility in a less than fully reflective and rational way. We do need to think carefully about terrorist attacks, not reactively, but with our System-2 critical thinking skills fully engaged.

The disadvantage of basing judgments on the availability heuristic is that we will wrongly estimate the actual probabilities that a given outcome will occur.[xvi] In the aftermath of the horrendous killings of over 30 people at Virginia Tech (VT) in April 2007, parents, students, faculty, and staff at the nation's more than 4,200 colleges and universities sharply revised their estimates of the probabilities of a similarly deranged killer's assault on their own campuses. Campus security increased, counseling centers received more funding, legislators held hearings at the state and national levels, and campus authorities updated emergency plans and conducted readiness drills. Although these might have been good things to do, resources are finite. Were these the most urgent things for a campus to do, given all the other risks and threats out there? Probably not. Fire preparedness, weather disaster preparedness, theft detection and prevention, rape and assault protection, food poisoning prevention, and flu epidemic preparedness are just a few projects that address events with higher probabilities. But all the attention was on the VT situation. It was vividly in mind for administrators, students, parents, and the media. Those other more likely dangers were not on their minds right then. Hence, the disproportionate allocation of time, money, and attention.

6. Representation

"Uncle John did not smoke cigars at the track, he chewed them. Today he liked the filly—a sleek three-year-old who looked fast. He would have to find her name in the racing form. But just watching her in the paddock, she reminded him of a horse he'd seen run so well at Bay Meadows a couple of years back. Same markings, same look of a winner in her dark, intense eyes. Hadn't he'd won a couple of Benjamins at 8 to 1 on that filly? To Uncle John it only made sense to put down a bet on this one to win." Uncle John made the snap judgment that because this horse looked like that other horse, this horse would perform like the other horse.

The *Representation Heuristic*: Making the snap judgment that X is like Y in every way upon noticing that X is like Y in some way. A perceived

similarity becomes the basis for assuming that there is an analogical relationship between two things, an analogy that may or may not be warranted.[xvii] For example, someone might say, "My father and I were alike in so many ways—in our lifestyles and how we thought about things. Dad died a few years ago of lymphoma. He was only 69. You know, as much as I don't like the idea, I probably have about 30 years before lymphoma gets me, too." The speaker in this example is overestimating the probability of contracting a fatal lymphoma or even of dying at age 69. This thinking is disconnected from any System-2 analytical reflection on the scientific evidence regarding the genetic and environmental factors that estimate a person's cancer risks. But absent that self-corrective reflection, we risk allowing the analogical representation heuristic to influence our beliefs and choices unduly.

If the similarity between two things is fundamental and relevant, it's more likely that the analogy will be reliable. For example, suppose your co-worker was fired for missing sales targets. You might draw the reasonable conclusion that you are no different in relevant respects from your co-worker. Thus, if you miss your sales targets, you'll be fired too. Good thinking.

Thinking Critically Estimate Your Chances

Watch the local news on TV this evening and look for the story in which the victim of a crime, a disease, an economic misfortune, or an accident is interviewed. The more empathetic the victim, the better. The more the victim is like you in terms of age, gender, socioeconomic status, the better. On a scale of 1 to 1,000, with 1,000 being "extremely likely," estimate the chances of the same or a similar event happening to you. After making your estimate, look up the actual statistical likelihood that such an event will happen to you. Is it less than 1 chance in 1,000? For example, if the event is poisoning from contaminated food, the U.S. government estimates that there are about 5,000 deaths nationally each year. So, if you are living in the United States, your chances are 5,000 divided by 306,000,0000 (estimated population of the United States), which is less that 1 in 60,000. On a 1 to 1,000 scale, that is too small to register. But the sales of peanut butter, tomatoes, and spinach have not recovered from the nationwide food poisoning scares that were so well publicized by the media. In 2009, if you estimated your chances of an event happening at a higher rate than 1 in 1,000 after watching the vivid personification of the danger on the evening news, and then learned that your actual chances were less than 1 in 1,000, this would help you appreciate how our System-1 thinking can be wrongly influenced by the availability heuristic. And it reinforces the need for the use of the System-2 critical thinking skill of self-regulation to balance our natural impulse to misestimate the actual risks.

Or the similarity might be superficial or not connected with the outcome, which would make the analogical inference much weaker. For example, we see a TV commercial showing trim-figured young people enjoying fattening fast foods and infer that because we're young, too, we can indulge our cravings for fast foods without gaining excess, unsightly poundage. This is another example showing that heuristic thought needs to be monitored when it is used to make important decisions. As we develop our critical thinking skill of self-regulation, we become more adept at noticing when our decisions hinging on the analogical representation heuristic. And we can correct ourselves before making a decision that is not well thought out. Self-monitoring and self-correcting one's thinking can help assure that conclusions are warranted. In Chapter 11, we will explore comparative reasoning and the criteria for the evaluation of analogical inferences in detail.

might suggest, "Let's take our drinks outside to the picnic table." To which someone else might respond, "Remember the picnic three years ago when Grandpa had his heart attack? I'm never going to that park again." The representativeness, or associational heuristic maneuver, is triggered when a word or idea reminds us of something else. Typically, this is System-1 thinking: reactive, associational, and not critically reflective. For example, one person might associate sunshine with happiness, and another person might associate sunshine with sweaty work picking strawberries. Or, as in the example above, "picnic" with Grandpa's heart attack. The salient negative experience brought to mind by the mere use of the word "picnic" influenced the speaker to assert the decision never to return to the park where the sad event occurred. This unreflective decision emerged from the System-1 reaction triggered by the word association in this person's mind.

Associational thinking, an unmonitored nearly stream-of-consciousness twitter-blab of ideas, is of very little value, logically speaking. But if the associational thinker is also saying out loud every thing that comes to

7. Association

"We were having a good time, probably on our third beer, ESPN's *Sports Center* was on TV someplace nearby but we're not really paying attention because Bill was talking about

∧
∧ **Looking like a winner doesn't make this horse a**
∧ **winner.** Finding the key points of comparison which really make a difference requires sound critical thinking, as we'll see in Chapter 11.

how the girl he was seeing really liked dogs, and he did, too. So, he's saying that she has a pit bull. And I have no idea what Harry was thinking but he says, 'Didn't Michael Vick just get out of jail?' So we all look at Harry because he's on some other planet and say, 'Where did that come from?' And he's like, 'Pit bulls, dogs, dog fights, Michael Vick.' And then I'm like, 'I heard Vick might sign with Baltimore, Buffalo, or maybe Philadelphia.' And now they're all looking at me. Hey, Vick, quarterback, football, teams that need help. Baltimore! Buffalo! How about the Lions? Now there's a team that has gone to the dogs!"

The *Association Heuristic*: Connecting ideas on the basis of word association and the memories, meanings, or impressions they trigger. We all have experienced conversations in which one comment seems connected to another by nothing more than word association. Someone

mind, it can be creative, frustrating, and entertaining all at the same time. And way too personal! It is rather commonplace in today's culture, and yet we seem unconcerned that judgments made using associational thinking can be very flawed. Instead the media report the results of causal twitter fests and "instant polls" as though these represented our best and most informed thinking on a given topic.

8. Stereotyping

"Did I tell what happened when I went to D.C.? So I rented a car and Hertz gives me a Toyota Venza. Never drove one before, won't drive one again. I thought Toyotas were supposed to be good cars. Forget that. So, anyway, I get to the Hampton Inn and that night while I'm sending e-mail I see some bug walking across the bedspread. A roach! What kind of

>>> **From "pit bull" to "eagle"?** System-1, loosened from sound critical thinking, takes full flight with the association heuristic.

Twitter encourages discrete observations, like pixels flashing randomly across a TV screen. As a result, the full image is always disjointed and incomplete. The flurry of tweets surrounding the Iranian presidential election in 2009 is one such example.

People marching and chanting "Down with the dictator" July 17 Tehran http://bit.ly/NUEWS #iranelection

5:54 AM Jul 17th from web

Crowd outside Tehran University Friday Prayers today July 17 Tehran http://bit.ly/Qv9fd #iranelection

5:45 AM Jul 17th from web

http://bit.ly/HakOb more footage July 17 Tehran #iranelection

5:43 AM Jul 17th from web

Footage of military helicopter hovering over Tehran streets July 17 http://bit.ly/44Uoe #iranelection

5:42 AM Jul 17th from web

July 17th after Friday Prayers, more footage http://bit.ly/hsVYO

5:15 AM Jul 17th from web

Just got call from reliable source: interior ministry IS SURROUNDED! ppl are fighting the basijis back, how long can we last? #iranelection

5:11 AM Jul 17th from web

Mass of people marching from Friday prayers July 17th http://bit.ly/hsVYO #iranelection

5:06 AM Jul 17th from web

RT At least 20 thousands right now outside of Interior Ministry in Fatemi, more ppl coming JOIN THEM. TODAY IS THE DAY #iranelection

5:01 AM Jul 17th from web

"Marg bar Russiye" meaning "Death to Russia" from today July 17th http://bit.ly/UeidU #iranelection

5:00 AM Jul 17th from web

dumps are those Hampton Inns? Won't stay in one of them any more, I'll tell you. But, on the good side, I met this Marine, a young corporal, and he was an impressive young man. I could tell just talking to this young soldier that our service men and women are wonderful people."

The *Stereotyping Heuristic*: Making a snap judgment about an entire group based on a single instance. Although an anecdote is not data, we have all heard people draw conclusions about whole groups of people based on their experience with only one or two people who are members of that group. We call this stereotyping or profiling. There are advantages to stereotyping, because it is a highly efficient way of thinking. For example, I enjoyed the Grand Slam breakfast at Denny's the first time I ordered it, and I'll order it again and again. From that one experience, I make the snap judgment that it's the breakfast for me. On the other hand, there are risks associated with stereotyping. Profiling groups of people based on a single unfortunate experience with one member of that group can lead to bigotry, prejudice, misunderstanding, and mistrust, to name only a few.

Humans do not have the time to make systematic scientific surveys of everything we may need to know. So, we take the shortcut of basing decisions on relatively few instances. This is what we are doing when we ask a friend if she or he knows a good dentist, doctor, real estate broker, or lawyer. Or if we ask an alumna to tell us how good her college experience was when we are trying to decide where to go to school. The trade-off between effort expended and the reliability of the information derived makes this approach risky. Yes, it's a starting point to get some preliminary information, but it is not an ending point of a thorough investigation. Here again, monitoring one's habits of mind is a good idea.

The tendency to think that our personal experience of a single instance is predictive of what we would find were we to sample more systematically a whole class of individuals can undermine decision making in almost any context. We eat a burger at a fast food restaurant and make a snap judgment about everything on the menu there and at every other restaurant in the same chain. Does this work for paintings by a given artist, songs by a given songwriter, and novels by a given author? What about courses taught by a given professor, patient problems treated by a given health care provider, or decisions by a given manager?

Recall the situation in July 2009 involving a black Harvard professor, Henry Louis Gates, and the white police officer who arrested him, James Crowley. One interpretation of that event was that each man's reactive System-1 decision making made a snap judgment about the other man based on the stereotyping heuristic. Eventually, President Obama invited both of them to the White House for a beer, so they could get to know each other as individuals.

9. "Us vs. Them"

"I went to Congress to lobby for the reauthorization of the Higher Education Act and to support increased funding for Pell Grants and other forms of

---

Thinking Critically   Last Word to First Word

Listen attentively to a conversation. But do not focus on the topic being discussed, instead focus on the words as they are said. Pay special attention to the last word or expression in a sentence and count how many times the next speaker uses that word or expression as the first thing they say. An associational thinker—and we use the term "thinker" advisedly—often interacts conversationally by connecting what he or she says to the last word in the sentence that the previous speaker

uttered. No, this doesn't make any logical sense. But listen for it nonetheless. Keep a log of which person in the conversation does it the most frequently. And keep track of whether or not the topic of the conversation is actually altered from whatever it was before to whatever topic the associational thinker introduces. Put a clock on the topic. See if any topics at all can last more than three minutes when the associational thinker is in full form.

Thinking Critically

Have You Ever Been Stereotyped?

Were you ever the object of someone else's use of the stereotyping heuristic? To answer this, think of a time when you might have been treated a certain way, either positively or negatively, by someone else simply because of something about your age, gender, style of clothing, race, or accent.

∧
∧ **Resolving our differences at a "beer summit"**—a new
∧ American tradition.

student aid. I explained that higher education is a benefit to the person who is fortunate enough to afford to go to college. Research shows consistently higher earnings for college graduates than for those who have not gone to college. But, I said, college education provides benefits to society as a whole. The teachers, nurses, business people, engineers, journalists, and social workers, etc., who attained access to those professions through their college education provide much needed services for everyone in the community. I was told by one member that he simply did not agree with that. His reason was simple: 'I've heard all that before because it's what the other side says.' I asked the member to help me understand his thinking better and he replied, 'You see, on the Hill, it's good guys vs. bad guys. They're the bad guys. Whatever they say, whatever they want, whatever argument they make, I don't buy it."

The **"Us vs. Them" Heuristic**: Reducing decisions to the choice between two starkly opposing options and then rejecting the option your opposition favors. This could be named the "good guys vs. bad guys" heuristic as well because applying this heuristic results in an

2004 Electoral Count

TOTAL
538

BUSH
286

KERRY
252

∧
∧ **Wedge issues,** like gay marriage, immigration, and flag burning, play on our System-1 us
∧ vs. them heuristic. Can our collective System-2 critical thinking overcome the divisiveness with reasoned judgment?

territory with caution thrown to the wind is seldom likely to be the optimal choice. An advantage of this heuristic is that it orients our thoughts and actions in support of our family, our team, our platoon, our business, our community, "our kind." And, obviously, the disadvantage is that we lose objectivity and impartiality, and we can be prone toward bias and prejudice if we are not reflective. In instances like these, our critical thinking (System-2) must override the pull toward prejudice arising from the misapplication of the us vs. them heuristic.

Go to **www.TheThinkSpot.com** and view the three-minute "Pep Talk" scene from *Glory Road*. The coach begins by antagonizing his play-ers with racial stereotyping, and their gut response (affect heuris-tic) is silent anger and resent-  ment. The coach says that they cannot win the national championship, because they cannot think. He describes them losing the game, they can see it happening (simula-tion) in their minds, and they become even more agitated because he is the authority figure and he is saying they will lose. They do not want to lose. This is not "just a game." Then the coach changes his tone and evokes the us vs. them heuristic to rally the players and unify the team. The short scene ends with one of the players making the point to his teammate that he needs to play good defense (not satisfice), because the usual effort will not be good enough.

> How does the coach use the us vs. them heuristic to motivate the team? **Is this manipulation or good leadership?**

automatic competitive and oppositional relationship. And our tendency, evolv-ing from the earliest survival instincts of our species, is to band together with "our own people" to fight "those other guys." Battle lines are drawn with phrases like "Those who are not with me are against me"; "There can be no middle ground"; "Never compromise"; and "There can be no negotiations."[xviii]

Once our minds apply the us vs. them heuristic to a situation, many other decisions about the people or issues involved become very simple. We have no obligations toward "them" or toward anything they want or anything they represent. But, if you are one of "us" we will stand by you through thick and thin.[xix] In its most extreme manifestations, the us vs. them heuristic can set up the tendency to regard "them" as non-persons, objects off the ethical radar screen, "others" who can be manipulated or removed without ethical concern. As a nation, we saw this in the torture and prisoner abuses at Abu Ghraib. Called the false polarization effect,[xx] this tendency to divide the world into two opposing camps can be a very dangerous approach to problem solving and a potentially explosive and negative strategy for a society or a leader to take.

Let us not be naïve about this. If humans are strongly influenced by us vs. them thinking, then it would be foolish of us not to take that into con-sideration when approaching others for the first time. Generosity of spirit and openness are wonderful virtues, but venturing into potentially hostile

Journalists, politicians, zealots, coaches, and evangelists of all stripes use our natural tendency to mistrust "those other people"—the ones who are not part of "us"—the ones who are different, the ones with whom we disagree. Unscrupulous people make an enemy of the opposition and ascribe to them evil and dangerous intentions. This ral-lies the troops against the external threat and makes it unnecessary to take seriously what "they" have to say. In the cut-throat competition for high office, campaigners strive to marginalize or even demonize their opposition, engender fear in "us," lest "they" should "get what they want," "come to power," or "take what is rightfully ours." The risks associated with dualistic thinking are serious, and these risks are com-pounded when fear and mistrust are set in opposition to loyalty and group identity.

10. Power Differential

"I once worked on a senior management team that was headed by a CEO who was the personification of the 'alpha male.' I recall one meet-ing where the other nine vice presidents and I were sitting along both sides of a conference table, with the CEO at the head of the table. He wanted us to discuss a proposal he had come up with the night before. He presented his idea by handing out five pages single-spaced and

---

Thinking Critically   Closer to Home

Clubs, community groups, and professional organizations are not immune to the dangers of the misapplication of the us vs. them heuristic. On the other hand, the benefits of this heuristic include that it gives people energy and a sense of urgency to be working to defend their own, to compete for resources, and to feel justified in their beliefs and actions. Recall the last decision-making meeting of a club or organization to which you belong. In what ways did the us vs. them heuristic influence your group's thinking about people, about threats or opportunities, about problems or issues? Reflect on those influences. How might your group's decisions have been dif-ferent had it not been for the sense of "us" vs. "them" that this heuristic engendered?

talking non-stop for half an hour. Then he said, 'OK, now I'd like to hear from you.' Nobody spoke. Nobody believed he actually wanted to hear our views. Nobody wanted to rock the boat or risk crossing him by pointing out even the smallest flaw or raising even the most tentative counterargument. The CEO waited less than two seconds. When nobody responded, he said, 'OK, then. That's it. We'll implement this. Now, next topic."

The *Power Differential Heuristic*: Accepting without question a belief as stated by, a problem as presented by, or a solution as proposed by, a superior authority. Social hierarchies abound at home, at work, in government, in religion, and even in recreation. Many are benevolent and respectful. But even in these cases, and certainly in those that are manipulative and abusive, there is a tendency to defer to the individual (or subgroup) in charge. It may be something as benign as agreeing on when to eat dinner or which TV show to watch. The decision to defer, that is, not to dispute or challenge, the decisions of others higher in the social pecking order is natural. It manifests itself in our accepting what "those above us" may decide to have us do. This heuristic leads us to see the world and how our leaders see it and to understand problems and issues the way our leaders describe them to us. Middle managers in a corporate culture are susceptible to similar pressures from

senior executives, as are second children from their elder sibling, or junior officers relative to their superiors. But "pressure" is not exactly the correct word, for this heuristic makes compliance with authority the automatic reaction. Thus, when one is out of step with one's "higher-ups," one often feels more discomfort than when one is "going along to get along." In a gang, for example, the power differential between the gang leader and his or her followers, when combined with the us vs. them heuristic for viewing the world, can strongly influence gang members to internalize gang rivalries and to agree with violent responses to perceived threats.

There are some advantages to recognizing the realities of power differentials and not bucking the system. Not only can this save cognitive resources, it might save your job and your domestic happiness as well. After all, if the boss wants the client list updated, why not update it? And if your partner wants to go to a movie that might not have been your first choice, why not go anyway? Having people see things your way may not be the highest of all values, even if you are smarter than they are about some things. Societal harmony and domestic tranquility are values, too.

On the other hand, how many times have we seen clearly that the boss was heading the department in the wrong direction, that the team captain was employing an ineffective strategy, that our elder sibling was wrong, or that our leaders were motivated more by self-interest than the common good? Any full evaluation of the reasoning presented by those in power over us—coaches, teachers, ministers, managers, governmental authorities, or otherwise—should include consideration of whether the benefits derived from the current power structure relationship warrant continuing that relationship or whether it is time to consider seriously other options. In reviewing one's options, do not forget the influence that the satisficing heuristic, discussed earlier, can have on our sense that, however flawed our current situation may be, it is "good enough."

11. Anchoring with Adjustment

"The first book report I wrote as a ninth grader was about a novel entitled *Space Cadets*. My report earned a C-. The teacher, a lover of 18th- and 19th-century British literature, found scant merit in the silly novel I had chosen and even less merit in my futile attempt to state its theme and explore how its author had developed plot and characters. A friend of mind received an A on his report on George Elliot's 1863 novel, *Silas Marner*. About halfway through the academic year I was consistently making C-, C, or C+ on my work, and my friend was doing A- or A work.

<<< **A Student Body president champions a new resolution. How does the power differential within student organizations affect the work of the group and the sense of group unity?**

Thinking Critically Fostering A Group Culture of Critical Thinking

The capacity to cultivate a group culture that fosters reflective, respectful, and fair-minded decision making and problem solving can be a great asset to a leader. The leader, if trusted not to revile, belittle or ridicule subordinates for their ideas and suggestions, can benefit immensely. Decisions can be openly discussed and refined before being implemented. Problems can be analyzed and options considered, with each person feeling encouraged to bring his or her best thinking forward. Based on your own experience, what are some specific things leaders can do to foster a climate that is highly receptive to critical thinking and self-regulation? What are some things that undermine that good climate? Give examples.

So, we switched. I started writing reports using his name and he wrote reports using my name. My grades (that is, the grades he earned for me) edged up into the C+ and B- range. His grades (that is, the grades my reports earned for him) held steady except for one B+ late in April. Our analysis: In the mind of our teacher from the first paper we submitted in September and throughout that whole year, I was a C student and my friend was an A student."

The **Anchoring with Adjustment Heuristic**: Having made an evaluation, adjust only as much as is absolutely necessary and then only if new evidence is presented.[xxi] When we are making evaluative judgments, it is natural to locate or anchor our evaluation at some point along whatever scale we are using. If we are being more reflective, we may have established some criteria and we may be working to apply them as fair-mindedly as possible. As other information comes our way, we may adjust our evaluation. The interesting thing about this cognitive maneuver is that we do not normally start over with a fresh evaluation. We have dropped anchor and we may drag it upward or downward a bit, but we do not pull it off the bottom of the sea to relocate our evaluation. First impressions, as the saying goes, cannot easily be undone.

One advantage of this heuristic is that it permits us to move on. We have done the evaluation; there are other things in life that need attention. We could not long endure if we were to constantly re-evaluate every thing anew. Part of developing expertise is learning to calibrate and nuance one's judgments, refine one's criteria, and adjust the criteria to fit the complexities of the circumstances of judgment. Anchoring with adjustment can reflect a progression toward greater precision, a way to refine not only judgments about particular things, but the criteria applied when making those judgments.

The unfortunate thing about this heuristic, however, is that we sometimes drop anchor in the wrong place; we have a hard time giving people a second chance at making a good first impression. How often have we seen it happen that a co-worker's performance is initially evaluated as sub-par (outstanding) and almost nothing that happens subsequently can move that initial evaluation marker very far from where it started? Subsequent outstanding work (poor work) is regarded as a fluke or an anomaly, not as genuine counterevidence that should result in a thorough re-evaluation.

12. Illusion of Control

"They hired me because I was known as a corporate gunslinger. I know how to take a failing organization and turn it around in short order. I kick ass and take names. I hire people who want to bust their butts to get the job done, and I fire the deadwood and anyone who gets in the way of what we're trying to do. Within 90 days I had reorganized the finance division and the technology division. Sales needed major work. That took another three weeks, but I put in the right people and revised our marketing approach. Then it was time to increase productivity and decrease costs in our manufacturing operation.

∧
∧
∧ Our opinions of celebrities often anchor on our first impressions and
then adjust, but oh so slowly. Robert Downey, Jr., drug addict and criminal?
Or Robert Downey, Jr., Oscar nominated movie star? Which was your anchor?
How can some reflective thought help us hoist anchor and reposition our thinking?

In six months I had stopped the bleeding. In nine, we had bottomed out and were starting to see the signs of a turnaround. We posted our first net profits at the end of my fourth quarter with the corporation. I stayed another two years and then the job got so boring that I had to move on. So, now I'm on the market looking for another company that needs my skill set to save its cookies." The gunslinger's constant references "I did this" and "I did that" gives no credit to the team effort it really takes to turn an organization around. Perhaps the gunslinger deserves praise and credit for his or her leadership contributions. But from my own personal experience, I assure you that turning around a large organization that is in real trouble is a group project, not a one-person show. The gunslinger in this example is looking back on the project with an exaggerated and illusory sense of his or her own personal control over how events turned out.

The ***Illusion of Control Heuristic***: Estimating the control you have over events by the amount of energy and desire you put into trying to shape those events. When used correctly, this heuristic helps calibrate estimates of our effectiveness and thus it helps us gauge how hard we should try. When misapplied, the illusion of control heuristic leads us into snap judgments that are nothing more than wishful thinking. We frequently overestimate our actual ability to control the outcomes of events because we consistently fail to account for contingencies.[xxii] We overestimate our control of a situation because we underestimate the influences of other people and events. As a result, we imagine wrongly that there is a very strong relationship between whatever we might do and how things are going to ultimately turn out. Wanting a given outcome strongly, we tend to think that decisions we make or actions we take are genuinely instrumental in bringing about or failing to bring about that outcome regardless of the actual contingencies, forces, and factors at work.

13. Optimistic Bias and
14. Hindsight Bias

Please answer these two questions: Are you any more or less likely than others just like you to contract cancer at your age? Are you more or less likely than others just like you to suffer a debilitating injury in a traffic accident?

The ***Optimistic Bias Heuristic***: Tendency to underestimate our own risks and overestimate our own control in dangerous situations.[xxiii] On the two questions above, approximately 75 percent of us will

estimate our risks to be lower and about 25 percent will say higher. But, the true answer is that our risks are neither higher nor lower than persons just like us. This natural tendency toward optimistic bias has the evolutionary advantage for our species of providing us with the courage to move ahead in life. The constant dread of serious hazards could be mentally detrimental and debilitating. However, since our risk of hazard is actually no better and no worse than others', all things being equal, this built-in bias results in poorer and perhaps more risky judgments in some situations. Our sense that we will succeed where others have failed, or that we are not as likely as others to suffer misfortune or the ill effects of bad decisions can lead us to take unnecessary risks.

Please answer these questions: Have you ever felt that perhaps you did not receive your fair share of the credit for successful projects that you worked hard on? Were you unfairly blamed when things went wrong that were actually beyond your control?

The *Hindsight Bias Heuristic*: Tendency to remember successful events as being the result of the decisions we made and actions that we took and past failures as having resulted from bad luck or someone else's mistakes.[xxiv] Our human need for accuracy, predictability, and self-justification is believed to motivate this hindsight-biasing behavior.[xxv] Hindsight bias adds fuel to the fire of our false confidence, for it inclines us to believe that our decisions and actions had a strong positive impact on the outcome of events, or, if things did not turn out as hoped, the fault was not ours. The tendency to take undeserved credit for good outcomes or to shift responsibility to others for undesirable outcomes is something we humans seem to have in common.

We do not mean to suggest that we are mistaken every time we feel unfairly blamed nor that we are mistaken every time we feel in control of a situation. By noting these potentials for wrong judgments, however, we are able to anticipate the possibility of a mistake and correct our thinking before we dig in too deeply to the feelings of pride or resentment that come with being mistakenly praised or blamed. We can use our self-regulation critical thinking skills to monitor ourselves for optimistic bias and hindsight bias so that our estimations about how much we really can control or how much blame or credit we deserve are made more reflectively, and hopefully, more accurately.

15. Elimination by Aspect: "One Strike and You're Out"

"I went on four job interviews, which was great because many of my friends were having trouble getting any interviews. The interviewers all wanted me to make a PowerPoint presentation. And, of course, there was a lot of meeting individuals and groups of people. And the mandatory lunch when you have to remember to order lemonade instead of

anything alcoholic. All those parts went fine. But at one place there was this guy who kept interrupting my PowerPoint to ask questions. I don't want to work there, not with jerks like him in my work group. This other place was OK, great new computers in fact, but the cubicles were gray and so was the carpet. I just didn't like how blah it looked—too institutional, you know. So, really, it's down to the other two places, and I'm hoping to get an offer from one or both of them real soon."

The *Elimination by Aspect Heuristic*: Eliminating an option from consideration upon the discovery of one undesirable feature. There are simply too many choices! The Excalibur Hotel in Las Vegas boasts a 500-dish smorgasbord. DirecTV offers hundreds of channels, as does XM radio. Want to buy a car, a downtown condo, a fancy watch, or enroll in an MBA program? There are thousands from which to pick. How do we move efficiently through this maze of opportunities? Certainly not by giving our full attention and due consideration to every aspect of every option. Rather, we hack through the choices individually or in whole bunches at a time, pushing the clutter out of our cognitive path as quickly and efficiently as possible. Elimination by aspect is our heuristic strategy. As soon as we identify a "reason why not," we dump that option and options like it. The reason does not have to be monumental. I don't like brown cars or used cars. That's it. For me, the car-buying choices have just been reduced by tens of thousands. Don't like cream sauces? Great, that cuts the smorgasbord problem down by a huge percentage. Don't like to wait behind other folks grazing through the food line? Fine, step around them to an open spot along the smorgasbord and never worry about looking back at the dozens of culinary delights you may have skipped.

In situations where we enjoy a plethora of acceptable choices, the cognitive utility of elimination by aspect cannot be overestimated. However, the price we pay for conserving all that energy and time is clear, too. Applying this heuristic may result in a final selection that does not reflect the best holistic choice we might have made. The used car I refused to consider may have been just as good in every way as a new car of the same make and model, but thousands of dollars less expensive. I will never give that car its due consideration, having eliminated it entirely from view when I rejected it along with all others that were labeled "used." In situations where our choices are limited and where no option is perfect, this heuristic can be a major liability. Because nobody is perfect, balancing the good with the bad is a sign of wisdom. The one strike and you're out approach denies this reality. Political litmus tests, for example, could paralyze a pluralistic democracy. We would all soon become hermits if we tried to select our employees, friends, and leaders on the principle that any one flaw is a fatal flaw.

16. Loss and Risk Aversion

"Early in my career I was offered an entry-level management position with a new company in a new industry. The company was called Cingular Wireless. I didn't seek the job. And I was a bit surprised when the offer was extended one evening during a dinner party. It would have meant a lot more money than I was earning as a part-time instructor. A job like that would have been the ticket to a lucrative corporate career. But I had a job in the field of higher education, and, with a couple years of

<<< How does our natural optimistic bias affect our decision making in contexts of risk and uncertainty? In *Business Week*, Dan Ariely, says it is great for society but a disaster for individuals![xxvi]

Reflect on how often you approach key decisions with your own personal litmus test, sorting choices by looking for a single flaw or reason to eliminate as many as possible as quickly as possible. For example, reducing the list of job applicants this way, "Let's eliminate every applicant whose GPA is less than 2.70." In this example, the first important System-2 question is why should we look at GPA at all, and the next reflective question is why does 2.70 make the cut, but 2.69 misses? What is the evidence that GPA is such a precise measure as that? Going back to your own personal litmus test decisions, apply your critical thinking skills, and ask yourself whether there is good evidence to support using that single criterion as a make-or-break decision point?

experience, I was becoming comfortable in the role of college teacher. I didn't want to lose the identity I had just begun to create for myself. I wasn't sure what it would be like to work in the corporate sector, having all my life been either a student or a teacher, and recently a new mother. My daughter was less than a year old at that time. What if the job with Cingular didn't work out? Somehow the idea of remaking myself into a corporate junior executive seemed too risky and there was too much to lose. So, I thanked the person but declined her offer."

The **Loss and Risk Aversion Heuristic**: Avoiding risk and avoiding loss by maintaining the status quo. Not losing anything, not going backward, at least staying where we are, for most humans, is the preferred default outcome, particularly under conditions of uncertainty. Research demonstrates that most humans are more likely to pass up an opportunity to make a gain rather than risk a loss.[xxvii] Humans psychologically privilege the status quo. Whenever possible, humans take an incremental approach, seeking to avoid uncertainty and the difficult cognitive tasks of weighing and combining information or trading-off conflicting values, rather than opting for more dramatic change. Muddling through personal decisions, attempting to avoid any loss, is the norm rather than the exception. We've all heard the old adage "A bird in the hand is worth two in the bush."

Making decisions on the basis of what we do not want to risk losing can have advantages in many circumstances. People do not want to lose control, they do not want to lose their freedom, and they do not want to lose their lives, their families, their jobs, or their possessions. And so, in real life, we take precautions. Why take unnecessary risks? The odds may not be stacked against us, but the consequences of losing at times are so great that we would prefer to forgo the possibilities of gain not to lose what we have. Can you think of an example of this in your life?

We are more apt to endure the status quo, even as it slowly deteriorates, than we are to engage in change that we perceive as "radical" or "dangerous." Loss and risk aversion have the disadvantages of leading to paralysis or delay precisely when action should be taken. Having missed that opportunity to avert a crisis, we discover later that it requires a far greater upheaval to make the necessary transformations once the crisis is upon us. Worse, on occasion, the situation has deteriorated beyond the point of no return. In those situations we find ourselves wondering why we waited so long before doing something about the problem back when it might have been possible to salvage the situation. History has shown time and time again that businesses that avoid risks often are unable to compete successfully against those willing to move more boldly into new markets or into new product lines.

Uncertainty, risk, and fear of loss are the tools of those who oppose change, just as optimistic bias and simulation are the tools of the proponents of change. Consider the debate over health care reform in the United States. The August 2009 onslaught of organized opposition to health care reform legislation tried to prevent Congress and the Obama administration from "foisting expensive, risky, and ineffective programs" on the American people. More than "If it ain't broke, don't fix it," their campaign was "Leave well enough alone!"

WHO'S YOUR CITY?
by Richard Florida

place finder

Would you like to integrate the *Who's Your City? place finder widget* into your site? *Here's how...*

Take the place finder to find your city.

Please use the complete city name (ie. "London, UK" or "London, Ontario")

Which city do you currently live in?	Your choice Base city
A city you would consider moving to?	Your choice A city
Another city you would consider moving to?	Your choice B city
Another city you would consider moving to?	Your choice C city
One more city you would consider moving to?	Your choice D city

< Back   Next >

start over

creative class group   home   book overview
praise   articles & reviews   excerpt
Richard Florida   place finder   best cities   maps
who's YOUR city?   contact

∧∧∧ **When considering where you should live,** what characteristics do you consider vitally important? Instead of tossing away a good choice just because it is less than perfect on every important characteristic, Sociologist Richard Florida's "Who's YOUR City" quiz seeks to put all of your requirements in context. Take the quiz yourself at: http://creativeclass.com/whos_your_city/place_finder/.

17. "All or Nothing"

"I heard that there were going to be budget cuts and layoffs. We all knew that the economy was in the tank. But this is a big university with an annual operating budget over $230,000,000 and more than 1,800 faculty and staff members. So, I figured that the chances that they would cut the course that I was going to take next semester out of the budget had to be about 100,000 to 1. I mean they probably offer thousands of courses here every year. And there are so many other places to save money at a university without cutting academics. So, I planned my work hours and day care around taking that course. And then I go to register and it's not in the schedule. I learned they

Reflect on a recent experience in your life that involved making a decision that included some element of risk and potential loss. In a purely objective analysis the *status quo* is only one possibility among many and should not be given any more value than any other state of affairs. But, as you saw in the "Loss and Risk Aversion" section, for human beings, built as we are with an aversion to loss and risk seemingly in our DNA, that is easier said than done. How did you handle the decision you faced? Were you able to give the status quo no more nor less value than any other possible state of affairs? How might a stronger application of the critical thinking skill of self-regulation have affected the decision? In other words, what steps can you take to monitor your own decision making for loss aversion? Write out some questions a person might ask himself or herself that would help the person be able to make a good decision in contexts of risk, uncertainty, and potential loss.

dropped it for budget reasons. Can you imagine! How am I supposed to complete my program if they cut required courses like that one?"

The *"All or Nothing" Heuristic*: Simplifying decisions by treating remote probabilities as if they were not even possibilities. By and large, when making decisions, we do not calculate Bayesian probabilities. Computers might, but humans do not. But over the millennia as a species, we humans have done reasonably well for ourselves (so far) by operating as if the exact probabilities did not really matter. Instead of thinking that there is precisely a 92 percent chance of this occurring or a 12 percent chance of that occurring, we tend to simplify our estimations and move them toward the extremes. In fact, we behave as if the odds were either 0 (no possibility at all), or 1 (it definitely will happen). Whether the chances are 1 in 100, or 1 in 10,000, do we really think about the mathematical differences in those situations? No. Instead we tend to treat both of them as if the odds were the same, and, in fact, as if they were both zero. The all or nothing heuristic treats these remote possibilities as if they were, for all practical purposes, "impossible." That is, as if the actual odds were 0 in 100 or 0 in 10,000.

When we stop and really think about things, there are all kinds of risky situations. A person could be hit by a car walking across the street. But, really, what are the chances? They are in fact *not* equal to zero. But if even the smallest risk of such a great loss as the loss of one's life were perceived, some of us might never venture out into the world. So, we push that decimal point out further and further in our minds, nullifying the risk, treating it as if it were not present at all. I've ice-skated hundreds of times, so what are the chances that tonight I'll fall and crack my skull? There are thousands of commercial flights each day, so what are the chances of a near miss involving my flight? Sadly, if one of those remote and unfortunate possibilities were to occur, we often think, "I never thought that would happen to me." A main advantage to the all or nothing heuristic is that it balances the paralyzing influences of loss and risk aversion.

HEURISTICS IN ACTION

In real-world conversations in which we focus on our own issues, cognitive heuristics expedite our thinking by generating ideas, but not necessarily reflectively. Here is an example of a person explaining why he decided to invest in high-tech stocks in late 2007. What could go wrong?

- "I know some businesses fail, particularly those based on technological innovation. But only three percent of new ventures failed last year, so I decided that the risk of failure was actually pretty small [All or Nothing], and I decided to go for broke and invest, and . . . you know. . . I'm pretty good at what I do, and I am really watching things closely now so that nothing happens that will threaten my investment. [Illusion of Control] I just don't think I can miss on this one. [Illusion of Control as Optimistic Bias]

True, it was smart to consider the percentage of businesses that failed, and to do all that one can to run a business well. And the business may not fail, but even the speaker himself would not be likely to invest with confidence were it not for the misuse of heuristic thinking, providing hope, a bit of confidence, and a sense of being in control of the investment. The economic recession of 2008 and 2009 demonstrated that the previous reasoning was a house built on sand.

In the following example of a casual family conversation over morning coffee, several heuristics are in play, including association, affect, and stereotyping:

- Husband to wife: "I'm looking forward to retiring. I've worked for 35 years in offices without windows, and, when I'm retired I want to be outside. I can see myself on the fifth tee right now!"

- Wife replies: "Same as my Dad; he used to say how much he hated the winter especially—going to work when it was dark outside, working in a windowless office all day, and then coming home when it was dark."

- Mother-in-law: "That senior's apartment you showed me was terrible. Only one window! I need more light. I'm never moving to an apartment! You're going to have to drag me out of my house."

In the first paragraph, availability and simulation influence the husband to link the idea of being outside immediately to his vivid and happily remembered hobby [availability]. He sees himself golfing [simulation]. projecting how much easier it will be to play golf when retired. As is common with the availability heuristic, he may be overestimating his opportunities to be on the fifth tee. Meanwhile, his wife is still thinking about the original topic, namely retirement. However, she connects her husband's expressed distaste for his windowless office with her father's similar expressions of distaste for the

Heuristics and Possible Errors from Their Misapplication

Heuristic	Cognitive Shortcut	Possible Error from Misapplication
Satisficing	Having found an option that is good enough, take it. We humans typically do only what must be done to achieve our purposes.	Underestimation of how much is required to satisfy objective.
Temporizing	Decide that a given option is good enough for now.	Underestimation of the growing problems associated with failing to make a long-term adjustment in a timely way.
Affect	Decide based on your initial affective ("gut") response.	First impressions and gut feelings may mislead.
Simulation	Estimate the likelihood of a given outcome based on how easy it is to imagine that outcome.	Overestimation of one's chance of success or likelihood of failure.
Availability	Estimate the likelihood of a future event on the vividness or ease of recalling a similar past event.	Mistaken estimations of the chances of events turning out in the future as they are remembered to have turned out in the past.
Representation	Make the snap judgment that X is like Y in every way upon noticing that X is like Y in some way.	The analogy may not hold.
Association	Connect ideas on the basis of word association and the memories, meanings, or impressions they trigger.	Jumping from one idea to the next absent any genuine logical connection and drawing confused and inacurate inferences.
Stereotyping	From a single salient instance, make a snap judgment about an entire group.	Profiling and misjudging individuals based on one's beliefs about the group.
"Us vs. Them"	Reduce decisions to the choice between two starkly opposing options and then reject the option your opposition favors.	Unnecessary conflict, disrespect for others, polarization, undermining of the possibility of reasonable compromise.
Power Differential	Accept without question a belief as stated by, a problem as presented by, or a solution as proposed by a superior authority.	Working on the wrong question or problem, applying a mistaken or inadequate solution.
Anchoring with Adjustment	Having made an evaluation, adjust only as much as is absolutely necessary and then only if new evidence is presented.	Failure to reconsider thoroughly, failure to evaluate fair-mindedly.
Illusion of Control	Estimate the control you have over events by amount of energy and desire you put into trying to shape those events.	Overestimation of one's actual power to control or manage events—confusion of desire and effort with effectiveness.
Optimistic Bias	The tendency to underestimate our own risks and overestimate our own control in dangerous situations	Taking unnecessary risks, putting one's self in unnecessary danger.
Hindsight Bias	The tendency to remember successful events as being the result of the decisions one made and actions one took, and to remember past failures as having resulted from bad luck or someone else's mistakes	Misjudging the actual extent to which one's actions contributed either positively or negatively to past events and outcomes.
Elimination by Aspect	Eliminate an option from consideration upon the discovery of one undesirable feature.	Failure to give due and full consideration to all the viable options.
Loss and Risk Aversion	Avoid risk and avoid loss by maintaining the status quo.	Paralysis of decision making, stuck in the deteriorating status quo.
"All or Nothing"	Simplify decisions by treating remote probabilities as if they were not even possibilities.	Failure to appreciate the possibilities that events could actually turn out differently than expected—the remote possibility may actually occur.

same work environment [representation]. At that point the mother-in-law introduces a new topic, her mind having jumped from "windowless" to an association with darkness [association] and from there to her vividly recalled [availability], negative [affect] experience of recently seeing one dark apartment. Clearly, she is overestimating the likelihood that all apartments will be dark. And, given that she has introduced this new topic, rather than join the conversation, this comment has the ring of a bolstering argument for a long-term debate about whether she will agree to move to an apartment. The option of moving to an apartment is off the table as far as she is concerned. And more, not wanting to lose control [loss aversion] over her own life, she expresses her decision to her children—regardless of their obvious age in this context—as a decision she will not permit them to override.

REVIEW

Human decision making uses two cognitive systems: System-1 is reactive and automatic, System-2 is deliberative and reflective. System-1 enables us to get through the routine parts of our lives so automatically that we can focus mental energy on difficult problems using the deliberative and reflective powers of System-2. Argument making is an effort to be logical and to rely on relevant reasons and facts as we make deliberative decisions and as we explain our decisions to others. Heuristic thinking is the often quite useful tendency to rely on highly effective cognitive shortcuts when making judgments. This chapter examined seventeen common cognitive heuristics, noting the advantages and disadvantages of each. At times, we misapply one or more of those heuristic shortcuts and, so, run the risk that our snap judgments will be mistaken. We can avoid the misapplication of heuristics by applying our self-regulation critical thinking skill to monitor and to correct our judgment-making process.

KEY TERMS

System-1 thinking is reactive thinking that relies heavily on situational cues, salient memories, and heuristic thinking to arrive quickly and confidently at judgments. *128*

System-2 thinking is reflective critical thinking that is useful for judgments in unfamiliar situations, for processing abstract concepts, and for deliberating when there is time for planning and more comprehensive consideration. *128*

cognitive heuristics are human decision-making shortcuts people rely on to expedite their judgments about what to believe or what to do. *129*

FIND IT ON THE THINKSPOT

The "Pep Talk" scene in the film *Glory Road* (p. 138) is a classic "us vs. them" psychological ploy. I invited you to watch this scene at **www.TheThinkSpot.com**.

The coach's challenge the evening before the championship game was not only to motivate the team to give its best effort. He also wanted his players to know that they deserved to win and that their victory would mean something to a nation wrestling with a legacy of racial discrimination. The coach used critical thinking to identify a strategy whereby he might accomplish his motivational goal.

- There are other scenes in *Glory Road* where the coach needs to solve problems and make important decisions—for example, in his conversations with his wife, with the players individually, and with their parents. The coach's wife also displays strong critical thinking in how she deals with the pressures on her husband and family that come with the coach's recruiting and playing black athletes at a time and

place in our history when racial prejudices and discrimination were strong. Watch the film in its entirety and pay special attention to how the coach and his wife think their way through socially awkward and personally stressful situations. Notice too the way that the screen writers rely on our heuristic expectations so that we viewers can sense the nature of the problems and feel the urges of our own heuristic responses.

Several things contributed to the basketball success chronicled in *Glory Road*. But one thing is for sure, had the coach or his wife, as depicted in the film, simply responded to events based on their unreflective heuristic guided responses, the championship would not have been won and their story never told.

Exercises

TWO- OR THREE-PERSON SMALL GROUP EXERCISE

Reflect on the choices you made today, for example, your choices of what you ate at one of your meals. Replay in your minds how you made that decision. Assuming that you are like the rest of us, you probably did not really give equal and due consideration to all of your potential options. That's OK. Heuristic snap judgments can be good things, for one, they are highly efficient and they conserve time and energy. Think now about the foods that you could have eaten, but decided not to choose. Share with the others in your conversation group the basis upon which you eliminated the ones you did not select. Was it by weighing all the pros and cons of each choice? Or was it via a snap judgment to reject a given option? For example, did association (memory of prior bad experience), affect ("looked gross"), or elimination by aspect ("too large a portion") play a role in your System-1 decision making? Talk about the choices you did make. Which cognitive heuristics played a role in those? For example, representativeness ("reminded me of something my Mom makes that tastes really good, so I thought this would taste good, too."), or satisficing ("I was in a hurry and I just grabbed the first thing that looked halfway edible").

REFLECTIVE LOG: TWO HOURS

Today or tomorrow keep a written record of all your actions, judgments, and decisions occurring within a two-hour window that begins one hour before your main meal of the day. Make eight very brief log entries, one every 15 minutes. For each entry, list all the actions, judgments, and decisions you made in the prior 15 minutes. Keep track of what you are doing using your System-1 and System-2 thinking. Continue right up through preparing your meal, eating it, and what ever you do afterward until the two-hour period is completed. For example, did you send a text, use the lavatory, think about a relationship, plan what to do on the weekend, open a can of soda, talk with a friend, imagine what it might be like to have more money, listen to music, fret over a problem, or go for a run? Whatever you did and whatever decisions or judgments you made, write them down.

Later, after a couple more hours have passed, go back and review your list of all your actions, judgments, and decisions you made. Count the number that you would classify as System-1 and the number you would classify as System-2. Are there any that you classified as System-1 that, in retrospect, you wish that you had reflected about more before acting or deciding as you did? In view of this little personal experiment, are their ways to build more critical thinking self-monitoring and self-correcting into your daily life?

CHALLENGE EXERCISE: EXPLAIN IT TO GRANDMA

Critical thinking is nothing new. Human beings have been relying on our reflective System-2 thinking from—well—from our beginning. Today we call this purposeful reflective judgment about what to believe and what to do "critical thinking." And we talk about its core skills and the positive habits of mind that incline us to use those skills. We caution ourselves against relying too heavily on snap judgments and we discipline ourselves to be reflective and thoughtful. The question is, do our grandparents use critical thinking or not?

If you are fortunate enough to be able to talk with one of your grandparents, please ask him or her if he or she uses critical thinking to solve problems and make decisions. Since the chances are overwhelming that he or she will not understand your question if you use the expression "critical thinking," you will have to find some other way to ask the question. If you are not able to talk with any of your grandparents about critical thinking, then your challenge is to find someone else with whom you can have the conversation. The catch is that the person has to be at least 40 years older than you.

The challenges of this exercise, in addition to simply having the conversation, are to explain what you are learning about critical thinking and to see how much of what you describe is something that the older person may have also learned. Is there something the older person knows about strong critical thinking that you may not yet have learned?

WHY DO WE FEEL SO CONFIDENT IN OUR CHOICES THAT WE SELDOM CHANGE OUR MINDS?

HOW CAN WE USE CRITICAL THINKING TO MAKE BETTER DECISIONS?

WHAT SPECIFIC CRITICAL THINKING STRATEGIES CAN WE USE TO IMPROVE OUR DECISION MAKING?

"Going to

war in Iraq was the right decision then, and it still is today." Former Vice President Dick Cheney was interviewed on ABC's *Good Morning America* in December 2008 about his 40 years of public service to this nation. He was our Secretary of Defense, Chief of Staff for former President Ford, and our Vice President for two terms. His influence on decision making at the highest levels of government is unmistakable. As you will see in the clip, when asked about the decision to go to war in Iraq, he gives five reasons why that was and remains a good decision today. Watch the two-minute interview at **www.TheThinkSpot.com** and list Cheney's five reasons.

In early 2003 President Bush and Vice President Cheney gave the American people two main reasons to go to war with Iraq: (1) Saddam Hussein possessed weapons of mass destruction, and (2) Iraq was linked to the Al-Qaeda terrorists who attacked the World Trade Center in New York in 2001. Later, the facts that Saddam Hussein had no WMDs and that there was no link to Al-Qaeda emerged. With both main reasons gone, should the decision to go to war be reversed or sustained?[i] With the facts refuting the main reasons to go to war, the original decision-makers, including Cheney, could have said that going to war, in retrospect, appeared to be a mistake. Instead, they vigorously affirmed that the decision to go to war had been the right decision. In the 2008 interview, Cheney offered five reasons that bolster the 2003 decision. In that interview he made no mention of arguments for any other point of view. An overwhelming dominant cognitive fortress has been constructed around that decision.

I selected this politically charged example intentionally. In order to strengthen our critical thinking, we must develop the capacity to entertain ideas without necessarily agreeing with them or rejecting them. Moreover, in this case, like the others in this chapter, the focus is on the commitment people have to their ideas, not the ideas themselves. This chapter is about how critical thinking can improve decision making. We need specific examples, but our focus is, again, on the decision-making process, not on the issue being decided about. To appreciate the example about Vice President Cheney, please do not focus on the war, the initial justifications for the war, or any of the five reasons the former vice present advanced for the war in 2008. But

continued on next page

DECIDING WHAT TO DO AND DOING IT

CHAPTER 10

continued from previous page

please do notice how self-assured he remains in the correctness of the decision. The reason this example fits our needs so well is that Mr. Cheney, a shrewd and articulate individual, vividly displays a psychological capacity that we all share. Our species has the psychological capacity to make a decision, particularly one involving risk and uncertainty, and then to move forward on the basis of that decision without looking back. We become convinced we are right and that those who do not see things our way are wrong. We all are able to sustain our decision, reaffirm it, bolster it, and defend it. And many of us will keep right on believing that our decision is right even if our original reasons no longer apply. Yes, it is possible that we might reconsider or change our minds, but once we have locked in on our choice, the chances of that happening are remote.

This chapter explores our natural human tendency toward **dominance structuring**. This is an extremely valuable characteristic. With confidence in the choice we have made, we are able to take action. Believing our decisions are right, we can persevere during difficulties. We would hardly be able to accomplish anything were we to constantly reconsider every decision and change our minds. Our natural tendency toward dominance structuring helps us to be resolute and to sustain our commitments. But with the benefits come risks. Because dominance structuring tends to lock us into a decision, this tendency can occasionally lock us into an unwise decision. The critical thinking skill of self-regulation and the habit of truth-seeking are our best hopes for identifying those occasions and guarding against hanging onto poor decisions. In this chapter we'll first unpack dominance structuring so we can see how it works. Then we'll consider critical thinking strategies for managing the occasionally negative influences and consequences of dominance structuring.

Dick Cheney, a Republican, was not the first high-ranking government official to argue that America's role in a controversial foreign war was the right thing to do. Robert McNamara, the Secretary of Defense for John F. Kennedy and Lyndon B. Johnson (both Democrats), made the same effort with regard to the Vietnam War. Challenge Exercise: Compare and contrast the arguments made by McNamara and Cheney as they explain why the decision to go to war remained the correct one. Robert McNamara is interviewed in the 2004 Oscar-winning documentary by Errol Morris, *Fog of War*. Access it at **the THINKSPOT** www.thethinkspot.com **www.TheThinkSpot.com**.

Dominance Structuring: A Fortress of Conviction

Once human beings have made a decision, they almost never change their minds. Looking back on our choice as compared to other options, we often feel that ours was so obvious and others were so poor that it is a wonder that we considered them possibilities at all. Maybe we do not need to work on the skill of self-regulation after all because we're seldom, if ever, wrong. We are likely to say to ourselves, "Others may disagree, but that's their issue." Things may not turn out as we had expected, but that's just bad luck or someone else's screwup. Right? Be honest; there are plenty of times when we all have thought exactly that. Why? Part of the answer may be that we really do a good job of making sound decisions. And part of the answer, whether our decisions are objectively wise or foolish, is our tendency toward dominance structuring. To appreciate the thought-shaping influences of dominance structuring, consider the arguments presented in this next example.

"I WOULD DEFINITELY GO TO THE DOCTOR"

This example is about a woman who, like Mr. Cheney, has made a decision. She has been asked to describe her decision making in detail to a trained interviewer. The narrative below is a brief excerpt from the transcription of that much longer interview.[ii] The interviewer and the woman are talking about the possibility that she might discover a worrisome lump during a breast self-examination. The excerpt begins with the interviewer asking the woman whether she would go to see her health care provider if she were to discover a change in her body that caused her to worry about the possibility of breast cancer.

Interviewer: "You're very religious. Could you see yourself waiting a while before going to the doctor and praying instead?"

Respondent: "Oh, no. For one thing, God is a wonderful God; he made doctors. You know, my mother-in-law—I'm divorced, I was married then—she had had a heart attack. And, she definitely would pray instead of go to the doctor. She loved the Lord, and she remained in God's will [and was fortunate not to die]. But at times people have to understand that God doesn't make things as complicated as people kind of want to make it. And it's not about religion; it's about God, your personal relationship with Him. And God, He made some become doctors to want to help. You know that's how I feel. You know, I'll say this until the day I die and go back to the Lord. I'm a practicing Christian; I love the Lord. I just know God works within common sense. That's why He gave us a brain, you know. And I would definitely go to the doctor."

Review the decision map on page 151 showing the respondent's arguments. For this individual the option not selected ("I would pray for a while instead of going to the doctor") has virtually no support. She considers whether going to the doctor means that she is not being sufficiently trusting in God, but abandons that line of reasoning. She is pulled by the availability heuristic as she recalls what her mother-in-law would do, but she resists that pull, saying that God does not make things that complicated. Although in the end she offers only two arguments directly supporting her decision, it is clear from the interview and the map that all her thinking has moved inexorably and confidently in that direction. Not going to the doctor is, for her, not really an option. The problem in her mind was how to explain that to her deeply religious friends.

Were we to evaluate the arguments the woman makes using the standards and strategies presented in Chapter 7, we would find them

MAP > it > OUT 1

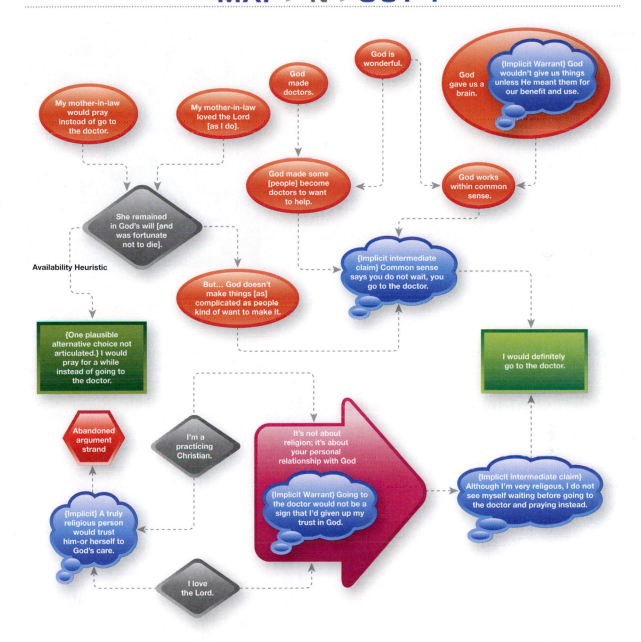

wanting. Had she followed the similarities, her comparison to her mother-in-law could well have led the respondent to infer that she did not need to see the doctor right away. The mother-in-law, a close family member, and, like herself, a woman of faith with a potentially severe illness, would delay seeking medical help. Ergo, following out the analogy, the woman being interviewed should also delay. The other arguments rely on belief statements about what God intends or how complicated God wishes things. But humans cannot know the mind of God. Therefore, we cannot establish the truth of premises about what God may be wanting, intending, or thinking. This makes the soundness of those two arguments highly questionable. And yet, whatever their individual logical weaknesses might be, taken together her arguments are, for her, persuasive explanations that she would indeed go to the doctor. She is firm in that decision. From the longer narrative, which is not reproduced here, we can infer that she is not an uneducated or illogical person, therefore to understand what is

happening we have to dig deeper into her purposes for telling the story as she does.

As it turns out, this woman is using her reasoning skills to explain a decision, not to make a decision. Going to the doctor was always to her the more sensible of the two choices. For her this was a System-1 decision—Sick? Go to the doctor! What she needed to do was explain that choice in the light of her deeply religious views and in the context of having relatives (and perhaps friends) who use religion to delay seeing a doctor for a possibly dangerous symptom. Her cognitive challenge was actually rather formidable. She had to deal with the issue that some of her friends and the people at her church would interpret her going to the doctor as showing that her faith was weak. Notice that she does not bother to explain why going to the doctor would be valuable to her health, only why it's OK not to leave it to God. And also notice that she is not doubting her faith. But she does achieve her goal of creating a rationale to support her preferred option.

Thinking Critically   Pro or Con

Let's try a little thought experiment. Indicate whether you are pro or con on each of the following issues:

		PRO	CON
1	Legislation permitting assisted suicide	_____	_____
2	Banning abortion	_____	_____
3	The right to bear arms	_____	_____
4	Government-run health insurance programs	_____	_____
5	Legalization of prostitution	_____	_____
6	Capital punishment	_____	_____

Pick one of the six issues. Write down all the good reasons for your position, pro or con. All of them, please. After you have finished, write down all the good reasons for the other position, the one that is not your view of the matter. Thank you, and we'll come back to this in a moment.

EXPLAINING AND DEFENDING OURSELVES

Our thinking capacities helped us survive as a species through the many millennia when we were anything but the most formidable species on the planet. Today our capacity for problem solving and decision making helps us achieve our personal goals, whatever they may be. If learning the truth helps achieve our goals, then we apply our skills to the problem of learning the truth. If needing to feel justified that we have made the right decision, particularly if that decision cost people their lives, is vital, we will apply our thinking skills toward creating and sustaining that justification.

Objectivity in decision making is something we prize. Yet objectivity can be very difficult for us when we already have a strongly held opinion on a given issue. Truth-seeking and open-mindedness incline us toward objectivity in the application of our skills of analysis, interpretation, evaluation, inference, and explanation. But unless we also invoke the sixth critical thinking skill, self-regulation, we may fail to achieve the objectivity we seek.

A Poorly Crafted Assignment

For many years when I taught critical thinking, I would give my students assignments not unlike this: I would say, "Gun control is a controversial issue in our nation. I want you to take a position for or against legislation banning all sales of handguns. Research the issue and defend your position with the best arguments possible. In doing so, please consider the arguments for the other side and explain why they are mistaken."

As it turned out, that was a terrible way to give a critical thinking assignment. And the reason was that my students would do *exactly* what I had asked, in *exactly that order*. If they did not already have a point of view on the matter, they would first take one side or the other. Often their System-1 heuristic thinking played a big role in determining which side they took. Some were "pro guns" and some had poignant personal stories of gun violence that made them "anti gun." Some would knock one side or the other out of contention in their minds using the one-rule decision-making tactics of elimination by aspect, "If she'd had a gun to protect herself, she'd be alive today" or "You don't need an automatic pistol to hunt deer." Then after

they had taken a side in their minds, they would search for reasons and information that supported their point of view, but not reasons or information that opposed the view they had adopted. This was energetic investigation, but it was neither truth-seeking nor fair-minded. Their minds were pretty much already made up on the subject. Next they would write a paper laying out all the good reasons for their points of view. But, no matter which side they took, they struggled to say anything good about the opposing point of view. Their papers, by the way, were often well organized and logically presented. Like the woman talking about her decision to see the doctor, my students could explain their decisions and defend them. But they had not reflected on whether or not they were the best decisions. Critical thinking is not the holding of a belief; it is the process of reflective judgment by which we come to the belief.

> It is the mark of an educated mind to be able to entertain a thought without accepting it.

Aristotle

The problem was my own, not my students'. I wanted my students to give due consideration to both sides of a controversial issue and to think about it in a fair-minded, objective, informed, and well-reasoned way. But that was not the instruction I gave. What I had done instead was invite them to build a dominance structure around one option and to bolster their perspective by fending off all counterarguments. I should have said, "The right to bear arms has become a major issue in our country. Come to class on Monday next week prepared to discuss this issue. I may ask you to take either the pro side or the con side with regard to a possible piece of legislation relating to gun control. Open your mind to either possibility. Be ready to present either side effectively. And be ready for the third possibility, which is that I will assign you to listen and then to

Pro or Con Revisited

Let's go back to the exercise in which I requested that you write down all the good reasons for your side of one of those six issues. Please count up the number of good reasons you put down for your opinion and then do the same for the other side. If you are like most of the rest of us, it was easier to list more reasons in favor of your point of view than against it. Was that true? Did you list more in favor of your view than the opposing view? Most of us would have. Do you think you listed the strongest reasons against your point of view? Most of us do not take the time necessary to discover exactly what those are. Most of us act as if those who disagree with us have flimsy arguments when compared to our own. Never assume that those who disagree with you are idiots. That could be a costly error.

adjudicate the class discussion by evaluating objectively the reasoning presented by your peers. Study the issue, inform yourself about the arguments in favor of and opposed to gun control. Be ready to speak intelligently and fair-mindedly on the topic of the right to bear arms and gun control legislation, no matter which of the three jobs I give you on Monday in class." If critical thinking is a process, then I should have found a way for my students to demonstrate that they are able to interpret, analyze, infer, explain, evaluate, and self-regulate. Only after the full, informed, and fair-minded discussion would it have made sense to invite students to then take a reasoned position on the matter.

The challenge for critical thinking is not unlike the problem of building a new house on a lot where an older house already stands. Without doing damage to the land or the neighborhood, we need to remove the old house, salvaging anything that may be of value, before we can build the new house. It takes similar skill and sensitivity to perform the same operation on opinions. Truth-seeking and open-mindedness need to be cultivated as much as possible so that we can be prepared to revisit our opinions with objectivity and judiciousness. In my life there have been more than a few times when my dearly held but ultimately mistaken opinions on controversial matters had to be abandoned so that

Poor Reflective Decisions

Reflective decisions are not always good decisions. Although reflective decision making often results in better choices, there are occasions when we make mistakes reflectively. Obviously, if we lack relevant knowledge, we are apt to make mistakes. Or if we do not anticipate the severe consequences that some options might produce, we are apt to make mistakes.

The tragic drowning deaths of three men off the coast of Florida in March 2009 illustrate these problems. You may recall the incident because it received national attention. *The Tampa Tribune* summarized the basic facts this way: "Feb. 28: Two professional football players and two who played at the University of South Florida, are lost at sea when their 21-foot boat capsizes about 35 miles west of Clearwater. Marquis Cooper, Corey Smith and Will Bleakley are lost at sea and rescuers find Nick Schuyler clinging to the hull two days later." Months later, the lone survivor, Nick Schuyler gave an interview to HBO's *Real Sports*. In that interview, which aired on August 18, Schuyler, clearly suffering emotionally from the tragic loss of his friends, told how the men, seeing a storm coming, made a series of decisions that resulted in their boat capsizing. The anchor had become stuck. They decided not to cut the rope because it would have cost a couple of hundred dollars to replace the anchor. Instead they moved the anchor line from the bow to the stern so they could try to pull the anchor free using the power of the boat's outboard motor. When they gunned the motor the anchor did not move; instead, the stern submerged and then their craft capsized. The men were thrown into the ocean. The storm hit, and over a period of two days three men succumbed to hypothermia. Had any of the men known that moving the anchor rope to the stern and gunning the engine would result in capsizing the boat, they would not have done that. But without the relevant knowledge the men made a poor decision. Or had they anticipated that deciding not to cut the anchor rope would put them at risk of dying, they certainly would have cut that rope.

The decision a 19-year-old driver made in Michigan on July 14, 2009, is a second equally tragic example of a poor decision made reflectively. The *Detroit Free Press* reported that five young people were killed when an Amtrak train hit their car. A video camera mounted on the train captured the horrible final moments. Apparently, the car driver could see up ahead that the train signals were flashing and a train barrier had lowered blocking the right lane. One car had already stopped behind the barrier. As he approached the intersection, the driver had several seconds to consider his options. Instead of stopping behind the other car, he decided to try to cross the tracks. He accelerated into the left lane to go around the stopped car, intending to cut back into the right lane as he passed over the tracks. But the train, moving at high speed, collided with the car before it cleared the tracks. The train dragged the vehicle over 100 yards, crushing its five young passengers. Was it overconfidence that led the young driver to risk his life and the lives of his four friends? Or was it that he did not anticipate the dire consequences of failing to clear the intersection? We shall never know. But we do know that he had plenty of time to consider his options. And we know that the decision to risk everyone's life could have been changed at any second as he raced toward the intersection and began maneuvering around the stopped car and the train barrier.

Why are stories like these so important? Because it would be a mistake for us to believe that deliberation, in and of itself, is sufficient to assure that we do not make mistakes. It may be our best hope, but without relevant knowledge, without the capacity to anticipate consequences, and without a good sense of what's at risk if we are wrong, we are apt to deliberate ourselves into major difficulties.

One final point: These are two tragic examples. We should have only compassion and sympathy for the victims, the survivor, and their families and friends. The analyses offered here are not intended as criticism of the people involved. We all can learn from these misfortunes.

sounder, more informed, and better-reasoned opinions could take their rightful place. But it is never easy to change one's mind about an opinion that has been firmly held, which makes the job of self-regulation that much more difficult. To understand why most of us have a very hard time changing our minds, let's explore the psychological process of deciding on "the best available option."

MOVING FROM DECISION TO ACTION

Whenever we are presented with a problem, our cognitive heuristics and our capacity for logical reasoning play critical roles in the natural human quest to find some resolution that we can assert with plausible confidence to be our best available option. We shall call this option the dominant or superior option in any given context. In decision making we move, more or less quickly, through a process that includes sorting through options. We discard the implausible ones, identify one or more promising options, evaluate it or them on the basis of our decision-critical criteria,[iv] and select the option we come to judge to be superior.[v] Psychological research by Henry Montgomery and others, as we shall see, is consistent with the idea that both argument making and cognitive heuristics are central factors in our search for a dominant option on the basis of which we move from cognition to action. In times of uncertainty when action is needed, dominance structuring is a necessary strategy for deciding between alternatives and swinging into action. Montgomery describes the human search for a single dominant option among our many possible choices in any given context as having four phases:

- pre-editing,
- identifying one promising option,
- testing that promising option for dominance, and
- structuring the dominance of the option selected.[vi]

Phase 1: Pre-editing

In the pre-editing phase, we start by selecting a group of possible options and a number of attributes that we think are going to be important as we decide which option to finally pick. Take, for example, the problem of hiring one new employee from a large applicant pool. We want to interview only a small group of highly qualified candidates. We want them to have relevant work experience, education, letters of reference, and the like. We may have a concrete set of characteristics in mind for the final choice: someone with strong communication skills, enthusiasm for the position, and a schedule that permits that person to work the hours we might require. Our selection of these criteria shows good reasoning, for they are in fact crucial to finding the best person for the job. And we expect further evidence of reasoning in the systematic approach taken to identify potential candidates by advertising the position and screening the applicants to cull the list down to a group of interviewees. But when the applications come in, we don't exhaustively rate every candidate on every decision-critical attribute. Rather, at this early pre-editing stage we look for reasonable ways to make the decision easier and more efficient. We eliminate as many alternatives as possible with as minimal an expenditure of effort as must be committed to the task.

Typically, we use the elimination by aspect heuristic and the satisficing heuristic to make our work go more quickly. We toss every applicant who is missing any single qualifying condition (no letters of reference, insufficient education, or no relevant work experience), and we retain only those we judge to be good enough for a second look. We may cluster the applications into broad categories such as "well-qualified," "qualified," and "marginal." If we do cluster them like that, we will quickly eliminate all but the "well-qualified." Pre-editing can be brutally expeditious, and yet there is good reason for this. In real life we do not have the time or the resources to deliberate in detail about the cases we already know are not going to make the cut. What's the point?

Phase 2: Identifying One Promising Option

The second phase of the search for dominance is the identification of a promising option. We do this by finding *one* alternative that is more attractive than the others on at least one critically important attribute. There are many reasons why one choice may emerge as very attractive and be judged optimal. Perhaps this choice is most in tune with our values or current desires. Or perhaps the choice is the least threatening or the most economical. Whatever the source of the attraction, once this choice is identified, it becomes our superior or dominant option. Using our hiring example, suppose there are four finalists who have passed

Job Candidate Options

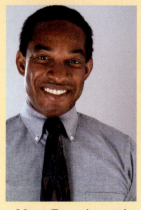

Most Experienced

Most Energetic

Most Analytical

Most Congenial

Consider a time when you needed to deliberate over a decision under conditions of uncertainty about an important issue. Perhaps, for example, you pondered the question of which college to attend, which apartment to rent, or whether to accept a job offer. How well does the four-stage process described on pages 154–156 fit with your decision-making experience in that case? Were a number of conceivable options quickly eliminated in pre-editing? Did one option begin to appear rather attractive to you for some particular reason? Did you weigh that option against a few other possibilities to be sure that yours did not have any major disadvantages? Did you do any mental trading off, bolstering, grouping of criteria, or de-emphasizing of criteria that might initially have seemed important? In the end, after you had made your decision, do you recall thinking that the choice you made was rather obviously the best option among those realistically available at the time? If you answered "yes" to all the questions, which would be fine, then it would appear that you dominance structured around that option. If you answered "no" to one or more of these questions, then reflect on what happened to derail the natural tendency toward dominance structuring in your particular case. If you do not feel that you were dominance structured around your preferred option, what new information or new considerations would have led you at the time to have made a different decision?

through our initial screening process, and we plan that a committee will interview them all. And suppose that candidate number one has the most job experience, number two is most energetic, number three is most analytical, and number four is the most congenial. It is possible the committee will immediately discover its consensus candidate. But it is more likely that different members of the committee will find different candidates to be optimal for different reasons. Each member of the committee has a different favorite. Thus, the stage is set for a difference of opinion as to which candidate should be the one hired.

Phase 3: Testing the Promising Option

Having identified a promising option, we begin almost immediately to test it against the other options. We do this by comparing our promising alternative to the other options in terms of the set of **decision-critical attributes**. Typically, we focus on seeing whether our promising option has any salient disadvantages or major drawbacks. Returning to our hiring example, suppose that five years of relevant work experience is a decision-critical criterion. If our favored candidate has seven years of relevant work experience, we will interpret that to mean that our candidate is not at a disadvantage on that criterion. That our candidate may not have as many years of experience as some other candidate is not a problem. We are not going to argue the potential positive advantage of more years beyond the minimum five. Our focus will only be to assure ourselves that our favored option does not fall short of the mark on any decision-critical factor. But what if our candidate does fall short? In that case some of us may argue that the disadvantage is not fatal to our favorite's candidacy. In fact, if we are attracted to candidate number four because of his or her congeniality, we are likely to argue that even if candidate four has only two years of experience, this is really more than enough. At this point, we are not looking to prove that our candidate is the best; rather we want to be sure that our candidate has no fatal flaws.

If our promising alternative is "comparable to the others," "about as good as the others," "neither better nor worse than the others," or "good enough" on the other decision-critical attributes, the promising alternative becomes the "to be chosen" alternative. Our initial preference for that candidate, *who was the first one we found whom we liked*, wins out. We become more and more firm in our choice. We will not abandon our "to-be-chosen" option easily. Once we begin to appraise and anchor on a given promising option, we seek to establish a rationale for selecting this promising or "to-be-chosen" option over the others, and this means we transition nearly seamlessly into phase four.[vii]

Phase 4: Fortifying the To-Be-Chosen Option

In the final phase, we restructure our appraisals of the options so as to achieve the *dominance of one option over the others*.[viii] This restructuring can be more or less rational, more or less in touch with reality, and, hence, more or less likely to lead to the intended and desirable results.[ix] One way we restructure the decision so that our "to-be-chosen" candidate comes out on top is by de-emphasizing those decision-critical attributes on which our promising candidate may be weaker. Another way is to bolster our candidate by increasing the significance of an attribute on which our candidate is stronger. A third way is to collapse attributes into larger groupings; for example, we could combine education and job experience into the single attribute, "background experience." Now we can hire someone with more education but very little job experience, overriding our concern for job experience *per se*. Or, because we do not favor candidate number one who has the most job experience, we may need to diminish this apparent strength. We might argue that work experience is an advantage of candidate number one, but some detail about that work experience (for instance, that the person had never served in a supervisory role) is a disadvantage, so the one can be said to cancel the other. And, because of this, we might argue, candidate number one is not the person to hire.

The process of *de-emphasizing, bolstering, trading off, and collapsing* attributes continues until we find that one alternative stands above the others as the dominant choice. Acute reasoning skills are vital to this complex and dynamic process of making comparisons across attributes. Obviously, one might be able to quantify within a given attribute, for example, by comparing two candidates on the basis of their years of relevant background experience. But it is not clear how one would compare, for the purposes of possible trade-offs, communication skills against, say, energy or loyalty. And yet, we will make arguments in support of the to-be-chosen alternative as the decision-maker's search continues for a dominance structure to support this choice above all others.[x] When the decision is being made by committee, and the stakes are high, this process can become interpersonally difficult, stressful, political, and, in the worst situations, ruthless.

When is dominance structuring complete? Here are three indicators: First, unless they are intentionally dissembling, people who have made their choice will tend to describe themselves as having decided, rather than as still thinking or as undecided. Second, people who are locked into a given choice tend to dismiss as unimportant, refute, or abandon all arguments that appear to be leading to a decision other than the one they embrace. Third, when asked to explain their choice,

One more time, let's revisit the stance you took on one of those six issues where you were asked to list all the good reasons for both sides. Looking at your side of the matter, describe what information or what new considerations would lead you to change your mind. Please attempt to be as forthright and honest as possible. If nothing would lead you to change your mind, then write that down.

people who have built a dominance structure to fortify their selection often present with some enthusiasm a plurality of arguments supporting their chosen decision and they tend to recite rather unconvincingly a minimum number of arguments supporting any of the other possible options.

BENEFITS AND RISKS OF DOMINANCE STRUCTURING

The result of dominance structuring is confidence, whether reasonable or unreasonable, in the option we have decided upon. Dominance structuring supplies us with enough confidence to motivate us to act on our decisions and to sustain our efforts. Obviously, the more unreasonable, biased, irrational, and unrealistic we have been in our dominance structuring, the greater the risks of a poor decision. On the other hand, if we have made the effort to be reasonable, truth-seeking, informed, open-minded, and neither too hasty nor too leisurely in coming to our decision, then there is a greater chance that the decision will be a wise one. And we would be foolish not to be confident in it and not to act on the basis of such a decision. It is hard to know what more we could want when we need to make an important decision that involves elements of risk and uncertainty.

It would be a mistake to think of this human process as intentionally self-deceiving or consciously unethical or unfair. Rather, what cognitive scientists like Montgomery offer is a description of how human beings bolster confidence in their judgments under conditions of uncertainty. Humans seek to establish a strong and enduring rationale for the belief that one alternative dominates over others to such an extent that we can act and continue to act on the basis of that belief in the enduring superiority of that option. We surround our choice with a rationale for its being superior to the others, and this strategy allows us then to move forward with that decision.

Understanding the power of dominance structuring explains why it is so difficult for us to reconsider a choice once it has been made or why the criticisms of our choices seem unpersuasive. Once we have dominance structured around a choice, the virtues of other options are less compelling and their vices appear larger than they may in fact be. When the dominance structure has been created, it is not uncommon to hear people describe the results of their deliberations with phrases like "When we looked at it, we really didn't have any other choice," or "Hey, at the end of the day it was a no-brainer!" These mantras are evidence that the decision-maker has elevated one option to the top position and discredited or discounted all other options, so at this point, it is unclear to the decision-maker why any of the other options were ever considered viable in the first place.

Proponents of organic foods maintain that they're natural, they taste better, they are healthier for us, they are more environmentally sustainable, and purchasing them supports local small farmers. We should put aside the first reason, "they are natural." The Black Plague was natural, as are tornadoes, polio, and selfishness; thus, the argument "It is natural, therefore it is good" is fallacious. But the other reasons, well, those seem plausible. Of course, there's the issue of cost. Organic foods are expensive. So, for the sake of this exercise, let's eliminate that factor from the other side of the equation. Assume that you have plenty of money to spend on food. So, for this exercise, money is no problem. This leaves four reasons to go organic. And we only need one good reason to accept the claim that going organic is what we ought to do. Would you buy organic, if you had enough money? Yes or no? If no, why not? If yes, what would it take for you to change your mind? What if all four reasons were knocked down, would you still buy organic? What if all four reasons were knocked down and the assumption that you had plenty of money was removed? After you write your answers for this exercise, watch the clip "Organic" from *Penn and Teller: Bullshit!* (Showtime, Season 7, Episode 6). As with the opening example with Mr. Cheney, our focus in this chapter is not on the pro or con arguments about buying organic. For our purposes, what this video shows is that ordinary people can hold onto a decision (in this case, to buy organic foods) even though they come to believe that their reasons for doing so are misguided. Unscripted, they display how our shared, human psychological tendency to dominance structure around a decision continues to have the power to influence our behavior even after we no longer accept our original reasons for that decision. Access the video at **www.TheThinkSpot.com**.

Searching for dominance in conjunction with elimination by aspect, satisficing, and anchoring with adjustment involves cognitive risks. First, the risk is in making poor decisions due to a lack of due consideration of all reasonable alternatives. Second, we risk that we are blind to the chance that our choice might be seriously flawed or need revision. At some level, we recognize these potential problems in human decision making. Our judicial system, for example, generally provides for appeals to be made to some person or judicial panel other than the one that rendered the initial decision. We know that once people have fixed their minds on given results, it is very difficult for them to change their judgment. In everyday life, who is there to review our decisions for us if we do not do have the habit of truth-seeking and the skill of self-regulation so that we can review them ourselves?

O. J. SIMPSON'S VIGOROUS DEFENSE

There are countless examples that display our natural human tendency toward dominance structuring. People engaged in group decision making have been known to revisit, and, at times, modify or reinterpret virtually every element involved in judging what to believe and what to do. Even if we assume that the decision-makers are paragons of intellectual honesty, we should not underestimate the risks of dominance structuring around a mistaken choice if we are not careful. Although it may not make logical nor ethical sense to do so, there is no psychological limit on renegotiating the decision-critical attributes. We all want to be successful and solve our problems, and thus we are inclined, at times, to change our evaluations of competing options simply to reach a solution.[xi] And when it comes to our enthusiasm for our to-be-chosen option, objectivity requires cognitive discipline—that is, strong critical thinking habits of mind.

So, we have two drivers to consider. One is our desire to achieve closure by making a decision. And the second is our psychological capacity, whether it is logical and ethical or not, to revisit and renegotiate every aspect of a decision to advance the to-be-chosen option. How might these two, in combination, make group decision making challenging? Well, consider what it might have been like to be a member of the jury for the O.J. Simpson murder trial.

Mr. Simpson, at that time, was one of the most widely known and admired college and professional American football stars of the era. Retired from football, he was an international celebrity who made movies and commercials. Then he was accused of murdering his wife and her lover, and a celebrity trial of the kind that perhaps only Los Angeles can produce filled the airwaves throughout 1995. People watched on television, and news reports appeared daily in the tabloids and the mainstream media. Mr. Simpson retained a stellar defense team to represent him and vigorously defend him from the accusations.

In Chapter 2, we said that critical thinking gave reasoned consideration to *evidence, methods, conceptualizations, standards,* and *contexts of judgment.* One way to interpret the "not guilty" verdict the jury returned for Mr. Simpson is to see how each of these five elements was addressed by the defense team:

O. J. Simpson's Murder Trial Defense Team

During Mr. Simpson's murder trial, the DNA *evidence* was questioned. "Was this really Mr. Simpson's DNA?" Some on the jury may have found it lacking. During the trial, the defense lawyers attacked the *methods* of the police investigation. "Was the chain of evidence secure or could there have been tampering?" Some on the jury may have judged those methods to be inadequate. The defense lawyers shifted the *context* of concern away from the violence done to the murdered people and onto the motives of potentially racist police officers and the moral character of those who were killed. Some on the jury may or may not have been distracted by this shift of attention. The *concepts* that were used by the defense went beyond jurisprudence to include those ideas and theories some associate with the politics of race. Perhaps some on the jury accepted that analysis and were influenced to be more sympathetic toward the accused because of that. The *standard* for a conviction— "beyond a reasonable doubt"—appeared to be given a new meaning by the defense team in which virtually every doubt might be conceived of as reasonable. Perhaps one or more of the jurors found the phrase problematically vague, resulting in a misapplication of the standard. Critical thinking in the context of group decision making is challenging even when the question is not as high-stakes as a potential murder conviction and even when the circumstances are less politically charged.

It would appear that to some of the jury members, the to-be-chosen alternative was that the accused was not guilty. Dominance structuring would suggest from that point forward some on the jury may have done whatever might psychologically be needed to restructure interpretations of evidence, analyses of motives, or the meaning of "reasonable doubt" to bring the option to dominance. To achieve this, it took more than just will power. It took considerable creativity and reasoning prowess to provide the jurors with the language and the conceptualizations that would permit them to go in the direction of the to-be-chosen alternative: "innocent." Arguments had to be made, data presented, reasons (contrived or otherwise) given, claims supported, and counterarguments refuted. Alternative explanations of the crime had to be simulated, effective responses favorable to the accused had to be engendered, options eliminated by aspect, and countless other opportunities for heuristic thinking made available. Eventually, the drive to come to a conclusion may have moved the jury to render the "not guilty" verdict, given that it became clear during their deliberations that one or more members of the jury were never going to be able to vote for "guilty." The drive for closure meant that the jury would not, could not, deliberate indefinitely.

Mr. Simpson's defense team fulfilled its duty of putting on a vigorous defense. In so doing, the team demonstrated outstanding skills at being able to reframe the entire problem in the mind of at least some jurors. They got some on the jury to believe that in deciding Mr. Simpson's guilt or innocence they were also sending a valuable message about the systematic oppression of African Americans in a society that tacitly condones a criminal justice system rife with racism, incompetence, brutality, and evidence tampering. I am not suggesting that some jurors thought Mr. Simpson was guilty but voted "not guilty" simply to make a political statement. Dominance structuring does not work that way. I am saying that some jurors built a psychological dominance structure around the belief that the state had failed to meet its burden of proof, "guilty beyond a reasonable doubt," because of the racism, incompetence, etc., in the system. And these jurors could not, in good conscience, vote a defendant guilty having dominance structured around the belief that the burden of proof had not been met by the state.[xii]

Dominance structuring is a powerful influence on individual and group decision making, as the Simpson murder jury example illustrates. Our last discussion may seem a harsh critique of human decision making. However, no criticism is implied or intended. Nor is any praise. The description of dominance structuring is meant to be exactly that: a description of how human decision making works based on empirical investigations. At times we do well, at other times not.

OK, given that we humans engage in dominance structuring, and given that the process has many benefits but some risks, is that the end of the conversation? No. Developing strength in critical thinking is about improving our decision making. We are human beings, not machines, so we are not going to replace dominance structuring with some other process. The question for strong critical thinkers with a positive disposition toward truth-seeking becomes "What steps can we take to improve our decision making outcomes given that we tend toward dominance structuring?"

Self-Regulation Critical Thinking Skill Strategies

Because dominance structuring is an automatic System-1 tendency, we do not ask ourselves whether we wish to engage in dominance structuring or not. We just do it. And, again, for the most part that is a good thing, particularly in contexts of uncertainty when a decision is needed and action is required. But, sometimes, premature dominance structuring is a mistake. It can lock us into a less than optimal decision. Fortunately, System-2 is capable of overriding and intervening. There are many strategies to mitigate the risks of dominance structuring around a less than optimal choice. These strategies rely on the critical thinking skill of self-regulation. Using self-regulation we can monitor our individual and group decision making, and we can make corrections in our decision-making processes to protect ourselves against prematurely dominance structuring around a lesser option. Some of these strategies will be familiar and obvious, but others may be new to you. What's important is that we use our self-regulation skills to monitor decision making and make mid-course corrections should we begin to waver. And that can happen, because our preferred option, after all, appears to be rather strong as compared to the others. So, we will be tempted to take short-cuts and to achieve closure prematurely on our preferred option,

"Apartment Must Haves"

✓ Under $900/mo

✓ Two bedrooms

✓ Near campus

✓ Near metro stop

✓ Safe neighborhood

fortifying it psychologically even against the onslaught of our original precautionary intentions.

CRITICAL THINKING PRECAUTIONS WHEN PRE-EDITING

Be Sure about "the Problem"

What we take to be the problem can limit our imaginations about possible solutions. For example, if the problem is "Our team is not going to meet the deadline," our solutions include working harder, putting in more time, or reducing the quality of the work to complete it on time. But if the problem is "Roy is not doing his share of the work," then our solutions include talking with Roy about the importance to the team of his fulfilling his responsibilities, giving some of Roy's work to other team members, replacing Roy on the team, or excluding Roy from the work effort and the resulting credit for the team's accomplishments. As we saw in the video that introduced Chapter 3, the crew of *Apollo 13* was able to identify the right problem; it was the oxygen. But if they had interpreted the problem to be instrumentation, it is difficult to see how they would have survived. Through training and experience, we learn all sorts of ways of solving all kinds of problems. But if we interpret the problem incorrectly, we are very apt to decide upon a solution that will be ineffective or inappropriate.

Specify the Decision-Critical Attributes

Before beginning to work on a solution, be clear about the standards to be applied when evaluating options and minimum thresholds that an acceptable option must meet. If two years of work experience is an expectation for hiring, then say so and stick to it. If a non-stop flight is, in your judgment, a requirement for your next vacation trip, then don't compromise on that standard. On the other hand, if a non-stop flight is desirable but not essential, then don't elevate a secondary criterion to the level of "mandatory." If the decision must be made after you hear from your friend next week on Monday, but before the opportunity lapses next week Thursday, then hold to that time frame. People with strong critical thinking skills and habits of mind protect themselves from making suboptimal decisions by establishing primary and secondary criteria and negotiating the secondary ones but holding firm to the primary ones.

Be Clear about Why an Option Is In or Out

Even at the pre-editing phase, make a reflective and deliberative judgment as to why each option should remain in contention or be eliminated. It will be impossible in most cases to give full consideration to every conceivable option. We need to eliminate large numbers of options early in the process so we can conserve time and energy to focus on those that remain. Real estate sales people know this, and so they will ask prospective buyers and renters about their price range and how many bedrooms they need.

These two parameters alone will enable agents to avoid wasting their own time and their clients' time on properties that are too expensive or not the right size.

Suppose you are looking to rent a two-bedroom apartment for less than $900 per month near school. A computer search or a friend who is a real estate agent can provide a list of a dozen apartments within minutes. Because you were clear about why an option was in (near the campus, two bedrooms) and why an option was out (cost more than $900), each and every one of the apartments will be a viable possibility. Your chances of making a poor decision or falling in love with a place you cannot afford or that does not meet your needs are reduced considerably. Suppose that a safe neighborhood and proximity to the metro system are also major considerations for you. Now, with clarity about five criteria, the choices become fewer and the next step, identifying the promising option, is more manageable.

CRITICAL THINKING PRECAUTIONS WHEN IDENTIFYING THE PROMISING OPTION

Scrutinize Options with Disciplined Impartiality

When you first start considering a problem, it is too soon to become the champion of one alternative over another, and you'll need to discipline yourself to assess strengths and weaknesses without becoming enamored of any specific option. If there are four apartments to look at, prepare your mind to look objectively at each. In practice, this can be more difficult than it seems, especially because many professional real estate agents often use the following tactics. First, an agent shows an acceptable property, a weaker one second, the best one third, and a lesser-quality property fourth. Psychologically, this puts the client at ease because, after two less-than-fully-desirable options, the third option looks really good, adjusting upward from where the client had first anchored. Seeing a less-acceptable fourth option helps lock the client in on the third option. Although the sales person may never have heard of Professor Montgomery and dominance structuring, he or she knows how to wield these decision behaviors. The agent might ask the client to note the positives of one apartment over the other, guiding the dominance structuring process along. The agent will have a fifth to show, if the client insists, but the agent is hoping that the client will lock in on one that is "good enough." The way *not* to be shepherded into a decision we might later regret is to decide beforehand that we will not let ourselves make any decision about the options, not even a tentative decision, until we have examined each with equal scrutiny.

Listen to Both Sides First

A variation on the previous strategy is the mental discipline not to decide until we have heard the other side of the story. Judges instruct juries not to decide until after the prosecution and the defense have both completed presenting their cases and made their closing arguments. Parents discover that it is not good enough to hear one child's story about who started the fight and why. They know that they must hear the other child's side of the story. We all have a natural tendency to believe the first credible report we hear and then use that belief to critique subsequent reports. In the August 2009 political battle over health care reform legislation, those opposed predicted dire consequences should reform legislation pass. It was very difficult after that for the proponents to clarify exactly what the proposed legislation would do. Most of us had decided what we believed based on the first thing we heard. It would have taken a set of practiced critical thinking self-regulation skills and a strong habit of open-mindedness to resist coming to a premature decision regarding which side to believe.

CRITICAL THINKING PRECAUTIONS WHEN TESTING THE PROMISING OPTION

Use All the Essential Criteria

As obvious as this seems, we often do not use all the decision-critical criteria after identifying our preferred option. We like the apartment in the complex that has the well-equipped workout room, and so we elevate that new factor to the status of a major consideration. But our initial set of essential factors did not include that consideration. It may have been on our desirable list, but it was not on the essentials list. Instead, we err by neglecting one or more of our initially essential criteria, for example, the proximity to the university or the cost. Strong critical thinking disciplines of mind incline us toward sticking to our initial criteria and applying all of them to this candidate and to all the other candidates. If a new and important criterion emerges during the decision-making process, then we would want to revise the list of decision-critical criteria and initiate a new search. There may be others that have great recreational spaces. As we first envisioned our set of criteria, great recreational space was not among them. Until we saw this apartment, that consideration was not an essential factor. No matter whether we stick with our initial set of criteria or initiate a new search with a new set of criteria, the important thing is that we apply all of them if they are all considered essential.

Treat Equals as Equals

The tendency toward dominance structuring privileges the promising option over all the other candidates by orienting our thinking around whether that one option has any obvious disadvantages. If the favored option has no obvious disadvantages, then it will become the to-be-chosen option. I like the apartment in the complex with the great fitness room. So, I ask myself whether it has any major disadvantages as compared to the other choices. It's pricy, but I can stretch. It isn't as close to

Thinking Critically   Your Candidate in 2008

One's orientation toward a political party, either Democratic or Republican, runs deep. People often find themselves consistently voting for candidates from the same party. Dominance structuring explains part of this, and obviously the quality of the candidates and what they stand for explains part, too. Consider the candidate you supported in the 2008 presidential election, Obama or McCain.

What would it have taken for you to support the other candidate? Make a decision map of

your reasons for supporting your favored candidate and the reasons for voting for the other candidate. After you have finished your map, inspect it to see whether your decision map reveals a larger clustering of arguments around your favored candidate, with relatively fewer arguments supporting the other candidate. Evaluate the quality of those reasons using the standards presented in Chapter 8.

the university, but it's not too far either. I wish the second bedroom were bigger, but I can live with that. Nope. No major disadvantages. Notice that in this process I did not give all four options a fair-minded evaluation, seriously comparing them on each criterion. Instead of truth-seeking, I threw objectivity to the wind and settled for a apartment that was more expensive, further from the university, and too small. And I did not even look at the other two criteria, safety and proximity to the metro.

Diligently Engage in Truth-Seeking and Remain Impartial

Truth-seeking helps us follow reasons and evidence wherever they lead, even if they go against our preferred or favored option. This is an active process. We must discipline ourselves to go out and find the needed evidence and consider all the reasons, pro and con. Being diligent in truth-seeking means that we give fair-minded consideration to options and ideas even if they go against our preconceptions or cherished, but perhaps unreflectively held, beliefs. Impartiality helps us maintain our objectivity. But we all know that it is

hard to be impartial in some situations. If the stakes are high for us or if people we care about are involved, it is very difficult. Strong critical thinking demands that we recognize contexts in which impartiality is difficult to maintain. In those cases, if others are involved, the judicious thing to decide is that someone else should decide. In legal matters, when a potential juror is deemed to be at risk of not being impartial, that person is excused from being a juror. A judge who is at risk of not being impartial in a given case asks that the case be moved to a different judge. But in our daily lives, we cannot remove ourselves from judging or excuse ourselves from the responsibility of making decisions. We must, instead, make a conscious and deliberative effort to decide objectively. The habit of truth-seeking and the skill of self-regulation are irreplaceable assets in doing this.

CRITICAL THINKING PRECAUTIONS WHEN FORTIFYING THE TO-BE-CHOSEN OPTION
Be Honest with Yourself

The complex processes at this stage are difficult to manage unless one is deeply committed to making honest evaluations. But, if there are good reasons, we can de-emphasize a given decision-critical criterion relative to another. In the apartment example, price may be more important than proximity to the campus. At other times, a criterion cannot be de-emphasized. Safety, for example, might have been a major consideration in the pre-editing phase. If that were the case, then it would be intellectually dishonest to argue at this point that it is no longer a factor to consider seriously. When bolstering we may be tempted to exaggerate the virtues of

our to-be-chosen option and exaggerate the vices and shortcomings of the other options. But exaggeration would be less than fully honest. Yes, our favored candidate does have advantages, and yes, the other options have flaws, but we should use self-regulation to monitor our evaluation so that we do not blow these advantages or these flaws out of proportion. Trading off one criterion for another can be straightforward if the two have the same metric. For example, proximity to the university and proximity to the metro can both be measured in time and distance. So, we can more easily decide whether being a little closer to the metro and a little further from the university is acceptable or not. But when two criteria are measured on different metrics, the tradeoffs can be more difficult. How much safety should one trade to get a lower rent? How much smaller can that second bedroom be in order to live closer to the university? Again, we need self-regulation skill to monitor and correct, if needed, our tendency to trade away too many important things to get that one feature that attracts us so much. Collapsing criteria is not going to work when the criteria are as different as those in the apartment example. It is hard to imagine price and safety as one criterion. But in the hiring example earlier in the chapter, it could be reasonable to collapse work experience, volunteer experience, and maybe service learning experience. If we can expect that the person learned job-relevant skills even though he or she may not have had a paying job, then collapsing makes sense.

CRITICAL THINKING STRATEGIES FOR BETTER DECISION MAKING
Task Independent Teams with the Same Problem

Military commanders, realizing the risks of poor decisions, occasionally set two independent teams to work on the same problem. The theory behind this strategy is that if the two teams make the same recommendations, then that recommendation is probably the best option. If the teams make divergent or conflicting recommendations, then that provides the commanding officer the opportunity to listen impartially and objectively as each team explains why its recommendation is superior.

Decide when It's Time to Decide

Particularly in group decision-making situations, there is a tendency to decide prematurely. Time for discussion is short, and some people always seem ready to decide faster than others. People can become impatient, and the urgency of other matters can lead us into the trap of "Ready, Fire, Aim." We can mitigate the tendency toward premature decision making by first setting out a plan for making the decision that identifies all the steps that will be taken first. In group decision making, this can be very helpful, for it establishes a set of expectations and assures

Deciding Whether or Not a Man Should Die

In December 2005, Arnold Schwarzenegger, Governor of California, was faced with a difficult decision. Should he grant clemency to a high-profile inmate on death row, Mr. Stanley "Tookie" Williams? The death penalty, as a social policy, had come under considerable criticism. Many well-known Californians called for Governor Schwarzenegger to commute Mr. Williams' sentence to life without possibility of parole. Many Californians believed that Mr. Williams had demonstrated for several years that he was a "changed man." As a convicted murderer he deserved life in prison, but he was not the same person he had been decades earlier, and he did not, in their view, deserve at this time to be punished with death. Some saw him as a symbol of why the death penalty should be abolished. After deliberating on the matter, Governor Schwarzenegger decided against clemency, so Mr. Williams was executed. The governor posted a document on the Internet describing his decision-making process. Access that document at **www.TheThinkSpot.com**.

The governor's statement explains his decision. First, map that decision. Your map will show that the Governor provides two primary

lines of reasoning supporting his decision. One ends in the claim that Mr. Williams is, in fact, guilty (as determined by the jury at his trial), and that there is no other basis for clemency given

that he is guilty. The map should also show additional bolstering arguments supporting the conclusion that Mr. Williams should not be granted clemency: The gangs he formed continue to do violence; his attempted escape risked the lives of law enforcement officers; and the murders he committed were brutal in nature. The governor entertained five considerations which indicated that a decision would be needed [mapped using diamond shapes]: 1) claimed innocence, 2) claimed redemption, 3) a lack of apology, 4) fairness of the trial,

and 5) good works while in prison. Several of these were endorsed as important considerations in the public debate prior to the governor's decision.

Second, examine the map that reflects your interpretation of this document to see if there is a discernible dominance structure surrounding and supporting the chosen option. Were the strongest arguments for the option not chosen identified and given due consideration? Does the map reflect that the governor applied appropriate standards in an appropriate way? Discuss your response to these two questions with due consideration to maintaining your own objectivity, truth-seeking, and fair-mindedness. These are not easy questions because the chances are that you, like most of the rest of us, have an opinion about the death penalty. And, if so, then you, like the rest of us, have probably built a dominance structure to support your opinion on that policy question. Thus, objectivity and impartiality must be self-monitored during this discussion.

Third, evaluate the governor's arguments individually and his decision holistically. Apply the criteria for evaluating arguments presented in Chapter 7, the Holistic Critical Thinking Scoring Rubric presented in Chapter 1, and what you have learned about heuristic thinking and dominance structuring in Chapters 9 and 10.

time for the diligent inquiry and deliberation that is due an important decision. Obviously, it would be equally unwise to fail to make the decision when opportunities are being missed and the costs of delaying are mounting up. Sticking to an initial plan for when and how a decision needs to be made, including the time frame, fact finding, option development, and consultation, can be very helpful.

Analyze Indicators and Make Mid-Course Corrections

Health care and business professionals employ this strategy. They frequently measure progress and make necessary adjusts if the relevant outcome indicators do not show the expected improvements. This strategy is the critical thinking skill of self-regulation made operational. When a patient is in the hospital, the clinicians monitor all the patient's bodily systems to be sure that the treatment plan is having the desired effect. If any of the many tests that are performed show that the patient's condition is not improving, then the medical team makes changes in the patient's treatment. In business settings, people monitor sales revenues, expenses, cash flow, accounts payable, and accounts receivable on a regular basis. They review data to monitor progress toward revenue targets or to be sure they are staying within budget allocations. If any of

the numbers look problematic, they make mid-course corrections. The same idea applies to decisions we make to improve or change our life situations. If we monitor the effects of those decisions and we do not see the results we planned, we need to make mid-course corrections.

Create a Culture of Respect for Critical Thinking

All of us, and leaders in particular, can increase the likelihood of better decision making by creating a culture of respect for critical thinking. We do this by modeling and encouraging positive critical thinking habits of mind. We do this by inviting, acknowledging, and rewarding the constructive use of critical thinking skills. We do this by showing respect for people even if they advance ideas and opinions that differ markedly from our own. We can model respecting people's effort to think well even if we do not accept their ideas. As leaders we would be wise to invite people to supply their reasons for their recommendations, rather than only their votes or their recommendations, as if the reasons were unimportant. As leaders we must give truth-seekers enough latitude to raise difficult questions without fear of reprisals. We must be willing to listen, to reconsider, and to be persuaded by good arguments. At the same time, we must use these same tools when presenting our final decisions—sharing not just the choice made, but providing the reasons for that choice.

CHAPTER REVIEW

Dominance structuring is the natural tendency we have to fortify our decisions in our own minds so that we can move forward with confidence to act on those decisions, particularly in contexts of risk and uncertainty. The many advantages of dominance structuring include persistence when the going gets tough, confidence that we have made the right choice, and the courage to act even though some uncertainty may remain. With these advantages there are also risks. The choice may not have been a good decision in the first place. Or conditions may have changed, making the choice no longer optimal. But unless we are monitoring our decision making and self-correcting along the way, dominance structuring can lock us into a bad decision or prevent us from making needed changes. There are many critical thinking strategies that we can use to guard against the pitfall of poor decision making. These strategies share two common themes: cultivate and practice the critical thinking habits of mind, especially truth-seeking, and apply strong critical thinking skills, especially self-regulation. You can use these strategies to monitor decision making every step of the way and correct the process as often as needed.

KEY TERMS

dominance structuring is the psychological process through which humans achieve confidence in their decisions. The four phases of dominance structuring are pre-editing, identifying one promising option, testing that promising option for dominance, and structuring the dominance of the option selected. *150*

decision-critical attributes are those criteria the decision-maker deems to be important and relevant for the purpose of evaluating options. *155*

FIND IT ON THE THINKSPOT

The decision to take the nation to war is an extremely serious one. Everyone agrees that good reasons are essential before such a momentous option is chosen. The first two www.TheThinkSpot.com references in this chapter focus, however, on how two people deeply committed to their decision to go to war continued to maintain that commitment even after new facts emerged that showed that their original reasons were seriously flawed. Dick Cheney, a Republican (p. 149), and Robert McNamara, a Democrat (p. 150), displayed the power dominance structuring has over our thinking.

   Since our convictions provide the basis for sustaining a decision once we've made it, I am all the more mindful of the need to make reflective well-reasoned judgments before I lock into a choice. I urge you to consider what you see and learn from watching how these two powerful figures in U.S. history, Cheney and McNamara, dealt with their decisions after the fact.

- Life and death decisions are not limited to wartime combat. Governor Arnold Schwarzenegger wrestled with the question of whether or not to commute the death sentence of a man convicted of murder (p. 161). The governor's reasoning is revealed in the document at www.TheThinkSpot.com. Is this only a legal question? When does it become a question of conscience?

- On a lighter note, popular culture abounds with deeply held, almost unshakable beliefs for which we have precious little hard evidence. The entertaining clip from one of Penn & Teller's broadcasts (p. 156) reveals that many of us have built almost impenetrable mental dominance structures around a belief in the superior quality, benefit, and value of organic foods. After seeing their analysis, I found myself seriously questioning some of my prior beliefs about organics. Perhaps you will too. Access the clip at www.TheThinkSpot.com.

Exercises

REFLECTIVE LOG: POTENTIALLY LIFE-ALTERING DECISIONS

Picking an apartment is a relatively benign matter compared to decisions that have the potential to radically alter the course of your life. Imagine these four possibilities:

1. Considering whether you should get married
2. Deciding whether you need help with a drinking, gambling, or drug problem
3. Deciding whether to make an embarrassing apology to someone
4. Dealing with another request from a member of your family for a loan

Step 1: Select one of the four possibilities. Think about the problem as it might play out in your life and how you would go about deciding what you should do. Simulate the entire decision. Then, draw it out in a decision map or write a free-flowing essay.

Step 2: Examine your completed map or essay for dominance structure. Evaluate your decision process to see whether you applied the critical thinking strategies to assure that you make as good a decision as possible.

SMALL GROUP DISCUSSION: WHAT WOULD IT TAKE?

You are on the governor's select committee of senior advisors, and the governor has asked you to make a recommendation and supply your reasons. Here's the situation: A serial killer who brutally rapes and tortures for days before murdering his victims was cornered by FBI agents and, while trying to escape, was shot and suffered a non-lethal head wound. Now lying in a private room in a state hospital, the killer, who is in a coma, is being kept alive by a feeding tube. Doctors say that he will never recover from the coma because of the severity of the head wound he suffered. Although there is no doubt about his guilt, he has never been arrested, indicted, or put on trial. The governor has been receiving political pressure from many sources saying that the killer should not be kept alive. They want the governor to order that the feeding tube be removed, which will cause the killer to starve to death. Others, hearing of this, have sent a flurry of messages to the governor that say that all human life must be respected, reminding the governor that this person has not been convicted of any crimes by a jury.[xiii] The governor has asked you to advise on the question: "Withdraw the feeding tube or not?" After discussing this with your group, write down your recommendation and your reasons. Also write down your reasons for *not* recommending the opposite.

After you have written down your recommendation, write down what it would take for you to change your mind and recommend the opposite. If that is not a possibility, explain why not.

PREPARING FOR YOUR BIG DECISION

Consider a decision coming up in your life. Reflect on the issues and concerns that are leading you to make this decision. What exactly is "the problem" you must resolve with this decision? What are your decision-critical criteria? Which are essential and which are important but only desirable? Are there any minimum thresholds that must be met for an option to be considered viable? How do you plan to scrutinize your options? How will you be sure that you have heard all sides? Is there a way for you to assure yourself that none of the essential options will be dropped out of the equation before you make your decision? How do you plan to assure that you have diligently engaged in truth-seeking, maintained your objectivity, and impartially evaluated all the options prior to selecting a favorite? How will you determine when the time has come to make the decision? What factors will you monitor after you have made your decision so that you can know whether a mid-course correction is needed? This exercise does not invite you to make that important decision. It invites you to lay the groundwork for making that decision by applying the critical thinking strategies of self-regulation.

SMALL GROUP DISCUSSION: WISHY-WASHY FLIP-FLOPPERS

If judiciousness is a positive critical thinking habit of mind and if strong self-regulation skills and honest truth-seeking can guide us to revisit our decisions and change our minds, why is it that, in the United States, a leader who changes his or her mind is criticized for being wishy-washy? And why is it that a politician who learns new information and comes to a new position on an issue is criticized for flip-flopping?

OPTIONAL BONUS EXERCISE: *DEATH IN THE WEST*

In 1979, the BBC aired a documentary on smoking. It featured gut-wrenching interviews with American cowboys from Montana and other Western states who were dying of lung cancer, emphysema, and heart disease. Their doctors were interviewed and hypothesized that smoking was the cause of these men's illnesses. The documentary also shows interviews with executives from Phillip Morris, the manufacturer of Marlboro cigarettes, which used the "Marlboro Man," a handsome, rugged, healthy, independent-minded cowboy, on all their advertising. The executives offered reasons why we should not believe that cigarettes were causally connected to these diseases. Phillip Morris sued the BBC. The documentary  was suppressed as part of the court settlement. It may be that only underground copies are available. If you happen to find a copy to watch, you will see dominance structuring in action. Even the independent clinical psychologist who is interviewed suggests that the Phillip Morris executives needed to think of themselves as people doing worthy labor, not as ruthless purveyors of disease and death. And this insight came several years before the initial research on dominance structuring was published. Watch the documentary, if you can locate a copy, and map the arguments made by the Phillip Morris executives in favor of smoking and opposed to those who would argue that smoking is dangerous.

WHAT ARE THE THREE MOST FUNDAMENTAL REASONING PATTERNS?

HOW CAN WE RECOGNIZE COMPARATIVE REASONING?

HOW CAN WE EVALUATE COMPARATIVE REASONING?

WHAT ARE THE USES, BENEFITS, AND RISKS OF COMPARATIVE REASONING?

"The reporter

is supposed to shout, 'Americans, these guys are about to attack you,' and then you die. Is that the problem here?" demands veteran CBS News anchor Mike Wallace of Air Force general Brent Scowcroft. "Yes, you should warn our troops!" is the answer the general wants to hear. But that is not the answer Wallace gives. The hypothetical—you are an American TV news journalist who is embedded with enemy troops who are about to ambush a platoon of American soldiers. Your options—videotape the ambush for the evening news or warn the American platoon.

The program *Ethics in America* brought together military officers, journalists, and government officials to debate this hypothetical as a way of exploring the relationship between one's responsibilities as a professional journalist and one's responsibilities as a fellow American. Mike Wallace and Peter Jennings—at the time two of the best-known, respected, and widely watched TV journalists in the nation—struggled mightily with the high-stakes hypothetical. As Mike Wallace is speaking, another panelist, USMC colonel George M. Connell, is seething with contempt for the journalist. The Marine colonel is wondering if he should order American Marines to rescue a reporter pinned down by enemy fire if that same reporter didn't have the courage to risk his own life to save a platoon of Americans. To see how Wallace answers the general and whether the colonel would in fact send Marines to rescue a journal-

ist for whom he has "utter contempt," watch the video clip at **www.TheThinkSpot.com**.

The clip begins with Harvard Law School professor Charles Ogletree presenting the hypothetical to Peter Jennings. After clarifying the question that Ogletree has put to him, Jennings refines the question; he struggles with the ethical dilemma. At one point, about three minutes into the clip, Jennings pauses nearly 12 seconds to ponder what he would do. No experienced television personality would knowingly create that much "dead air time." But, for Jennings, the problem is very high stakes. He infers that should he decide to warn the Americans about the ambush, the enemy will immediately kill him. Ogletree turns to Mike Wallace and presents the same problem. He too struggles. Unsure how to get a handle on the dilemma, Mike Wallace tries to use an analogy—he proposes that the ethics of the situation in the combat zone are comparable to ethical standards that would apply to a similar situation in a U.S. city. If a reporter knew that a murder was about to be committed on the streets of an American city, then the reporter would be ethically bound to call the police or to try to warn the victim. "Now," says Wallace, nervously moving his hands along the top of the table, "now. . .you take that and apply it to a war zone. And. . ." The video clip is a moving display of the challenges associated with reasoning through a novel high-stakes problem.

165

COMPARATIVE REASONING: "THIS IS LIKE THAT" THINKING

CHAPTER 11

After you have watched Colonel Connell tell whether he would or would not "send Marines to save a couple of journalists," ask yourself if the comparison that Mike Wallace tried to make—between warning the soldiers and warning the potential murder victim—is a good analogy or not. Why or why not? In your arsenal of tools from Chapter 7, you already have the four tests for the acceptability of an argument. You also have the self-regulation skills we talked about in the last two chapters. Use those skills to keep your evaluation of Wallace's analogy tentative, at least for now. Moving forward, we will explore the specific criteria for evaluating comparisons, so let's put this analogy on the back burner for now.

Comparative, Ideological, and Empirical Inferences

The final part of our work on developing our critical thinking skills addresses the three most fundamental ways we make explanations and inferences. The three ways are by using comparative reasoning, ideological reasoning, and empirical reasoning. **Comparative reasoning** (or **this-is-like-that thinking**) enables us to make interpretations, draw inferences, or offer explanations by relying on something that is more familiar in order to understand something that is less familiar. For example, I have never driven an 18-wheeler, but I have driven a U-Haul rental truck and can infer that the 18-wheeler is probably more like a rental truck than a sports coupe. I'm thinking about the most important similarities, at least to me, between an 18-wheeler and a rental truck: a larger vehicle with limited maneuverability, a cab higher off the ground, and heavier. The two are not exactly alike, but they have a lot of characteristics in common that relate directly to what it probably would be like to drive them.

We use comparative reasoning when giving advice by using a story that relates the current problem to a similar one we have experienced in the past. Legal reasoning uses this strategy in the appeal to precedent. Imaginative engineers and scientific investigators use this way of reasoning when they develop and apply theoretical models in the creative search for novel solutions to problems. We will explore the creativity, complexities, and uncertainties of comparative reasoning in this chapter.

So that you know the plan, and so that you can get a preliminary sense of the contrasts between the three modes of reasoning, here's what we'll do in the next two chapters: In Chapter 12, we'll consider ideological reasoning, which is drawing inferences from axioms, principles, or fundamental truths to determine their specific applications. In high school plane geometry, for example, we begin with a set of first principles or assumptions about lines and points, and from these we infer the theorems they imply. A person with strongly held political or religious principles will use this mode of reasoning to draw inferences about specific legislative proposals. For example, if I begin with the principle that all human life is sacred, I am likely to oppose specific legislative proposals that would permit euthanasia because of the belief that euthanasia, the taking of a life, ought not to be permitted. As we shall see in the next chapter, ideological reasoning is largely deductive, because we are looking for what the implications of our core beliefs must be. Ideological reasoning leaves little

or no room for any doubt or possibility that the application may be mistaken.

Then, in Chapter 13, we will explore empirical reasoning, which moves from particular observations toward generalizations and theories intended to explain those observations. Because of the possibility that our theories, generalizations, and explanations might be false, this mode of reasoning is commonly associated with induction. In its most refined and sophisticated form, empirical reasoning is scientific investigatory reasoning progressing, as we saw in Chapter 8, from coincidence to correlation toward causal explanations so accurate that we can predict and control events. Chapter 13 extends that discussion by exploring the rigor, power, and limitations of scientific investigatory reasoning.

"This Is Like That"— Recognizing Comparative Reasoning

When using comparative reasoning, we make an interpretation, explanation, or inference about that which is less familiar by comparing it to that which is more familiar. As we saw in Chapter 9, comparative reasoning can be automatic, reactive System-1 thinking. The representativeness heuristic, the simulation heuristic, and occasionally the affect heuristic are examples of times that we make quick, reactive comparisons. The fruit of System-2 comparative reasoning, with its more deliberative effort to explicitly consider points of comparison and contrast, is often an analogical argument. Mike Wallace's effort in the opening video clip is an attempt to find a useful comparison when trying to solve a difficult and unfamiliar problem. Mike Wallace tried to understand his ethical responsibilities in a combat situation by considering his ethical responsibilities in a comparable, but not identical, situation he has experienced before, namely warning an innocent person that he or she is about to become the victim of a crime.

Comparative Reasoning: This is like that

Breaking Down Comparative Reasoning

Elements	Mike Wallace's Example	18-Wheeler Example
Feature or features of interest	A journalist's ethical responsibilities	Maneuverability, vision of the road, size, and weight of vehicle
Less familiar object, event, concept, or experience	An American journalist warning an American platoon in a combat zone that it is about to be ambushed	Driving an 18-wheeler
Assertion of useful likeness or similarity	is analogous to	is probably like
More familiar object, event, concept, or experience	an American journalist warning an innocent person in a U.S. city when the person is about to become the victim of a crime	driving a U-Haul rental truck

Comparative reasoning, whether System-1 or System-2, is basically the reliance on a more familiar image, idea, or experience to shape or guide how we think about something that is less familiar. I am using the word "reasoning" broadly in order to include comparisons used to illustrate our ideas as well as comparisons used to draw conclusions. There are many ways to express comparative reasoning, and not all of them are fully developed arguments with reasons and claims. But because they all can shape our judgment about what to believe or what to do, judicious critical thinkers must be alert to the rich variety of ways we use comparisons to express our thinking. Here are several examples. Each is a bit different than the others, but they do have one important feature in common: In each example, the speaker is attempting to interpret or to explain something, or to draw an inference about something, by comparing that thing to another thing the speaker believes to be more familiar to the listener.

- Think of the world as a clock. Just as a clock could not have come into existence unless there was a clockmaker, so there also must be a God who made this wonderfully complex world.

- You can make John the club's treasurer, if you want. But with the way he manages money, that would be like skydiving without a parachute.

- Time is a great river. We float on that river, like leaves borne along by the rush of seasons, spun by the turbulence of events beyond our control, knowing only that we are being carried into the infinite sea of eternity.

- How do I know that my old fireside friend, Blue, understands when I tell him it's time to go out for a walk? Well, I think that your average dog is about as smart as your average two-year-old.

- The proposed metro line will ribbon around the downtown business district and then shoot north to the airport. This will save commuters a lot of time.

- Like a knife in the heart of our town's economy, the proposed new freeway will slice this city in two, severing the commercial district from the residential neighborhoods.

- The people at the Family Bank care about each other. And we care about you. When you bank with Family Bank, you're not just customers, you're family.

- God forgives the sinner who repents in the same way that a loving father forgives a prodigal son who returns to the family.

- Former president George W. Bush, speech to the U.S. Congress, September 20, 2001: "Al Qaeda is to terrorism what the Mafia is to crime."[i]

- Animal rights activist: "We did not steal any animals from the lab. We rescued those monkeys because they were the helpless victims of torture."

- Last year, the CEO said everyone who worked here was on the same team. Then the economy goes south and he wants everyone's suggestions for downsizing. Sort of reminds you of asking for volunteers to play Russian roulette.

- Michael Douglas in the movie *Traffic*: "If there is a war on drugs, then some of the enemies are members of our own families. And I don't know how to wage war on my own family."[ii]

- You pull the trowel over the wet cement with the same kind of motion you would use to apply frosting to a freshly baked cake.

One productive way of thinking about how our minds work is by using the computer model of list processing, as suggested by Allen Newell. Just like computers, our minds store problems and tasks as lists, and our mind always works on the first thing in a list, the others coming to the fore only after the first is dealt with.[iii]

As the examples on page 167 illustrate, comparative reasoning can rely on images, comparisons, parables, allegories, fables, models, metaphors, and similes. We can use comparative reasoning to illustrate ideas, to offer interpretations, to make arguments, to give reasons, to explain our thinking, and to simplify concepts. As Mike Wallace did in the video clip, we can use these skills to help ourselves understand new ideas, unfamiliar objects, and abstract concepts. Comparisons have the power to persuade people, to shape expectations, to alter attitudes, and to evoke emotions.

When former president George W. Bush compared Osama bin Laden's al Qaeda organization to the Mafia in 2001, he communicated that al Qaeda is responsible for terrorism on a very large and organized scale, in the same way that the Mafia is responsible for crime on a large and organized scale. In addition, the former president's comparison evoked the same loathing toward al Qaeda that the public at large feels toward the ruthless, criminal Mafiosi. As a tool for communicating his ideas, Mr. Bush's comparison was powerfully effective, for it touched the American public at both an intellectual and an emotional level. Because they often communicate at the emotional level as well as the intellectual level, comparisons are among the most persuasively powerful devices in our culture.

Evaluating Comparative Inferences

Comparisons are like a fine set of carpentry tools—you have to know a tool's purpose, or else it will be useless to you. Several factors contribute to the merit of a comparison (like the one in the previous sentence). Before specifying the evaluative criteria more formally, let's first look informally at how we might evaluate a couple of examples.

- "Competition in today's business climate is like war. Companies that have good strategic plans will out-compete their opposition; they will gain market share the way an army gains ground in a battle. Lean, mean, and nimble, they will be ready to attack new opportunities and defend against threats and assaults from all sides. Their loyal troops will do whatever it takes to make the business successful, including doing battle with marketing campaigns and orchestrating superior manufacturing productivity. And in the end, they will prevail. So if you want your company to win out over the competition, hire our consulting firm. We have the know-how to make you a winner."

- "A seagull is like a sailboat. The gull's tail is like the boat's rudder. The gull's body is shaped like the boat's hull. A lot of gulls are white, and so are a lot of sailboats. Gulls often fly in flocks, and sailboats are often seen in bunches, too, called regattas. The gull's feathery wings remind me of the billowing sails. Gulls probably float on the surface of the air the way a sailboat floats on the surface of the water."

The first comparison, "business is like warfare," is the stronger of the two. It is based on several points of comparison that seem both apt and central, specifically the struggle to gain market share, the importance of being able to adapt quickly to changing conditions, and the assets of good communications, efficient manufacturing, and loyalty. The analogy is productive in another way as well, for the maker of the analogy could have extended the comparison by adding comments about corporate espionage and sabotage but did not.

The second comparison is weaker. Yes, the gull's tail functions like a rudder. But the gull's body does not function like a hull; it only looks like a hull—and then, not very much like one, given the legs hanging down. Gulls do not float on the air by displacing their weight in that gaseous medium the way a boat displaces its weight in water. The similarities of color and visual appearance are superficial, not structural or functional. The hull of a sailboat holds up the mast, which lifts and holds the sail. When birds are in flight, the lifting is done by the wings, not the body. The physics of how a wing functions is the opposite of a sail. A sail catches wind and is pushed along. In contrast, the speed of the air passing over the top of a wing, as compared to the speed of the air passing under the wing, creates lift and pulls the wing upward. The physics of flight is not the same as the physics of floating. All in all, it is a rather poor analogy indeed.

DO THE FOUR TESTS OF ACCEPTABILITY APPLY?

The analyses and evaluations offered may appear to stray a bit from the four tests for the worthiness of arguments presented in Chapter 7. Let's apply those four tests to our two examples to see if they are as useful for evaluating comparative reasoning as they are for evaluating inductive and deductive reasoning.

Are the premises all true? The key premises in these two cases are the sentences that assert the similarities "business is like war" and "a seagull is like a sailboat." Based on the analyses, our first thought when applying this test would be to evaluate "business is like war" as true and "a seagull is like a sailboat" as false. Unfortunately, the words "true" and "false" are not optimal for evaluating a sentence that asserts a comparison. The terms "true" and "false" offer us only two options when, in fact, our evaluations are more nuanced. Going back to our examples, we would want to say that "business is like war" is *more true* than "a seagull is like a sailboat." But expressions like "more true" or "more false" have no place in the world of logic. In addition, the two (waging war and sailing) are not connected in any way that would permit us to say that one is "more true" than the other. Words like "apt," "insightful," "vivid," "silly," and "superficial" are better words for evaluating sentences that assert comparisons. As we shall see, we use these insights to come up with more precise criteria for evaluating comparisons than "true" or "false."

Are there counterexamples and how difficult is it to image them? Given that comparative inferences are inductive, this question helps gauge the logical strength of the analogy. We do not have refined statistical tests to apply to comparative inferences. But we can categorize comparisons as more or less plausible. And, yes, there are counterexamples to consider. Let's look at the stronger of the two analogies. Some businesses form partnerships with other businesses, and some acquire and merge with their competitors by purchasing their stock. Behaviors like these suggest that business is not always like war. Do these observations mean that the analogy is illogical? No, that would be too negative. What this does show is that comparative reasoning shows points of dissimilarity as well as points of similarity. We will need to make a more refined judgment about the utility of the points of comparison. Again, we will build this insight into our more refined set of criteria below.

Are the premises relevant to the truth of the conclusion? The conclusion is the assertion about the characteristics of the unfamiliar object (business in the first case and gulls in the second). At first, we may not see how warfare is relevant to understanding business or how boats are relevant to understanding gulls. The burden is on the maker of the analogy to show that the comparison is relevant. In both of our examples, the argument maker offers observations to establish the relevance of the comparison.

Does the truth of any premise depend on the truth of the conclusion? This can be tricky, because for many of us, business is more familiar than warfare, and gulls or birds in general may be more familiar than boats. But comparative inferences should flow from what we know about war to what we can project to be true about business, and from what we know about boats to what we can project to be true about gulls. Both of our examples have problems with this test. Many businesspeople have never been in combat. Likewise, many people within the general public have no firsthand combat knowledge. Therefore, for many people, the comparison depends more on imagination of what war might be like than on actual warfare experience.

Based on the application of the four tests we developed in Chapter 7, neither comparison establishes that its conclusion is true or justified. But the purpose of comparative reasoning is to illustrate, illuminate, suggest, or hypothesize, rather than to prove that a conclusion is true. Our four tests of acceptability may be a little heavy-handed. Comparative inferences will almost always come up short on those four tests. Yet some comparisons appear to be stronger and more useful than others. Why is that? Because in some cases, the points of comparison are based on shared functional, structural, central, and essential features. However, in other cases, the points of comparison are based on shared features, but they are unimportant, trivial, superficial, decorative, or happenstance. We'll analyze this generalization in the next section to come up with five specific criteria to use when evaluating comparative inferences.

FIVE CRITERIA FOR EVALUATING COMPARATIVE REASONING

Why is comparative reasoning so potentially valuable? Its value comes from the possibility that comparative reasoning offers for suggesting new insights, hypotheses, and dimensions of something unfamiliar that we are trying to understand better. If the comparison is reasonable, then some salient feature of the more familiar object is also a salient feature of the less familiar object. Evaluation depends on the congruence between the two objects. "Are they alike enough in important ways or not?" *The more pervasive the essential similarities are, the more relevant the comparison is, and therefore the more credibility a conclusion based on those similarities will have.* Comparative inferences, including analogical arguments, are inductive and probabilistic. They draw their power from the perceived relevance and pervasiveness of the fundamental parallelism between the situations or objects being compared. Superior comparative inferences are *familiar*, *simple*, *comprehensive*, *productive*, and *testable*.[iv] Let's break down each of these features in turn.

Familiarity

Suppose that a speaker offers this analogical argument: "Don't put John in charge of buying groceries! That would be like asking Queen Cleopatra to do the laundry." But suppose that the listener has no idea who Queen Cleopatra was. This lack of familiarity with the object of the comparison would quash the analogy like an elephant stepping on a snail. Familiarity is the first criteria for a successful comparative reasoning process. Successful comparisons direct the listener's attention to that which is more familiar. Consider this example:

- A coach trying to teach an eleven-year-old how to swing a baseball bat: "The right way to swing a baseball bat is with the same motion you use when you swing a long-handled ax into the trunk of a pine tree."

These days, the number of children who learn to swing a baseball bat is higher than the number who learn to swing a long-handled ax. The coach's comparison fails because the child is probably entirely unfamiliar with ax swinging as the object of comparison. Maybe if the child was at summer camp and the camp counselor was trying to teach about chopping trees, the camp counselor could say, "Swing the ax like you would a baseball bat." This might work, because there is a better chance that the child is familiar with how to swing a baseball bat.

Earlier in this chapter, we looked at the following example about hiring John as the club treasurer.

- You can make John the club's treasurer, if you want. But with the way he manages money, that would be like skydiving without a parachute.

This comparison works, but not because most of us have ever personally experienced skydiving. It works because most of us have seen people skydiving on television, so we can simulate the process. And we can easily realize that it would be suicidal to skydive without a parachute. The simulation heuristic makes skydiving familiar enough that we can

Clichés

Like wearing good clothes to a wedding, comparisons dress up our conversation with memorable images and useful illustrations. At times, however, a given comparison can become so commonplace and overused that, like an old blouse or tie worn too often, it deserves to be retired. Here are a few that are simple, familiar, and, unfortunately, so overused that they have become clichés.

Can you add another five clichés to this list?

like riding a bike	costs an arm and a leg
tastes like chicken	luck of the draw
out on a limb	old as the hills
crazy like a fox	

 Reserving a room online is like buying a book online.

understand the comparison. But for most listeners, it would be far less effective for the argument maker to have made this comment:

- You can make John the club's treasurer if you want to, but if you ask me it would be like ingesting massive quantities of sodium chloride.

The point is the same, but this comparison is less effective because most people are not as familiar with consuming toxic amounts of salt as a means of self-destruction. **Familiarity** is the quality of a comparison that expresses the degree of knowledge the listener has about the object to which the unknown is being compared.

Simplicity

Simplicity, a virtue for comparisons, is a measure of the relative complexity of the comparison. The less complicated—that is, the simpler—the comparison is, the better the comparison. Simpler comparisons are often more readily understood and remembered.

- Today our nation is declaring war on drugs.

The comparison of a policy to a war is simpler, more familiar, and easier to remember, and has more emotional impact than this description of the policy.

- Today I would like to announce a policy of concerted, long-term, resource-intensive, multi-agency interdiction of illegal substances and the associated criminal prosecution of persons found to be importing, manufacturing, distributing, selling, shipping, or possessing those substances.

Using a simple but effectively memorable image of "WAR!" the argument maker can more easily capture the imagination of the listener.

Consider the situation of a young American couple wanting to take a romantic vacation in Italy. Seeking advice about places to go and hotels to stay at, the couple is told, "You'll want to see Venice, Florence, Rome, and the Amalfi Coast. Not to worry, these days making hotel reservations in another country is as easy as buying books at Amazon.com." Suppose that the young couple is familiar with buying books on the Internet at Amazon.com, and because of that familiarity the couple knows that there are several initial steps. They had to establish an account and, in so doing, they had to enter a lot of personal data, such as their address and credit card information. Then they had to search for the book they wanted and wade through the ads and the suggestions, which appeared on their computer screen as they did so. Then they had to navigate through the checkout process. Familiar, yes. And, for this couple it is simple enough too. They have been through the Amazon.com registration and purchasing process successfully.

Comprehensiveness

The process of booking hotel reservations in another country may seem daunting for people who have never done it before. Comparing that process to the process of using Amazon.com offers another benefit. It provides the young couple with a single comparison that includes all the major steps in the process. The virtue of simplicity must be balanced with the importance of **comprehensiveness**. One comparison is more comprehensive than

Thinking Critically   Keeping It Simple and Familiar

How are subscribing to podcasts and newspapers similar and how are they different? How would you describe subscribing to podcasts to a less media-savvy friend or relative?

Andy Manis/The New York Times

another to the extent that it captures a greater number of central or essential features. The question is, "Does the comparison capture enough of the critical elements?" Let's revisit the example about the camp counselor teaching someone how to swing a long-handled ax into a tree.

- Counselor to the camper: "Hold the handle like you would a tennis racket. Set your feet apart like you would if you were getting ready to push something heavy. And swing like you would if you were going to hit a nail with a heavy hammer."

Swing a long-handled ax like you would a baseball bat.

Three comparisons were needed because none was comprehensive enough to apply to the whole effort. On the other hand, the counselor might have said:

- "Swing an ax like you swing a baseball bat."

That single comparison covers everything relevant, including how to hold the ax, how to stand, and how to swing.

Suppose that the counselor and the camper are in a gymnasium, not at the campground. And suppose that the camp counselor does not have an ax, but has a broom handle. And suppose instead of a tree, in the gym there is a volleyball net held up by two steel poles. The camp counselor could simulate the skill using the broom handle and pretending that one of the poles is a tree. The counselor might say, "Swing the ax like this." This demonstration would rely on the camper's capacity for comparative thinking, just as do the verbal explanations. This demonstration works as a comparative explanation because the camper can see the grip, the positioning of the feet, and all the relevant movements of the legs, hips, torso, arms, and wrists, even without an ax in hand or a tree in sight. And although swinging a broom handle into a steel pole only simulates swinging an ax into the soft wood of a living pine, the demonstration is a more comprehensive comparison than the words alone are.

Productivity

Productivity is the capacity of a comparison to suggest consequences that go beyond those mentioned in the initial comparison. Productive comparisons are so rich that exploring the comparison more deeply reveals or suggests additional possible implications. For example, comparing the government's policies on illegal drugs to a war allows us to predict that there are going to be "innocent victims" of the war on drugs. Harm to innocent victims, collateral damage, is a foreseeable consequence of waging war. Innocent victims of war deserve our compassion. Using the comparison to war also suggests that some people are going to be regarded as "the hated enemies." In war, we use all of our military might to destroy the enemy. Wartime propaganda engenders hatred for a nation's enemy. So if we are waging war on drugs, we can expect to commit considerable effort to destroying the hated enemy—whomever that may turn out to be. This, in turn, raises an interesting problem: At times, a productive comparison can suggest something that is both unexpected and troubling. In non-metaphorical wars, the innocent victims are not the hated enemies. But what if one's brother or sister becomes a drug user and then, to support his or her habit, becomes a pusher? In situations like that, the "war on drugs" comparison does not help us understand what has happened or how we should behave toward our brother or sister. Should we have compassion for the person, hate the person, help the person, report the person to the authorities, or what?

Testability

The "war on drugs" comparison productively suggests consequences, including the unexpected and confusing one we just talked about—that a member of our own family might be both an "innocent victim" and a "hated enemy." Should we treat our addicted siblings or children who become small-time pushers as the hated enemy? We may not approve of what they are doing, and we may seek treatment for them, but most of us are not likely to think of them as "the enemy" or to treat them as such. That the comparison would lead us to do so diminishes its value. It is a weaker comparison because it implies this unacceptable consequence.

Thinking Critically   Side-by-Side Comparison

Make a list of the major steps in the process of registering, locating, and buying a used copy of Agatha Christie's *Murder on the Orient Express* or Stephen King's *The Stand* on eBay. Locate a travel Web site, like Orbitz or Travelocity or one of the many European hotel reservation Web sites. Make a list of the major steps involved in registering, locating, and reserving a room at a three-star hotel in Paris, France. Place the two lists side by side. On the criterion of comprehensiveness, evaluate the comparison that says "reserving a room for a night at a three-star hotel in Paris is as easy as buying a used copy of an Agatha Christie or Stephen King novel on eBay." Were there any major steps involved in reserving the room that were not in the list associated with buying the book?

Mike Wallace's Analogy

Reconsider the analogy Mike Wallace attempted to draw between warning American soldiers about the ambush and warning a person that he or she was a murderer's intended target. This time, apply the five criteria by asking:

1 How familiar, as compared to the combat zone situation, is the prospect of warning someone about a crime that is about to be perpetrated?

2 Is the comparison simple and straightforward enough for us to understand the basic idea and simulate what it would be like to warn the victim of the crime?

3 What are the critical elements in the two situations and how well are they captured by the comparison?

4 Is the comparison productive enough to provide useful guidance or indications of how we might behave in the unfamiliar combat zone situation?

Practice Using the Five Criteria on Two Analogies

5 Are there any crucial incongruities that undercut the comparison of the behavior of a civilian journalist in a combat zone to the behavior of journalists at home?

Father Tom's Story about the Man Who Lived by the River

Episode #14, "Take This Sabbath Day," from season 1 of *The West Wing*, first aired on February 9, 2000. In that episode, President Jed Bartlet, played by Martin Sheen, must decide whether or not to commute a murderer's death sentence. He has less than 48 hours to make his decision. The episode features an array of powerfully presented arguments—economic, ethical, political, religious, and legal. Pushed and pulled by those considerations, President Bartlet, a Catholic, eventually calls his wise old friend, a priest, played by Karl Malden, for guidance. The priest tells the president, "You remind me of the man who lived by the river. He heard a

radio report that the river was going to rush up and flood the town. . ." The story is, of course, meant as an analogy to Bartlet's situation. Evaluate that comparison using the standards of familiarity, simplicity, comprehensiveness, productivity, and testability. Access that episode at **www.TheThinkSpot.com**.

We call this criterion testability. **Testability** is the capacity of a comparison to project consequences that have the potential to be shown to be false, inapplicable, or unacceptable. If there is a war on drugs, then our siblings and children might be our hated enemy. For most of us, "hated enemy" does not apply to family members.

One tactic for testing a comparison is to ask if there are crucial incongruities between the objects being compared. Going back to an example from the beginning of the chapter, suppose that in response to the idea that stealing experimental animals is really a kind of rescuing of innocent victims, a person objected by saying, "No, under the law, animals are property, not persons. Therefore, they cannot be considered victims in any sense that would excuse you from the legal consequences of your having taken property without authorization." This objection points out that one of the consequences of that comparison does not apply—under the law, animals are property, not persons. This might change someday, but that day is not yet upon us. One of the other examples at the beginning of the chapter compared the CEO's request for downsizing options to Russian roulette. That comparison can be criticized as false

in this way: "Not really, because in Russian roulette, you have to hold the pistol up to your own head, but what I plan to do is to recommend eliminating someone else's department, not my own."

The criterion of testability enables us to evaluate the acceptability of a proposed comparison. In general, we should prefer comparisons that have the potential to be testable as false, inapplicable, or unacceptable. Some comparisons simply cannot be falsified in principle. Consider this example: Like having a loving aunt or uncle, each of us has a guardian angel who watches over us, protects us from danger, and helps us know right from wrong. This comparison is familiar, simple, and productive. The many ways that a loving aunt or uncle might help us in our lives suggest a reasonable level of comprehensiveness as well. Unfortunately, there is no way, in principle, to test whether or not the comparison is true, applicable, or appropriate, at least none that this author has been able to imagine so far.

SHAPING OUR VIEW OF THE UNIVERSE FOR TWO THOUSAND YEARS

Imagine a wooden wheeled cart, loaded with fresh vegetables, standing still on a flat and level country road. There are two ways to get the cart moving and keep it moving. One is to push it; the other is to pull

British Library, Picture Desk, Inc./Kobal Collection

how the universe worked came undone. And who would have thought that it would be about the motion of Mars and the arc of cannon-balls? Go to **www.TheThinkSpot.com** and watch this clip from episode 5, "Infinitely Reasonable," of the BBC series *The Day the Universe Changed* to see how the Aristotelian model of the universe was unraveled. The clip begins with the astronomer-priest Copernicus and continues through Galileo and a letter he wrote to a female friend saying that Aristotle, and everything that depended on his view of the universe, was wrong. What do you imagine would be the immediate aftermath once Church authorities realized that bulwark, upon which rested all European civil and religious power in those days, was wrong?

The comparative inference used by Aristotle—understanding the cause of motion in the way that you understand how a man pushes or pulls a cart—was a powerfully valuable comparison. It endured for two millennia as a scientific principle. The idea that an object is predictable because of how it is made remains a powerfully valuable idea, although today we do not appeal to an object's "nature." Instead, depending upon what the object is, we talk about its organic composition and function, its chemical structure, or its physical properties.

THE MANY USES OF COMPARATIVE INFERENCES

Comparative reasoning is widely used in legal argumentation. Attorneys will appeal to precedents when arguing about the interpretation or the applicability of points of law. The basic character of the appeal to precedent is the assertion that the case now in question is so much like the prior case that the ruling that applied there should apply here. That argument depends on how much the new case is analogous to the prior case.

The short version of the appeal to precedent is used whenever we make an argument structured like this: "We had a situation sort of like this before and that time we did such-and-such." As in this example:

- Someone said we should turn off the air conditioner when we are stuck in a traffic jam on a blisteringly hot summer day. We didn't believe it until last summer when our car overheated on a day just like this. We were stuck in traffic and we kept the AC running. Not too smart of us. So I say this time we close that puppy down and just deal with the heat!

Comparative reasoning is used in discussions of ethics, such as to compare cases and infer obligations.

- Making a promise to help your sister rake the leaves is the same as when Daddy made the promise to take you to the zoo. Even though he was tired, Daddy had to keep his promise to you. He took you to the zoo. Remember? So you have to keep your promise to your sister. You go outside now and help her rake the leaves.

it. Being very familiar with carts and the effort required for a man to push a cart along muddy country roads, Aristotle, and those influenced by his philosophical writings prior to Copernicus, drew comparative inferences about the movements of the sun, the moon, the planets, and the stars. The common sense, late 15th-century European view of the universe, which everyone in those days took to be God's design for things, placed Earth firmly in the center. Everyone could see these heavenly bodies moving in great circles above our heads. Like the horse cart, they needed to either be pushed or pulled along their paths. A good job for angels, perhaps. How could we see them, if they were being pushed along a hard surface? The answer was that the surface was transparent, a "crystal sphere," totally encompassing Earth. Not familiar with crystal spheres? Think of a giant glass fishbowl. The heavenly object—for example, the moon—was resting on a crystal sphere. An angel pushed it along, like a man pushing a cart. When we looked up, we saw the moon through the transparent crystal. And we could note the path it had traveled and predict where it was going because the path was a perfect circle. Heavenly motion was perfectly circular. On Earth, however, if you propel a cart along a flat and level path or drop a rock from a tower, you can see that the cart or the rock will move in a straight line. For two thousand years, Aristotle's views dominated our understanding of how the natural universe worked. Every object had its own particular nature, and it always behaved in certain predictable ways because its nature made it act that way.

Circular motion in heaven, straight-line motion on Earth, some Greek who's been dead for 2500 years or so—who cares? Well, as it turned out, just about everyone of European heritage was affected in one way or another when the Aristotelian comparisons for understanding

Thinking Critically Simplicity and Hypothetical Entities

In the video clip from *The Day the Universe Changed*, the writer and presenter, James Burke, notes the application of the simplicity criteria by Copernicus. Can you spot how Copernicus used this criterion? First the Catholic Church was unconcerned about the "mere lines and circles" drawn by the astronomer-priest. Why? How are the hypothetical orbits of Earth and the sun, which Copernicus introduced, similar to other scientific ideas, like "atoms" and "germs"? Hint: Think of objects that exist "theoretically" and are used to explain observations but cannot themselves be observed—angels, for example. Can one test the existence of orbits, atoms, germs, and angels? In each case, why or why not?

Chris Rock's Comparative Inference

People are capable of driving a car with their feet only, but that does not imply that they should drive that way.

Women have the capability to raise their children alone.

Children need fathers as well as mothers.

Just because you can do something a certain way does not imply that you should do it that way.

Women should not insist on raising their children alone.

Often, comparative reasoning is used in public policy arguments. In this example, the genetic similarity of human beings and human stem cells is used as a basis for the policy proposal that the rights we accord to human beings should be accorded to stem cells.

- Because human stem cells can be cultivated and grown into human organs and potentially cloned into whole persons, we should think of stem cells as potential human beings. We are never justified in taking the life of an innocent human being. So geneticists should not be allowed to experiment with human stem cells.

In business and professional life, arguments like the following are commonplace.

- The CEO's misuse of corporate funds was bad enough, but the way upper management lied to keep the board from learning the truth was far worse. That deceit was a cancer that spread throughout upper management. And, like a cancer, it had to be mercilessly eradicated. Everyone had to go, even if it meant firing some people who never had any idea about what was going on. When you cut out a tumor, you have to remove good cells too, because you can't risk leaving a single bad cell or the cancer will return.

One of the greatest benefits of the use of comparative inference is its power to persuade. In the previous example, if we accept the characterization of the board's deceit as "a cancer," then it follows that we should treat that deceit with the same aggressive therapies. If we were to be persuaded that upper management did not lie to the board but that its failure to notify the board could be explained in some other reasonable way, then using the "cancer" word would only inflame passions and impel us toward responses that were disproportional, if not inappropriate.

A comparison's persuasive power depends heavily on the suggested parallelism. For example, consider this argument for the claim, "Women should not insist on raising their children alone."

- "Women, I know you *can* raise your children by yourselves. But children need fathers. And just because you can do something don't mean you should. You *can* drive a car only with your feet, but that don't mean you *should* drive a car only with your feet."[v]

The response to this argument that comedian Chris Rock received from the audience at the Apollo Theater was loud and enthusiastic. The clever comparison brought home his point. It was an easy and humorous image for the audience to imagine. And, if raising children alone is like driving your car with your feet, you can see how awkward, clumsy, risky, and foolish that would be.

To balance and complement the work done by the comparison on the negative side of the claim, the comedian bolstered the affirmative aspect of the claim with the observation, "But children need fathers." From the other remarks he had made in the same context, it was clear to that audience that Chris Rock was really speaking to both of a child's parents, calling for them to stay in a parental relationship with their child.

The persuasive power of comparisons, analogies, and models derives in part from our natural propensity to use heuristics like simulation, representation, and association, which were explained in Chapter 9. Comparisons are built into the language we use. We say that standard household electric current *flows* through the wiring in our homes and businesses. We know that if the wires are not connected to the sources, the electricity would not flow through them to our computers, lights, and appliances. The comparison is to water flowing through pipes. But if that were true, then electric current should be gushing out of every open socket in the wall. Obviously, there is more to it than what the simple and familiar image of flowing water conveys.

Logically speaking, comparative inferences are not acceptable proofs of the truth of their conclusions. Comparing electricity to flowing

Creative Suggestions vs. Solid Proofs

Comparative inferences are best used when making initial and tentative assumptions about new situations. They suggest explanations and hypotheses, which then should be analyzed and tested before being relied upon. Comparisons, termed "models," are relied upon in engineering to imagine possible solutions to structural puzzles. Models, not in a physical but in a conceptual sense, are used in science to suggest promising hypotheses for further testing. While creative comparisons can be richly suggestive of new ideas, comparative inferences are notoriously inadequate to the task of serving as final proofs of those ideas.

Group Discussion: The "Free Enterprise System" Model

One of the basic economic beliefs associated with doing business in the free enterprise system is the "law of supply and demand." When the supply of goods or services is greater than the demand, prices go down. When the demand is greater than the supply, prices go up. For example, in times of weather emergencies, merchants selling ordinarily plentiful commodities like food, electric generators, fuel, flashlights, tarps, and fresh water are beset by unquenchable demand because people are trying to stock up. So prices rise. Showing the reverse process, the prices of homes and automobiles dropped during the 2008–2009 recession because consumer demand fell sharply.

Two areas of our economy seem to defy the law of supply and demand. One is public higher education, where tuition and fees do not increase to the level that market demands would sustain. If this fit the free enterprise model, then the consumers—that is, the students—would be charged much more. The second area that does not appear to fit the model is health care. In the case of health care, the consumers, sick or injured people in need of care, do not "shop around" looking for the best deal. Also, the charge for a medical procedure is the same whether a lot of people or only a few people need that service.

First, evaluate the comparison of public higher education to the classic model of the free enterprise system. How can comparing public higher education to a business operating in the free enterprise system help us understand higher education better, and in what ways does the idea not fit? Second, evaluate health care services against the classic model of the free enterprise system. How does comparing the services provided by health care professionals, hospitals, emergency rooms, insurance providers, and pharmaceutical companies to businesses functioning in a free enterprise system help us better understand health care services? How might the comparison cause us problems because it does not fit?

A third enterprise that may or may not fit the model of the free enterprise system is organized religion. Organized religion provides services for the benefit of the faithful, including prayers and religious ceremonies. Many people give money to those organizations and receive those services. In some cases, the money is given voluntarily as contributions; in other cases, the money is in payment of a fee. In still other cases, the money is given voluntarily, but the amount is established by the religious organization on the basis of some metric, like 10% of a person's income. Religious organizations need the money they receive in order to pay their employees, rent or buy buildings used for worship, and acquire the equipment and supplies needed to provide services. Evaluate the comparison of organized religion to the free enterprise model and the applicability of the law of supply and demand.

water, as useful as that image might be for some purposes, does not prove that electricity can be expected to behave just like flowing water in all contexts. Comparisons are helpful for suggesting initially promising approaches to understanding unfamiliar things. Comparisons can be memorable and persuasive. They have the power to shape individual and group decisions. Comparisons can be humorous, emotionally evocative, and powerfully motivating. Their simplicity and familiarity often lead to a false sense of their relevance and applicability. The strong critical thinker with a healthy sense of skepticism and a good nose for weak logic will be cautious when comparisons and metaphors, rather than sound arguments, are used as substitutes for solid explanations or as calls to action.

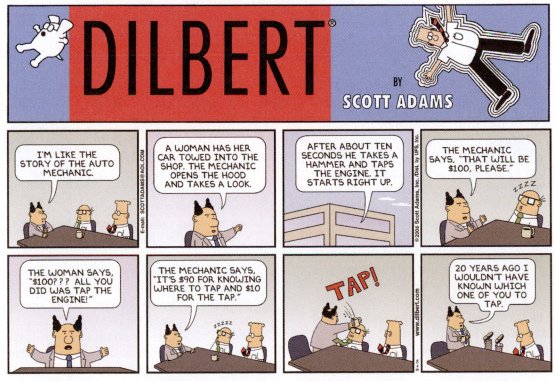

© Scott Adams/Dist. by United Media Feature Syndicate

Comparative reasoning projects aspects of things that are more familiar onto things that are less familiar. Using comparative inferences, we extend our understanding and our expectations about less familiar things by comparing them to things that are more familiar to us. Comparative reasoning is best used to make tentative projections, to propose hypotheses, and, at most, to offer imprecise probabilistic explanations. Although powerfully persuasive because of their appeal to familiar things and their connections to cognitive heuristics, comparisons are risky. Their soundness, logical strength, and relevance can easily be questioned. They are useful for suggesting new directions of inquiry or pointing the way to possible solutions to problems, if the comparison of the current problem to the past one is sufficiently parallel in its essential elements. But comparative inferences are notoriously weak and unreliable, from a logical point of view. We can evaluate comparative inferences using five criteria: familiarity, simplicity, comprehensiveness, productivity, and testability. The most useful comparisons are those that base their comparisons on structural, functional, central, and essential features in order to *suggest* how we might understand that which is less familiar based on what we know about that which is more familiar.

KEY TERMS

comparative reasoning (or **this-is-like-that thinking**) is the process of using what is more familiar to make interpretations, explanations, or inferences about what is less familiar.   *166*

familiarity, in the evaluation of comparisons, is the degree of knowledge the listener has about the object to which the unknown is being compared.   *170*

simplicity, in the evaluation of comparisons, is a measure of the relative absence of complexity.   *170*

comprehensiveness, in the evaluation of comparisons, is the extent to which a comparison captures a greater number of central or essential features.   *170*

productivity is the capacity of a comparison to suggest consequences that go beyond those mentioned in the initial comparison.   *171*

testability is the capacity of comparisons to project consequences that have the potential to be shown to be false, inapplicable, or unacceptable.   *172*

FIND IT ON THE THINKSPOT

As delicate shade-loving plants wither in direct sunlight, analogies and comparisons, while perhaps beautiful, at times cannot stand the bright analytical light of close logical examination and evaluation. And yet they seem so helpful, at least at first. I invite you to watch the *Ethics in America* video clip that opens this chapter (p. 165). In it, the veteran TV journalist Mike Wallace struggles with the question of warning American troops that the enemy is about to ambush them. Access this remarkable *Ethics in America* segment of the episode "Under Orders Under Fire – Part II" at **www.TheThinkSpot.com**. Start the clip at 30:13, which is where the interlocutor first asks Peter Jennings to consider what he would do if he realized that enemy troops were about to attack a platoon of American soldiers. The clip is 12 minutes long.

- I found *The West Wing* episode about capital punishment to be terrific, start to finish (p. 172). You can access the culminating highlight of that episode, a conversation between President Bartlet and his old friend, Fr. Tom, played by Karl Malden, at **www.TheThinkSpot.com**. What do you think of the allegorical tale that the wise confessor spins?

- The entire *The Day the Universe Changed* series is worth watching through at least twice. It is perhaps the greatest and most readily understandable digest of the history and philosophy of science ever produced. I invite you to go to **www.TheThinkSpot.com** and view a short clip from the episode where we learn about the power of Aristotle's "like a cart being pushed along its path" analogy (p. 173).

This way of explaining why the sun, moon, and stars move about in the sky controlled how Europeans thought about the solar system for two millennia.

- The fourth video clip for this chapter found at www.TheThinkSpot.com is from an HBO special about the slaughter of animals for human food production. Called *Death on a Factory Farm*, it is the basis for a Bonus Exercise. You'll find the exercise at www.TheThinkSpot.com in the supplementary materials for this chapter. Some of the images in this HBO special report can be disturbing for some people.

Exercises

REFLECTIVE LOG: TIME TRAVEL—EVALUATE THE EVALUATIONS

Time travel—the stuff of great science fiction! Is time travel really possible? If the time-space continuum loops back upon itself, like tangled yarn, then perhaps there are places so close together that passages from one point in the string to another point in the string would not be impossibly distant. Consider the following two comparisons. The first is by an advocate of the dynamic view of time, and the second is by an advocate of the static view of time.

Advocate of the dynamic view of time: Like wind rushing by our faces, time whisks from the past to the future, pausing but for the smallest instant in this moment we call the present. The past is unreal and the events it contains are no more. The future is unreal, and the events that will become are not yet. Only the fleeting present—that place where past and future join—is real. And even that reality is lost into the past as quickly as it is conceived. Think, you who flit on life's stage for your one tiny moment of existence—how should you use what precious little time you have?

Advocate of the static view of time: Time doesn't pass; we do. We move through time as if we were driving along an interstate highway. The highway stretches ahead of us and behind us to places we may never visit. We get on the highway at birth and exit at death. We move along, like those in the cars beside us, at a constant rate of speed. So, looking from car to car it seems we are not moving, but looking at the mileposts flashing by, like the weeks and months of our lives; we are steadily going along. Along this highway, there are places that came *before* or *after* or that occurred *simultaneously* with others. The past and the future are real places.

Before reading further, stop for a moment and write your own evaluation of the two comparisons, "time is like the wind" and "time is like an interstate highway."

After entering your own evaluations into your log, read the following two critiques. The first applies to the dynamic view and the second to the static view.

Critic of the dynamic view of time: Your analogies are charming, but your thinking is confused. If only the present is real, how can we measure the *passage of time*? Any measurement must be against some external standard. But do you want to argue that there is some kind of time outside of time? Also, consider the present. According to you, it is the point at which the unreal past touches the unreal future. In that case, it is so infinitesimally tiny as to have no duration in itself. Thus, the present is unreal too. But if time is the accumulation of present moments, you might as well say that time is entirely unreal. There is no past, future, or present.

Critic of the static view of time: You make it sound like all I have to do is make a U-turn and I can go back in time. That's absurd. Also, by your analogy, if I step on the accelerator, I can shoot ahead of the other cars and, in effect, speed myself into the future. That is also absurd. Your problem is that you are thinking of time as analogous to your concept of space. However, our movement in space from one place to another does not imply we can move in time from one present to another.

Evaluate the critics' evaluations. In what respects are the two critiques strong or weak? How might an advocate of each of the two views of time respond reasonably to the criticisms offered? If you disagree with both of the critics or if you agree with both of the critics, then explain what your view of time is. Just for fun: Is time travel possible?

GROUP EXERCISE: ARE VIRUSES LIVING THINGS?

We tend to compare "germs" to living things, like bugs, that infect our bodies and cause illnesses. Bacteria fit that comparison, except that not all bacteria are harmful. Digestion, for example, relies on bacteria in our mouths and gastrointestinal tracts. Without those bacteria, we would be less well nourished. But what about viruses? Are viruses living organisms? Do they reproduce, move around, and take in nourishment?

In a science textbook, locate a contemporary and scientifically precise definition of "living organism." Determine whether viruses are living organisms. What other comparisons might be useful to help the general public understand what viruses are?

HOW CAN WE RECOGNIZE IDEOLOGICAL REASONING?

HOW CAN WE EVALUATE IDEOLOGICAL REASONING?

HOW ARE THE USES, BENEFITS, AND RISKS OF IDEOLOGICAL REASONING?

"Only marriage

between a man and a woman is valid or recognized in California," read Proposition 8, a ballot initiative that was approved by California voters 52 percent to 48 percent on November 4, 2008. And then the controversy really started to heat up.

Less than six months before that, in June 2008, the California Supreme Court had ruled that same-sex marriage was a fundamental right. More than 8,500 couples sought marriage licenses in the first week the ban was lifted, which was "more than two and a half times an average June week," reported the *Los Angeles Times*.[i] The California court's decision and the thousands of marriages it permitted deeply offended and angered religious conservatives who believed that marriage could only be a sacred bond between a man and a woman. The Alliance Defense Fund, a consortium of religiously conservative attorneys, drafted Proposition 8.[ii] At first, support for the proposition lagged far behind in the polls. But as the election approached, the movement gained momentum. In the media, in churches, in civic clubs, and on street corners throughout the state, backers and opponents presented their case to the voting public. An unprecedented $83 million was raised by backers and opponents of Proposition 8, the largest amount ever for a battle over a single proposition in California history.

179

IDEOLOGICAL REASONING: "TOP DOWN" THINKING

CHAPTER 12

"Top Down" Thinking: Recognizing Ideological Reasoning

After California's Proposition 8 passed in November 2008, supporters of the ban were delighted that their efforts had prevailed. But in the week after the election, angry opponents of Prop 8 marched in protest of the outcome in Los Angeles, San Francisco, Sacramento, San Diego, and other California cities. Immediately, legal challenges were filed with the California Supreme Court. One case requested that the court invalidate the same-sex marriages that had taken place between June 17 and election day. Another case asked the court to invalidate Proposition 8 itself.

Go to **www.TheThinkSpot.com** and view an analysis of the legal issues by CNN commentator, civil rights attorney Avery Friedman. Notice how Friedman frames the issue as a conflict of rights. On the one hand, there is the *right of the people of the state* to pass amendments to their state constitution. On the other hand, there is the *right of individuals* to marry the person whom they choose. If the court views the individual's right to marry the person of his or her choice as an "inalienable" right, then the court will reject Proposition 8. Inalienable rights cannot be stripped away, even by majority vote. But if the court determines that same-sex marriage is not an inalienable right, then Proposition 8 will stand, because of the right of the majority to amend the Constitution of the State of California. We can map out the court's decision, as envisioned by Friedman, this way:

Notice that Friedman's arguments begin with the idea that both sides in this issue have certain rights. This is an important first principle, for ascribing a right to a person implies that others cannot bar the person from exercising that right. The freedom to exercise one's rights is a core value in our society. Whenever the rights of different people come into conflict, it is necessary to consider which rights take priority. To help resolve the matter, Friedman suggests that the court will consider another high-level first principle, namely that inalienable rights cannot be removed from a person by any agency of

government, including by majority vote. This is one of the basic principles of the American democratic system; it is affirmed in our Declaration of Independence. From these two broad and powerful absolutes ideals ("honor all rights" and "give priority to inalienable rights"), Friedman reasons down to the specific case at hand. If X is an inalienable right, then X cannot be removed by majority vote. Otherwise, it can be. In May 2009 the California Supreme Court handed down its rulings. CNN reported the outcomes of these two cases. Friedman's ideological reasoning appears to have been strongly in the

MAP > it > OUT 1

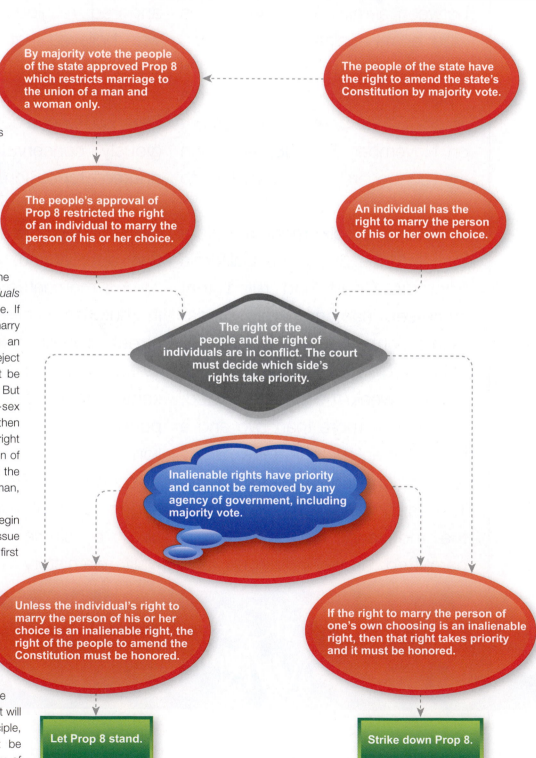

minds of the justices on the California Supreme Court.

After the California Supreme Court made its pronouncement, legal challenges were filed forthwith with the U.S. District Court. As I write these paragraphs, the judge who has been appointed to hear the case has asked both sides to prepare their arguments. Whatever his ruling, we can expect an appeal to the United States Supreme Court.

In this chapter we will focus the kind of thinking that we shall call **top-down reasoning** or **ideological reasoning**. This kind of reasoning begins, as illustrated by the previous arguments, with abstract generalizations and proceeds to apply these initial principles to specific situations. Ideological reasoning is a very important and widely used way of thinking. It offers many benefits, such as in the practice of law. As we saw in the argument map on page 180 discussing Proposition 8, both sides in the same-sex marriage debate use ideological reasoning when making their respective cases in the courts. Lawyers for one side argue the ideals associated with personal liberty and civil rights imply that same-sex marriage should be permitted. Lawyers for the other side argue that our democratic ideals imply that the majority's right to pass laws and constitutional amendments takes priority. Other people approach this question

∧∧∧ **Is a single-parent family worse for children than a two-parent family?**

of same-sex marriage with their religious ideals in mind, or from a perspective based on fundamental beliefs about the purpose of marriage. Here is another example of an argument, as reported by CNN, that employs ideological reasoning:

- Miles McPherson, pastor of the Rock Church in San Diego, said the court "did the right thing." Voters in 28 other states have approved constitutional bans on same-sex marriages, and none has been rejected, he said. "God didn't create the family that way," McPherson said. "You can't have a family with a mother and a mother, because [children] need a mother and a father to nurture their personality and their character."[iii]

In August 2009, the Evangelical Lutheran Church of America decided to allow congregations to support non-celibate same-sex relationships among their members and to allow individuals in same-sex relationships to assume positions as active members of the clergy. Here are two arguments, both of which begin from a religious ideology, the first in opposition to the decision, and the second in support:

- "Brothers and sisters, I ask you, before you dig yourselves deeper into this hole, if you are so absolutely certain that these behaviors are not sinful that you are willing to place yourselves and this church at the spiritual risk that comes from encouraging sin," said the Rev. Steven Frock of the Western Iowa Synod.

- Among those on the other side was Alan Wold of the Northern Illinois Synod. "If according to some I am going to be in err for supporting this. . . Let me err on the side of mercy, grace, justice, and love of neighbor. Let me err on the side of gospel, which makes all things new."[iv]

Ideologically based reasoning, exemplified by both sides in this heated controversy over same-sex marriages, is pervasive and important in human affairs. We use it to make inferences and to

Thinking Critically News Reporting, Ideologies, and Objectivity

We often hear that news coverage of ideologically controversial events, like the battle over Proposition 8, is biased and slanted, rather than objective and fair-minded. People accuse news organizations of pandering, sensationalizing, and confusing hype and entertainment for solid reporting.

Back in the day, when there were only three national television networks, TV news departments could operate at a loss because ABC, NBC, and CBS made money from the other shows they produced. Entertainment revenues covered the expensive newsroom operations. Today, networks like CNN do not produce dramas, sitcoms, game shows, and variety shows. They cannot sell commercial time using entertainment

programming. To survive, news networks need to find sponsors who will advertise on news shows. And, given that many advertisers do not want to be associated with political or

ideological positions that they do not endorse, how can a news network, such as CNN, FOX News, or MSNBC, survive economically without positioning itself either to the left or to the right of the political spectrum?

On a scale of 1 to 10, with 10 being "objective" and 1 being "biased," rate CNN's coverage of the Proposition 8 issue. Access the CNN story "California High Court Upholds Same-Sex Marriage Ban" at **www.TheThinkSpot.com**. Explain your reasons for the evaluation you assign. Show

how you would edit the CNN story to make it more objective, if you did not assign it a 10.

explain our point of view on specific issues of the day. As strong critical thinkers, we must understand how it works, what its uses are, and what its potential benefits and risks are. Above all, we must learn to appreciate ideological reasoning for what it can achieve and, at the same time, be able to apply it and evaluate it objectively and fair-mindedly. Before we look at its evaluation and applications, both reasonable and unreasonable, we must learn to recognize ideological reasoning so we can distinguish it from comparative reasoning and from empirical reasoning. To help us be able to recognize ideological reasoning, we will first look briefly at three more sets of examples and then, based on the examples we've developed, we will be able to identify three distinguishing characteristics of ideological reasoning.

∧
∧ If being parented by two adults is good for children, would having
∧ three parenting adults be even better?

EXAMPLES OF IDEOLOGICAL REASONING

Consider the following pairs of ideological arguments. Beginning with broad axiom-like first principles and generalizations, each speaker reasons to specific applications. As is often the case with opposing ideological positions, there is precious little room for compromise.

Immigration Policy

1(a) By definition, if a person enters this country illegally, that person is breaking the law. All lawbreakers are criminals. Criminals should be prosecuted. I support legislation that is tough on crime. That is why I support a Constitutional amendment that requires the incarceration and deportation of all illegal immigrants.

1(b) Government policies and laws that destroy the family unit are bad. The family is sacred, and it is fundamental to our American way of life. That is why I oppose the Constitutional amendment, which would rip a family apart by deporting a parent, or even a child, if the person is not in this country legally.

>>> **Is this a dad or a criminal?** Blocking illegals vs. supporting families—**exactly how should we frame the immigration policy question?**

God's Existence

2(a) The space-time continuum extends outward, forward, and backward infinitely from the present-here-and-now moment. It follows that there can be no reality whatsoever other than the universe, for there can be no time nor space outside the infinite vastness that is the space-time universe. Ergo, there is no God sitting outside our naturally infinite time-space continuum. Nor is there any such place as Heaven or Hell, nor any time when we shall receive eternal happiness or eternal pain. There is no place outside space nor any time after the end of time.

2(b) Every natural thing that exists today—the matter and energy that is this universe, this galaxy, this solar system, this planet, all the animals and plants, each one of us—every natural thing comes from prior natural causes. We would not exist were it not for our parents, for example. If we could go back and back in time, we would never find anything that came into existence on its own without a prior cause. Given that natural world exists, it follows that something had to get this whole huge chain of causes going. Something had to set it all in motion. And that something had to be outside of the natural universe, for without a force outside nature, the whole long causal process would never have begun. Thus that first creative mover had to be supernatural. We call that First Cause by the name "God." Ergo, God exists.

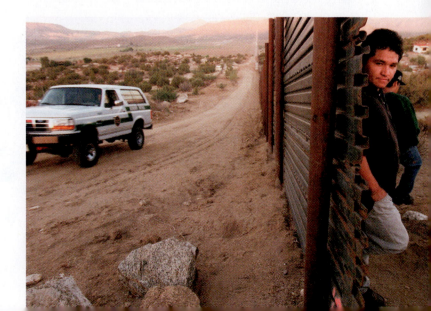

∧ ∧ ∧ **What would the world have been like if God had created Eve first?**

Human Nature

3(a) People are fundamentally good. Most people will keep their word and to try to do what is right for their fellow human beings most of the time. It is wrong to take away our freedom. This is why I support those who would maximize individual liberties and reduce the number of bureaucratic rules and regulations that legislators and administrators are constantly trying to impose on our personal and commercial interactions.

3(b) People are fundamentally bad. If they can get away with something they will, they can be counted on to exploit every advantage in an effort to advance their own interests. This is why we need tougher laws and detailed regulation of commerce. More individual liberty will lead only to greater societal disintegration and the inevitable exploitation of the poor by those who have the means to do so.

In the first pair of arguments about immigration policy, one speaker appeals to the value of enforcing our laws while the other appeals to the value of the family. Each comes up with a different conclusion. The first would deport people who entered the country illegally, without reference to the fact that a given person might be the parent or the child of someone else who is in the country legally. The second would attend to that family relationship and not deport the person. Starting the policy discussion from those two opposing positions will make a legislative compromise a challenge to negotiate. On the other hand, perhaps both speakers share both values. A first step might be agreeing that enforcing the laws and protecting families are both core commitments.

The second pair of arguments take on a challenge that many regard as intellectually impossible, that is proving beyond a doubt either that

>>> **How do our untested beliefs about human nature** affect our behavior toward others?

God does exist or that God does not exist. Theological conceptualizations of God are not static; they have changed throughout human history and from culture to culture. So have our scientific conceptualizations and theories about the nature of the universe. Thus, in different historical eras and in different cultures, we may or may not find people making arguments for or against the existence of God or gods, as conceived of in those times and places. The Judeo-Christian monotheistic view of the universe dominated European culture for centuries. From that cultural perspective, many philosophers proposed arguments for God's existence. One question this pair of arguments raises for the critical thinker is "To what extent does or should our understanding of the universe influence our theological ideas?"

The third pair of arguments both begin with a core belief about human nature. One says human nature is fundamentally good, another that it is fundamentally bad. The debate about our fundamental moral character goes back millennia. Are we the innocent creatures originally designed for life in a Garden of Eden, or are we self-indulgent brutes never more than the collapse of a government away from barbarism? The truth is probably some place between the two extremes. The issue is not likely to be resolved any time soon. And although there are anecdotes and historical examples, which might be cited to support both sides of that dispute, it is difficult to know when, how, or whether it can ever be fully resolved. But notice that, at the purely ideological level, one's stance on this question tends to propel one toward specific applications. If we're basically good, then trust us and give us more freedom. If we're basically bad, then protect us from each other with more governmental or religious controls on our behavior. Ideological reasoning, even about ideas that cannot be resolved, has important consequences for policies and practices that profoundly affect our lives.

183

Ideological Reasoning: "Top Down" Thinking

<<< These images of Adam and Eve and the Vietnam War depict very different sides of human behavior. Are we all potentially devoted lovers or brutal warriors—or both? Explain why.

Ideological Reasoning Is Deductive in Character

For the most part, the conclusions of ideological arguments are presented as certainties. Qualifiers like "probably," "maybe," or "perhaps" are seldom, if ever, found in ideological arguments. There might be a citation of a book, author, or other "authoritative" source. There will seldom be references to correlations, data, experimentation, or systematic investigation unless those support the author's preconceived ideas. Unlike courageous truth-seekers, ideologues look for facts that support their points of view, not facts that disagree. If research is cited, an example used, or a comparison made, the purpose is anecdotal or illustrative, not evidentiary. For example, "Same-sex couples do not make good parents. Let me tell you about the sad case of little so-and-so who had two mommies, until they wanted to get a divorce."

Not all deductive reasoning is ideological. To categorize ideological reasoning as deductive is like categorizing trees as plants. Doing so does not imply that all plants are trees. Describing ideological reasoning as deductive focuses on the certainty with which ideological thinkers endow their conclusions. In Chapter 2 we defined "deductive" as "drawing an inference in which it appears that the conclusion cannot possibly be false if all of the premises are true." Ideological arguments fit that definition. Ideological thinkers have a strong sense that their conclusions must be true because their arguments move from general ideas to specific applications. If the general ideas are true, then their specific application must be true, too. We talked about this kind of deductive argument in Chapter 8's "Applying a Generalization." There are other kinds of deductive arguments that have nothing to do with "general-to-specific," as the examples and discussions in Chapters 2 and 8 illustrate. In fact, our definition of deductive reasoning, cited above, never mentions "general" or "specific." The observations in this chapter about ideological reasoning, particularly about its benefits and risks, do not apply to all deductive arguments. There are many kinds of deductive arguments that are not ideological.

THREE FEATURES OF IDEOLOGICAL REASONING

There are three distinguishing features of ideological reasoning: (1) It is deductive in character; (2) the ideological premises are axiomatic; and (3) the argument maker takes the ideology to be true more or less on faith. Before unpacking each of the three, we need to take note of the word "ideological." The root of "ideological" is "idea." The concept behind our use here of "ideological" as applied to reasoning is that the reasoning begins with ideas that express concepts, opinions, beliefs, or principles. The contrast would be reasoning that begins with descriptions of events, observations, or experiences. The use of the term "ideological" is meant to be value-neutral. In other words, thinking is neither good nor bad simply because it is ideological as we are using the term here. Some people hear the word "ideological" or "ideology" and associate negative connotations with those words. And there is no question that some specific ideologies are quite dangerous. But ideological thinking, as we use the term, is not about a specific good or bad ideology. Rather, it refers to the way in which arguments are made beginning with general ideas, such as concepts, opinions, beliefs or principles, and moving down from these abstractions to their specific applications.

Ideological Reasoning or "Top-Down Thinking"

Abstract axiomatic ideas, convictions, core beliefs, principles, definitions, and generalizations on any topic taken on faith.

Deductive inferences including applying a generalization and applying an exception described in Chapter 8.

Specific applications to issues, event, questions, or controversies of the moment.

About Metaphysical Claims

The term "metaphysical" refers to assertions that are regarded as being true or false, independent of physical facts or circumstances. A claim is metaphysical if there is no conceivable evidence that could establish whether the claim was true or false. The claims might be true, they might be false, or they may be nonsensical. But whatever they are, scientific inquiry cannot confirm or disconfirm them. The eight example claims in the "Ideological Premises are Axiomatic" section below are all metaphysical in this sense of the word. Only one of them, "All lawbreakers are criminals," appears to be a tautology.

It may be impossible given the technology or the resources at hand in a given time or place to confirm or disconfirm a given claim, but those kinds of practical limitations alone do not make a claim metaphysical. For example, at one point it was technologically impossible to confirm or disconfirm the claim, "There was water on Mars." But today we have the technology and the resources to gather evidence to evaluate that claim. By contrast, there is no conceivable way, even if we had the technology and the funding, to confirm or to disconfirm a claim like "Pet cats have the same rights as pet angelfish." Some may wish to argue that the claim is true, but such an argument would depend on another metaphysical claim, perhaps, "All pet animals have the same rights." That argument would then qualify as ideological reasoning. And when we evaluate that argument, we would have problems with the very first test, the Test of the Truthfulness of the Premises, because we cannot know whether the axiomatic first principle about the equality of the rights of all species of pets is itself true.

Ideological Premises Are Axiomatic

As in high school plane geometry, axioms are simply a set of first principles, starting points, or assumptions. For example, two straight lines on a plane can intersect at one and only one point. From the axioms we proved that other statements (theorems) were true. In ideological reasoning the key assumptions, whether spoken or unspoken, are those that embody a community's or individual's deeply held beliefs and core values. These, for that person and that community, are axiomatic. The ideas, concepts, principles, or beliefs that ideological thinkers use to initiate their arguments represent the axioms from which other ideas or specific applications follow, much like theorems in geometry. We saw absolute convictions, including those listed here, in the previous examples:

- Everyone should have the right to marry the person whom he or she chooses.
- God intended that marriage should be between a man and a woman.
- All lawbreakers are criminals.
- The family is sacred.
- The space-time continuum extends outward, forward, and backward infinitely.
- Every natural thing that exists today comes from prior natural causes.
- People are fundamentally good.
- People are fundamentally bad.

The Argument Maker Takes the Ideological Absolutes on Faith

To the person or the community making an ideological argument, the first principles are so profoundly obvious that they require no demonstration. Ideological thinkers do not require or expect independent scientific confirmation of their first principles. Ideological reasoning begins with the conviction that the axiomatic first principles express good ideals and true beliefs. Similarly, ideological thinkers consistently regard their absolutes as immune from disconfirmation. Evidence scientifically gathered cannot, in principle, demonstrate to the argument maker that these absolutes are mistaken. Recall in our discussion

about evaluating claims, back in Chapter 6, when we talked about the strategies of confirmation or disconfirmation as two independent ways to evaluate a claim. We might, for example, ask a person who believes that people are fundamentally good, "What would it take to convince you that you are wrong about that?" If the opinion is held by that person as a matter of faith, then the person would probably reply quite honestly, "Nothing. You could never convince me otherwise." We would expect the same reply from a person who holds as a matter of faith that people are fundamentally bad. The same holds for people who believe any of the other six statements in our list as matters of personal faith.

Because the argument maker sees the truth of his or her own ideology as self-evident, that person might at times become impatient, frustrated, or even angry with a listener who disagrees. A listener who cannot see the truth of those axiomatic first principles may appear to the argument maker to be uneducated, unintelligent, or perhaps even malevolent. This would be an unfair assumption on the part of the argument maker, of course.

Consider what we learned in Chapter 10 about how dominance structuring gives us confidence to act on our choices and convictions. Applying axiomatic convictions that are held to be true independent of potential confirmation or disconfirmation, it is even easier to understand how powerfully convinced a community can become that its view of the

>>> **"Do unto others as you** would have others do unto you."

Thinking Critically   Assessing Our Convictions

All of us have beliefs that we hold with such conviction that they might be considered "immune" from being proven wrong, at least in our own minds. But a strong conviction might still be mistaken. Strong critical thinkers strive to protect themselves from the error of being strongly committed to mistaken beliefs. Critical thinkers ask themselves what evidence or arguments might be developed that should lead reasonable and fair-minded people to realize that one or another of their strongly held opinions is mistaken. Or they ask what possible life experience might come along to dislodge the dominance structuring that they have built in their minds to prop up a mistaken belief. This exercise invites you to ask yourself these same questions relative to your beliefs about each of the statements listed below. Some of the statements address serious topics; others address matters that may not be of great concern to you. But, whether the issue is profound or trivial, we can find ourselves holding beliefs with unwarranted conviction. And that is something that strong critical thinkers seek to avoid. This exercise unfolds in five steps.

Step 1: Mark "True," "False," or "Uncertain" by each statement below to reflect your current opinion about each.

1 Same-sex couples make excellent parents.

2 America is the greatest nation in the world.

3 Freedom is a fundamental right.

4 Every human being has a soul.

5 Every child deserves a high-quality free education.

6 The good of the many is more important than the good of the one.

7 Cheating on an exam is unethical.

8 Pets are people, too.

9 Children should honor and respect their parents.

10 Lazy people don't deserve handouts.

11 You should never wear a polka dot tie with a Hawaiian shirt.

^^^ **Poker, as in Texas Hold'em,** is not a sport.

12 Promises are meant to be kept.

13 Socialism is bad.

14 Geminis can't make decisions.

15 Cabernet goes better with beef than with fish.

16 Poker, as in Texas Hold'em, is not a sport.

17 Ronald Reagan was one of the five best presidents in U.S. history.

18 Our nation has an obligation to stop ethnic cleansing wherever it might happen.

19 Democracy is the best form of government.

20 God is love.

Step 2: Having asserted your opinion about each statement, reflect on the risks associated with dominance structuring and create some mental space for yourself so that you can complete this exercise with your habits of truth-seeking, open-mindedness, and objectivity fully engaged.

Step 3: Looking only at the ones you marked "True," write down what evidence or arguments you would accept as proof that each statement is *false*. If no possible evidence or argument could persuade you that the statement is false, is there any experience you could imagine that would lead you to abandon your commitment to the truth of that statement?

Step 4: Looking only at those that you marked "False," write down what evidence or arguments you would accept as proof that each statement is *true*. If no possible evidence or argument could persuade you that the statement is true, is there any experience you could imagine that would lead you to abandon your commitment to the falsehood of that statement?

Step 5: Looking now only at the statements that you marked "Uncertain," write down the process you could use to gather information and make an informed, fair-minded, and reasoned judgment about what to believe with regard to the truth or falsity of that statement. That is, how would you use your critical thinking skills and habits of mind to make that purposeful reflective judgment?

world is right and every other view is wrong. So powerful can a community's world view be that from within that community some are moved to become martyrs or warriors. They are willing to make the ultimate sacrifice to protect and defend their community's worldview.

Our level of faith and conviction is no measure of the truth of the beliefs we hold so dear. Nor is our devotion to the cause a measure of the worthiness of the values for which we may be prepared to die. We might be tragically mistaken, believing something that is not true, prizing something that is not worthy. Aristotle and the people of ancient Greece

believed that slavery was an ethically acceptable practice. The economics of ancient Rome depended on slave labor as a given. Sending her mighty legions to conquer and enslave others was righteous and self-evidently reasonable. Slavery was accepted as part of the cultural fabric of several of the original 13 colonies that formed the United States. There were men and women of those times and places who were as convinced of the rightness of slavery as we, today, are convinced that it is wrong. By no means am I advocating relativism in this matter. Recall the "Levels of Thinking and Knowing" chart in the section on cognitive development

Applying the Test of Truthfulness of the Premises

If argument maker asserts that a given premise is to be accepted as self-evident... 	...evaluate the premise as a claim made in the absence of any supporting reasons or credible expert source. Use the methods in the "Assessing the Substance - What Should I Believe?" and "Independent Verification" sections of Chapter 6.
If argument maker asks the listener to accept the argument maker himself or herself as the source of the truth of a given premise... 	...evaluate credibility of the argument maker by applying the twelve criteria for trustworthy expertise learned in Chapter 6.
If argument maker cites some other source or sources as basis for believing that a given premise is true... 	...evaluate credibility of the other source or sources by applying twelve criteria for trustworthy expertise learned in Chapter 6.
If the speaker gives an additional reason to establish that a given premise is true, then the speaker has made a new argument. 	Map the new argument (reason + claim) using the methods learned in Chapter 5. The "claim" in this case is the premise which the speaker had initially asserted without any supporting reasons. Then evaluate the new argument using the methods from Chapters 7 and 8, or use the criteria from Chapter 11 if the new argument happens to rely on comparative reasoning.

in Chapter 6. There we said that "Truth-Seekers" and "Sages" were at higher and more sophisticated stages of intellectual development than "Relativists." To move beyond relativism, we need to expand the domain of critical thinking by courageously and objectively examining those beliefs that we hold as articles of faith. Perhaps some of the things that we hold to be true and righteous are as wrongheaded as slavery. That we believe them does not make them true.

The importance of applying the critical thinking skill of self-regulation, guided by the habit of truth-seeking and a healthy sense of skepticism, becomes more urgent for me as I consider not only the ideological reasoning of others, but my own ideological reasoning. Am I so blind to my own wrongheadedness on some issue that I am critical about the tiny speck in my brother's eye but miss the branch in my own?

Evaluating Ideological Reasoning

To evaluate ideological reasoning, we will apply the four tests for the worthiness of an argument that we developed in Chapter 7. Recall that the four questions those tests ask are these: (1) Are all the premises true? (2) Is the argument logically strong? (3) Are the reasons relevant to the claim being made? and (4) Is the argument non-circular? Let us consider each question in sequence.

ARE THE IDEOLOGICAL PREMISES TRUE?

The test for the truthfulness of the premises is perhaps the most important test for ideological reasoning. If the premises are taken as true, then the listener could be well down the path to believing the conclusion. To apply this test, one must consider all the premises one after another. Some will be spoken and others will be implicit. Each needs individual attention. Given that strongly held beliefs and core values often function as the implicit but unspoken guiding ideology, it may be challenging to bring all the unspoken assumptions to the surface for examination. And yet, for ideological inferences, the key issues revolve around the truthfulness of those axiomatic ideological premises themselves. These are the very premises that the argument maker takes on faith and expects the listener to take on faith as well. For critical thinking, the question is, "How can we tell whether the premises expressing the speaker's ideology are true or false?"

The speaker may or may not wish to defend any given premise. The first possibility to consider in applying the Test of the Truthfulness of the Premises is that the speaker would provide no further backing. Instead, the speaker may regard the premise as self-evidently true. In this case we can use the methods described in Chapter 6 for evaluating claims to see whether or not we should agree that it is true. Asking the listener to have faith too is not likely to persuade a strong critical thinker with a healthy sense of skepticism.

Thinking Critically   Faith in Adversity: The Book of Job

Critical thinking is not something invented by scientists or philosophers of the modern or postmodern eras. There is evidence of vigorous critical thinking, including lively debates and arguments, in many historically significant documents, the Bible among them, and in many religious traditions as well. The reasoning, as we would expect, particularly in prescientific times, tends to be ideological in character, but the skills of analysis, interpretation, inference, self-regulation, evaluation, and explanation are all evident. Consider, for example, the question "Why does God, who is all good and all powerful, permit innocent people to suffer evil?" The question has been around for thousands of years, and there are no easy answers. To say that evil is unreal is playing with words. To say that all evil is natural, like the tragic consequences of bad weather or unfortunate accidents, is to ignore the evil that men and women do to each other intentionally on occasion. To say that God gives us free choice so the evil we do is something God is permitting, but does not approve of, seems to contradict God's goodness. No loving parent would permit his or her children to rape and murder one

another. This issue, known as "the problem of evil," is a classic concern of people raised in the Judeo-Christian tradition. It is addressed early in the Judeo-Christian Bible

in a book called Job. That book contains the story of a wealthy and blessed man named Job. One day Satan and God decide to test his faith. They have a bit of a wager over the question of what it might take for Job to abandon his conviction and trust in God. Their approach is to test him by visiting upon him and his household all manner of evil and misfortune.

Read Job and consider how Job behaves in response to the adversity sent his way. Apply your critical thinking skills to the arguments used by the three main characters in the story: God, Job, and Satan. Map and evaluate their arguments. In the final analysis, is Job's faith an example of ideological reasoning or not—that is, does it have the three characteristics of being deductive, axiomatic, and immune from both confirmation and disconfirmation? Would God and Satan have given Job a tougher challenge were they to have filled his life with ease and comfort? Is there any experience or set of circumstances that can logically lead one to infer that if God does exist, then God is not currently taking an active interest in the lives and fortunes of all the individual human beings.

The second possibility is that the argument maker would present himself or herself as the source that stands behind a given premise. The person might say, "Trust me when I tell you . . ." or "Based on all my experience I know that . . ." If the speaker wants us to believe the premise is true because of his or her own credibility, then we can apply the lessons from Chapter 6 about the twelve characteristics of a credible expert. We can use those lessons to assess whether the maker of an ideological argument is, in fact, a credible source whose word we should trust regarding the truth of a given premise.

The speaker's third option is to cite a source that the speaker trusts and that the speaker is asking the listener to also trust. Strong critical thinkers will then turn their evaluative attentions toward that source and inquire as to its worthiness. Suppose, for example, that the argument maker states, "It is in this reference book that XYZ," "I saw it on the Internet that XYZ," "My buddy at work says that. . .," or "Someone on *Oprah* said XYZ." We would then demand reasons why any of these sources should be trusted as experts on the topic XYZ. In Chapter 6 we developed a full set of expectations for evaluating the credibility of sources, and we can apply those to see whether we should or should not trust the source that the speaker now offers.

The fourth possibility is that the argument maker could offer a reason why the ideological premise is true. In effect, this creates a new argument. The premise we had been questioning is now the conclusion of this new argument. Its reason is the reason newly given. This tactic of providing an additional reason simply pushes the problem one step back. For example, "I believe that chimpanzees and humans have the same rights because all animals that are self-conscious and can feel pain do

have the same rights." Providing a reason for an ideological claim invites strong critical thinkers to evaluate that new argument. The first question might be "Why do you believe that all self-conscious animals that can feel pain have the same rights?" The next question might test the implications of that conviction by asking, "Do you really believe that worms, sparrows, kittens, small children, and carpenter ants have the same rights?" If the argument maker offers a reason or reasons why a given premise is true, we would simply apply our tools for evaluating arguments. We could map the argument, then use the four tests. If the speaker happens to use comparative reasoning to make a new argument that his or her original premise was true, we would apply the criteria from Chapter 11 for evaluating comparative thinking.

Depending on the context and the importance of the issue, we may decide not to push things this far. Good judgment is always a virtue. If the issue is trivial, we may not want to keep asking, "Why should I believe you about that?" so aggressively that we end up risking an important friendship or relationship. But if the ideological argument is going to be costly and risky, then good judgment requires that we push the Test of the Truthfulness of the Premises with vigor. It is too easy to let ideological first principles slip by unchallenged. Strong critical thinkers do not want to do that. But because these first principles often express beliefs and values that we happen to share, we can drop our guard at times. And it is exactly in those times that we are vulnerable to making mistakes. We do not want to sing the critical thinker's lament, "Oh, but I should have asked more questions before I believed so-and-so or agreed to such-and-such. But it all sounded so sensible at the time."

19th-Century Ideologies and 20th-Century Wars

During the 19th century, remarkably different ideologies took heart from the expression "survival of the fittest" and the scientific weight that Darwin's evolutionary theory had already garnered. In the 1800s three writers whose ideas greatly influenced world leaders and world events a century later—Ernst Haeckel, William Sumner, and Karl Marx—pressed Darwinian ideas, misinterpreted and wrongly applied, into the service of their ideologies. To appreciate how each invoked evolution, watch the clip "Fit to Rule" from *The Day the Universe Changed*. You can access this clip at **www.TheThinkSpot.com**.

The 20th century saw tens of millions of human beings killed as these global ideologies clashed. Nazism, with its theory of Aryan supremacy and programs of "racial hygiene," manifested Haeckel's misuse of Darwin's ideas. Capitalism, which free of government regulation produces an ever widening gap between the very rich 1 percent and everyone else, mani-fested Sumner's misapplications of Darwin. And Communism, with its belief in the inevitability of the rise of the proletariat working class, revealed Marx's misconceptions about Darwin. As history has demonstrated, the power of ideologies like these not only to shape policies but to destroy tens of millions of human lives cannot be overestimated. Science made subservient to ideology will always pose a grave danger for us all.

<<< Haeckel's 19th-century misinterpretations of Darwin spawned the brutal genocides perpetrated by 20th-century Nazism.

∧ Sumner's 19th-century misinterpretations of Darwin ∧ spawned the greedy dog-eat-dog excesses ∧ and recurring market collapses of unrestricted 20th-century capitalism.

∧ Marx's 19th-century misinterpretations ∧ of Darwin spawned failed economics ∧ and the crushing misery of 20th-century communism.

LOGICAL STRENGTH AND IDEOLOGICAL BELIEF SYSTEMS

Ideological arguments, which are often the product of deductive reasoning, generally display reasonable levels of logical strength. By and large, they will pass the second test for evaluating arguments—the Test of Logical Strength. Many of the arguments used follow the patterns described in the section on deductive arguments in Chapter 8, and in particular they often use the templates for "applying a generalization" and "applying an exception." For example:

• Lazy people don't deserve handouts. Cecelia and street people like her who don't have regular jobs are lazy. So, you shouldn't give her any pocket change when you see her begging for a handout.

• Cheating on an important exam is unethical. But this course is not in my major and it's only a midterm, not the final. This exam is not important. So, this one time it's OK to cheat.

• Jesus has made it clear that the most important commandment is to love our neighbors as we love ourselves. No nation that structures its health care policy so that 40 million of its citizens are systematically denied access to adequate health care is practicing love of neighbor.[v] Jesus would be very disappointed in all of us, voters and leaders alike, for our part in permitting so many millions of our neighbors to be treated so badly. Good Christians should be among the strongest advocates of universal health care.

When considering these examples, keep in mind that one or more of the premises may be false. But for the sake of illustrating the logical strength often found in ideological reasoning, let us, only for the moment, assume that they are all true.

Ideological belief structures often contain internal contradictions. Buddhism, Islam, Taoism, Newtonian physics, Aristotelian cosmology, Scientology, communism, fascism, democracy, Marxism, and feminism can all be reasonably described as ideological belief systems of one kind or another. Each contains inconsistencies, small or large, as is evident from the internal disagreements that theorists and proponents of those systems experience. Some, like Buddhism and Marxism, embrace inconsistency. Some, like Newtonian

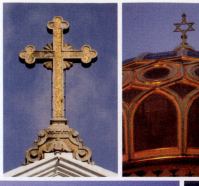

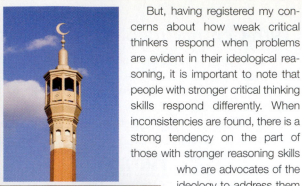

^^
^
When should an ideology be set in stone?

physics and Aristotelian cosmology, give way to superior conceptualizations, such as the theory of relativity. Some, like democracy and feminism, struggle with inconsistencies.

As a rule of thumb, all ideological belief systems that are "isms" are prone to internal inconsistencies. It is always possible that internal inconsistencies can be explained or resolved. As we shall see in the next chapter, the internal inconsistencies called anomalies, in scientific belief systems often provide the impetus for further research and the generation of new knowledge. In ideologies that do not employ empirical investigation as a source of new knowledge, inconsistencies can be resolved by debate and the examination of founding documents. One belief will survive and be embraced as dogma, and the other will be branded a heresy.

What should we do if our beliefs lead to contradictions? In that case, strong critical thinking would require us to revise or abandon one or more of our beliefs. That is the only logical way to resolve the contradiction that inconsistent beliefs create. Unfortunately, in my opinion, too often proponents of ideological systems give themselves permission not to think critically about their own beliefs. Instead, they use escape clauses when challenged about the internal contradictions in their beliefs, using phrases such as "Well, we call that a mystery" or "If your faith were stronger, you would understand." The other unfortunate tactic ideological thinkers at times employ is resorting to donkey cart terms, "You see, true freedom means. . ." "True racial supremacy means that we have. . ."

If the truth of their absolute convictions is challenged, weak critical thinkers are likely to try to fend off those challenges with fallacious or unverifiable rationales such as: "It's just common sense; everyone knows that. . ."; "Our tradition has always taught that. . ."; "It is a fundamental principle of our founders that . . ."; "Inspiration and revelation are the sources of . . ."; "I was brought up this way"; "It's what my parents always told me"; "It's what I learned in kindergarten"; or "We'll all find out the truth some day after we're dead."

But, having registered my concerns about how weak critical thinkers respond when problems are evident in their ideological reasoning, it is important to note that people with stronger critical thinking skills respond differently. When inconsistencies are found, there is a strong tendency on the part of those with stronger reasoning skills who are advocates of the ideology to address them and remove those inconsistencies. Understanding the power of dominance structuring to bolster their preferred opinion, we would expect those advocates not to abandon ship if they can plug the leak. Their efforts generally take the form of reframing the definitions of key terms, modifying or qualifying core beliefs, or refining the language used to express the ideology to remove the "apparent" contradiction. Notice that in this paragraph, I'm talking about advocates who are devoted to the ideology and who have strong thinking skills. I did not say that they had strong critical thinking habits of mind or a healthy skepticism. If they did, then their responses would also have to include the possibility of abandoning the ideology.

RELEVANCY, NON-CIRCULARITY, AND IDEOLOGICAL REASONING

For the big "isms," our third test for evaluating arguments, the Test of Relevancy tends to yield unambiguously positive results. Why? Proponents of large-scale ideological systems, like religions, metaphysical worldviews, and political and economic worldviews declare their ideologies to be relevant to everything. In the United States, commentators advocating liberalism and conservatism provide strongly held opinions on virtually all topics. The initial problems that some Christian theologians had with Darwin, for example, grew out of a belief system that presumed that, in the act of creation, God must have made every animal at the same time. Later theologians refined their theory of creation so that it would be consistent with the scientific evidence. The inconsistency was resolved, and the Church and its belief system could continue to be presented as relevant to all God had created, which of course, is everything. We saw in one of the previous examples that a plausible case can be made that Jesus would have expected his followers to support universal health care.

Our fourth test, non-circularity, produces consternation as well. The arguments used by ideological thinkers typically pass this test. They are not circular for the most part. Yes, it would be circular to argue that God exists because the Bible says so, and then to argue that the Bible is true because it is the word of God. But that is not generally how strong critical thinkers who are religious people would frame their arguments. And, yes, it would be circular for a Marxist to argue that

> I do not feel obligated to believe that the same God who has endowed us with sense, reason, and intellect has intended us to forgo their use.

Galileo Galilei[vi]

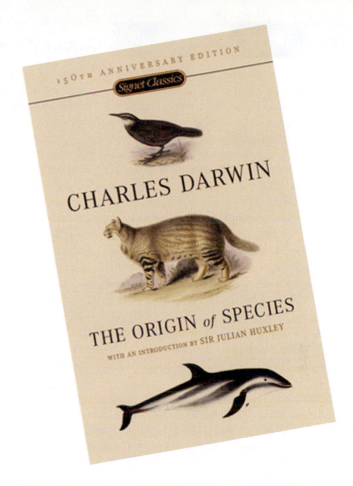

∧
∧ **How could a study of beetles and birds** cause so
∧ much trouble?

the proletariat will prevail over other economic classes because that is the inevitable result of world historical economic forces, and then to argue that belief in those forces is based on the expectation that the proletariat will prevail. But, again, that is not how strong critical thinkers who are Marxists would frame their arguments. But I have to tell you that for me, conversing with advocates of ideological systems often feels like a ride on a merry-go-round—a lot of movement but not much progress! To those watching from the side, the riders appear to be going no place fast, but they are generally enjoying the experience. To those riding, the spectators seem to be rushing by, while the merry-go-round represents the steady and predictable force of their well-ordered universe with every other horse and rider exactly in the place where they belong.

Uses, Benefits, and Risks of Ideological Reasoning

Ideological reasoning offers many benefits. First and foremost, our shared ideologies define and shape our communities and give individuals a strong sense of identity. We know who we are by reference to our ideological belief systems. For example, "I am a liberal, a member of the Democratic Party, and a Christian." Second, ideological convictions enable us to escape the suffocating malaise of relativism. The core values of an ideological belief system guide our thinking about right and wrong, good and bad, and obligatory and optional. Third, ideological reasoning offers an efficient way of addressing novel questions. Our "isms" often provide ready answers to new questions we may not have the time

Thinking Critically

Group Project: Conflicting Principles and Conflicting Positions

Select one of the following conflicts and prepare a well-researched report on the core beliefs, values, and assumptions that fuel each side in the dispute:

1 The conflict between Israel and Palestine in the Middle East

2 The conflict over legislation permitting assisted suicide

3 The conflict between property developers who want to build communities and create jobs and preservationists who want to protect the environment by limiting development

Thinking Critically

About Value Judgments

We all make judgments that express priorities. I prefer clean water to impure water, moderate exercise to a couch potato's sedentary existence, and intelligent discourse to loudmouthed stubbornness. And, as you know, I give priority to all of the positive critical thinking habits of mind over their negative polar opposites. But I have not asked you to agree with me about the positive critical thinking habits of mind as a matter of faith. Instead, in Chapter 1, we considered several reasons why critical thinking was valuable for you individually and for us as a society. We connected the skills and the habits of mind to that core idea of critical thinking in Chapters 2 and 3. Therefore, the value of the habits of mind, like the value of the skills, comes from the value of critical

thinking as purposeful reflective judgment. If there are superior ways to judge what to believe and what to do, I do not know what they are.

Taking it a step further, I have recommended that you should strengthen your skills and fortify your habits of mind. These recommendations are based on the value that I see for you and for all of us in using critical thinking. More than that, this book contains a number of other value judgments about critical thinking. I have urged that we try to be more reflective and use self-regulation to protect ourselves against premature dominance structuring and from risky reliance on System-1 judgments when more reflection should be used. To support my advice and explain my value judgments, I have used

arguments, examples, and research. Some people might think that value judgments are automatically unreliable, false, or nonsense. I do not agree with that assumption. And I do not know how a rational person could argue for that assumption. Arguing that value judgments should neither be made nor accepted is arguing for a specific value judgment! So, let's agree that people make value judgments. The question critical thinking raises is the question of judiciousness. Are our value judgments reasonable, well founded, carefully considered, and thoughtfully applied with sensitivity to the complexities of real-world situations? Recall the "Sage" level of cognitive development we talked about in Chapter 6. That is the quality of value judgment we should be striving to attain.

---

or the expertise to answer for ourselves. Suppose, for example, that we genetically modify food grains so that rice, corn, and wheat provide nourishment that is the equivalent of the protein from eating meat. People with deep convictions that anything God did not create naturally is probably bad might advocate bans on the genetic manipulation of foods. People deeply convinced that God intended human beings to use their powers of reason to solve problems, like world hunger, might advocate expanding the use of genetically altered foods.

The benefits are also the risks. Ideological reasoning is pervasive in our culture, and it can be powerfully persuasive. We noted that our ideologies shape the character of our communities and our personal identities as members of those communities. Ideological belief structures are socially normative—those who disagree are seen as outsiders, ignorant, mistaken, abnormal, or dangerous. Socrates

(470–399 B.C.E.) was convicted of the capital offense of corrupting the youth of ancient Athens because he taught them to reason for themselves and to question the unsubstantiated beliefs of the leaders of that city-state.[ix] Take heed, you who write books about critical thinking!

> *Fix reason firmly in her seat,* and call to her tribunal every fact, *every opinion.* Question with *boldness...*

Thomas Jefferson[x]

Thinking Critically

Group Exercise: Why Do We Believe What We Believe?

Discuss each statement below in turn and, as a group, examine as objectively as possible the reasons why it may be true or may be false.

1 Just like people, computers can think for themselves.

2 Chimpanzees have the same rights as humans.

3 Life is fundamentally unfair.

4 Management and labor are natural adversaries.

5 Over 2 million aliens, originally from some other planet, are being secretly held in a concentration camp 200 kilometers outside Johannesburg, South Africa.[vii]

6 The world will end on the winter solstice in 2012.

7 God has a purpose for everything that happens.

8 And now these three remain: faith, hope, and love. But the greatest of these is love.[viii]

The world will end on the winter solstice in 2012! Really? And we know that how?

The Courage to Challenge the Ideologue

It takes courage to challenge powerful people who are using their ideological stance to cause harm. That decision is never an easy one, because there is always the risk that you will be targeted. The film *Good Night and Good Luck* reenacts a conversation that might have occurred at CBS when the journalists Edward R. Morrow and Fred Friendly decided to take on Senator Joseph McCarthy. This clip also includes actual footage of the Senator using innuendo and insinuation when questioning people whom he had called to testify before his Committee. Access this clip at **www.TheThinkSpot.com**.

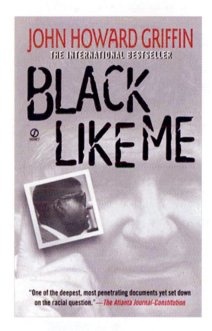

JOHN HOWARD GRIFFIN
THE INTERNATIONAL BESTSELLER
BLACK LIKE ME
"One of the deepest, most penetrating documents yet set down on the racial question." —*The Atlanta Journal-Constitution*

<<< **What would today's parallel be to the ideology-busting,** truth-seeking courage Howard Griffin displayed?

Because our ideological convictions generally operate in the background of our consciousness, we do not often question our fundamental axiomatic beliefs. And yet, they are powerful but subtle influences that shape our interpretations of events and experiences. For example, it is easy for a person with an ideological belief system to interpret questions that challenge that system as hostile and to regard the person who asks those questions as an enemy. Belief structures determine the scope of what we imagine to be possible. If we believe that all human beings have immortal souls, then we can imagine that it is possible that our souls might survive after our bodies die. Ideological systems shape the questions we ask. If we believe in souls surviving after bodily death, then it makes sense to ask where they go and what that disembodied survival might be like. Our belief systems, like filters on a camera, color our view of the world.

Because ideological convictions often seem to be immunized against scientific confirmation or disconfirmation, it can be difficult for us to see them as mistaken. For example, we know of no scientific test to determine whether the individual is more important than the social collective. We have not found a scientific way to verify or falsify the belief that knowledge is superior to ignorance, but most of us believe it is. There is no scientific way to investigate the claim that it is the will of God that America be destroyed. Ideological convictions that are neither testable nor falsifiable can be called "metaphysical."

Ideological reasoning constrains and empowers. Our axiomatic core convic-tions have life-shaping consequences. Differing political orientations generate dramatically divergent visions of human society. Not surprisingly, people who are deeply convinced that their way is "the only right way" often seek to change or to destroy those institutions and people who threaten "the only right way." History offers many examples: the Christian Crusaders, the Taliban, the Nazis, the Stalinists, the Klan, racists, zealots, true-believers, and bigots of all stripes, shapes, and stenches who use ideological reasoning to motivate their followers and try to destroy those who disagree.

The benefits and risks of ideological thinking revolve around the power of ideologies to structure our individual and collective way of seeing the world. In the middle of the 20th century many Americans saw the world as a place of conflict between two global powers, the United States and the Soviet Union, each dominated by opposing ideologies: constitutional democracy and communism. The film *Good Night and Good Luck* shows what can happen when unscrupulous ideological bullies, like Senator Joseph McCarthy, gain political power. True, McCarthy regarded himself as doing battle against the communists, who were regarded as ideologues and enemies of the United States. Although his goal may have been consistent with the defense of the rule of law and individual freedom, McCarthy's methods turned out to violate those very ideals.

Hundreds of years ago, the English statesman and philosopher John Locke described the habit of talking and listening only to those who agreed with the beliefs and opinions one already holds as a basic type of flawed thinking.[xi] Today the critical thinking community refers to the habit first described by Locke as a failure of courageous truth-seeking. James Howard Griffin's extraordinary book, *Black Like Me*,[xii] describes the power of ideologies to shape our perceptions of reality. In that book, he tells about his life-shaping experiences as a white man living as a black man in America's deep South in the late 1950s. There are many other powerful examples in literature and film that help us simulate what the world is like from another's perspective. Trying to see the world through the eyes of another is a valuable way of expanding our sensitivities and monitoring our tendency to accept beliefs uncritically.

<<< **David Strathairn won an Oscar for his portrayal of Edward R. Morrow in *Good Night and Good Luck.***

REVIEW

Ideological reasoning begins with our deeply held convictions, core values, and assumptions about the world. From these we reason, top-down, to specific implications about how we should live and what to think about issues of the day. Ideological reasoning is deductive in character, the ideological premises are axiomatic, and the argument maker takes the ideology to be true more or less on faith. Ideological reasoning is important and useful because it shapes our community and individual identities. It guides our thinking on policy questions and reflects our value judgments. It helps us know what we should think when we do not have the time or the expertise to address new questions on our own. The risks associated with ideological reasoning are as great as the benefits. Because strong convictions may be mistaken, we can easily find ourselves advocating and defending views that are ill-conceived and harmful. History shows the dangers of ideological reasoning though the wars, genocides, and human misery caused by ideologues and their followers.

KEY TERM

ideological reasoning (or **top-down thinking**) is the process of thinking that begins with abstractions or generalizations that express one's core beliefs, concepts, values, or principles and proceeds to reason top-down to specific applications. Ideological reasoning is deductive and axiomatic. The argument maker takes the ideological premises on faith.   *181*

FIND IT ON THE THINKSPOT

We open this important chapter with CNN reports about California's divisive Proposition 8. By visiting **www.TheThinkSpot.com**, you can access the legal analysis CNN's Avery Freeman provides (p. 180). There, too, you can access the CNN news story describing the protests and demonstrations sparked by the court rulings. Wherever you live, I invite you to follow the issue of same-sex marriage closely. This could turn out to be one of those issues we will all look back on decades from now with wonderment. I can imagine a conversation about same-sex marriage in the year 2050 that includes the sentence, "What were they thinking back then in 2010?"

The "Fit to Rule" episode (p. 189) from the series *The Day the Universe Changed* is an insightful analysis of how Darwinism was misused to advance ideological preconceptions. Visit **www.TheThinkSpot.com** to access this remarkable video, and then ask yourself whether hundreds of millions of us are today being guided toward mutual destruction by "true believers" and unexamined ideological worldviews. Is our consumerist culture ideologically driven too? Why do we believe that we need to own so many nice, new things? Are we being led to believe that we can purchase happiness? If so, why and by whom?

Not all bullies lurk in playgrounds. Unfortunately, some are ensconced in government agencies, religious organizations, workplaces, universities, medical centers, health clubs, and corporate offices. That clip from *Good Night, and Good Luck* I invited you to watch (p. 193) offers a look at considerations that often come to mind when one contemplates confronting a bully. Access this clip at **www.TheThinkSpot.com**. In fact, I urge you to watch the entire movie. It is an excellent film. Do we have any journalists with the truth-seeking courage, ethical strength, and powerful skills of an Edward R. Murrow or a Fred Friendly today?

Exercises

REFLECTIVE LOG: THE MILITARY DRAFT

A nation can legislate mandatory service in the armed forces. Known as "the draft," the United States used forced conscription to build the armies it needed to fight World War II, the Korean War, and the Vietnam War. If drafted, a person must leave his or her school, job, and family to serve for a specified period of time, typically two years, in the armed forces. Draftees become soldiers. And some soldiers give their lives in combat. Those who try to escape their duties, known as "draft dodgers" are prosecuted and imprisoned. Assume that the nation's military leaders evaluate the readiness of the armed forces and determine that the national defense requires that a military draft should be established now. Assume that men and women between the ages of 18 and 35 will be subject to the draft as recommended to the President and the Congress. Assume that the proposal to institute a draft is going to be taken up by Congress next week and that you have the opportunity to offer your advice to your state's representatives and senators. Although the nation may or may not be at war at the moment when the legislation is being considered, it is reasonable to assume that the nation could be at war at some point in the future. Considering what you know about the nation, its ideological convictions and its history, what would you recommend and why? Assume that you are the right age to be drafted into the military and that you are otherwise fully qualified and eligible to serve. That is, assume that whatever law is passed, if there is a draft, you may be one of the people conscripted to serve.

GROUP DISCUSSION: WHAT IDEALS WOULD YOU GO TO WAR TO DEFEND?

Throughout history people have gone to war. On many occasions, religious ideologies, political ideologies, or economic ideologies have been at the root of those conflicts. The Crusades, World War II, and the American Civil War might be seen as examples of such conflicts, at least in the minds of some leaders and some combatants; ideological reasoning played a major role in explaining why each war was unavoidably necessary. Discuss with your peers the ideological beliefs and core values that, in your considered judgment, would make war unavoidably necessary. Beyond self-defense and the defense of the lives of your family and other members of your community, are their principles, fundamental beliefs, and core values worthwhile to defend with your life and the lives of those you love by waging war? Is freedom worthwhile? Is democracy? Would you go to war to end slavery, to prevent genocide, to free children from forced labor, to rescue fellow citizens from illegal detention in a foreign country, to protect commercial shipping on the high seas, or to save whales from being slaughtered for human food? Would you fight to regain your homeland, or to gain access to clean water? Would you go to war to free your ethnic group from an oppressor nation? If none of these is a worthwhile endeavor to you, is there anything that you personally would go to war to defend or to protect? Remember that whatever your group's answer might be, you should expect that your answer works in reverse as well. That means that you should expect others to do no more and no less, should they perceive your behavior as demanding from them an identical bellicose response. Be prepared to give the very best reasons possible for either the view that war would be the appropriate response of last resort in a given situation or that war is never an appropriate response no matter what the situation. When considering the "no matter what" alternative, be sure to include in your reflections "self-defense and the defense of the lives of your family and other members of your community."

WHEN IDEOLOGIES CLASH

In the 2009 film, *Capitalism: A Love Story*, writer Michael Moore strongly suggests that contemporary American Capitalism is at odds with Christianity, Socialism, and Democracy. Whatever your personal beliefs, these four ideologies are in fact influencing your life, your leaders, and the laws by which we live. I recommend you view the film as part of your effort to learn about these major ideologies. But, keeping and open mind, do not limit your learning to one filmmaker's interpretation of these four ideologies. Develop a reasoned and factually informed analysis of each. In light of your learning and in light of the actual facts as can be demonstrated by trustworthy scientific studies, evaluate the claim that contemporary American Capitalism is at odds with Democracy, Christianity, and Socialism. If it is your view that it is at odds with any one of them (and it cannot be compatible with all of them because of the differences between the three), then how should we reconcile these ideological conflicts in real life—that is, what government policies and personal practices would be the wisest to pursue?

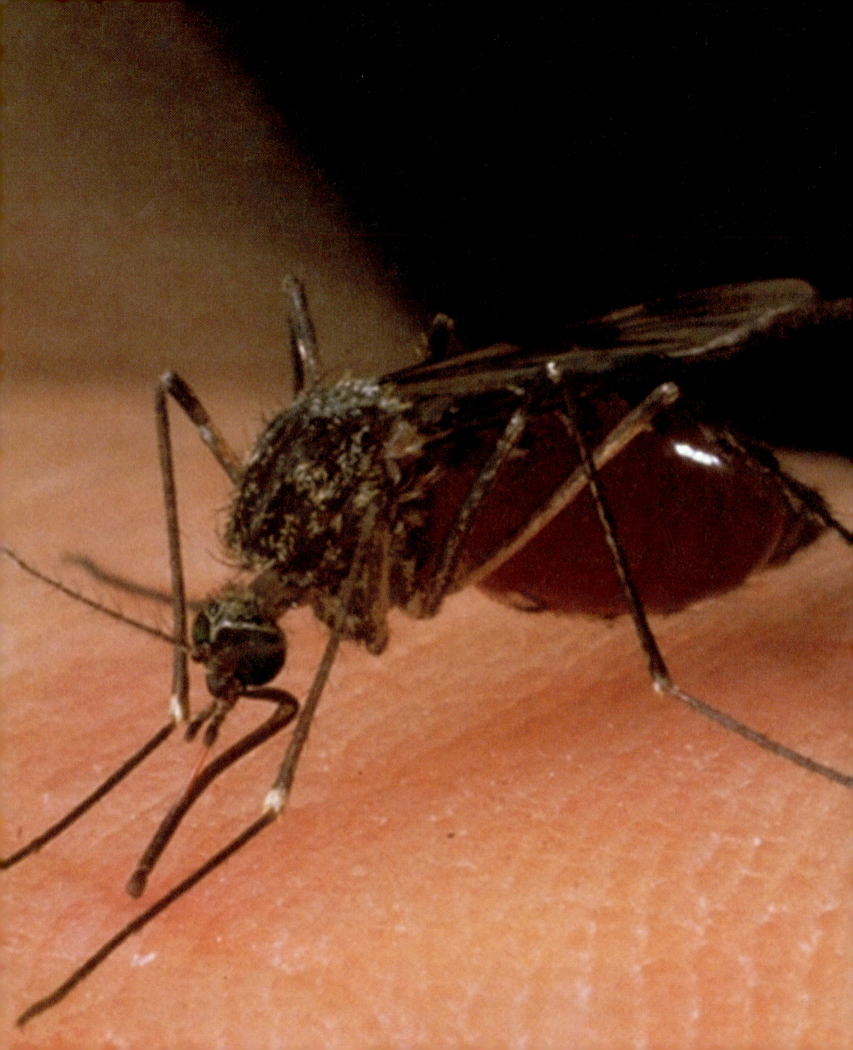

HOW CAN WE RECOGNIZE EMPIRICAL
REASONING?
WHAT ARE THE STEPS IN CONDUCTING
AN INVESTIGATION SCIENTIFICALLY?
WHAT ARE THE BENEFITS AND RISKS OF
EMPIRICAL REASONING?

"Yellow fever!"

The cry struck dread and panic into the hearts of the residents of port cities from New Orleans to Philadelphia during the 18th and 19th centuries. Epidemics of yellow fever ravaged the population. Its symptoms include nausea and vomiting, chills, headaches, restlessness, prostration, and pain throughout the body. Victims suffer irregular fever, jaundice, bleeding from every bodily orifice, delirium, convulsions, coma, and death.[i] Once the disease took hold of a city, it spread throughout, mysteriously killing some but not others. The epidemics raged, and tens of thousands died until the first frosts of late autumn.

Called "Yellow Jack," no one knew where the disease came from, how to treat it, or how to stop its spread. Quarantines did not work. Closing doors and windows did not work. Burning tar to "disturb the miasma" did not work. The disease seemed to jump from house to house through the city, afflicting men and women, old and young, black and white, prosperous and poor.[ii] People fled cities by the thousands in fear. Commerce collapsed; cities declared bankruptcy. Ministers advocated moral reform and closing dance halls. Physicians treated the sick with purging and bleeding. Nurses and family members tried to ease the pain, to comfort, and to console. Many, but not all, of those physicians, ministers, nurses, and family members contracted the illness themselves. Why? Was it by touching the sick person, by breathing the same air, by handling the filthy bed linens? Was the contamination in the blood, the feces, the food, the furniture, or the air? Nobody knew. But unless someone could figure out exactly how the disease was transmitted, there would be no hope of containing or controlling it.

In the late 1870s a Cuban physician, Carlos Juan Finley, presented a theory about the cause of the disease. He hypothesized that the dreaded fever, which annually plagued his homeland, was carried from person to person by, of all things, a mosquito. He had gathered empirical data and mapped the locations where the mosquito was prevalent and where the fever occurred. Looking at the two maps, he realized that the locations correlated. But a correlation is not a cause, and the physicians of his day did not believe a disease could be transmitted by a mosquito. He presented his work in 1881 at a scientific meeting in Havana and was completely ignored.

That is, until 1900. That year the U.S. Army marched into Panama and faced the same enemy that had destroyed other armies sent by Spain and by Napoleon. The generals knew that the U.S. troops being sent to Panama risked annihilation by Yellow Jack. To lead the effort to combat yellow fever, the Army appointed a young major named Walter Reed. Reed and his colleagues thought that the mosquito transmission theory might have some value. They worked to refine the theory, but in October 1900 there had been only two cases to examine. Without more data, Reed's group could not rule out other possible causes. One particular explanation was regarded as much more plausible: The idea that germs transmitted

continued on next page

EMPIRICAL REASONING: "BOTTOM UP" THINKING

CHAPTER 13

197

continued from previous page

by the filthy clothing and bedding of yellow fever victims caused the epidemic. *The Washington Post* labeled Reed's ideas about mosquitoes "silly and nonsensical."

To test his hypothesis that mosquitoes were the cause, Reed needed to create an experiment that would show two things: First, that the disease was transmitted by contaminated mosquitoes and, second, that it was not transmitted by contact with filthy, germ-infested clothing and bedding. To obtain the volunteer human subjects his experiment would require, he offered each willing person $100 in gold. At a remote location known as Camp Lazear, Reed set up two identical huts and divided the volunteers randomly, sending some to live for several days in Hut #1 and others to live for several days in Hut #2. Both huts were screened to prevent the entry of any mosquitoes. Hut #1 was loaded with filthy clothing and bedding in which yellow fever victims had slept, bled, vomited, and died. No one in Hut #1 became sick with yellow fever. Hut #2 was divided into two chambers by a screen that permitted the air to circulate between the two chambers. Infected mosquitoes were released into one side but not the other. As predicted, only the volunteers in the chamber where the infected mosquitoes had been released became ill. None of the other volunteers in Hut #2's other chamber contracted yellow fever, even though they were breathing the same air as the sick volunteers. Walter Reed was able to design a test that demonstrated that a widely held idea was probably false and that another idea (mosquitoes can bring sickness and death to humans) must be regarded as a vital new insight. It was an insight of great importance to public health. Go to **www.TheThinkSpot.com** for details about the objective, preparation, protocol, data, and conclusions from Walter Reed's classic use of empirical reasoning in his Camp Lazear experiment.

Recognizing Empirical Reasoning

Our capacity as a species to anticipate what comes next and then to devise ways to affect the outcomes of events and processes is absolutely fundamental to our survival and our current planetary dominance. We look for cause-and-effect relationships to explain, and hence to predict and control. The opening sequence of *2001: A Space Odyssey*[iii] dramatizes the basic idea: You hit your rival over the head hard enough and he dies! But your arm is not long enough and your fist is not hard enough, so you make a tool, a club, to get the job done. The film suggests that progress from the bone used as a club to interplanetary space travel is simply a matter of filling in the blanks.[iv]

Tens of thousands of years later we are still working on filling in those blanks. Today our species is using the map of the human genome and research on gene expression to mount a genetic counterattack on diseases like cancer. Advances gained through empirical reasoning permit us to ask ourselves questions that eclipse the understanding of scientists working in Reed's or Finley's day. What makes a cancerous cell's DNA express itself in different ways at different points in the tumor's growth? What are the mechanisms that turn off and on the protein receptors and, hence, make one kind of therapy effective and another ineffective at different points along the way?

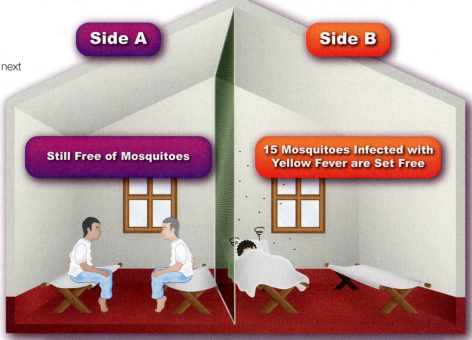

Side A

Side B

Still Free of Mosquitoes

15 Mosquitoes Infected with Yellow Fever are Set Free

J. MORAN ENTERS SIDE B AND DEVELOPS YELLOW FEVER IN 4 DAYS. MEN IN SIDE A REMAIN WELL. THE PRESENCE OF CONTAMINATED MOSQUITOES INFECTED SIDE B.

 Interior of Walter Reed's experimental Hut #2. Why the screen creating Chamber A and Chamber B?

The correct answers to these questions and to others like them come only as the fruit of empirical arguments. Investigators, using the same kind of reasoning that Reed and Finley used, begin with a theory about how or why something happens in the natural world. They form a testable hypothesis, gather data by observation and experimentation, and use those data to confirm or disconfirm their hypothesis. In the process, they strive to disconfirm competing hypotheses. In this chapter we will explore this kind of "bottom-up" thinking, known as empirical reasoning.

CHARACTERISTICS OF EMPIRICAL REASONING

Empirical reasoning contrasts with ideological reasoning on all three key characteristics. Recall that in the previous chapter we described ideological reasoning as deductive, axiomatic, and taken on faith. By contrast, **empirical reasoning** is inductive in character, open to self-corrective revision, and the argument makers take their empirical premises to be true on the basis of interpersonally verifiable experience.

Empirical Reasoning Is Inductive

Describing scientific investigations as inductive in character means that the conclusions reached are probabilistic. Scientists would be the first to insist on this. They strive to remain open to the possibility that the conclusions they reach based on empirical reasoning might need to change! Recall our discussion of coincidences, correlations, and causes in the section on inductive reasoning in Chapter 8. We noted there that the analytical and inferential tools used in empirical reasoning, like statistical tests, produce confidence levels that approach 1 in 100 or 1 in 1,000. But even with such high levels of confidence, the conclusions drawn remain inductive. Scientists use observations and statistical analyses to draw inferences with varying levels of confidence. The inferences drawn remain probabilistic even when our statistical analyses permit us to have very high levels of confidence.[v] Although it turned out that Finley was right about the mosquito being the vector that transmitted the yellow fever virus from one person to another, he might have been wrong. His correlations that mapped the mosquito's habitat and the areas where the disease was found may have been correct, but there just might have been some third factor he had overlooked.

Just as not all deductive reasoning is ideological, not all inductive reasoning is empirical. In Chapters 2, 8, and 11 there are many examples of inductive arguments that are not instances of empirical reasoning. Just as deductive reasoning is not defined in terms of "general" and "specific," neither is inductive reasoning. Examples of comparative reasoning illustrate

that induction can also go from general to general ("Fashion models are like thoroughbreds, beautiful to see but expensive to maintain and difficult to control") or from specific to specific ("Bill's tastes in deserts is like his sister's, so if Sue doesn't like rhubarb pie, Bill probably doesn't like it either"). The characterizations in this chapter about empirical reasoning do not necessarily apply to all of inductive reasoning because empirical reasoning is only one kind of inductive reasoning.

Empirical Reasoning Is Self-Corrective

The second important feature of empirical reasoning, namely that it is self-corrective, is vital to the progress made using investigative methods. Crime dramas like *CSI* and *Law & Order* unfold like mystery novels. They reveal clues and bits of information along the way so that the viewer can form hypotheses about "who done it." Clever writers arrange the story so that the criminal's identity is concealed as long as possible. But the writers organize the flow of information to the viewer so that various characters can be ruled out as the possible criminal. The viewer then revises his or her theory of the crime so that it explains all the data, old and new. The process of scientific inquiry is similar, except that there is nobody orchestrating the moment at which the data will be made known to the investigating researcher. The researcher himself or herself must devise the means to acquire the kind of data that will be relevant and revise his or her hypothesis, if necessary, as new information is gained. To answer empirical research questions, investigators examine data gathered using instruments specifically designed to find the kinds of data that they expect might exist. We would not have invented the microscope had we not thought that perhaps there were important things to learn by looking at objects in more detail than the unaided human eye can reveal.

Empirical Reasoning Is Open to Independent Verification

A third feature of empirical reasoning is that premises that report data or the results of statistical tests are open to scrutiny and independent verification by the entire scientific community. Investigatory inquiry is a community activity. Other scientists are welcome to gather additional data, to recreate experiments, and to recalculate statistical findings. The observations, databases, and findings scientists use and report are subjected to the scrutiny of other investigators. Other scientists are welcome to scrutinize a colleague scientist's arguments, data-gathering methods, statistical analyses, and every other aspect of the empirical reasoning. Replication is a way of verifying that the observations and findings reported by the original scientist are true. If we were to replicate today the experiment Reed conducted in 1900, we should expect to find, as he did, that the only people who become infected are those who are exposed to yellow fever by the infected mosquitoes. Our belief in the truth of the premises, observations, and findings, does not depend on whether we

Empirical Reasoning or Bottom-Up Thinking

General statements expressing hypotheses which are intended to explain and to predict observable phenomena.

Inductive inferences, including correlations and causal reasoning as described in Chapter 8.

Specific data gathered carefully and systematically from representative samples

Chapter 13

> ## One is always a long way from solving a problem until one actually has the answer.
>
> Stephen Hawking[vi]

have faith and trust in Reed. Science is not a matter of faith in the word of others. Science is based on the fact that if others conducted the same experiments, they would get the same results.

HYPOTHESES, CONDITIONS, AND MEASURABLE MANIFESTATIONS

An empirical investigation begins with a hypothesis. The hypothesis often can be expressed as a hypothetical, such as "If things of a certain kind are placed under certain conditions, then we will be able to observe certain phenomena." Or a hypothesis can be expressed as a general statement: "Certain kinds of objects behave in certain ways under certain conditions." Here are some example hypotheses.

- If the *Salmonella* bacterium is exposed to temperatures greater than 140 degrees Centigrade for more than 30 seconds, it will die.

- Married couples who experience unanticipated severe financial problems will argue and fight more than they did prior to their financial problems.

- The reflexes of a person who drives a motor vehicle for five or more hours without a rest period will have deteriorated by 30% or more as compared to his or her reflexes after only one to four hours of driving.[vii]

- In our new program, we train sixth graders to tutor third graders in reading and math. Our hypothesis is that the test scores of the sixth graders and the third graders will be significantly higher than the scores of their peers who were not involved in this tutoring program.

- Green is big right now. So, if we promote the belief in the general public that our company has a sincere concern for the environment, we will see an increase in our market share.

- If the Federal Reserve reduces the prime interest rate, there will be a proportional reduction in short-term interest rates on consumer credit card purchases. And, if this happens, it will stimulate the economy, since consumers will tend to spend more, thus leading to an increase in manufacturing and the creation of more jobs.

Arguments expressing empirical reasoning include statements describing the particular states of affairs that the researchers strive to create experimentally or to measure in their natural settings. The advantage of creating specific conditions in the lab is that potential influences of extraneous factors can be reduced. Yet that tends to weaken the generalizability of the findings because the highly controlled conditions achieved in a science lab might not be found in the real world. The scientist's ultimate purpose is to explain and to predict real-world phenomena. There is always a trade-off between the strict controls possible in a laboratory experiment and the generalizability of that experiment to the real world. Automobile companies crash test their vehicles in lab experiments controlling for speed, mass, and direction of impact, and using computerized mannequins instead of human beings. That's good enough for me. They do not have to kill a lot of innocent people in "real-world" experiments to prove that one way of designing an airbag or door frame is better than another. Here are two examples in which the investigators note the difference between the controlled experimental environment and the real world. Under the circumstances, trade-offs must be made.

- Rather than risk accidents on the open road where our subjects and other people as well might be injured or killed, we can check the reflexes of men and women of different ages by having them drive on a closed track in dry weather. Of course, driving on a closed track in dry weather is boring compared to driving on the open road under differing weather and traffic conditions.

Thinking Critically — Measurable Manifestations

The six example hypotheses above illustrate measurable manifestations of hypotheses in six different subject areas: biology, psychology, human performance, education, marketing, and economics. Here are five more examples that are only partially completed. Please complete each one by expressing one or more measurable manifestations of the hypothesis proposed. Add additional statements that clarify or expand upon the descriptions of the exact conditions under which the behavioral manifestations you predict will occur. Explain, in your own words, why the clarifications or expanded descriptions are helpful.

- If we apply a solution made up of water and laundry bleach to mold growing on the surface of a glass dish, then the mold, which is a fungus, will _____.

- In our experimental teacher training program, we have each college student spend a semester as a math and science tutor for seventh or eighth grade students. Our regular teacher training program does not include the semester tutoring. Our hypothesis is that the college students in our experimental program will _____, as compared to the students in our regular program.

- One of the sources of energy consumption is household electricity usage. Electricity is used to heat water, cook or refrigerate food, and to operate lights and consumer appliances. Compact fluorescent lightbulbs last six times longer than comparable incandescent bulbs and use less energy. So, we can predict that if the average consumer were to replace household lightbulbs with compact fluorescent bulbs, he or she would save _____.

- Fashion magazine models, many of whom are teenagers, risk malnourishment and severe eating disorders. If the fashion industry were to adopt mandatory body mass requirements to protect the health of these people, _____.

- Domestic dogs, like their pack animal ancestors, behave in accord with a social hierarchy. The lesser animals in a pack will follow the lead of the dominant animal. Obedience and subservience are expected, and violation of the rule of the pack is punished. We can expect that if dog owners displayed more _____, then their pet dogs would _____.

Small Group: Physical Symmetry, Sexual Attractiveness, and Smell

Hypothesis: Women find men whose faces are more physically symmetrical to be more sexually attractive and to smell better than men whose faces are less physically symmetrical.

What is your first reaction to this hypothesis? How might we test it?

Suppose you had access to a sufficient number of willing volunteers including men whose facial and physical symmetry you could measure and women who were willing to provide you with their opinions about which of these men looked more sexually attractive and smelled better. Design an experiment to test the hypothesis expressed above. The challenge is to describe the steps your experiment would follow, if it were conducted. You do not have to actually conduct this experiment, just design it.

Remember to find some way not to let extraneous factors confound your data. For example, control for the possible influences of cologne or certain foods, like garlic. Be sure too that the women are not influenced by a man's facial expressions, weight, height, or personal charm. Find a strategy for gathering data, which will prevent the women from being influenced by something that a lab assistant might say or do.

After you have recorded the design for your experiment, visit **www.TheThinkSpot.com**

to access recent articles on symmetry and sexual attractiveness, including one peer-reviewed published study conducted by a Stanford undergraduate.

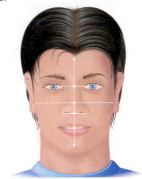

- If we divide the sixth graders and third graders into two groups each, we can train one group of sixth graders to tutor one group of third graders. If we assure that all other known relevant factors are held constant (for example, that otherwise they receive instruction in the same subjects and by equally competent teachers and in identical learning environments), then we should see statistically significantly higher test scores for the experimental group students [third graders who were tutored and their sixth grade tutors] as compared to the control group students [third graders who were not tutored and sixth graders not in the tutoring program]. But how can we assure that the other known relevant factors are held constant?

Conducting an Investigation Scientifically

There are many steps involved in investigating an empirical question logically, systematically, and in a way that allows others in the scientific and professional community to verify the results through replication. Any place along the way an investigator can introduce error though technical, conceptual, methodological, or reasoning mistakes. And yet, because the process can be monitored and corrected by the investigator or others on the research team, science is exceptionally robust from the perspective of the reasoning to be used. All our critical thinking skills and habits of mind are engaged when we set out to determine, using empirical reasoning, what we should believe. As it turns out, as in Reed's situation, a measure of cleverness and bit of creativity are needed just to figure out how to test one's hypothesis.

PERHAPS THE FIRST RECORDED EMPIRICAL INVESTIGATION

Consider, for example, that a driving sense of scientific curiosity impelled the Head Librarian of Alexandria in North Africa to wonder how to explain the observation that at noon on June 21st in a city 800 kilometers to the south, the sun cast no shadows. "Would I see this same lack of shadow

> " There are in fact two things, science and opinion; the former begets knowledge, the latter ignorance. "

Hippocrates, Greek Physician[viii] (460–377 BCE)

everywhere?" To approach an answer to this question, the librarian first had to ask the question with more specific detail. "Do sticks, towers, columns, and obelisks cast shadows in Alexandria at noon on the summer solstice?" wondered that librarian. He experimented and observed that they do. "But how is that possible?' he wondered, given that the Earth is flat?"

That librarian, whose name was Aristophanes, was a person of extraordinary accomplishment and learning. Although 2,200 years ago, science as we know it did not yet exist, inference, analysis, and truth-seeking were alive and well in Egypt and its greatest center of learning, Alexandria. Aristophanes drew the inference that the only way that there could be a shadow in the one city and not in the other is if the Earth were curved, instead of flat. He needed more data to either disconfirm his idea that the Earth was curved or to find evidence that supported his insight. It was easy to measure the length of the shadows in Alexandria at the appointed date and time. But, without any other way to measure the distance, Aristophanes had to hire a man to pace out the exact distance between Alexandria and the city to the south where the sun caste no shadows on June 21st at noon. Aristophanes needed that datum to calculate the curvature of the Earth. Then by using geometry (thank you, Euclid), he could estimate the Earth's circumference. Watch the explanation provided by Carl Sagan in the

---

<<< At high noon on June 21st, the sun casts no shadows down the walls of this well. But it casts shadows at other places at that same date and time. Aristophanes asked why 2,200 years ago.

series *Cosmos* to appreciate Aristophanes' empirical reasoning as he tried to explain the phenomenon he was so curious about. Access this clip at www.TheThinkSpot.com. As it turned out, Aristophanes was able to infer that the Earth was approximately 40,000 kilometers in circumference, an amazingly accurate calculation. (Oh, and for some reason we forgot and then needed to rediscover more than a millennium and a half later that the world was round. Oops! Our bad!)

STEPS IN THE PROCESS OF AN EXTENDED EXAMPLE

At some point during their college years or soon after, many college students find themselves working in an office as an administrative assistant. They may work in an office on campus, or during a summer job, perhaps after graduation to pay the bills before they land a job closer to their intended career field. Many people work in group office environments for many years. The job can have its good points and its bad points. Lately, the collective productivity of office workers, which in the past may have been taken for granted, has become a serious concern for cost-conscious employers. With millions of men and women working in group offices, even a small increase or decrease in productivity can have an unexpectedly large impact on the nation's economy as well as the company's bottom line. How much does the workplace environment affect the motivation and the productivity of group office workers?

Some might leap to the conclusion that improvements in the workplace environment would mean predictable increases in motivation and productivity. Others might be skeptical about that. Whatever one's initial thoughts, the question cannot be satisfactorily resolved without investigating the facts. Spending money to improve the workplace environment for group office workers may or may not make cost-effective positive changes in their motivation and productivity. Merely speculating about the issue is not an adequate response, not if you are the owner of the company and greater productivity would mean more profits for you.

The "Steps in a Scientific Investigation" table on pages 203–204 describes in detail how a team of researchers would scientifically investigate this question.[ix] One column describes the steps in an empirical investigation. The next column applies that step to our example question. In the first step, the investigators articulate the question they are expecting to investigate. Unless the investigator expects to fund the research work himself or herself, simply raising a question is not adequate to secure the funding for conducting that research. Today researchers must explain why a question is significant enough to warrant attention and a commitment of resources. This real-world financial reality is reflected in the table. Critical

> ## Measure what is measurable, and make measurable what is not so.
>
> Galileo Galilei[xi]

thinking is the tool one uses to take into consideration all the problems that need to be overcome in order to engage in a productive empirical inquiry.

In the earlier paragraphs we already addressed Step 1, the importance of the question of the productivity of workers in group office settings. Investigating a factor that might improve motivation and productivity for millions of people is a worthy inquiry. Undertaking an investigation that involves the application of our knowledge of psychology to answer this question could be useful to millions of people and businesses.

If all the work described in the table looks difficult, that is because it is difficult to design a strong plan to test a complicated idea. But the table shows that reasoning through the process is not impossible. Within each step along the way, we benefit from the refinements made because previous investigators may have learned the hard way that this or that step was essential to making a tightly reasoned empirical inquiry. We can ask important questions and we can test important ideas using empirical methods. It takes training in research methods, often a requirement of undergraduate and graduate programs, to learn how to apply the broad sketch of empirical science provided here to the specific context of one's professional field and academic discipline. But, in general, the specific investigatory steps are more or less the same for empirical disciplines.[x] The critical thinking skills and habits of mind apply across the board.

EVALUATING EMPIRICAL REASONING

A rigorous and thorough investigatory process, like the one described in the "Steps in a Scientific Investigation" table, takes into consideration all four tests for the worthiness of an argument.[xii] The truthfulness of the premises is in part assured by the accuracy of the measurements made and the descriptions of the conditions under which the investigation was conducted. There are additional theoretical assumptions being made, of course. In the example, which showed how to apply the psychological theories about human motivation and productivity to a workplace setting, the theoretical assumptions were presented as true. One might wonder if they are, of course. In the example we could choose to measure noise, distractions, and views of exterior windows, but not the color of the flooring or the height of the ceiling. When we do this we are making certain assumptions about whether those factors we choose not to measure could plausibly be relevant. Perhaps we should also measure the air temperature, on the theory that it is difficult to work when you are too cold or too hot. In an empirical investigation, even one that is tightly controlled and designed, there will always be assumptions that may be questioned. That said, any issues about the truthfulness of any of the premises should have been addressed by the investigator when the study was being designed and by the reviewers who evaluated the merit of the project's possible contribution to knowledge development. If all of those checks fail, empirical investigations are still open to independent verification through replication.

The test for logical strength is also addressed in the research design of a study. That is why the investigators consider which statistical tests are the appropriate ones to use, given the kinds of data they are gathering. That is also why they consider any and all possible factors that might have a relationship on the outcome of the investigation. The investigation, if it is tightly designed and conducted well, should supply ample grounds for an

Steps in a Scientific Investigation

The Steps in the Investigation		Group Office Example	The Investigator's Argument-Making Responsibilities
Identify a problem of significance.	(1)	How does the office environment affect the productivity and job motivation of employees working in a group office setting?	Explain why this problem is important. We did this in the text leading up to this table.
Form a hypothesis that describes what we can expect to happen under certain conditions.	(2)	The more noise and distractions, the more confined and the less personal the workspace, the lower the productivity and motivation of workers will be.	Explain that the hypothesis asserts that as the environment deteriorates, productivity and motivation decrease, but as the environment improves, productivity and motivation improve. This is a correlational hypothesis at this point, not a causal hypothesis.
Review the scientific literature to see what can be learned from the work of others about this hypothesis or similar hypotheses.	(3)	The lit review is for the purpose of informing our investigation. It can help with many practical problems in future steps, e.g., we may learn how those investigators measured "noise" "distractions" "productivity," and "motivation." The lit review is not for the purpose of proving we are right.	Before accepting its conclusions, evaluate the scientific merit of each study. Are the premises true? Are the arguments logically strong? Were all the relevant factors considered? Was the research noncircular?
Identify all the factors related to the hypothesis and the phenomenon of interest that it will be important to measure, control, or monitor.	(4)	We will measure noise, distractions, personalization of the workstation, window view, productivity and motivation. And we will measure things about the workers that might also affect motivation and productivity (e.g., years of experience, knowledge of the job, the importance which the worker attaches to his or her assignments).	Explain why each of the factors to be measured is potentially relevant to the hypothesis (e.g., people with more experience may be more productive. People who are new to the job may be more motivated. People who think their assignments are "unimportant" may be less motivated.).
Make each factor measurable.	(5)	We will measure noise as decibels, personalization of the workstation as number of family pictures and personal knickknacks displayed, window views as simply the presence or absence of an unobstructed view out through an exterior building window located within seven feet of the person's chair. Productivity as phone and e-mail messages sent and received in a randomly selected one-hour period, and motivation as statements affirming desire to work as recorded during a personal interview.	Justify the chosen method of making each factor measurable. For example, why use an interview, instead of a survey questionnaire, to gather data about motivation?
Assure that the experimental conditions can be met.	(6)	We will determine that there will be a sufficient number of office workers about whom data can be collected, that their supervisors have authorized the research, that the research has been reviewed and approved by relevant human subjects review boards, that the provision has been made to secure the informed consent of the persons who will be the experimental subjects. We will decide how we will gather the measurable data, including the information on work experience, who will conduct the interviews, who will count the personal items in each workstation, who will count the phone calls and e-mails, etc.	Answer why and how questions for every decision made about setting up these experimental conditions.
Design a procedure to assure that the data gathered will reveal the full range of possible observations.	(7)	We will study an equal number of workers in three settings: Group A will remain at their current workstations and data regarding noise, personal items, distance from exterior windows, and productivity will be gathered without any change in their work environments. Group B will be assigned new workstations	Explain why and how the three groups will be created. Show that the investigator has considered all the ways that the data being gathered might be discounted as irrelevant or as misleading, and then has taken steps to guard against those problems.

continued

The Steps in the Investigation		Group Office Example	The Investigator's Argument-Making Responsibilities
		that are optimally configured for the purposes of this study and encouraged to personalize those workstations to suit their own tastes. Group C will be assigned new workstations that are negatively configured according to the hypothesis of this study (noisy, no-window, not private) and be advised that they are not allowed to personalize those workstations.	
Construct reliable measuring devices and test them.	(8)	E-mails processed will be measured by an automated count of messages opened and messages sent from each person's desktop PC through the network servers. Messages greater than 100 words will be counted as 1.5 messages. Privacy will be measured by counting the number of persons who pass within three feet of the person's chair. Interviews will follow a protocol of questions to be asked, etc.	Demonstrate that whatever amounts of error the measurement tools themselves might introduce is an acceptably small amount.
Conduct the experiment/gather the data.	(9)	Divide the workers into three groups. Make all the measurements and conduct the interviews. Record the data for future analysis.	Anticipate practical problems and justify the decisions about those problems (e.g., explain why in one case a person who sent an unexpected long, 300-word e-mail was given credit for 2 messages).
Conduct appropriate analyses of the data.	(10)	Statistical analysis shows that productivity for Group B is statistically significantly higher than for Group C. Distractions and noise together account for 31 percent of the variance in productivity. Differences in motivation were not statistically significant, etc.	Demonstrate that the experimental conditions were satisfied, that the data were recorded correctly, that the correct analyses were used.
Interpret the findings and discuss their significance.	(11)	If workplace distractions are limited, noise is reduced, and privacy is assured, then one can expect modest increases in productivity. These findings may be of interest to interior design architects and supervisors who configure group workplace settings.	Demonstrate that the interpretations being made are reasonable and justifiable, given the data. The claims must not exaggerate the findings.
Extend the research by articulating new hypotheses.	(12)	We might inquire whether higher productivity will reduce costs of employee recruitment through increased retention of productive workers. Or might it reduce costs potentially by increasing the ratio of workers to supervisors on the assumption that fewer supervisory personnel are needed to manage an office staffed with more productive and satisfied workers?	Explain why the additional research would be valuable in its own right or because of its potential to refine applications of the current findings.
Publish the research. Contribute to our better understanding of the world by making the investigation known to others in the scientific and professional community.	(13)	We will submit a paper reporting this investigation for possible publication in the *XYZ Journal of Office Productivity*. Our paper will describe each step of our question, or methods, our measurement tools, our results, and our interpretation of those results.	The investigator must reason through questions such as "Who may need to see the results of this investigation?" in order to decide on an appropriate scientific or professional journal in which to seek publication.

inductive inference with regard to the probable truth or falsity of the hypothesis. But, again, if there are errors in logical strength, they should emerge when independent investigators endeavor to replicate the study. Suppose, for example, that an independent inquiry determines empirically that the air temperature (something not measured in our study) had an impact on productivity and more of an impact than any of the other environmental factors we measured. In that study, workers in a group office were less productive when the office was too hot or too cold. In this case we would refine our collective understanding about the relationship of workplace environment and worker productivity. Instead of saying that environment does not count, we would say that it continues to make a difference, but that the element in the environment that is most important to control appears to be the air temperature. We would suggest that management makes sure it is warm enough, but not too warm, in the winter, and cool enough, but not too cold, in the summer.[xiii] The same observations can be made about the test of relevancy and the test of non-circularity. All the factors relevant to testing the hypothesis or to observing the phenomenon in question should have been identified by the investigators as they designed their empirical research. If the investigators missed any or were not able to account for one or more factors, they should note this in their discussion of their research findings.

Similarly, a well-designed and well-executed project can be expected not to be circular. But expectations can be mistaken. Ideally, if the empirical reasoning behind the research plan fails the test of relevancy or the test of non-circularity, that should be picked up by the investigative team or project reviewers very early in the process and the research study should not move forward until those issues are addressed.

Errors happen. From time to time poor research ends up being published. So, it is always a good idea not to take for granted that any of these four tests are somehow automatically passed simply because the reasoning is empirical, or simply because a study appears in print. That would be a mistake. Just because something is published in a professional or scientific journal does not mean it passes the four tests. Of course, with all the checks and balances, especially the process of independent peer review, the chances are high that the material published in professional and scientific journals can be trusted. Even so, note that the table, in Step 3 calls for the investigators to make their own independent evaluation of the merits of the arguments in other published papers that may be found in the literature.

Benefits and Risks Associated with Empirical Reasoning

Empirical reasoning is used when we want to explain, predict, or control what happens. These are three powerful ideas. Explanation helps us understand why.

- Why do some people catch yellow fever and not others?
- Why does the sun cast a shadow at one place and not at another?
- Why does environment affect workplace productivity?

Predictions, accurately made, enable us to anticipate what is likely to happen under certain conditions.

- If we eliminate the mosquitoes that carry yellow fever, we can prevent the disease from spreading.

- If we travel to a place 1,600 kilometers south of Alexandria, we will see shadows cast by the sun in the opposite direction of those we see in Alexandria on June 21st.

- If we eliminate distractions and keep the air temperature moderate, we will increase employee productivity among workers in group office settings.

We human beings want to assure our health, safety, survival, and, to the extent possible, our happiness by controlling our lives and the world around us.

- If we can prevent the spread of the disease, we will save a lot of lives.

- Because the Earth is a sphere, we can save fuel by taking a polar route when flying from Chicago to Moscow.

- If we can increase employee productivity, we will make more money.

Empirical reasoning offers the promise of explanation, prediction, and control, but empirical reasoning can be complicated. And errors can occur. It would be a mistake to think that a hypothesis was not true simply because an empirical inquiry failed to provide us evidence that supports that hypothesis. Empirical reasoning is inductive and probabilistic. So, it would be a mistake to think that findings that have been established with a high level of confidence can never be rejected, revised, or refined. Confirmatory findings *support* a hypothesis. The scope of questions that guides empirical investigations is very broad, but not universal. For instance, some questions, like those involving policy matters, require good judgment in addition to good information.

Those caveats in mind, the scientific approach, when executed by fair-minded, truth-seeking people, is exhaustively systematic and unwavering in the honesty of the inquiry. It anticipates the consequences of choices and intermediary judgments and decisions, demanding well-reasoned justifications at every step from the beginning through all the intermediary stages in the investigation, all the way to the presentation of the results. The cognitive skills required are the critical thinking skills of analysis, interpretation, drawing reasoned inferences, explanation, evaluation, and reflective self-correction. The habits of mind, such as following reasons and evidence wherever they lead, courageously pursuing the inquiry, being systematic, being confident in the power and process of reasoned inquiry, and so on, are the ideal attributes of a critical thinker.

Empirical investigation and the application of our critical thinking skills and habits of mind to scientific inquiry are fundamentally group endeavors. It is the community that determines what is most important to study. Science progresses when the entire scientific community can evaluate the merits of a scientific investigation through replications and refinements of the original investigation. Replication and refinement yield either disconfirmation of the original investigation's findings or generation of support and possible improvements of the original findings. Thus, the scientific community uses a process of reasoning that has a built-in capacity for objective self-monitoring and self-correcting through independent inquiry. It is this capacity that gives empirical reasoning an advantage over comparative reasoning and ideological reasoning. Empirical reasoning calls for the application of the four tests of the logical quality of arguments at every stage of scientific investigation. The results are evident in our increasing knowledge of how the natural world works, and in the technological, biomedical, and engineering benefits humans have achieved over centuries by using scientific inquiry.

> "Nothing in all the world is more dangerous than sincere ignorance and conscientious stupidity."
>
> Martin Luther King, Jr.[xiv]

Empirical reasoning moves bottom-up, from specific observations and measurable data to generalizations that explain why things happen. Empirical reasoning is inductive in character and open to revision. The argument makers take their empirical premises to be true on the basis of observations which other persons can verify and replicate. The steps in an empirical inquiry require the formation of a hypothesis, and the specification of the conditions under which the truth or the falsehood of the hypothesis would be manifested in measurable phenomena. Using strong critical thinking, the investigator must identify the factors that, according to prevailing understandings and scientific theories, might affect the phenomenon of interest. In experimental contexts, the investigator will endeavor to control and vary these factors to most accurately observe the phenomenon being studied. In empirical investigations that do not involve experiments, the investigator will observe and measure the natural variations in the factors and note their effects. Empirical investigators analyze and interpret their measurements, using those analyses and interpretations to draw inferences leading to an evaluation of their hypothesis. Good science requires connections to past research, which is the purpose of a solid literature review, and it requires the production of reports for the advancement of knowledge and to aid one's scientific and professional community.

The purpose of empirical investigation is to generate new knowledge through which we can explain, predict, and possibly control what happens. **Critical thinking** in real life is also about explanation, prediction, and control. The "purpose" in purposeful, reflective judgment is deciding what to believe and what to do. There would be little benefit in that were it not that what we believe and what we do have meaning in our lives and in the lives of others we care about or who care about us. From the time our hominid ancestors first clubbed their way to the top of the local food chain to today, we have been using our oversized brains to try to figure out what to believe and what to do.

My hope for you is that you would expand the scope and range of critical thinking in your problem solving and decision making, and, as the preface says, that you would be "forever young."

KEY TERMS

empirical reasoning (or **bottom-up thinking**) is that process of thinking that proceeds from premises describing interpersonally verifiable experiences in order to support or to disconfirm hypotheses, which, in turn, are intended to explain and predict phenomena. Empirical reasoning is fundamentally inductive, self-corrective, and open to scrutiny and independent verification by the entire scientific community.   *199*

critical thinking is purposeful, reflective judgment in the real world concerning what to believe or what to do.   *206*

FIND IT ON THE THINKSPOT

I invite you to visit **www.TheThinkSpot.com** three times in this chapter: first to learn more about Walter Reed's experimental inquiry into the cause of yellow fever (p. 198); second to examine some of the research exploring the connections among facial symmetry, beauty, sex, and mental health (p. 201); and third to watch the clip from the *Cosmos* series in which Carl Sagan recounts the empirical investigation Aristophanes designed and carried out to satisfy his driving desire to know why there were no shadows down a well (p. 202). Critical thinking skills and positive habits of mind—vital tools for everyone who would seek to know… anything.

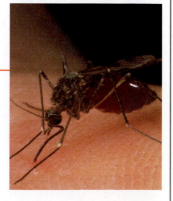

Exercises

GROUP EXERCISE: DESIGN THE INITIAL STEPS IN A SCIENTIFIC INVESTIGATION

Some claim that because of global warming, the sea level will rise by as much as 10 feet, or perhaps more, during the next two decades.

1. Is this a significant problem? Why do you make that judgment?

2. What testable hypotheses are implied by the claim, if it were true?

3. Let's assume that you have performed a thorough review of the scientific literature and that it has been helpful in suggesting factors to measure and ways of measuring them. And let's assume that, through this literature review, you have learned what other investigators have discovered about the potential implications of the sea level rising.

4. What factors related to these hypotheses should we measure either to disconfirm a given hypothesis or to acquire evidence that tends to support the hypothesis? Remember to think about all the ways that various factors which might confound the evidence you seek to gather.

5. How could those factors be measured?

EVALUATE REPORTS OF EMPIRICAL RESEARCH

Scientific studies are constantly being reported in newspapers, magazines, television, and the Internet. Because television synopses tend to provide the findings but not describe the methods or the data, we will focus this exercise on the fuller descriptions provided in newspaper, magazine, and Internet reports. Locate an article published within the last 30 days that reports on the findings of a scientific study. Read and analyze that article carefully. Using the table "Steps in a Scientific Investigation," determine how many of the steps are covered in the magazine or newspaper article. Based on what you learn about the scientific study from the article, evaluate the quality of that scientific research. To inform your evaluation you will want to judge how well the study, as reported by that magazine or newspaper, fulfills the demands of each step in the table. Remember that you are reading another person's synopsis of someone else's research.

Advanced students only: Find the scientific publication in which the research was originally reported. Evaluate the scientist's presentation of his or her research findings in light of the "Steps in a Scientific Investigation" table. Each step should be addressed some place or other in that scientific publication, unless the scientific journal placed word limits on reports it would accept for publication.

A FINAL REFLECTIVE LOG: COMPARATIVE, IDEOLOGICAL, AND EMPIRICAL REASONING

Chapters 11, 12, and 13 describe comparative, ideological, and empirical reasoning. Each of these major strategies of thinking is best suited for some applications, but not for others. Each has its strengths and weaknesses. As you probably detected from reading these three chapters, from the perspective of strong critical thinking, I have major reservations about two of the three forms of reasoning. But even in my own life, I cannot do without using all three, at least on occasion. I love comparative reasoning because of the insights and new ways of looking at things it generates. I worry, however, that comparative reasoning can confuse people unless we keep in mind that just having a new idea does not automatically make that new idea a good idea. I admire empirical reasoning because it is self-corrective and is open to independent verification. But even the highest levels of confidence do not provide some people the certitude that they crave. And I understand that some arguments, including those that capture my political and ethical stance on many issues I regard as vitally important, are best expressed using ideological reasoning. Yet ideological reasoning has many drawbacks when it comes to achieving accord among people. Perhaps this is because the starting points for ideological arguments must ultimately be taken on faith.

My comments are hardly exhaustive of the strengths and weaknesses of these three most common and powerful forms of human thinking. I ask you to reflect on what you have learned in Chapters 11, 12, and 13, and on everything you learned about critical thinking while studying this book. All things considered, what are the relative strengths and weaknesses of comparative, ideological, and empirical reasoning? As a truth-seeker who must make reasoned and purposeful judgments about what to believe or what to do in real life, which of these forms of reasoning is the most valuable? Explain why, give examples, and present your perspective as clearly as possible in your own words.

Using and Extending Argument Mapping

In **Chapter 5**, we said that our mapping techniques make the reasoning used in complex decision making clearer and easier to follow. That certainly is one very important use of mapping. But there are additional practical and scholarly ways of using argument maps and decision maps. This section will build upon the skills and habits of mind that you've already learned about arguments, and will show the finer points at play in the decision-making process. The key is that the map works at a practical level to help reveal the thinking being used and, where beneficial, your interpretation and evaluation of that thinking—once you have secured a correct analysis, of course.

The following map displays an interviewee's explanation of why she cannot quit smoking at this time. As you can see, the map displays two possible conclusions and three watershed realizations that a decision was called for. One argument strand leading from one of the watershed ideas is abandoned. The full decision map is rich with data for interpretation.

For example, inspection of the figure reveals that the interviewee offered more arguments supporting quitting smoking now (5) than quitting later (4). This suggests that the dominance structuring (discussed in **Chapter 10**) around the "continuing to smoke" option may not be impervious.

I augmented this map by adding numbers inside the shapes. This preserves the chronology of the interview, revealing how the interviewee first argues for quitting smoking (phrase 2: Smoking is dangerous to life). And although the person never declares that she must stop smoking, it is an implicit statement in four of the five argument strands for quitting now. But as the interview progresses, the person's defenses begin to build. The interviewee starts rather early in the interview to explain why this was not the time to try quitting (phrase 5). The interviewee's arguments also reveal unwarranted beliefs that there are beneficial effects of the nicotine addiction (phrase 13 "To function, I've gotta' smoke").

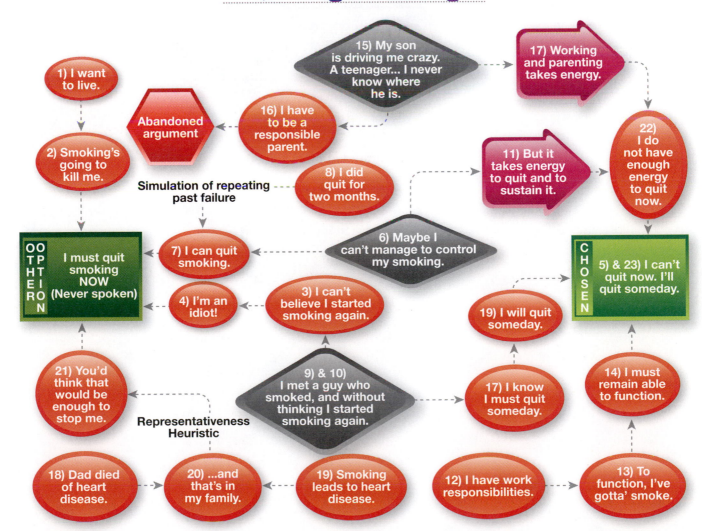

You may have noticed the simulation heuristic from **Chapter 9** noted on the arrow line between phrase 8 and phrase 7. On the arrow line between phrase 20 and phrase 21, you can see that I have noted the interviewee's apparent use of the representativeness heuristic, as the memory is fresh in her mind and close to her life. We can augment our mapping techniques by adding key information on the arrow lines— for example, the way the two heuristics are displayed here. But we can add more notes too. We can recognize other habits of mind in argument maps and insert the names of any fallacies, deductively valid argument templates, or inductive statistical tests that the argument maker uses. Here is an example indicating the critical thinking skills used.

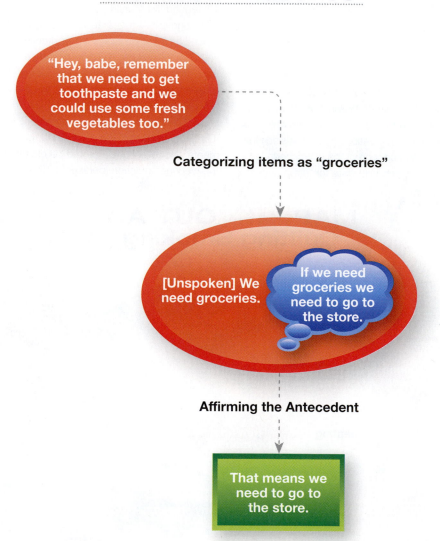

In the previous example, one of the deductively valid rules for drawing inferences we discussed in **Chapter 8**, affirming the antecedent, is noted on the arrow line leading directly to the conclusion. The argument maker logically infers the conclusion without needing to speak aloud the two implicit statements in the intermediate claim. The argument maker reaches the first of those, "We need groceries," by applying a basic critical thinking sub-skill listed in **Chapter 2**, categorization. Here's another example. I use overlapping ovals, creating something that looks like an upside-down "Mickey Mouse" hat, in order to show that the data in the large central oval are supported by good methodology—specifically that the sample was representative, as discussed in **Chapter 8**, and that the survey instrument used to gather the data was itself a valid and reliable tool, something we talked about in **Chapter 13**. To show the close connection of these supporting methodological claims, I drew overlapping ovals.

Here I've noted a commonly used analysis called a Chi-Square Test for statistical significance, which is another way of saying "a test to determine the likelihood that the observed results happened to come about merely by random chance." Another option would have been to put all three into one larger oval. Either way works to communicate the basis for the statistical analysis that, itself, then justifies our confidence in the conclusion. By the way, the expression p < .000 means that the chances that the relationship is merely random are less than 1 in 1000.

MAP > it > OUT A.3
Which Students Value Truth-Seeking?

In a survey of the beliefs and values of students at a given university it was found that 25.5% of the freshmen and sophomores endorsed truth-seeking, whereas 40.4% of the juniors and seniors surveyed endorsed truth-seeking.

The students surveyed are a representative sampling of the students at the university.

The survey of beliefs and values used was a valid and reliable instrument for measuring truth-seeking.

Chi-Square Test for Statistical Significance
X=30.648, p<.000

CLAIM At this university juniors and seniors are statistically significantly more likely to endorse truth-seeking than are freshmen and sophomores.

Here's an example of an augmented decision map that draws from what we learned in **Chapter 9** about systems of reasoning. Here, the notations of System-2 and System-1 reasoning are both present. The application of the rule called "substitution" is the more reflective System-2 inference that *would* have led the person to buy the car, but the System-1 negative affective response to its color gave the buyer pause. Ergo, this car was not purchased by this decision maker!

MAP > it > OUT A.4
Buying a Car

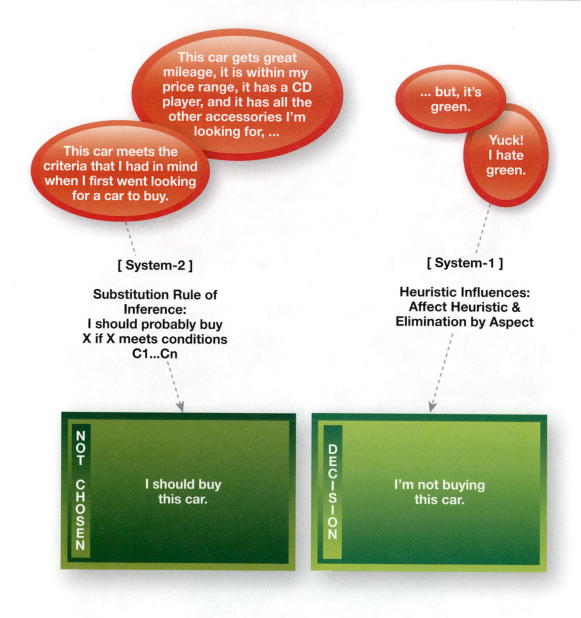

In this next example, I have stripped out the arguments so that the map reveals the overall pattern of the decision making divorced from the specific content of the argument. The numbered "P" ovals are the reasons the speaker gave in favor of ("pro") attending a given college, and the "C" ovals are "con" arguments the speaker made concerning attending that college. And I've added my evaluations of the arguments (discussed in **Chapter 7**) as "sound" or "unsound" based on the truthfulness of the premises and the logical strength of the speaker's original arguments. Now the map clearly shows which of the options was the one that was best supported, in my judgment, by the decision maker. The dominance structuring we talked about in **Chapter 10** emerges strongly in this next map too. In the end, this person decided to attend Michigan State. What was particularly interesting was that a few of the arguments the person considered both for and against attending MSU were not sound. This is an instance of the fourth stage of dominance structuring, as we learned in **Chapter 10**, by a person who does not seem to be the world's best critical thinker.

MAP > it > OUT A.5
Which College Should I Attend?

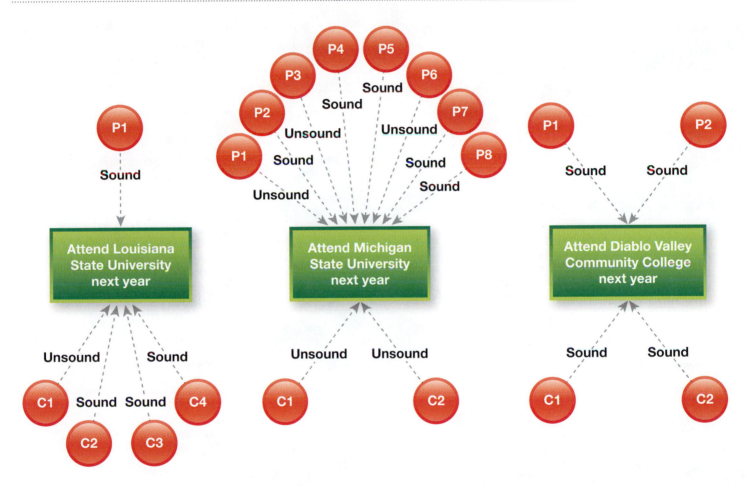

In **Chapter 10**'s exercise about Governor Schwarzenegger's denial of clemency for Stanley "Tookie" Williams, on page 161, I invited you to map his reasoning as expressed in the statement he published. The map you produced would likely have been rather complex, since the reasoning you were mapping was itself rather complex. And you would probably have had to make more than a couple drafts before you were satisfied that your analysis was reasonable. Here I've provided a map of the governor's reasoning. Assuming this map is reasonably accurate, how would you evalu-

MAP > it > OUT A.6
Governor Arnold Schwarzenegger's Argument for Denying the Death Row Appeal for Clemency of Stanley "Tookie" Williams

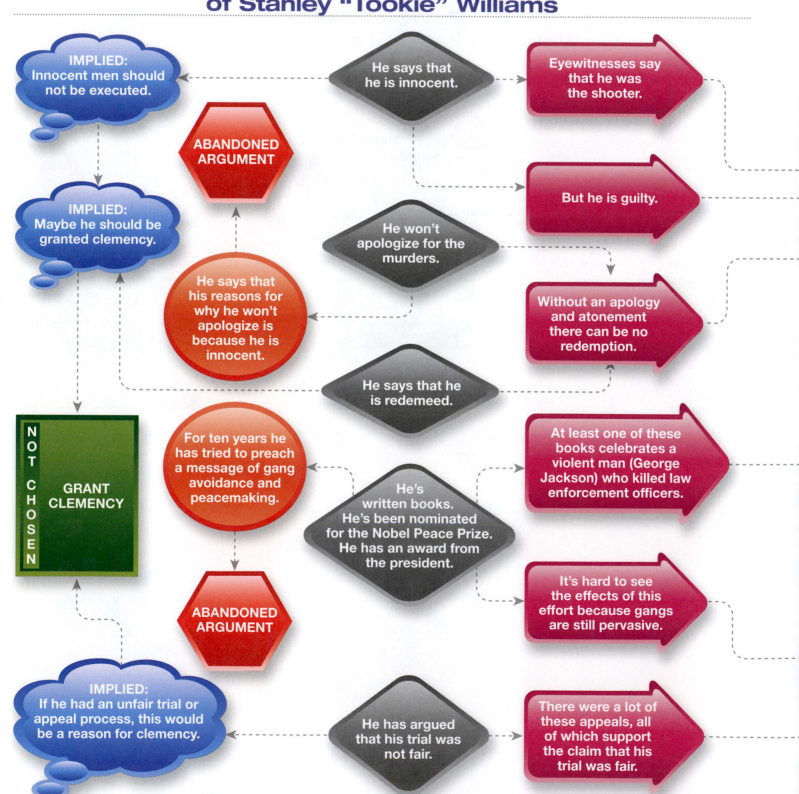

ate that reasoning? In particular, what should we make of the two abandoned lines of reasoning? What would have been the result had they been more fully developed? Or, why should we assume that a person should apologize if the person believes he is not guilty? Similarly, why would an attempt to escape be interpreted as a reason to suppose that a person is guilty? A good argument map reveals both the strong points and the weak points of a decision maker's thinking.

There are still other ways we can effectively use our mapping techniques for practical and for scholarly purposes. Advanced students interested in pursing the idea of using decision maps to compare how different people make comparable decisions, for example, would find

the book that I co-authored with Dr. Noreen Facione, *Thinking and Reasoning in Human Decision Making: The Method of Argument and Heuristic Analysis*, useful. The mapping techniques presented in this appendix and in **Chapter 5** are drawn from that book, from our many years of collaborative research, and from our shared goal of making the analysis, interpretation, and evaluation of complex human decision making more scientifically objective and open to replication by other investigators. In this work, critical thinking and scientific inquiry, as discussed in **Chapter 13**, go hand in hand. Using empirical reasoning, if our maps do not agree, we can compare our analyses to see what the best interpretation might be.

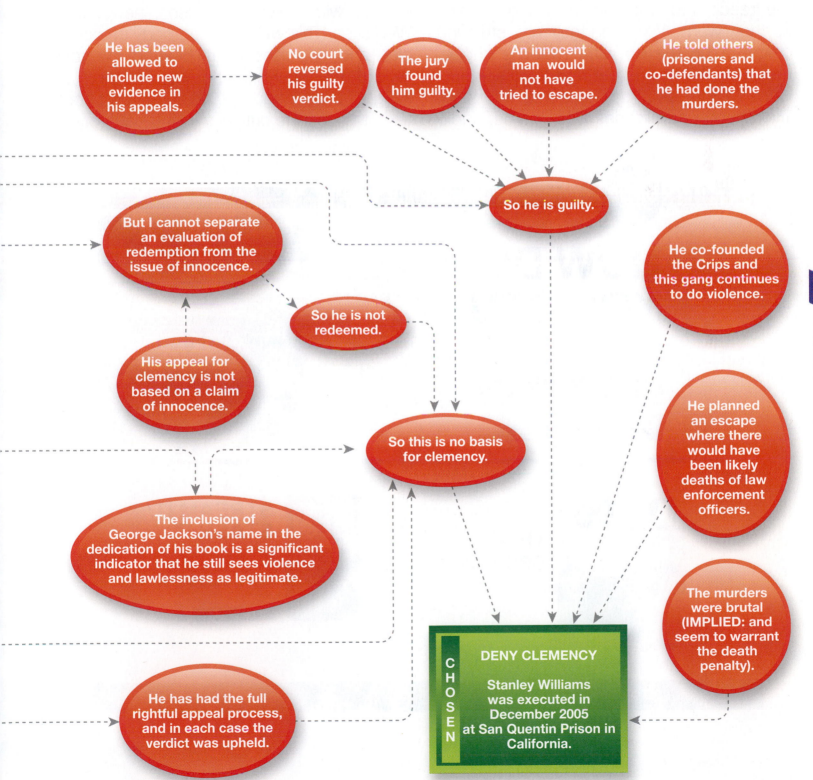

Using the 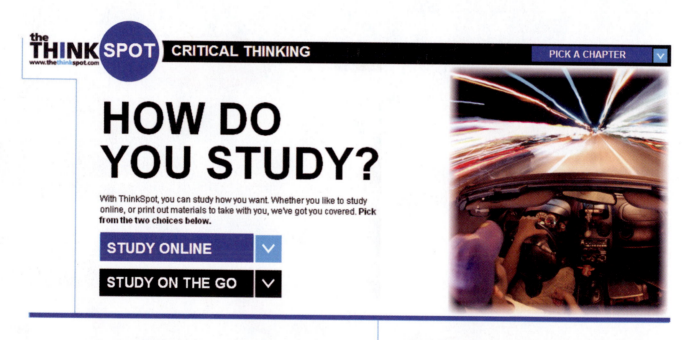 the THINKSPOT
www.thethinkspot.com

The THINKSpot is an open-access Web site for *THINK Critically* that gives students the freedom to study however and wherever they want. Whether they are studying online or on the go with a mobile phone, music player, or printout, this Web site provides all the resources students will need. The chapter summaries, flash cards, audio summaries, and chapter quizzes in the THINKSpot reinforce and build upon what is learned with exercises, videos, news, and Web sites. This well-rounded body of examples and exercises goes beyond the text toward the analysis and interpretation of images, body language, gestures, and contexts that real-life critical thinking calls for.

the **THINK**SPOT
www.thethinkspot.com **CRITICAL THINKING**   **PICK A CHAPTER**

HOW DO YOU STUDY?

With ThinkSpot, you can study how you want. Whether you like to study online, or print out materials to take with you, we've got you covered. **Pick from the two choices below.**

STUDY ONLINE ⌄

STUDY ON THE GO ⌄

THINK CRITICALLY

's 2011 Edition

STREAM IT/ STASH IT

Purchase audio chapters from the iTunes Music Store and study anytime, anywhere.

ITUNES STORE >

Whether online or on the go, students can access the same great study tools:

CHAPTER SUMMARY

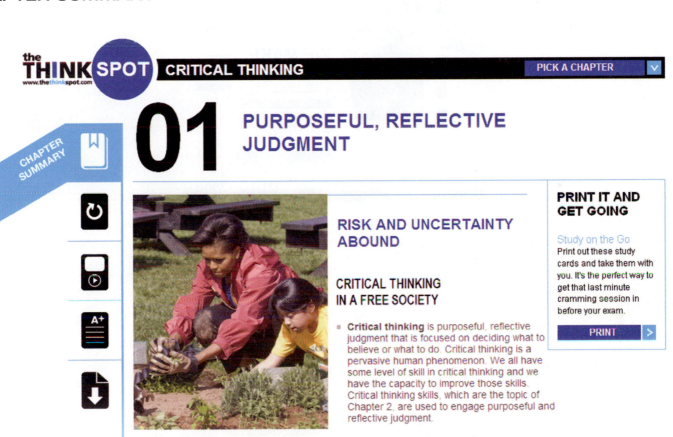

In addition to reviewing each chapter's central themes and key terms, the section called "Find It on the THINKSpot" contains nearly fifty links to video clips, news stories, and Internet URLs that are called out in the body of the chapters, in some of the exercises, and at the end of the chapter. The "Exercises" section contains a variety of questions, exercises, and activities because critical thinking is practiced both individually and with others in the process of group problem solving. A Reflective Log exercise for every chapter invites students to keep a continuing journal of the thoughtful application of their critical thinking skills and habits of mind.

FLASH CARDS

The flash card tool makes it easy for students to learn at their own pace. Customized flash card decks can be read online, exported to a mobile phone, or printed out.

AUDIO SUMMARY

Audio summaries of each chapter are available for streaming online or for purchase through the iTunes store.

CHAPTER QUIZ

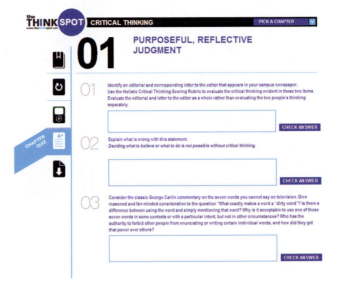

The chapter quizzes feature short-answer questions that ask students to apply the principles covered in the text.

DOWNLOAD FILES

All of the chapter summary material, audio, and flash cards are downloadable in one place.

GLOSSARY

Parenthetical numbers refer to the pages on which the term is introduced.

analysis   is the skill of identifying the intended and actual inferential relationships among statements, questions, concepts, descriptions, or other forms of representation intended to express belief, judgment, experiences, reasons, information, or opinions. (18)

analytical   means that a person is habitually alert to potential problems and vigilant in anticipating consequences and trying to foresee short-term and long-term outcomes of events, decisions, and actions. (30)

argument   is the process of giving a reason in support of a claim. (60)

claim   refers to the statement that the maker of an argument is seeking to show to be true or probably true. (60)

cognitive heuristics   are human decision-making shortcuts people rely on to expedite their judgments about what to believe or what to do. (129)

comparative reasoning (or **this-is-like-that thinking**)   is the process of using what is more familiar to make interpretations, explanations, or inferences about what is less familiar. (166)

comprehensiveness,   in the evaluation of comparisons, is the extent to which a comparison captures a greater number of central or essential features. (170)

conclusion   is another way of referring to an argument's claim. (60)

confident in reasoning   means that a person is trustful of his or her own reasoning skills to yield good judgments. A person's or a group's confidence in their own critical thinking may or may not be warranted, which is another matter. (30)

critical thinking   is purposeful, reflective judgment that manifests itself in giving reasoned and fair-minded consideration to evidence, conceptualizations, methods, contexts, and standards in order to decide what to believe or what to do. (4)

decision-critical attributes   are those criteria the decision-maker deems to be important and relevant for the purpose of evaluating options. (155)

deductive reasoning   is drawing inferences in which it appears that the conclusion cannot possibly be false if all of the premises are true. (23)

deductively valid argument   is an argument such that it is impossible for all of its premises to be true and its conclusion to be false. (110)

dominance structuring   is the psychological process through which humans achieve confidence in their decisions. The four phases of dominance structuring are pre-editing, identifying one promising option, testing that promising option for dominance, and structuring the dominance of the option selected. (150)

empirical reasoning (or **bottom-up thinking**)   is that process of thinking that proceeds from premises describing interpersonally verifiable experiences in order to support or to disconfirm hypotheses, which, in turn, are intended to explain and to predict phenomena. Empirical reasoning is fundamentally inductive, self-corrective, and open to scrutiny and independent verification by the entire scientific community. (199)

evaluation   is the skill of assessing the credibility of statements or other representations that are accounts or descriptions of a person's perception, experience, situation, judgment, belief, or opinion; also assessing the logical strength of the actual or intended inferential relationships among statements, descriptions, questions, or other forms of representation. (18)

expert   refers to someone who is both experienced and learned in a given subject matter or professional practice area. (80)

explanation   is the skill of stating and justifying reasoning in terms of the evidential, conceptual, methodological, criteriological, and contextual considerations upon which one's results were based; also presenting one's reasoning in the form of cogent arguments. (18)

fallacies   are deceptive arguments that appear logical, but upon closer analysis, fail to demonstrate their conclusions. (102)

familiarity,   in the evaluation of comparisons, is the degree of knowledge the listener has about the object to which the unknown is being compared. (170)

good argument (or **a worthy argument**)   is an argument that merits being accepted as a proof that its conclusion is true or very probably true. (96)

ideological reasoning (or **top-down reasoning**)   is the process of thinking that begins with abstractions or generalizations that express one's core beliefs, concepts, values, or principles and proceeds to reason top-down to their specific applications. Ideological reasoning is deductive and axiomatic. The argument maker takes the ideological premises on faith. (181)

inductive reasoning   is drawing probabilistic inferences regarding what is most likely to be true or most likely not true, given certain information. (21)

inductively justified argument (or **warranted argument**)   is an argument such that were all of its premises true then its conclusion would most likely or very probably also be true. (117)

inference   is the skill of identifying and securing the elements needed to draw reasonable conclusions; it forms conjectures and hypotheses, considers relevant information and educes the consequences flowing from data, statements, principles, evidence, judgments, beliefs, opinions, concepts, descriptions, questions, and other forms of representation. (18)

inquisitive   means that a person habitually strives to be well-informed, wants to know how things work, and seeks to learn new things about a wide range of topics, even if the immediate utility of knowing those things is not directly evident. An inquisitive person has a strong sense of intellectual curiosity. (30)

interpretation   is the skill of expressing the meaning or significance or a wide variety of experiences, situations, data, events, judgments, conventions, beliefs, rules, procedures, or criteria. (18)

judicious   means that a person approaches problems with a sense that some are ill-structured and some can have more than one plausible solution. A judicious person has the cognitive maturity to realize that many questions and issues are not black and white and that, at times, judgments must be made in contexts of uncertainty. (30)

language community   is a community in which people share an understanding of the meanings of words and icons. Dictionaries were invented to record a language community's conventions for what its words *shall* mean. (53)

open-minded   means that a person is habitually tolerant of divergent issues and sensitive to the possibility of his or her own possible biases. An open-minded person respects the right of others who have different opinions. (30)

premises   are the statements, explicitly asserted or contextually assumed and implicit, that comprise an argument's reason. Each reason is a separate set of premises. (61)

problematic ambiguity   is the characteristic of a word or expression as referring to more than one object or as having more than one meaning in a given context or for a given purpose. (46)

problematic vagueness   is the characteristic of a word or expression as having an imprecise meaning or unclear boundaries in a given context or for a given purpose. (45)

productivity   is the capacity of a comparison to suggest consequences that go beyond those mentioned in the initial comparison. (171)

reason   is the basis provided by the argument maker to show that the claim is true or probably true. (60)

self-contradictory statement   is a sentence that is false entirely because of the grammatical construction and the meanings of the words used to form the sentence. (85)

self-regulation   is the skill of monitoring and correcting one's own cognitive activities, the elements used in those activities, and the results educed, particularly by applying skills in analysis, and evaluation to one's own inferential judgments with a view toward questions, confirming, validating, or correcting either one's reasoning or one's results. (18)

simplicity,   in the evaluation of comparisons, is a measure of the relative absence of complexity. (170)

sound argument   is an argument with true premises that also passes the Test of Logical Strength. (97)

System-1 thinking   is reactive thinking that relies heavily on situational cues, salient memories, and heuristic thinking to arrive quickly and confidently at judgments. (128)

System-2 thinking   is reflective critical thinking that is useful for judgments in unfamiliar situations, for processing abstract concepts, and for deliberating when there is time for planning and more comprehensive consideration. (128)

systematic   means that a person consistently endeavors to take an organized and thorough approach to identifying and solving problems. A systematic person is orderly, focused, persistent, and diligent in his or her approach to problem solving, learning, and inquiry. (30)

tautology   is a statement that is necessarily true because of the meanings of the words. (85)

testability   is the capacity of comparisons to project consequences that have the potential to be shown to be false, inapplicable, or unacceptable. (172)

trusted source on topic X   is a person (or the words of a person) who is learned in X, experienced in X, speaking about X, up-to-date about X, capable of explaining the basis for their claim or their advice about X, unbiased, truthful, free of conflicts of interest, acting in accord with our interests, unconstrained, informed about the specifics of the case at hand, and mentally stable. (83)

truth-seeking   means that a person habitually has intellectual integrity and a courageous desire to actively strive for the best possible knowledge in any given situation. A truth-seeker asks probing questions and follows reasons and evidence wherever they lead, even if the results go against his or her cherished beliefs. (30)

worthy argument (or **good argument**)   is an argument that merits being accepted as a proof that its conclusion is true or very probably true. (96)

ENDNOTES

CHAPTER 1

i. Navy Admiral Mike Mullen to the graduating senior military officers at the U.S. National Defense University, June 11, 2009, Quoted according to a story by Fred W. Baker III of the American Forces Press Service.

ii. Ray Marshall and Marc Tucker, *Thinking for a Living: Education and the Wealth of Nations* (New York: Basic Books, 1992).

iii. Quoted according to a story by Fred W. Baker III of the American Forces Press Service.

iv. Karl Popper, *The Open Society and its Enemies*, Vols. 1 & 2 (New York: Routledge, 1945, 2002).

v. "Thurgood Marshall Quotes," Brainy Quote, 8 Jul. 2009 <http://www.brainyquote.com/quotes/quotes/t/thurgoodma115747.html>.

vi. Karl Popper, *The Poverty of Historicism* (New York: Routledge, 1957, 2002).

vii. Anne Rice, *The Vampire Lestat* (New York: Ballantine Books, 1985).

viii. The Delphi method begins by inviting all the experts to respond to an initial set of questions about the topic of interest. The project's coordinating research director, who cannot be one of the experts, has responsibility for compiling results, sharing those results with the roster of participating experts, and asking whether they agree, disagree, or want to propose clarifications or revisions. The research director also moves the project forward by asking questions that arise from the material being generated by the experts. This process is repeated over and over again as the group slowly comes to consensus on major points. The research director keeps track of those points of consensus. The research director invites more comment on areas that are still unclear or on which there is disagreement. The experts may end up not agreeing on everything. But after several rounds, there usually is enough accord on key points that the process can be drawn to a close. To do this, the research director writes up the points of apparent agreement and verifies that the experts are in accord. In this particular Delphi research project focusing on critical thinking, it took six rounds of questioning and 16 separate group communications back and forth before consensus was achieved. One very important thing about the Delphi process in general, which was true of this particular project as well: Because the group is made up of experts whose names and reputations are well known to the other experts, the Delphi process calls for omitting their names when the research director circulates their remarks and opinions to the other members of the group. That way the group sees each expert's arguments and explanations, but not knowing who the author is, the others in the group will not be overly influenced by any positive or negative opinions they may have about that other expert. The ideas speak for themselves. This account of the Delphi research process comes from the person who was the project director for the effort to achieve an expert consensus regarding the meaning of critical thinking, namely the author of this textbook. As such, he was not a contributing expert on that 46-person panel.

ix. American Philosophical Association, *Critical Thinking: A Statement of Expert Consensus for Purposes of Educational Assessment and Instruction*, Also known as *"The Delphi Report"* (ERIC Doc. No. ED 315 423) 1990, Executive summary and full report available through Insight Assessment/The California Academic Press, Millbrae, CA, <www.insightassessment.com>.

x. Some use the word "meta-cognitive" when referring to the skills of self-monitoring and self-correcting. We will unpack these ideas in much greater detail in Chapters 2 and 3.

xi. "George Carlin Quotes," Digital Dream Door, 8 Jul. 2009 <http://digitaldreamdoor.nutsie.com/pages/quotes/george_carlin.html>.

xii. "A Call to Service," From The White House Blog, The White House, 8 Jul. 2009 <http://www.whitehouse.gov/blog/09/04/21/A-Call-to-Service/>.

xiii. Ann Sanner, "Obama to Sign National Service Bill Today," Huffington Post, 21 Apr. 2009, 8 Jul. 2009 <http://www.huffingtonpost.com/2009/04/21/obama-to-sign-national-se_n_189407.html>.

CHAPTER 2

i. The findings of expert consensus are published in *Critical Thinking: A Statement of Expert Consensus for Purposes of Educational Assessment and Instruction* (ERIC ED 315 423). The research was undertaken originally as a project of a committee of the American Philosophical Association (APA). In 1993 and 1994, the Center for the Study of Higher Education at Pennsylvania State University undertook a study of 200 policy makers, employers, and faculty members from two-year and four-year colleges to determine what this group took to be the core critical thinking skills and habits of mind. That Pennsylvania State University study, under the direction of Dr. Elizabeth Jones, was funded by the U.S. Department of Education Office of Educational Research and Instruction. The Penn State study findings, published in 1994, confirmed the expert consensus expressed in the APA report.

ii. *12 Angry Men*, United Artists, 1957. This film was nominated for three Academy Awards. In 2007, *12 Angry Men* was selected for preservation in the United States National Film Registry by the Library of Congress as being "culturally, historically, or aesthetically significant." Do not miss DVD scene #10 where the two main protagonists argue about how a streetwise killer would hold a switchblade knife.

iii. American Philosophical Association, *Critical Thinking: A Statement of Expert Consensus for Purposes of Educational Assessment and Instruction*, Also known as *"The Delphi Report"* (ERIC Doc. No. ED 315 423) 1990.

iv. © 2007, Image from P. Facione "Critical Thinking: What It Is and Why It Counts," Rendition of an original design used with permission of the publisher, Insight Assessment.

v. Mathematicians and computer scientists would describe this as a "recursive function," meaning that the function can be applied to itself. We can analyze our analyses. We can evaluate our evaluations.

vi. Table © 2009. *Test Manual for the California Critical Thinking Skills Test*, published by Insight Assessment, Millbrae, CA, Used with permission of the publisher.

vii. M. Neil Browne and Stuart M. Keeley, *Asking the Right Questions*, 9th ed. (Pearson Prentice Hall, 2009).

viii. Table © 2009, *Test Manual for the Test of Everyday Reasoning*, Insight Assessment, Millbrae, CA, Used with permission of the publisher. Critical thinking skill definitions cited are from American Philosophical Association, *Critical Thinking: A Statement of Expert Consensus for Purposes of Educational Assessment and Instruction*, Also known as *"The Delphi Report"* (ERIC Doc. No. ED 315 423) 1990.

ix. © 2008, CBS Interactive Inc. All Rights Reserved.

x. William Calvert Kneale and Martha Kneale, *The Development of Logic* (Oxford, UK: The Clarendon Press, 1962).

xi. Albert Blumberg, "Modern Logic," *The Encyclopedia of Philosophy*, P. Edwards, ed., (New York: Macmillan, 1967) Vol. 5, 24–34.

xii. Jum C. Nunnally, *Psychometric Theory* (New York: McGraw-Hill Book Company, 1978).

xiii. S. E. Hankinson and W. C. Willett, principal investigators, Funding provided by the National Institutes of Health, 7 Jul. 2009 <http://www.channing.harvard.edu/nhs/>.

xiv. Nurses' Health Sutdy Newsletter, Vol. 16, 2009, p. 6. See also, The Nurses' Health Study, <www.nurseshealthstudy.org>.

CHAPTER 3

i. Allen Newell, *Toward Unified Theories of Cognition* (Cambridge, MA: Harvard University Press, 1990); Paul Slovic, Baruch Fischhoff, and Sarah Lichtenstein, "Behavioral Decision Theory," *Annual Review of Psychology* Jan. 1977, 28: 1–39; Henry Montgomery, "From Cognition to Action: The Search for Dominance in Decision Making," *Process and Structure in Human Decision Making*, ed. Henry Montgomery and Ola Svenson (Chichester, UK: John Wiley & Sons, 1989) 23–49; Allen Newell and Herbert Alexander Simon, *Human Problem Solving* (Englewood Cliffs, NJ: Prentice Hall, 1972).

ii. Peter A. Facione, Noreen C. Facione, and Carol A. Giancarlo, "The Disposition Toward Critical Thinking: Its Character, Measurement, and Relationship to Critical Thinking Skill," *Informal Logic* 2000, 20(1): 61–84; Peter A. Facione, Noreen C. Facione, and Carol A. Giancarlo, "The Motivation to Think in Working and Learning," *Preparing Competent College Graduates: Setting New and Higher Expectations for Student Learning*, ed. Elizabeth A. Jones (San Francisco: Jossey-Bass Publishers, 1997) 67–79; Peter A. Facione, Carol A. Giancarlo, and Noreen C. Facione, *Are college students disposed to think?* (ERIC Doc. No. ED 368 311, Apr. 1994); Peter A. Facione, Noreen C. Facione, "Profiling critical thinking dispositions," *Assessment Update* 1993, (5)2: 1–4; Carol A. Giancarlo and Peter A. Facione, "A Look across Four Years at the Disposition toward Critical Thinking Among Undergraduate Students," *The Journal of General Education* 2001, 50(1): 29–55.

iii. H. C. Triandis, "Values, attitudes and interpersonal behavior," *Beliefs, Attitudes, and Values. Nebraska Symposium on Motivation*, ed. Herbert E. Howe (Lincoln, NE: University of Nebraska Press, 1980); Icek Ajzen and Martin Fishbein, "A theory of reasoned action: Some applications and implications" *Beliefs, Attitudes, and Values. Nebraska Symposium on Motivation*, ed. Herbert E. Howe (Lincoln, NE: University of Nebraska Press, 1980).

iv. John Dewey, *How We Think* (Boston: D.C. Heath & Co., Publishers, 1910), Republished as *How We Think: A Restatement of the Relation of Reflective Thinking to the Educational Process* (Lexington, MA: D. C. Heath Publishing, 1933).

v. Peter A. Facione, Carol A. Giancarlo, Noreen C. Facione, and Joanne Gainen, "The Disposition Toward Critical Thinking," *Journal of General Education* 1995, 44(1): 1–25; Peter A. Facione, Noreen C. Facione, and Carol A. Giancarlo, *Test Manual: The California Critical Thinking Disposition Inventory* (Millbrae, CA: California Academic Press, 1992, 1994, 2001, 2007); Noreen C. Facione and Peter A. Facione, "Externalizing the critical thinking in knowledge development and clinical judgment," *Nursing Outlook*, 1996, 44: 129–136; Peter A. Facione, "Empirical methods of theory and tool development for the assessment of college level critical thinking and problem-solving," Report, Conference on Collegiate Skills Assessment, Washington, DC: NCES, U.S. Department of Education, 1992; Elizabeth A. Jones, Steven Hoffman, L. Moore, G. Ratcliff, S. Tibbetts, and B. Click, *Essential Skills in Writing, Speech and Listening, and Critical Thinking for College Graduates: Perspectives of Faculty, Employers, and Policy Makers*, Project summary, U.S. Department of Education, OERI Contract No. R117G10037, University Park, PA: National Center for Postsecondary Teaching, Learning, and Assessment, Pennsylvania State University, 1994; Elizabeth Jones, Steven Hoffman, L. Moore, G. Ratcliff, S. Tibbetts, and B. Click, *National Assessment of College Student Learning: Identifying the College Graduates' Essential Skills in Writing, Speech and Listening, and Critical Thinking*, Washington, DC: National Center for Educational Statistics, U.S. Department of Education, Office of Educational Research and Improvement, OERI publication NCES 93-001, 2005.

vi. Stephen D. Brookfield, *Developing Critical Thinkers: Challenging Adults to Explore Alternative Ways of Thinking and Acting* (San Francisco: Jossey-Bass Publishers, 1987); Lauren Resnick, *Education and Learning to Think* (Washington, DC: National Academy Press, 1987); Chet Meyers, *Teaching Students to Think Critically* (San Francisco: Jossey-Bass Publishers, 1986).

vii. The graphs shown, known as "scatter plots," show the dots arrayed in what appears to be an elongated cloud shape that stretches diagonally upward from the lower left to the upper right. This suggests a positive correlation between critical thinking skills and the disposition toward critical thinking. Stronger skills are associated with a more positive disposition. Weaker overall skills correlate with an ambivalent or negative overall disposition. What is remarkable, too, is that the lower-right quadrant of the graph is virtually empty. This suggests that the combination of strong skills with hostility toward the use of those skills is probably rarely found. George Andrew Ferguson and Yoshio Takane, *Statistical Analysis in Psychology and Education* (New York: McGraw-Hill, 1989); Emanuel J. Mason and William J. Bramble, *Understanding and Conducting Research: Applications in Education and the Behavioral Sciences* (New York: McGraw-Hill, 1989).

viii. "Mark Twain Quotes," Quote DB, 2 Jul. 2009 <http://www.quotedb.com/quotes/117>.

CHAPTER 4

i. Paul E. Koptak, "What's New in Interpreting Genesis," *The Covenant Quarterly*, Vol. LIII, No. 1 (February 1995), pp. 3–16, 13 Jul. 2009 <http://prophetess.lstc.edu/;rklein/Doc3/whatsnew.htm>.

ii. Jared Diamond, *Guns, Germs, and Steel* (New York: WW Norton & Co., 1997).

iii. *My Cousin Vinny*, Palo Vista Productions, dir. Jonathan Lynn, writ. Dale Launer, perf. Joe Pesci, Ralph Macchio, and Marisa Tomei. 1992.

iv. Roger Fisher, William L. Ury, and Bruce Patton, *Getting to Yes: Negotiating Agreement Without Giving In* (New York: Penguin Books, 1983).

v. Driving Under Influence of Drugs or Alcohol," California Department of Motor Vehicles, 25 Aug. 2009 <http://www.dmv.ca.gov/pubs/vctop/d11/vc23152.htm>.

vi. The findings of expert consensus are published in *Critical Thinking: A Statement of Expert Consensus for Purposes of Educational Assessment and Instruction* (ERIC Doc. No. ED 315 423). The research was undertaken originally as a project of a committee of the American Philosophical Association (APA). This report is often referred to as "The Delphi Report."

CHAPTER 5

i. "Measles Vaccination," Vaccines and Immunizations, Department of Health and Human Services: Centers for Disease Control, 20 Oct. 2009, 27 Oct. 2009 <http://www.cdc.gov/vaccines/vpd-vac/measles/default.htm>.

ii. "Argument," Merriam Webster's Online Dictionary, 22 Jun. 2009 <http://www.merriam-webster.com/dictionary/argument>.

iii. "Parents' Guide to Childhood Immunization," Centers for Disease Control and Prevention, 22 Jun. 2009 <http://www.cdc.gov/vaccines/vpd-vac/measles/downloads/pg_why_vacc_measles.pdf>.

iv. There is a contextual element relating to scientific research that a fuller analysis of the reason might include; if the question "But if even 1 case occurs, then why not call it a side effect?" were raised, then the premise added might be, "When two events occur together so rarely that their coincidence cannot be distinguished from pure chance, then we do not have sufficient reason to regard either as the cause of the other."

v. *12 Angry Men*, United Artists, 1957. This film was nominated for three Academy Awards. In 2007, *12 Angry Men* was selected for preservation in the United States National Film Registry by the Library of Congress as being "culturally, historically, or aesthetically significant." 39:30–43:00.

vi. That people make arguments in their efforts to reason through their decisions is clear. The number of arguments can vary widely, particularly if the decision is one of those important ones that needs to be reaffirmed on a frequent basis, like deciding not to seek a diagnosis for a worrisome symptom, or deciding not to take disciplinary action against a problem employee. Noreen C. Facione and Peter A. Facione, "Analyzing explanations for seemingly irrational choices: Linking argument analysis and cognitive science," *International Journal of Applied Philosophy*, 2002, 15(2): 267–286.

vii. The mapping conventions presented here are drawn from Peter A. Facione and Noreen C. Facione, *Thinking and Reasoning in Human Decision Making: The Method of Argument and Heuristic Analysis* (Millbrae, CA: The California Academic Press, 2007). That book offers additional conventions that enable the analyst to display the reasoning relationships (logical or statistical inferences) or the heuristic relationships (satisficing, association, anchoring with adjustment, etc.) that connect the reasons and claims.

viii. Peter A. Facione and Noreen C. Facione, *Thinking and Reasoning in Human Decision Making* (Millbrae, CA: The California Academic Press, 2007) 58.

CHAPTER 6

i. Maureen Boyle, "Massachusetts slayings touch Cape Verde community around the world," GateHouse News Service, 8 Feb. 2009, 27 Jul. 2009 <http://www.wickedlocal.com/ghsnewsservice/regional_news/east/x1851008485/Video-Massachusetts-slayings-touch-Cape-Verde-community-around-the-world>. Stories also in *The Examiner*, Brockton, MA, Jan 21–22, 2009.

ii. Larry Keller, "From Hate to Hurt," *Intelligence Report*, Summer 2009, 134: 50–54, Published by the Southern Poverty Law Center, Montgomery, Alabama.

iii. Patricia M. King and Karen Strohm Kitchener, *Developing Reflective Judgment* (San Francisco, CA: Jossey-Bass Publishers, 1994). My formulation presented here is a reformulation of work by King and Kitchener. Scholars who were instrumental in expanding our understanding of cognitive development include B. Bloom, W. Perry, L. Kohlberg, J. H. Flavel, M. Fischer, and J. Piaget, to name only a few of the many.

iv. "Expert," Wikipedia, the Free Encyclopedia, 27 Jul. 2009 <http://en.wikipedia.org/wiki/Expertise>.

v. In Chapter 9, we will revisit statements like this in the context of "heuristic thinking" and "system-1 decision making." Highly trained individuals have so internalized their problem-solving and pattern-recognition skills in the domain of their expertise that they make automatic, reactive decisions. Often, these are quite reliable and appropriate. The difficulty for critical thinking is that we cannot know that in a reflective and carefully explained way. But let's save this conversation for later.

vi. Plato, "*The Republic* Book III, 389 b-c," *The Collected Dialogues of Plato*, ed. Edith Hamilton (New York: The Bollingen Foundation, 1961) 634.

vii. Mark Silva, "Obama, McCain: U.S. Citizens," The Swamp: Tribune's Washington Bureau, 25 Oct. 2008, 27 Jul. 2009 <http://www.swamppolitics.com/news/politics/blog/2008/10/obama_mcain_us_citizens.html>.

viii. Alex Koppelman, "Why the stories about Obama's birth certificate will never die," Salon.com, 5 Dec. 2008, 27 Jul. 2009 <http://www.salon.com/news/feature/2008/12/05/birth_certificate/>.

ix. Stephen Barrett, M.D., "Q-Ray bracelet marketed with preposterous claims," Quackwatch, 6 Jan. 2008, 27 Jul. 2009 <http://www.quackwatch.com/search/webglimpse.cgi?ID=1&query=Q-Ray>.

x. Michael Higgins, "Placebo effect a key issue in trial over pain bracelet," *Chicago Tribune* 23 Aug. 2006.

xi. Benjamin Edelman, "Red Light States: Who Buys Online Adult Entertainment?" *Journal of Economic Perspectives*. Winter 2009, 23(1): 209–220.

xii. Enda Brady, "Image of Virgin Mary Found in Tree Stump," Sky News, 10 Jul. 2009, 21 Aug. 2009 <http://news.sky.com/skynews/Home/World-News/Virgin-Mary-Tree-Stump-Depiction-Found-In-Rathkeale-Ireland/Article/200907215334913>.

xiii. Steven Miller Design Studio, 27 Jul. 2009 <http://www.stevenmillerdesignstudio.com/>.

xiv. This exercise is based on Greg Brown, "Evaluating a Nutritional Supplement with SOAP Notes to Develop CT Skills," *Critical Thinking and Clinical Reasoning in the Health Sciences*, ed. Noreen C. Facione and Peter A. Facione (Millbrae, CA: California Academic Press, 2008) 198–201.

CHAPTER 7

i. Peter Facione and Donald Scherer, *Logic and Logical Thinking* (New York: McGraw-Hill Publishing, 1978).

ii. People studying logic learn that there are a couple of peculiarly paradoxical cases in which the premises cannot possibly all be true and the conclusion false. One is a case in which the premises are inconsistent with each other. In that case it is impossible for them all to be true, because if one of the inconsistent pair of premises is true, then the other in the pair will necessarily be false. In that odd situation, the argument will pass the test of logical strength. Not to worry—it will fail the test of the truthfulness of the premises. The other odd case is the situation in which the conclusion of the argument is a tautology, and again the argument will pass the test of logical strength, because it will not be possible ever for the conclusion to be false. Again, not to worry, because the test of relevance eliminates these kinds of arguments from being considered acceptable. The test of relevance requires that the basis for believing in the truth of the claim should be the reason given and not some independent consideration. A tautology is true no matter what reason is given; in fact, the reason is entirely irrelevant to the truth of the claim. Therefore, an argument with a tautological conclusion fails the test of relevance.

iii. Irving M. Copi and Carl Cohen, *Introduction to Logic* (New York: Macmillan Publishing, 1990) 52–53.

iv. "National Safety Council Calls for Nationwide Ban on Cell Phone Use While Driving," National Safety Council, 27 Jul. 2009 <http://www.nsc.org/news/cellphone_ban.aspx>.

v. John Searle, *Speech Acts: An Essay in the Philosophy of Language* (Cambridge, UK: Cambridge University Press, 1969).

vi. A couple of these may seem familiar because they were used as examples for other purposes in other chapters. This is the only place in the book, however, where you are being invited to evaluate them.

vii. William C. Rhoden, *Third and a Mile: The Trials and Triumphs of the Black Quarterback* (Bristol, CT: ESPN Books, 2007). This excerpt from Chapter 5 examines the fitful start to the 12-year NFL career of James Harris: William C. Rhoden, "The James Harris story: a long, painful road," 12 Feb. 2007, 27 Jul. 2009 <http://sports.espn.go.com/espn/blackhistory2007/news/story?id=2762569>.

viii. Many frequently repeated mistakes in reasoning have earned themselves names as fallacies. To list them all would not be possible. That is one reason for approaching the evaluation of arguments in terms of the four tests. There are many fallacies we will describe in Chapter 8 that fail the test of logical strength. Obviously, those seven fallacies described in this chapter are arguments that also fail the test of relevance. We could have named "circular reasoning" and a common fallacy as well, but we already have the test of non-circularity. Being able to recognize common fallacies is a way to become more proficient in applying the tests of logical strength, relevance, and non-circularity. And it is fun, too, to see how we all are, at times, misled by the clever fallacies that commonly infest everyday conversation.

ix. Aristotle, *On Sophistical Refutations,* trans. W. A. Pickard-Cambridge, 350 B.C.E., 27 Jul. 2009 <http://classics.mit.edu/Aristotle/sophist_refut.html>; J. Machie, "Fallacies," *The Encyclopedia of Philosophy,* ed. Paul Edwards (New York: Macmillan Publishing, 1967) 3(1): 169–79; C. L. Hamblin, *Fallacies* (London: Methuen & Co Ltd, 1970); John Chaffee, *Thinking Critically* (New York: Houghton Mifflin, 2003).

x. The prejudicial belief expressed in the first sentence was widely accepted for decades. Doug Williams went on to lead the Pittsburgh Steelers to victory in Super Bowl XXII. He received the 1988 Super Bowl MVP award for his performance that day as quarterback.

xi. A. Prior, C. Lejewski, J. F. Staal, A. C. Gram, et al., "The history of logic," *The Encyclopedia of Philosophy*, ed. Paul Edwards (New York: Macmillan Publishing, 1967) 4: 513–571.

CHAPTER 8

i. "The Cold Equations," a sci-fi classic, is a short story by Tom Godwin. It appeared in 1954 in *Astounding Magazine.* Later it was made into an episode of the CBS television series *The New Twilight Zone.* That episode, the 16th in third seasons, first aired January 7, 1989. Unfortunately, the episode was not available for viewing on any of the major Internet TV show Web sites, or through CBS.com. But with archival shows from this era appearing in ever increasing numbers on the Web, perhaps it is now available.

ii. The word "consequent" in "Denying the Consequent" refers to the second part of an "If ____, then ____" statement, that is the part after "then____". The part that comes before is the "if____" part, or the "antecedent." So, the hypothetical is constructed "If antecedent, then consequent."

iii. Logicians call this pattern *modus tollens.*

iv. Logicians call this pattern *modus ponens.*

v. The story is drawn from *CSI* episode 212, "You've Got Male" (episode #12, season 2), which first aired on December 20, 2001. The story as it is told in the *CSI* episode includes yet another twist that is not revealed as it is recounted here.

vi. Margaret K. Ma, Michael H. Woo, and Howard L. McLeod, "Genetic Basis of Drug Metabolism: Genetic Polymorphisms in the CYP Isoenzymes," *American Journal of Health-System Pharmacy* 2002, 59(21). Also found at Medscape Today, 10 Aug. 2009 <http://www.medscape.com/viewarticle/444804_5>.

vii. Raymond M. Lee, *Doing Research on Sensitive Topics* (London: Sage Publications, 1993); Delbert Charles Miller, *Handbook of Research Design and Social Measurement* (London: Sage Publications, 1991).

viii. Scott Maxwell and Harold Delany, *Designing Experiments and Analyzing Data* (Belmont, CA: Wadsworth Publishing, 1990).

ix. "Lighting Fatalities, Injuries, and Damage Reports in the United States from 1959–1994," National Oceanic and Atmospheric Association Technical Memorandum NWS SR-193, October 1997, 10 Aug. 2009 <http://www.nssl.noaa.gov/papers/techmemos/NWS-SR-193/techmemo-sr193-3.html#section3b>.

x. Karen B. Williams, Colleen Schmidt, Terri S. I. Tilliss, Kris Wilkins, and Douglas R. Glasnapp, "Predictive validity of critical thinking skills and disposition for the national board dental hygiene examination: a preliminary investigation," *Journal of Dental Education* 2006, 70(5): 536–44; Kenneth L. McCall, Eric J. MacLaughlin, David S. Fike, and Beatrice Ruiz, "Preadmission predictors of PharmD graduates' performance on the NAPLEX," *American Journal of*

Pharmacy Education, 2007, 15;71(1): 5; The CCTST total score is a prepharmacy predictor of successful licensure as a pharmacist (NAPLEX test). Age, advanced science education courses, and previous BS or MS degree were not significantly correlated with NAPLEX; J. Giddens and G. W. Gloeckner, "The relationship of critical thinking to performance on the NCLEX-RN," *Journal of Nursing Education,* 2005, 44(2): 85–89. CCTST total scores were higher in participants who passed the NCLEX-RN.

xi. The power of a correlation to predict results depends on how strong the correlation is. A correlation is reported as numbers between two-place decimals between 0 and 1—for example, "the correlation of X and Y is 0.31." Researchers use this number to calculate how much the change in X can predict changes in Y, and vice versa. That calculation is simple. Called the "variance," it is correlation squared. If college success (measured as GPA) is correlated at 0.30 with critical thinking skill, then we could infer that 9 percent of the variation seen in college GPA is predictable based on differences in critical thinking skills.

xii. Randy M. Kaplan, "Using a Trainable Pattern-Directed Computer Program to Score Natural Language Item Responses," Educational Testing Service, Research Report #RR-91-31, 1992, 10 Aug. 2009 <http://www.ets.org/portal/site/ets/menuitem.c988ba0e5dd572bada20bc47c3921509/?vgnextoid=7b34457727df4010VgnVCM10000022f95190RCRD&vgnextchannel=e15246f1674f4010VgnVCM10000022f95190RCRD>.

xiii. Donald E. Powers, Jill C. Burstein, Martin Chodorow, Mary E. Fowles, and Karen Kukich, "Comparing the Validity of Automated and Human Essay Scoring," Educational Testing Service, Research Report #RR-0010, 2000, 10 Aug. 2009 <http://www.ets.org/portal/site/ets/menuitem.c988ba0e5dd572bada20bc47c3921509/?vgnextoid=4301af5e44df4010VgnVCM10000022f95190RCRD&vgnextchannel=2af146f1674f4010VgnVCM10000022f95190RCRD>.

CHAPTER 9

i. Herbert Alexander Simon, *Models of Man: Social and Rational* (New York: Wiley, 1957).

ii. Peter Facione and Noreen Facione, *Thinking and Reasoning in Human Decision Making* (Millbrae, CA: The California Academic Press, 2007).

iii. Thomas Glovitch, Dale Griffin, Daniel Kahneman, eds, *Heuristics and Biases: The psychology of intuitive judgment* (Cambridge, UK: Cambridge University Press, 2002); Daniel Kahneman, Paul Slovic, and Amos Tversky, eds, *Judgment under Uncertainty: Heuristics and Biases* (Cambridge, UK: Cambridge University Press, 1982); Steven A. Sloman, "Two Systems of reasoning," *Heuristics and Biases: The psychology of intuitive judgment,* ed. Thomas Glovitch, Dale Griffin, and Daniel Kahneman (Cambridge, UK: Cambridge University Press, 2002) 379–396; Daniel Kahneman and Dale T. Miller, "Norm theory: comparing reality to its alternatives," *Heuristics and Biases: The psychology of intuitive judgment,* ed. Thomas Glovitch, Dale Griffin, and Daniel Kahneman (Cambridge, UK: Cambridge University Press, 2002) 348–366.

iv. My research colleagues and I recommend avoiding use of the word "intuition." We are puzzled by claims of justified true beliefs—knowledge—that go beyond observations or direct personal experience and yet are not preceded or preconditioned by some degree of interpretation, analysis, or inference, whether reflective or unreflective. Perhaps there is such a thing as intuitive knowledge, ineffable, immediate, mystical, and true. Even so, by definition such knowledge, if it is indeed knowledge, is beyond the scope of inter-subjective verification and science. That which is said to be "known" by intuition is, by definition, placed outside possible connections with other evidence-based, replicable, or falsifiable knowledge. Hence, other humans cannot, in principle, confirm or disconfirm that what is asserted to be known by means of intuition. "Special knowledge," available only to one, is always and ever to be suspect. Healthy skepticism demands that it be rejected. We respectfully decline to drink that Kool-Aid. Another reason we have deep ethical concerns about appeals to "intuition" as a basis for justifying beliefs as true or decisions as reasonable is that we seek accountability for knowledge and for action. In matters of importance, including the decisions made in professional practice contexts—such as medicine, law, government, business, and the military—some appeal to "gut feelings" or "intuition" because they are either unable or unwilling to explain their judgments. In effect, they seek the cover of "intuition" because they do not wish to explain their judgments, they cannot explain their judgments, or they do not want to permit others to evaluate those judgments or those explanations. How do we know this? Our research team includes people with many decades of professional practice experience involving health care, management, legal, and leadership responsibilities. We realize the fundamental inadequacies of appeals to intuition and gut feeling. These experiences, in part, motivated us to look more deeply into decision making.

v. Shelly E. Taylor, "The availability bias in social perception and interaction," *Judgment under Uncertainty: Heuristics and Biases*, ed. Daniel Kahneman, Paul Slovic, and Amos Tversky (Cambridge, UK: Cambridge University Press, 1982) 190–200; Baruch Fischhoff, "Attribution theory and judgment under uncertainty," *New directions in attribution research*, ed. John. H. Harvey, William John Ickes, and Robert F. Kidd (Hillsdale, NJ: Erlbaum, 1976); Herbert Alexander Simon, *Models of Man: Social and Rational* (New York: Wiley, 1957).

vi. Gerd Gigerenzer, Jean Czerlinski, and Laura Martignon, "How good are fast and frugal heuristics?" *Heuristics and Biases: The Psychology of Intuitive Judgment*, ed. Thomas Gilovich, Dale W. Griffin, and Daniel Kahneman (Cambridge, UK: Cambridge University Press, 2002) 559–581.

vii. Paul Slovic, Melissa Finucane, Ellen Peters, and Donald G. MacGregor, "The affect heuristic," *Heuristics and Biases: The Psychology of Intuitive Judgment*, ed. Thomas Gilovich, Dale W. Griffin, and Daniel Kahneman (Cambridge, UK: Cambridge University Press, 2002) 397–420; Norbert Schwarz, "Feelings as information: Moods influence judgments and processing strategies," *Heuristics and Biases: The Psychology of Intuitive Judgment*, ed. Thomas Gilovich, Dale W. Griffin, and Daniel Kahneman (Cambridge, UK: Cambridge University Press, 2002) 534–547.

viii. Oswald Huber, "Information-processing operators in decision making," *Process and Structure on Human Decision Making*, ed. Henry Montgomery and Ola Svenson (Chichester, UK: John Wiley & Sons, 1989) 3–21; Allen Newell and Herbert Alexander Simon, *Human Problem Solving* (Englewood Cliffs, NJ: Prentice Hall, 1972).

ix. Paul Slovic, Melissa Finucane, Ellen Peters, and Donald G. MacGregor, "The affect heuristic," *Heuristics and Biases: The Psychology of Intuitive Judgment*, ed. Thomas Gilovich, Dale W. Griffin, and Daniel Kahneman (Cambridge, UK: Cambridge University Press, 2002) 397–420.

x. Phillip Waite, "Campus landscaping in recruitment and retention: The package is the product," Presented at the 2007 annual Noel Levitz conference on enrolment management, Orlando, FL, 2007.

xi. Business students may be interested in how the Turning Leaf brand applied a "Blue Ocean" Business strategy to this and made tremendous gains in a very competitive market. W. Chan Kim and Renee Mauborgne, *Blue Ocean Strategy* (Boston, MA: Harvard Business School Corporation, 2005).

xii. D. J. Koehler, "Explanation, Imagination and Confidence in Judgment," *Psychological Bulletin* 1991, 110: 499–519; S. J. Koch, "Availability and inference in predictive judgment," *Journal of Experimental Psychology, Learning, Memory and Cognition* 1984, 10: 649–662.

xiii. Daniel Kahneman, Paul Slovic, and Amos Tversky, eds. *Judgment under Uncertainty: Heuristics and Biases* (Cambridge, UK: Cambridge University Press, 1982); Amos Tversky and Daniel Kahneman, "Availability: A Heuristic for Judging Frequency and Probability," *Cognitive Psychology* 1973, 5: 207–32.

xiv. Albert Bandura, "Self-Efficacy: Toward a Unifying Theory of Behavioral Change," *Psychological Review* 1977, 84(2): 191–215; Albert Bandura, "Self-Efficacy Mechanism in Physiological Activation and Health-Promoting Behavior," *Adaptation, learning and effect*, ed. J. Madden, IV, S. Matthysse, and J. Barchas (New York: Raven Press, 1989).

xv. Norbert Schwarz and Leigh Ann Vaughn, "The availability heuristic revisited: Ease of recall and content of recall as distinct sources of information," *Heuristics and Biases: The Psychology of Intuitive Judgment*, ed. Thomas Gilovich, Dale W. Griffin, and Daniel Kahneman (Cambridge, UK: Cambridge University Press, 2002) 103–19; Daniel Kahneman, Paul Slovic, and Amos Tversky, eds. *Judgment under Uncertainty: Heuristics and Biases* (Cambridge, UK: Cambridge University Press, 1982) 11.

xvi. Daniel Kahneman, Paul Slovic, and Amos Tversky, eds. *Judgment under Uncertainty: Heuristics and Biases* (Cambridge, UK: Cambridge University Press, 1982); Irving Lester Janis and Leon Mann, *Decision-making: a psychological analysis of conflict, choice, and commitment* (New York: The Free Press, 1977).

xvii. Paul Rozin and Carol Nemeroff, "Sympathetic magical thinking: The contagion and similarity 'heuristics.'" *Heuristics and Biases: The Psychology of Intuitive Judgment*, ed. Thomas Gilovich, Dale W. Griffin, and Daniel Kahneman (Cambridge, UK: Cambridge University Press, 2002) 201–216; Daniel Kahneman and Shane Frederick, "Representativeness revisited: Attribute substitution in intuitive judgment," *Heuristics and Biases: The Psychology of Intuitive Judgment*, ed. Thomas Gilovich, Dale W. Griffin, and Daniel Kahneman (Cambridge, UK: Cambridge University Press, 2002) 49–81. In the early heuristics literature, "representativeness" covered a wide range of things. Here we use "representation" as the name for some and "association" as the name for others. At times, these heuristics are found in the literature under the title "similarity."

xviii. Dualistic thinking divides the world into black and white with no shades of gray. For dualistic thinkers, all problems have right answers or wrong answers only. But psychological dualism is a broader construct. It is better understood in the context of cognitive development. The "Us vs. Them" dynamic, as cognitive heuristic, can influence decisions made by people whose cognitive development has progressed beyond dualistic thinking in many domains.

xix. David Berreby, *Us and Them: Understanding Your Tribal Mind* (New York: Little, Brown and Company, 2005).

xx. Robert J. Robinson, Dacher Keltner, Andew Ward, and Lee Ross, "Actual vs. assumed differences in construal: 'Naïve Realism' in intergroup perception and conflict," *Journal of Personality and Social Psychology* 1995, 68: 404–417.

xxi. Amos Tversky and Daniel Kahneman, "Judgment under uncertainty: heuristics and biases," *Science* 1974, 185: 1124–1131; Gretchen B. Chapman and Eric J. Johnson, "Incorporating the irrelevant: Anchors in judgments of belief and value," *Heuristics and Biases: The Psychology of Intuitive Judgment*, ed. Thomas Gilovich, Dale W. Griffin, and Daniel Kahneman (Cambridge, UK: Cambridge University Press, 2002) 122–138.

xxii. S. C. Thompson, W. Armstrong, and C. Thomas, "Illusions of control, underestimations, and accuracy: A control heuristic explanation," *Psychological Bulletin* 1998, 123(2): 143–161.

xxiii. T. R. Schultz and D. Wells. "Judging the intentionality of action-outcomes," *Developmental Psychology* 1985, 21: 83–89.

ENDNOTES

xxiv. Baruch Fischhoff and Ruth Beyth, "'I knew it would happen'—Remembered probabilities of once future things," *Organizational Behavior and Human Performance* 1975, 13: 1–16.

xxv. Irving Lester Janis and Leon Mann, *Decision-making: a psychological analysis of conflict, choice, and commitment* (New York: The Free Press, 1977).

xxvi. Dan Ariely, "The Curious Paradox of Optimism Bias," *Business Week*, Aug. 2009, 24 and 31: 48.

xxvii. James G. March and Chip Heath, *A Primer on Decision Making: How Decisions Happen* (New York: The Free Press, 1994); Daniel Kahneman, Paul Slovic, and Amos Tversky, eds. *Judgment under Uncertainty: Heuristics and Biases* (Cambridge, UK: Cambridge University Press, 1982); Irving Lester Janis and Leon Mann, *Decision-making: a psychological analysis of conflict, choice, and commitment* (New York: The Free Press, 1977); Slovic, P. (1989). *Op cit.*; Daniel Kahneman and Amos Tversky, *Choices, Values, and Frames* (Cambridge, UK: Cambridge University Press, 2000); Paul Slovic, "Limitations of the Mind of Man: Implications for Decision making in the Nuclear Age," *Oregon Research Institute Bulletin* 1971, 11: 41–49.

CHAPTER 10

i. This is a rhetorical question intended to focus attention on the process of decision making. Please do not interpret it as a comment on the war, the decision makers themselves, or national policy.

ii. The interview was conducted with the woman's informed consent and under a protocol approved by the Human Subjects Research Review Board of a major medical research university. The interview was audiotaped, again with the woman's full knowledge and consent. The interview excerpt and the associated decision map are published in Noreen C. Facione and Peter A. Facione, *Thinking and Reasoning in Human Decision Making* (Millbrae, CA: The California Academic Press, 2007) 108–111. Used with permission.

iii. "Quotations by Author: Aristotle," The Quotations Pages, 15 Sept. 2009 <http://www.quotationspage.com/quotes/Aristotle/>.

iv. "Decision-critical criteria" is a short phrase that refers to those criteria the decision-maker deems to be important and relevant for the purpose of evaluating options. Two people working together to make a decision often agree to use the same decision-critical criteria because they both think that the same things are important and relevant when evaluating options. That said, they may not agree on the relative priority or importance of their various criteria. "Tastes great!" NO, "Less filling!"

v. Henry Montgomery, "From cognition to action: the search for dominance in decision making," *Process and structure in human decision making*, ed. Henry Montgomery and Ola Svenson (Chichester, UK: John Wiley & Sons, 1989) 23–49.

vi. Henry Montgomery, "From cognition to action: the search for dominance in decision making," *Process and structure in human decision making*, ed. Henry Montgomery and Ola Svenson (Chichester, UK: John Wiley & Sons, 1989) 24.

vii. Henry Montgomery, "From cognition to action: the search for dominance in decision making," *Process and structure in human decision making*, ed. Henry Montgomery and Ola Svenson (Chichester, UK: John Wiley & Sons, 1989).

viii. Henry Montgomery "Decision rules and the search for a dominance structure: Towards a process model of decision making," *Analyzing and Aiding Decision Processes*, ed. Patrick Humphreys, Ola Svenson, and Anna Vari (Amsterdam/Budapest: North Holland and Hungarian Academic Press, 1983) 343–369.

ix. Henry Montgomery, "From cognition to action: the search for dominance in decision making," *Process and structure in human decision making*, ed. Henry Montgomery and Ola Svenson (Chichester, UK: John Wiley & Sons, 1989) 26.

x. Henry Montgomery "Decision rules and the search for a dominance structure: Towards a process model of decision making," *Analyzing and Aiding Decision Processes*, ed. Patrick Humphreys, Ola Svenson, and Anna Vari (Amsterdam/Budapest: North Holland and Hungarian Academic Press, 1983) 343–369.

xi. Oswald Huber, "Information-processing operators in decision making," *Process and Structure on Human Decision Making*, ed. Henry Montgomery and Ola Svenson (Chichester, UK: John Wiley & Sons, 1989) 3–21.

xii. I am not suggesting that Mr. Simpson was guilty. In fact, the jury's verdict was "not guilty." This example is intended as an interpretive analysis of how questions about the evidence, methods, concepts, standards, and context of a judgment can enter a group's decision-making dominance structuring.

xiii. This scenario about a serial killer was inspired by Michael Connelly's novel *The Scarecrow* (New York: Little, Brown and Company, 2008).

CHAPTER 11

i. Carolyn Lochhead and Carla Marinucci, "Freedom and fear are at war," The *San Francisco Chronicle*, 21 Sept. 2001, 1 Sept. 2009 <http://www.sfgate.com/cgibin/article.cgi?f=/c/a/2001/09/21/MN48614.DTL>.

ii. *Traffic,* Hollywood, CA: Universal Studios, dir. Steven Soderbergh, perf. Michael Douglas, Don Cheadle, Benicio Del Toro, Dennis Quaid, and Catherine Zeta-Jones, 2000.

iii. Allen Newell, *Toward Unified Theories of Cognition* (Cambridge, MA: Harvard University Press, 1990).

iv. Michael Scriven, *Reasoning* (New York: McGraw-Hill, 1976).

v. Chris Rock, *Chris Rock: Bigger and Blacker*, HBO Productions, writ. Chris Rock, perf. Chris Rock, 1999.

CHAPTER 12

i. *The Los Angeles Times* cites research on marriage statistics conducted by the Williams Institute of the UCLA School of Law, "Spike in marriage licenses statewide," *The Los Angeles Times*, 3 Feb. 2009, 2 Sept. 2009 <http://www.ltimes.com/news/local/la-marriagesmap,0, 6124834.htmlstory>.

ii. The group that drafted Prop 8 in California is the Alliance Defense Fund. Stuart Whatley in "The Group Behind Prop 8" described the ADF as a Christian conservative consortium of lawyers, founded in 1994 as an answer to the American Civil Liberties Union (ACLU). Whatley's article was published in *The American Prospect* on October 22, 2008. To view the full text, go to <http://www.prospect.org/cs/articles?article=the_group_behind_prop_8>.

iii. "California High Court Upholds Same-Sex Marriage Ban," *CNN.com*, 27 May 2009, 2 Sept. 2009 <http://www.cnn.com/ 2009/US/05/26/california.same.sex.marriage/index.html>.

iv. "Lutherans Accept Clergy in 'Lifelong' Same-Sex Relationships," *CNN.com*, 21 Aug. 2009, 2 Sept. 2009 <http://www.cnn.com/2009/US/08/21/lutheran.gays.index.html#cnnSTCText>.

v. "Access to adequate health care" is more than "has some level of health insurance" or "can go to an emergency room." Adequate health care, as defined by health care professionals, includes three things: screening, diagnosis, and treatment. These three are necessary not only to manage a person's care but also to prevent illness and to mitigate the morbidity and mortality associated with disease discovered at an already acute or advanced stage.

vi. "Galileo Galilei," Wisdom Quotes, 2 Sept. 2009 <http://www.wisdomquotes. com/003071.html>.

vii. The premise of the 2009 film *District 9*.

viii. *Paul's First Letter to the Corinthians*, The Holy Bible, Chapter 13, verse 13.

ix. Plato, *Euthyphro,* trans. Benjamin Jowett, 380 B.C.E., 2 Sept. 2009 <http://classics.mit.edu/Plato/euthyfro.html>; Ian Kidd, "Socrates," *The Encyclopedia of Philosophy* ed. Paul Edwards (New York: Macmillan Publishing, 1967) Vol. 7, pp. 480–486.

x. "Thomas Jefferson Quotes," Brainy Quote, 2 Sept. 2009 <http://www.brainyquote.com/quotes/quotes/t/thomasjeff141347.html>.

xi. John Locke, "Of wrong assent or error" in *Essay Concerning Human Understanding*, 1690, Book IV, Chapter XX.

xii. John Howard Griffin, *Black Like Me* (New York: Signet, 1961).

CHAPTER 13

i. Richard L. DeGowin, *Diagnostic Examination*, 6th edition (New York: McGraw-Hill, 1994) 945.

ii. Bob Arnebeck, "A Short History of Yellow Fever in the U.S.," 30 Jan. 2008, 3 Sept. 2009 <http://www.geocities.com/bobarnebeck/history.html>.

iii. *2001: A Space Odyssey*, Warner Brothers Studios, dir. Stanley Kubrick, perf. Gary Lockwood and Keir Dullea, 1968.

iv. At three key places in this film an obelisk is visible on-screen. One interpretation is that the obelisk's presence indicates moments of extraterrestrial intervention into human affairs; another is that these are moments of supreme insight, or perhaps divine inspiration. The first appearance of the obelisk is just before the man-ape creature realizes that he can use a leg bone as a tool to club another creature to death. This fictional depiction of the first realization of leg-bone-as-killing-tool includes moments intended by the filmmaker to show deliberation and stimulation. Whether the idea came to the man-ape by insight, extraterrestrial intervention, or divine inspiration is immaterial. What is important is that the man-ape considered the notion and decided to act on the hypothesis that a leg bone could be used to kill. Whatever its source, subsequent events supported that hypothesis.

v. Carl Gustav Hempel, *Philosophy of Natural Science* (Englewood Cliffs, NJ: Prentice-Hall, Inc., 1966); Stephen Edelston Toulmin, *The Philosophy of Science* (New York: Harper & Row, 1953).

vi. "Quotes on Education," Solina Quotes, 3 Sept. 2009 <http://www.inet.ba/~admahmut/quotes/1/education-quotes/>

vii. It is not necessary that a hypothesis be expressed as an "if. . .then" statement, only that it can be converted into one. For example, "The reflexes of a person who drives a motor vehicle for five or more hours without a rest period will have deteriorated by 30% or more as compared to his or her reflexes after only one to four hours of driving" can be rewritten as "If a person drives a motor vehicle for five or more hours without a rest period, then the person's reflexes will have deteriorated by 30% or more as compared with only one to four hours of driving."

viii. "Quotations by author: Hippocrates,"The Quotations Page, 3 Sept. 2009 <http://www.quotationspage.com/quotes/Hippocrates>.

ix. Delbert Charles Miller, *Handbook of Research Design and Social Measurement*, 5th edition (Newbury Park, CA: Sage Publications, Inc., 1991); John W. Creswell, *Research Design Qualitative and Quantitative Approaches* (Thousand Oaks, CA: Sage Publications Inc., 1994); Stephen B. Hulley, Steven R. Cummings, Warren S. Browner, Deborah G. Grady, and Thomas B. Newman, *Designing Clinical Research* (Philadelphia, PA: Lippincott Williams & Wilkins, 2001); Emanuel Mason and William J. Bramble, *Understanding and Conducting Research* (New York: McGraw-Hill, 1989).

x. The "empirical disciplines" as used here refer to the full spectrum of social, behavioral, natural, and physical sciences and all the other areas of study or professional fields, by whatever name, that fundamentally rely on empirical reasoning in the generation of new knowledge.

xi. "Galileo Galilei Quotes," Brainy Quote, 3 Sept. 2009 <http://www.brainyquote.com/quotes/authors/g/galileo_galilei.html>.

xii. Chapter 7 introduces and explains each test: truthfulness of the premises, logical strength, relevance, and non-circularity. Are all the premises true? If the premises were true, would the conclusion be true or very probably true? Does the truth of the conclusion depend on the truth of the premises? Does the truth of the reason (set of premises) not depend on the truth of the conclusion?

xiii. Critical thinking in real life: Since managers tend to wear jackets and administrative assistants do not, the wise office manager, on hearing this refined research finding, may wish to ask the administrative assistants, not the managers, whether or not the heating and cooling is set right.

xiv. "Classic Quostes,"The Quotations Page, 3 Sept. 2009 <http://www.quotationspage.com/quote/24972.html>.

CREDITS

PHOTO CREDITS

FRONT COVER: *The Science of Speed,* Drew Wilson

CHAPTER 01 PAGE 2: Everett Collection; **4:** Everett Collection; **5 (from top):** Everett Collection; Everett Collection; **8 (from top):** Corporation for National & Community Service; United Way of America; Courtesy of Volunteer Match; Courtesy of America's Promise Alliance; Corporation for National & Community Service; Corporation for National & Community Service; Corporation for National & Community Service; **12:** Everett Collection.

CHAPTER 02 PAGE 14: Landov Media; **16:** Everett Collection; **21:** Creative Digital Vision/Getty Images Royalty Free; **22:** Everett Collection; **23 (from top):** Photos.com; Creative/Brand X Pictures (RF)/Getty Images Royalty Free; **24:** Landov Media; **25:** Everett Collection.

CHAPTER 03 PAGE 26: Everett Collection; **32:** Everett Collection; **38 (from top):** Everett Collection; Everett Collection.

CHAPTER 04 PAGE 40: Everett Collection; **42 (from top):** Vincent O'Byrne/Alamy Images Royalty Free; Masterfile Corporation; Gary Vogelmann/Alamy Images Royalty Free; Joe Fox/Alamy Images; **45 (from top):** Kevin Chan; Everett Collection; **46 (left to right):** All Star Picture Library/Alamy Images; Jupiter Unlimited; **48:** The Granger Collection; **49:** Joe Corrigan/Getty Images; **51 (from top):** AP Wide World Photos; ©1991 Cindy Lewis. All rights reserved.; Kyodo/Landov Media; **53:** Kobal/Picture Desk; **54:** Tom Grill/Corbis Premium RF/Alamy Images Royalty Free; **55:** Pearson Education/PH College; **56 (from top):** Everett Collection; Everett Collection; Kobal/Picture Desk.

CHAPTER 05 PAGE 58: Everett Collection; **63:** © J. P. Wilson/Icon SMI/CORBIS All Rights Reserved; **65 (from top):** Getty Images, Inc.; AP Wide World Photos; **72:** Everett Collection; **73:** Getty Images, Inc.; **75:** Redux Pictures.

CHAPTER 06 PAGE 76: Editorial/Getty Images News; **78 (left to right):** Creative/Lifesize (RF)/Getty Images, Inc.; Creative/Stockbyte (RF)/Getty Images, Inc.; **80:** Everett Collection; **81 (from top):** Creative/Digital Vision (RF)/Getty Images. Inc.; Creative/Digital Vision (RF)/Getty Images, Inc.; Creative/Digital Vision (RF)/Getty Images, Inc.; moodboard/Alamy Images Royalty Free; **82:** Everett Collection; **84 (left to right):** Creative/Creative Photodisc (RF)/Getty Images; © Dorling Kindersley; **85:** Photos.com; **86 (left to right):** Getty Images; Julien Behal/PA Wire/AP Wide World Photos; **87:** Getty Images; **90 (from top):** Everett Collection; Everett Collection.

CHAPTER 07 PAGE 92: CHRIS SALVO/Getty Images, Inc. – Taxi; **95 (from top):** Stockbyte (RF)/Getty Images, Inc - Stockbyte Royalty Free; Scott Adams, Inc/United Media/United Feature Syndicate, Inc.; **96:** Everett Collection; **98 (from top):** Blended Images (RF)/Getty Images, Inc.; Acott Mansfield/UpperCut Images/Getty Images; **99:** Frederic Lewis/Hulton Archive/Getty Images; **103:** Private Collection/The Bridgeman Art Library; **104:** Landov Media; **106:** Everett Collection; **107:** Landov Media.

CHAPTER 08 PAGE 108: Jerry Lodriguss/Photo Researchers, Inc.; **110 (from top):** Getty Images; Time & Life Pictures/Getty Images/Time Life Pictures; **115:** Everett Collection; **118:** © Tony Phillips/CORBIS All Rights Reserved; **119 (left to right):** Digital Vision (RF)/Getty Images/Digital Vision; Image Source/Getty Images Inc-Image Source Royalty Free; **121:** Corbis RF; **122:** EYB/Imagebroker/Alamy Images; **124:** Everett Collection; **125 (from top):** Everett Collection; Everett Collection.

CHAPTER 09 PAGE 126: David R. Frazier/David R. Frazier Photolibrary, Inc.; **130 (from top):** Jim MacMillan/AP Wide World Photos; © Roger L. Wollenberg/UPI/Landov; Image Source/Jupiter Images Royalty Free; **131 (left to right):** Imagic Urban World/Alamy Images; Mode Ian O'Leary/Alamy Images; **133 (from top):** Dynamic Graphics Group/Jupiter Images Royalty Free; Larry W. Smith/Stringer/Getty Images; **134:** CNN America; **135 (from top):** T. O'Keefe/PhotoLink/Jupiter Images Royalty Free; Dave Porter/Alamy Images; David First/Stringer/Getty Images; UPI Photo/Haraz N. Ghanbari/POOL/Landov Media; Jim McIsaac/Getty Images; **136 (from top):** Stuwdamdorp/Alamy Images; Twitter, Inc; **137 (from top):** AP Wide World Photos; CNN America; **138:** Everett Collection; **139:** Bob Daemmrich/PhotoEdit Inc.; **140 (from top):** Jupiter Unlimited; AP Wide World Photos; All Star Picture Library/Alamy Images; **141 (from top):** Photos.com; Steven Lam/Taxi/Getty Images; **142:** City Living/Alamy Images; **143:** Creative Class Group; **144:** Image Source/Getty Images Inc-Image Source Royalty Free; **146:** Everett Collection.

CHAPTER 10 PAGE 148: Kevin Wolf/Fila/AP Wide World Photos; **152:** Joe Marquette/AP Wide World Photos; **154 (left to right):** Alamy Images Royalty Free; Blue Jean Images/Alamy Images Royalty Free; ©Business Office Career/Alamy Images Royalty Free; McPHoto/Alamy Images; **156:** Young-Wolff/PhotoEdit Inc.; **157:** Reed Saxon/AP Wide World Photos; **158:** Photos.com; **159:** Photos.com; **160:** SuperStock, Inc.; **161:** Robyn Beck/AFP/Getty Images; **162:** Kevin Wolf/Fila/AP Wide World Photos; **163:** Carl & Ann Purcell/CORBIS- NY.

CHAPTER 11 PAGE 164: Columbia University Graduate School of Journalism; **166 (left to right):** Erwin Bud Nielsen/Photolibrary.com; Jeff Greenberg/PhotoEdit Inc.; **167 (left to right):** Smit/Shutterstock; Everett Collection; **168 (from top):** Ulrich Baumgarten/Vario Images/Alamy Images; Nigel Hicks © Dorling Kindersley; **170 (from top):** John Heseltine © Dorling Kindersley; Alex Segre/Alamy Images; Andy Manis/The New York Times; PSL Images/Alamy Images; **171 (from top):** Alistair Scott/Alamy Images; Paul Spinelli/MLB Photos/Getty Images; **172 (from top):** Kim Sayer © Dorling Kindersley; Nancy G. Stock Photography, Nancy Greifenhagen/Alamy Images; **173:** British Library/Picture Desk, Inc./Kobal Collection; **175:** ©Scott Adams/Dist. by United Media Feature Syndicate; **176:** Columbia University Graduate School of Journalism.

CHAPTER 12 PAGE 178: C.J. Gunther/Zuma/CORBIS- NY; **181 (from top):** Morgan Lane Photography/Alamy Images Royalty Free; David McNew/Getty Images, Inc. - Getty News; **182 (from top):** Getty Images, Inc.; AP Wide World Photos; **183 (from top):** AKG-Images; Photolibrary.com; **184 (left to right):** NorthWind Picture Archives/Alamy Images; Eddie Adams/AP Wide World Photos; **185:** Hulton Archive/Stringer/Getty Images; **186:** Lee Foster/Alamy Images; **188:** William Baker/GhostWorxImages/Alamy Images Royalty Free; **189 (from top):** SPL/Photo Researchers, Inc.; Sean Sprague/AGE Fotostock America, Inc.; The

Granger Collection; Frances Roberts/Alamy Images; CORBIS- NY; AP Wide World Photos; **190 (from top):** Nigel Hicks © Dorling Kindersley; Sean Gallup/Getty Images; Alex Segre/Alamy Images; Peter Facione; Steve Allen/Brand X Pictures/Getty Images; **191 (left to right):** North Wind Picture Archives/Alamy Images; Penguin Putnam, Inc; **192 (left to right):** Mira.com/Artist Name; ©Mexico/Alamy Images Royalty Free; **193 (from top):** Penguin Putnam, Inc; Everett Collection; **194 (from top):** David McNew/Getty Images, Inc. - Getty News; Everett Collection.

CHAPTER 13 PAGE 196: William Brown/Photo Researchers, Inc.; **199:** Everett Collection; **202:** © Tom Wagner/Corbis; **206:** William Brown/Photo Researchers, Inc.

BACK COVER: istock

TEXT, TABLE, AND FIGURE CREDITS

PAGE xxiii: Copyright © 2007 by Peter A. Facione. Reprinted by permission of Peter A. Facione and Insight Assessment.

CHAPTER 01 PAGE 7: Reprinted by permission of Peter A. Facione and the California Academic Press / Insight Assessment; **PAGE 10:** Copyright © 1994, 2009 by Peter A. Facione, Noreen C. Facione, and Measured Reasons LLC, Hermosa Beach, CA USA. Published by The California Academic Press/Insight Assessment. Reprinted by permission of the authors and Insight Assessment.

CHAPTER 02 PAGE 17: Copyright © 2007 by Peter A. Facione. Reprinted by permission of Peter A. Facione and Insight Assessment. **19:** Copyright © 2008 by CBS News, a division of CBS, INC. Reprinted by permission of CBS News, a division of CBS, INC. **20:** From TEST MANUAL FOR THE CALIFORNIA CRITICAL THINKING SKILLS TEST published by Insight Assessment. Copyright © 2009. Reprinted by permission of the publisher. **21:** From CRITICAL THINKING: A Statement of Expert Consensus for Purposes of Educational Assessment and Instruction: The Complete American Philosophical Association Delphi Report by Dr. Peter A. Facione. Copyright © 1990 by The California Academic Press. Reprinted by permission of the publisher.

CHAPTER 03 PAGE 28: Copyright © 2009 by Measured Reasons LLC, Hermosa Beach, CA. Used with permission. **31:** Reprinted by permission of Dr. Peter A. Facione. **34:** Table 5, p. 25 from CRITICAL THINKING: A Statement of Expert Consensus for Purposes of Educational Assessment and Instruction: The Complete American Philosophical Association Delphi Report by Dr. Peter A. Facione. Copyright © 1990 by The California Academic Press. Reprinted by permission of the publisher. **35:** Reprinted by permission of Peter A. Facione and Insight Assessment. **36:** Copyright © 2009 by Insight Assessment. Reprinted by permission of The California Academic Press LLC, Millbrae, CA. **37:** Copyright © 2009 by Insight Assessment. Reprinted by permission of The California Academic Press LLC, Millbrae, CA.

CHAPTER 04 PAGE 50: Reprinted by permission of Dr. Peter A. Facione.

CHAPTER 05 PAGE 64: Excerpt from teleplay for 12 ANGRY MEN by Reginald Rose. Copyright 1954 by Reginald Rose. Reprinted by permission of International Creative Management, Inc.

CHAPTER 06 PAGE 79: Based on DEVELOPING REFLECTIVE JUDGMENT by Patricia M. King & Karen Strohm Kitchener, Jossey-Bass Publishers. San Francisco, CA. 1994. **91:** Based on pp. 198–201 from Brown, G.A., "Evaluating a Nutritional Supplement with SOAP Notes to Develop CT Skills", N. C. Facione and P. A. Facione (eds.) CRITICAL THINKING AND CLINICAL REASONING IN THE HEALTH SCIENCES. Copyright © 2008. Reprinted by permission of The California Academic Press, Millbrae, CA.

INDEX

Page numbers followed by *f* refer to figures. Page numbers followed by *t* refer to tables.